MEDIA STUDIES

This edition first published 2009
© 2009 Robert Kolker

Blackwell Publishing was acquired by John Wiley & Sons in February 2007. Blackwell's publishing program has been merged with Wiley's global Scientific, Technical, and Medical business to form Wiley-Blackwell.

Registered Office
John Wiley & Sons Ltd, The Atrium, Southern Gate, Chichester, West Sussex, PO19 8SQ, United Kingdom

Editorial Offices
350 Main Street, Malden, MA 02148-5020, USA
9600 Garsington Road, Oxford, OX4 2DQ, UK
The Atrium, Southern Gate, Chichester, West Sussex, PO19 8SQ, UK

For details of our global editorial offices, for customer services, and for information about how to apply for permission to reuse the copyright material in this book please see our website at www.wiley.com/wiley-blackwell.

The right of Robert Kolker to be identified as the author of this work has been asserted in accordance with the Copyright, Designs and Patents Act 1988.

Library of Congress Cataloging-in-Publication Data

Kolker, Robert Phillip.
  Media studies : an introduction / Robert Kolker.
    p. cm.
  Includes bibliographical references and index.
    ISBN 978-1-4051-5560-1 (hardcover : alk. paper) – ISBN 978-1-4051-5561-8 (pbk. : alk. paper) 1. Mass media. I. Title.
  P90.K587 2009
  302.23–dc22

                                                    2008041559

A catalogue record for this book is available from the British Library.

Set in 10/13pt Galliard by SPi Publisher Services, Pondicherry, India
Printed and bound in Singapore by Ho Printing Singapore Pte Ltd

001 2009

Contents

Illustrations

Preface

Media Studies: An Introduction examines a variety of media – journalism, advertising, radio, television, film, and digital – from a variety of perspectives. Its focus is on the historical and cultural place of media, and on our role – we as audience – in their creation, completion, and comprehension.

The following questions are asked in this book. Where do the varieties of media come from? How do they evolve? What do they ask of their audience, and how does their audience respond? As cultural expressions, what do media tell us about ourselves and our worlds, about class, race, and gender? How, finally, do we talk about media and develop our own discourse *about* the media that matches the media's discourse about us? How do we talk back?

Marshall McLuhan, in his groundbreaking book *Understanding Media*, considers media as extensions of human consciousness. But this implies that media are an add-on, an addition to our knowledge of ourselves and the world. I consider media in the root sense of the word, as the *mediations* of consciousness in culture. In the larger sense, anything that is made by someone in order to elicit a response from someone else, anything that represents something to us for our response, whether it is a poem, an advertisement for a cholesterol drug, or a page on MySpace – is a mediation. We live in a world of mediating images, words, and stories that have designs on us and are designed with us in mind. We, in turn, respond to them, and our response is informed by who we are and where we ourselves are placed in the media design. We attend, are moved, informed; we buy things, say things back; we tune in and out; we place value judgments on what is important, what is trivial, what is downright malicious or harmful; we create identities (mediations) for ourselves online. We are not always fully conscious of the mediating act, even as we answer our cell phone, respond to an email, read a newspaper, or watch a movie. But at some level of engagement our minds and emotions – our consciousness – are always at work decoding a message. That work – of understanding, of *mediating* media – is what media studies is about and what this book is about.

How does this book differ from a mass communications text? Rather than present an encyclopedic view of media from a sociological perspective, it presents instead a "reading" of media history and media texts – of texts within contexts – of the ways we are asked to respond and the ways we do respond. The book is written in a somewhat informal style, more congenial, I hope, than the average college textbook. It is opinionated and draws conclusions, and it tries to remain focused on the ways media are used and the ways in which they reflect their moments in history, their creators, and their audience. Its aim is to make the reader conscious, responsive, and intelligent about the designs of media. It offers the reader a voice.

Reference

Marshall McLuhan, *Understanding Media: The Extensions of Man* (Cambridge, MA, and London: MIT Press, 1994), p. 9.

Acknowledgments

Thanks to: Laura Berman, Professor Aniko Bodroghkozy, Professor Melvin Ely, Jayne Fargnoli, Helen Gray, Professor Jack Lindgren, Margot Morse, Helen Nash, Elsa Peterson, Ken Provencher, Eric Stangarone, and Joley Wood.

Acknowledgments for illustrations

Figure 1.1 George Du Maurier's 1879 cartoon *Punch*'s *Almanack*, 1879. Mary Evans Picture Library; Figure 2.1 Contemporary cartoon of Joseph Pulitzer. North Wind Picture Archives/Alamy; Figure 2.2 Cartoon of Joseph Pulitzer and William Randolph Hearst. Courtesy of the Library of Congress (LC-USZC4-3800); Figure 2.3 Robert Redford and Dustin Hoffman in *All the President's Men* (dir. Alan J. Pakula, 1976), *All the President's Men* © Warner Bros., 1976; Figure 2.4 A staged photograph from the Crimean War by Roger Fenton (1855). Courtesy of the Library of Congress (LC-USZC4-9174); Figure 2.5 Timothy O'Sullivan's 1863 photograph of the bodies of Federal soldiers, 1863. From *Gardner's Photographic Sketch Book of the War* (1865–6). Courtesy of the Library of Congress (LC-DIG-ppmsca-12558); Figure 2.6 Joseph Rosenthal's photograph of the raising of the flag at Iwo Jima, February, 1945. PA Photos/AP; Figure 2.7 Robert Capa's "Loyalist Militiaman at the Moment of Death, Cerro Muriano, September 5, 1936". ROBERT CAPA © 2001 By Cornell Capa/Magnum Photos; Figure 2.8 Bill Hudson's photograph of the dog attack on civil rights marchers, Birmingham, Alabama, 1963. PA Photos/AP; Figure 2.9 Senator Joseph McCarthy in the film *Point of Order* (dir. Emil de Antonio, 1964). Point Films © 1964; Figure 2.10 *The New York Times* front page, June 2, 2008. Courtesy of *The New York Times*; Figure 2.11 *The New York Post* printed page, June 2, 2008. Courtesy of *The New York Post*; Figure 2.12 *The New York Times* web page, June 2, 2008. Courtesy of *The New York Times*; Figure 3.1 Advertisement for the opening of Sears' first retail store, *Chicago Tribune*, February 1, 1925. Courtesy of Sears Holdings Archives; Figure 3.2 Art nouveau poster designed by Louis John Rhead (1857–1926) advertising the *Morning Journal*. Private collection/the Stapleton Collection/the Bridgeman Art Library; Figure 3.3 Poster for the 1933 Chicago World's Fair. Copyright © Swim Ink 2, LLC/CORBIS; Figure 3.4 Advertisement for Mercedes-Benz. Courtesy of Mercedes-Benz; Figure 3.5 An art deco pencil sharpener designed by Raymond Loewy. Raymond Loewy™/® by CMG Worldwide, Inc./www.RaymondLoewy.com; Figure 3.10 The model's gaze at the reader. Getty Images/Frazer Harrison; Figure 3.11 Dove's Campaign for Real Beauty. Olaf Kowalzik/Alamy; Figure 3.12 An early advertisement for Carter's Little Liver Pills. Wellcome Trust Medical Photographic Library; Figure 3.24 Product placement in the movie *The Weather Man* (dir. Gore Verbinski, 2005). *The Weather Man* ©Paramount, 2005; Figure 3.25 CBS comedy, *King of Queens*. *The King of Queens* © Sony Pictures Television and CBS Productions; Figure 4.1 Publicity photo *Amos 'n' Andy* radio show with Freeman Gosden and Charles Correll. Correll Family Collection; Figure 4.2 Publicity photo of Alan Freed, the disc jockey who, arguably, invented rock 'n' roll in the mid-1950s. Bettmann/CORBIS; Figure 4.3 Fats Domino from the film *The Girl Can't Help It* (dir. Frank Tashlin, 1956). *The Girl Can't Help It* © 20th Century Fox, 1956; Figure 5.1 Early advertisements for television sets pictured them as the center of the home and the cause of domestic tranquility. Mary Evans Picture Library; Figure 5.2 Still from *All That Heaven Allows* (dir. Douglas Sirk, 1955). *All That Heaven Allows* © Universal, 1955; Figure 5.3 Milton Berle with Dean Martin and Jerry Lewis in a 1950s television show. Milton Berle © Sagebrush Enterpises, Inc., 1989; Figure 5.4 Sid Caesar as one of his characters, the Professor, the world's greatest authority. Sid Caesar © Sidvid, 2000; Figure 5.5 One of Ernie Kovac's funniest gags. Ernie Kovacs © Ediad Productions, 1997; Figure 5.6 Amos 'n' Andy, and Kingfish, on television. Getty Images; Figure 5.7 Rod Steiger and Joe Mantell in *Marty*, broadcast live on May 24, 1953, written by Paddy Chayefsky, directed by Delbert Mann. *Marty* © Rhino Home Entertainment, 1995; Figure 5.8 Charles van Doren and Herb Stempel "competing" on the fixed quiz show, *Twenty-One* (1957). Everett Collection/Rex Features; Figure 5.9 Bruce falls ill on this installment of *Survivor* (2006). *Survivor* © Mark Burnett Productions, CBS, 2006; Figure 5.10 Michael gets a lesson in diversity on *The Office* (2005). *The Office* © Deedle-Dee Productions and Reveille LLC in association with Universal Media Studios, 2005; Figure 5.11 *Lost*: John Locke faces the "Others" (2007). *Lost* ©ABC Studios, 2007; Figure 5.12 Body parts on *CSI*. *CSI* © Jerry Bruckheimer Television, CBS Paramount Network Television, 2006; Figure 5.13 A victim of Nazi-like torture on *CSI* (February, 2006). *CSI* © Jerry Bruckheimer Television, CBS Paramount Network Television; Figure 6.1 One of the earliest photographs, made by Joseph Niépce. Science and Society Picture Library; Figure 6.2 Famous series of sequential images, made in 1872, by Edweard Muybridge. Science and Society Picture Library; Figure 6.4 The Kinetoscope. Science and Society Picture Library; Figures 6.10, 6.11, 6.12, 6.13 Frames from the film *Music and Lyrics* (dir., Mark Lawrence, 2007). *Music and Lyrics* © Warner Bros., 2007; Figure 6.15 Space travel in *2001: A Space Odyssey*, dir. Stanley Kubrick, 1968). *2001: A Space Odyssey* © MGM/Turner Entertainment, 1968; Figure 6.16 John Ford's *The Searchers* (1956), with John Wayne. *The Searchers* © Warner

Bros., 1956, 1984; Figure 6.17 The door opens in John Ford's *The Searchers* (1956) © Warner Bros., 1956, 1984; Figure 6.18 Buñuel's film of Jean Cocteau's *Beauty and the Beast* (1946). *Beauty and the Beast* © Comité Cocteau, 2000; Figure 6.19 *T-Men* (dir. Anthony Mann, 1947). *T-Men* © Eagle-Lion, 1947; Figure 6.20 Roberto Rossellini's *Open City* (1945). *Open City* © Film Preservation Association, 1997; Figure 7.2 *Donky Kong*, an early computer game. Museum of Computing (www.museum-of-computing.org.uk); Figure 7.3 *Second Life*. Second Life REUTERS/Ho New Figure 7.4 *Grand Theft Auto, San Andreas*, a first-person shooter. *Grand Theft Auto, San Andreas* REUTERS/Ho New.

Every effort has been made to trace all copyright holders, but if any have been inadvertently overlooked the publishers will be pleased to include any necessary credits in any subsequent reprint or edition.

Introduction

"What are you doing?"
"Watching television!"

This is a common enough exchange that contains a large amount of meaning. "Watching television," like "going to a movie," or "reading the paper," or "going online," even "reading a book," makes a very general statement about a relationship to a particular medium. In interesting ways, our relationship to various media is generic – that is, we engage with television, the movies, the Internet as objects unto themselves, sometimes without regard to content. They are time off from more particular, even more important, events – at least what we consider more important. We take part in something that engages us and gives pleasure. If we're "watching television," we pass our time with sounds and images, coming to us electronically, offering stories, news, adventures, even (we're told) "reality." We may settle in to watch a show, or we may actively pursue something that pleases us, punching through channels on the remote – in fact, channel surfing may, itself, be what we want to do with television. Similarly, if we go online, engaging in the newest form of mass media, we may spend time on a particular site or, again, surf through links on the Web, looking, resting on a page, or clicking through.

Many years ago, the media critic Marshall McLuhan famously said, "the medium is the message." The form itself, no matter what its content, creates the relationship between the participant and the medium, so much so that the relationship goes beyond the connection between an individual and program – movie, television show, website – and becomes part of an entire cultural event. As far back as the advent of books in the Renaissance, or as close as the invention movies at the turn of the twentieth century, the popularity of radio in the 1920s, television in the early 1950s, and the Internet at the end of the twentieth century, media have made and remade society in important and lasting ways. We are changed, individually and collectively, by the history of media, by the introduction of new media, and by the variety of ways we interact with it all.

Media involve not only a delivery system and an individual participant – a viewer, reader, listener, web surfer – but the entire complex of social, cultural, and economic events that are generated by and around the media themselves. We need only consider the changes in communication, commerce, legislation, and, indeed, a way of life, created by the Internet to realize how profoundly the influence of media and our relationship to them expands far beyond ourselves. Even the more established forms of film and television, of radio and journalism, have individually and collectively changed the life of the culture and continue influencing the lives of people who engage with them.

Media have multiple components. We can speak about our relationship to the larger forms – watching television, surfing the Web – but we also need to consider the particular content of those forms. So, let us return to the question, "What are you doing?" Another response would be: "I'm watching my show." *Your* show? From the general act of passive engagement with television, we jump suddenly to a sense of ownership. Content is foregrounded along with you and your status as viewer. "My show" implies, specifically, a show you particularly enjoy and may even watch with some regularity. It is on television, but, in a sense, transcends the medium because of the way you respond to it, personalize it – make it your show. But this form of personalization is different still from, for example, your home page, which is out there, sort of like a television show, but that is something you yourself created and that is theoretically available to anyone at any time. The relationship is different, though the differences converge in interesting ways.

Convergence is a key concept. As viewers, readers, or listeners, we interact with the media, the media with us, and all with the culture we are part of, including larger societal issues involving politics, law, regulations, and commerce. Together, they form a complex of objective entities, technological, economic, even political, events, and imaginative creations.

Let me offer an example. One of my shows is *Law and Order*, a venerable television series that started in 1990 and survives still, along with three spin-off shows – *Law and Order: Special Victims Unit*, and *Law and Order: Criminal Intent*. I like it for its narrative tightness – the way it tells often complex stories quickly and concisely – and for the ensemble acting that helps knit all its parts together. I like it as well as a kind of engineering feat, the way the narratives are turned out, assembly-line style, even recycled from show to show, season to season, and yet seem original (a concept we will examine in some detail as we go on). In other words, I appreciate the production skills that go into the making of the series and its spin-offs.

But my pleasure is only one part of the equation, the various terms of which move within and around the media complex. On the level of content, the *Law and Order* series combines two genres, two types of stories: linking both police thriller and court-room melodrama, which are as old as cinema and as old as television itself. Its cops and bad guys genre extends now to video games. Genre, a concept we will develop further, is a form that generates both the way stories are told and the ways we respond to them. We take pleasure in the safe, mediated observations of terrible crimes and their morally principled solution and prosecution. We enjoy observing the process of detection and prosecution. Our enjoyment, and this holds true for any genre, stimulates production. In other words, *Law and Order* has existed for as many years as it has, and spins off as many variations as it does, because a significant number of people watch it. Its popularity leads not only to spin-offs, the various flavors of *Law and Order* created by its own production company, but also the creation of somewhat similar shows made by other producers. Production, pleasure, response, more production: this is the cycle of programming that has moved from film and radio to television.

The *Law and Order* group is produced by a man named Dick Wolf for the National Broadcasting Corporation, which began life in 1926 as the radio broadcasting arm of the Radio Corporation of America (RCA), and is now one part of a huge conglomerate that is part of General Electric and includes many cable channels as well as Universal Pictures. It is rivaled by the three other networks, the American Broadcasting System (now owned by the Disney Company), the Fox Network (owned by media tycoon Rupert Murdoch), and the Columbia Broadcasting System. CBS was founded in 1927 as a rival to NBC. It has gone through many owners, including the Westinghouse company. CBS needed a counter-program, something "new," but not too new, that would bring audiences with a taste for the detection and prosecution genre to its screens. Jerry Bruckheimer, a movie producer known for films like *Top Gun, Con Air, Armageddon, Black Hawk Down*, and *Pirates of the Caribbean*, offered *CSI*, which reinvented and elevated the lowly crime lab technician into a super-sleuth in Las Vegas, a small city that has itself achieved a mythic cultural significance. Bruckheimer added into the mix elements of violent horror films – sometimes called "slice and dice" or "splatter" films – to portray various stages of violence, wounds, and decomposition. The popularity of the program allowed Bruckheimer and CBS to rapidly spin off the concept by locating it in other cities, namely Miami and New York, and to amuse everyone by making every episode of each program grosser than the previous.

We can begin to see how complicated this all gets. You and I are still sitting in front of the television watching a program. Behind and around it are large, competing entities, fighting (to use the phrase of the television and advertising business) for our eyeballs, our "monetized eyeballs," to be exact. We enjoy the free entertainment and gross-out of programs which are – again in the parlance of the business – the same only different. The networks enjoy the advertising revenue, while the advertisers enjoy the profit that comes their way when we buy the products they advertise.

Television's struggle for eyeballs and therefore advertising revenue is different from that of the movies. A diminishing fraction of a film's profits comes from ticket sales here and abroad. Most now comes from DVD sales and rentals. A relatively small part comes from advertising in the form of product placement in a particular film. The appearance in a film of, for example, an Apple computer or a can of Coke is not accidental, but is paid for by the companies who want their product seen. On-air television networks and local stations get profits directly from advertising. Companies pay to advertise on shows. The more popular the show, the more the network can charge. (Many cable companies, like HBO, get their financing directly from cable carriers, and this presents yet another element of complexity.) So, another part of the equation is that we put up with continual interruption to our show by advertising, each commercial being its own little narrative – its own genre, in fact – nestled in the larger narrative of the show itself.

There's more still. Television programs spin off variations of themselves, like *Law and Order: Criminal Intent* or *CSI: Miami,* but they are also syndicated to various other outlets. *Law and Order* reruns, for example, can be seen almost continually on Turner Network Television, a sponsored cable outlet that once belonged to the Atlanta media empire of Ted Turner, but now belongs to the New York-Los Angeles conglomerate Time Warner (which also owns AOL and the Warner Bros. studios, among many other media). *Law and Order: SVU* is syndicated on USA, a commercial cable network owned by NBC. USA also airs original episodes of *Law and Order: Criminal Intent.* It is not impossible, on a given day, to watch all the *Law and Order* shows all of the time. *CSI* reruns can be regularly seen on Spike, a new cable outlet owned by Viacom, a company that also owns MTV, Showtime, BET, and Nickelodeon). In all instances, money is made from the series, the spin-offs, and the repeats. We get to see our shows over and over again; the stars make money by what's known in the trade as "residuals"; and producer Dick Wolf earns about one billion dollars a year.

Like movies – like all media – television is a technological event. What enables us to see a particular show is a convergence not only of a variety of commercial interests, but the confluence of technologies of signal transmission, which, even as I write this, are changing dramatically, moving into the digital realm to converge with computers and the Internet. All popular programs and the networks that show them have Internet sites, allowing some interaction between viewer and program. All network and many cable channels are broadcasting digital signals, which is now the only broadcast technology. These same outlets are broadcasting in high definition, one of the newest technologies that moves the television image from the blur of low resolution to something close to a movie image. More and more television series, including *Law and Order* and *CSI,* are available on DVDs, a digital technology that has changed the way many see movies and that is now creating an archive of television programs to serve both fans and serious students of television.

Clearly, "watching television" is not a simple act. No more simple than any other engagement we make with media. Many forces are at work in creating the sounds and images we attend to; many more are involved in how we make our choices and what we make *of* our choices. This complexity, the interdependence of commercial, imaginative, technological, political, and personal forces at work to create the media we enjoy (or hate), is the subject of this book.

Definitions are needed. "Media," the plural of "medium," is a somewhat fluid and perhaps not always accurate term for what we are studying. Its root is shared by other words, like "mediate," "intermediate," "mediation," all of which derive from the Latin word for "middle." A medium is something that stands between one thing and another. It can be a passive, transparent object. A window is an intermediary between the outside and our looking from the inside, but, at the same time, it frames what we see. A medium can be a person who presumes to transmit messages or insights from the dead to the living, an act itself mediated by a great deal of imagination and willingness to believe.

A medium is a container, a transmitter, a conduit that always changes whatever passes through it and is always itself defined differently by those on either end of the transmission process. Our definition of media specifically refers to the transmission of information such as the news, and to works of the imagination like *Law and Order*. Of course, if we were to consider media in its widest sense, as the various means humans use to mediate or represent the world to one another, we would need to consider art itself, the act of human imagination that expresses or mediates insight, thought, and emotion through images, words, or music. Considering this wider notion of media, we could well begin with the dawn of humanity and those strange yet familiar images of animals painted on cave walls. More realistically, we can start in the middle of the fifteenth century with the invention of printing, a technology that, to use a well-worn cliché, changed the course of Western civilization.

But for now we need to step back for a more general view. We can assume that anything we see or hear is mediated in some way. Even everyday, one-to-one communication, talking to a friend, is mediated by a number of things, not the least of which is the way we present ourselves to our friend and how she does the same to us. We are slightly different in any conversation, our selves are differently tuned to hear or to speak in any given social situation. Even if we tell the same story to different people, it is slightly changed, differently mediated, according to the situation, the person we're talking to, and our mood at the time. We narrate and mediate our lives.

Art does the same. The artist mediates imagination by means of the forms used to express it: words in a novel or poem; musical notation in a composition; an actor's presentation in a performance; the painter's use of color and shape; the way a writer and director use the narrative and visual storytelling devices of film or television. In all cases, what we receive has been shaped by the media used, and any mediation has to be understood not as something that has become another thing, but an entirely new thing – a result of the mediation process.

Take photography as an example. The camera is a technological device, the product of a long series of inventions developed to capture an image that dates back at least to the seventeenth century. These inventions culminated in the mid-nineteenth century with the combined development of glass ground to the shape of a lens that would receive light, and a chemical base that would be changed by that light and produce the image delivered by it. The camera is a medium, standing between a person or object in the world and the eye of the photographer. The result is an image, a mediation or representation that is the end product of what the photographer saw, how she framed it in the camera, what lens was used, and what was done to the image after it was produced. A photograph can look like the thing photographed but it is not the thing itself. It is a processed representation of it.

Since its invention in the nineteenth century, the history of photography has traveled along a spectrum that helps us further define media and, especially, "mass" media. When you take a snapshot with your digital camera or your cell phone (and the fact that it is a digital and not an analogue process has great importance itself) and show it to friends and family, you have both used and created media. You have created a mediated representation of someone or something. An image. But what happens when you put your images on your website? Technically, a digital file sitting on a server is accessible by any computer that can find it. If a key word in your website or blog is picked up by a search engine, the chances of that accessibility increase. If you can be Googled, your pictures, in theory, are available to anyone who clicks on the link.

But this is not exactly what we ordinarily think of as "the media," especially mass media. To qualify as "mass," at least in the conventional sense, the medium must be consciously distributed to a large number of people by a profit-making entity. Early mass-mediated photographs appeared in newspapers and advertising, themselves part of an even larger mass-media complex that delivered news and provoked people to buy goods. These images were never simple snapshots, were rarely crafted for subjective, artistic expression, and were always made for a specific purpose. The purpose – and this is part of the defining characteristic of mass media – is to reach a large audience and give them information or persuade them to act. A journalistic photograph is often structured to communicate a point of view. A photograph of a labor strike, for example, can be taken to emphasize the unruliness of the workers who are striking. A political candidate not favored by the newspaper's editors may be photographed in an unflattering way. An advertising photograph will always be fashioned to persuade you to buy the advertised product.

This allows us to expand our definitions further. I said that mass media consisted of the collection of devices, strategies, and forms that mediate or transmit information to us. In fact, the mediation includes the material transmitted – pictures, sounds, stories, words, themselves constituting works of the imagination (and therefore could be considered a form of art) – and the act of reception, the way we individually or collectively respond to the transmission. Put another way, we ourselves are mediated by the media. No matter what the source, the media change and reconstruct the material that is sent our way. No matter what our disposition, we respond and in some minor way are changed by the response. If our response is to vote for a political candidate because of what a newspaper or blogger said about him, or if we buy a car because of our response to an advertisement, we have been changed in a major way.

Traditional studies of mass media, or mass communications, concentrate on the ways the media affect us, and try to quantify those effects by measuring them scientifically. Media Studies looks at the broader interactions of media, at all parts of the complex that makes up media, concentrating on how they are part of larger cultural and societal events. It addresses the individual "texts" the media produces – the websites, television programs, video games – and their contexts. In the course of this book, we will consider each of the major media – news, radio, and television, recorded music, advertising, film, and digital communication – and examine the cultural, economic, political, and personal interactions that they are part of. Our discussions will include a history of media technology from movable type to binary programming. We will address the notion of ownership – one of the most contentious issues in the study of media. All media are owned, often by enormous corporations. We need to understand this, but not let it obscure the fact that, no matter how big the corporate structure of ownership has become, we still respond to the media as individuals. We have "our shows." In the case of new digital media, we are able to influence the media, and even produce it, directly. At the same time, the possibility of individual influence has raised legal issues in the area of intellectual property. IP has added to the complexity of Media Studies and needs to be considered through analysis that will take us into the area of the law.

It is entirely possible to conclude that any aspect, any instance, of mass media has at its base a persuasive function with an economic outcome. We can reduce the phenomenon of *Law and Order*, of *CSI*, and of a reality show like *Survivor* to a two-step purpose: attracting an audience and selling a product. We will analyze newspaper photography for the ways it mediates and manipulates "reality" in order to express a certain editorial take on what is being photographed. Certainly we have no difficulty doing this with advertising, whose sole function is to persuade us to buy a product.

Traditional approaches to the study of mass media focus on its persuasive nature and how users of media respond to the persuasion or react to media messages, the measurable "effects" of the media. These studies, as noted earlier, depend upon scientifically organized surveys and statistical analysis of the results. They attempt to quantify response by turning it into data. This is a valuable approach, especially as it attempts to turn subjective response into apparently analyzable numbers. But, as we have started to see, there is a complexity to media and to our responses that may be beyond the tools available to survey research. If I choose a particular reality show, for example, because I like the stunts and the people who perform them; if I cheer on one contestant over another; if I purchase one product over another that's advertised in that show; if I stay tuned to whatever program follows or switch to another channel; if instead of switching, I turn on my DVR, leave the television and proceed to contribute to my favorite blog – how are these choices quantified beyond the facts of my having made them?

Media Studies doesn't quantify, but describes and analyzes, accounts for, and situates media within the even more complex matrix of the culture of which both the media and its audience are part. Media Studies seeks meaning not in numbers but within interactions and across diversity. It recognizes that the complex structure of mass media is not an undifferentiated mass any more than its audience. This is important. Traditionally, critics of mass media condemned it and its audience. They saw media as manipulative and its audience as an undifferentiated, passive mass whose tastes were lowered to the detriment of the whole culture. We can speculate that the rise of sociologically based quantitative mass-communication studies came about in order to bypass the notion of debasement. Of course, the producers of the media themselves depend upon such statistical analyses to determine who their audience is and what they might be thinking.

The media – particularly journalism, film, television, and (these days) that peculiar media subset, video games – have been accused of being base, biased, vulgar, corrupt, and in some instances responsible for lowering the intelligence and taste of the public and raising its level of violence. Such criticism reached its peak in the 1950s when comic books and rock 'n' roll were brought into the mix of media that corrupted young people. It is with us still, obvious in the outrage caused by nudity on television – accidental or otherwise – that caused the Federal Communications Commission to increase its censorship of broadcast TV, and in the negative responses to the violence evident in some hip-hop lyrics and pervasive in first-person shooter computer games.

Historically and currently, criticism and censorship, both real or threatened, have had little effect on any of the media. For every point of pressure applied to a suspected bad influence, another bubble of defiance and even excess appears somewhere else. When, in the early thirties, church groups threatened to boycott sex and violence in films, the studios co-opted the threat by forming their own industry censorship board that allowed film-makers to become imaginative and subtle in the ways they depicted sex and violence. Today, even with the Motion Picture Association of America's rating system, even with the FCC and right-wing lobbying groups breathing heavily down the backs of television producers, sex and violence continue to be represented in movies and television, and the search for cause and effect of computer-game violence continues.

More importantly, despite the content, despite the censorship, we continue to watch, listen, and partake. To be sure, the focus of our attention shifts and moves across various media. Not so many people are watching *Law and Order*. More are watching *CSI*. And, in general, viewership of the on-air networks is down, while cable is up. Movie attendance is declining. Newspaper readership, within the large numbers mass media producers demand, barely exists. Internet use continues to rise and rise, with broadband and wireless communications absorbing and reforming almost all older forms and genres. And what is to be done about this? The answer is not to condemn or ignore it, and certainly not to let it all flow over and by us without consideration. Nor should we rule out the pleasures of the media when we think of them in all their complexity. Serious analysis does not negate enjoyment; it only enhances it.

The pleasure of finding meaning in complexity is our aim.

The decision to organize this book by types of media may seem, at first glance, to go against the fact that, as you read this, all media are converging to the digital. It might, therefore, have made sense to organize our discussion by topic and issue, using digital convergence as the principle of order. But I wanted to maintain something of a historical context and a sense of specificity. Converging or not, each of the media chosen for discussion has its own history and cultural context. Organizing by type makes it possible to maintain that specificity, offer some history of the medium, analyze its cultural contexts, and "read" its texts.

The order of the chapters is likewise determined by history – in part – and the kinds of relationship one medium has with another. The first chapter lays out some basic principles, theories, and analytic tools for understanding media as industrial and cultural events. I've chosen "news and information" as the first subject of study (chapter 2) partly because in its print form it is the oldest mass medium and because it infiltrates all others. The history and analysis of the news – print, broadcast, online – provides an initial window on the ways in which media influence the culture and culture the media. Power and persuasion, the growing interaction between media producer and consumer, are contained within journalism's history and movement from print to broadcast to blog.

Advertising is the lifeblood of all media. Modern advertising and journalism grew up together. Chapter 3 on advertising examines the ways in which consumers and consumer culture are enveloped by media and at the same time push back by "reading" advertising according to individual needs. Because of the strong visual component of advertising, the chapter begins the discussion of visual media that will be carried over into the chapters on television and film.

Radio was the first entertainment medium to enter the domestic place. Its early history was an interesting mix of amateur engineering, the growth of commercial and governmental control, and an aural canvas on which race was painted in often-strange colors. Recorded music, which preceded, grew alongside, and finally became inextricably connected with radio, is a huge and complex field. I have narrowed the study in chapter 4 to include brief histories and analyses of the cultures of popular music, and recorded music's influence and eventual takeover of radio. The influence of African-American musical culture that is part of the discussion of radio is woven through the sections on recorded music.

To preserve a historical perspective and a link with in-home media, I've followed radio and recordings with chapter 5 on television. Its origins embedded in the nineteenth-century technologies of sight and sound, television slid out from radio in the late 1930s and by the 1950s dominated all other media as the source for news and entertainment. The chapter presents some of this history and then concentrates on the genres of television and their cultural influences.

Film presents an interesting problem in studying media cultures and histories. Of all media, it is treated as an art form that carries the potential for unique, personal expression, demanding close attention from its viewers. At the same time, film began as one of the technologies of the nineteenth century and took over as the entertainment of the *public sphere* – outside of the home – even before radio thoroughly infiltrated the private. Despite its claims to art, it is as mass-produced, profit and genre driven as are any of the media. At the same time, it permits continuation of the discussion of visual media begun in chapter 3 on advertising and elaborates many of the concepts discussed in chapter 5 on television.

Digital media is the logical place to conclude the study because it is the actual place toward which all media are converging. The final chapter looks broadly at the digital world, from the early days of the Internet to contemporary social networking, and provides a summary of all that has come before.

A Note on References and Websites

References appear at the end of each chapter. In the case of websites, I have tried, wherever possible, to use the most authoritative sites available. This means that, while not avoiding Wikipedia, I have tried to refer to a university site, or to an organization known for the quality of its research, or to an online version of a newspaper of record such as *The New York Times*. When citing articles that appear in the databases held by a university library, or in a newspaper that has an online version (and they all do), or that appear in a journal article that is available online, I have cited the article's URL. You can then discover whether your school subscribes to the online journal cited. Links were current at the time of writing – but links do go dead without notice.

Reference

Marshall McLuhan, *Understanding Media: The Extensions of Man* (Cambridge, MA, and London: MIT Press, 1994).

CHAPTER ONE
The Designs of Media

"The entertainment media is [sic] changing," said Allan Mayer, managing director at Sitrick and Company, a public relations firm. "The currency a movie star had was the ability to put people in the seats. They command enormous salaries. But simply having a star in a movie isn't enough. Young audiences don't have the same loyalties and interests that previous generations have. That's why there is so much panic in the industry."

New York Times, November 9, 2005

"Panic in the industry." An interesting place to start a discussion of media. The media are money-making events, and their producers are fond of thinking of themselves and their companies as an industry, perhaps like the Ford Motor Company. An industry is responsible for circulating money: investing in production, creating a product, selling it to consumers, making a profit, turning part of the profit back into production, salaries, and dividends for stockholders. The products of the Ford Company are automobiles: physical things. The product of the media is entertainment, itself a medium in the sense that it is a means for creating pleasure for its audience, who will like it enough to pay, which will in turn make the profit for its producers. The media's media are not automobiles or air conditioners or hair gel, but products of the imagination: movies, television shows, websites, games; or carriers of information, like newspapers. One of the media, advertising, attempts to manufacture a desire for other products and, in so doing, supports other media and the economy as a whole. Like the leaders of any other industry, the producers in media work in fear: whenever money is at stake, fear is involved. What will the audience want? How do we measure the audience and their desires? What do we do when the audience doesn't respond by buying tickets, watching TV and buying the advertised goods and services; doesn't click through to the advertiser's link; stops reading the newspaper? Panic in the industry.

The quote we started with comes from an article that dealt with two specific media events. Its main subject was the popular movie actor Tom Cruise, who had to hire a new agent in 2005 because his behavior during interviews, and his support of a controversial religious movement, were putting off his fans. More importantly, it addressed a concern that swept movie-making during the same year: a severe drop in movie attendance. Celebrity, pleasing an audience, attempting to craft products that will get its attention, are all part of the core of the media complex, part of its history and ours as well. It is that core and how it came to be formed, and the ways that we can open it up to our understanding, that constitute the subject of this book.

One thing must be kept in mind at the outset. The metaphor of a "core" suggests something tight and stable. In fact, media are not stable, nor – aside from making money – do they have a nucleus that can be clearly defined. By the time you read this, the article I'm referring to may have no relationship to anything regarding the media. Tom Cruise may be gone and forgotten, another celebrity grown old and discarded. Indeed, Paramount studio's boss, Sumner Redstone, severed the studio's contract with Cruise because they felt that his antics hurt tickets sales of his last movie for them, *Mission Impossible III*. He has since gone on to form his own production company. The movie business will most definitely change and will have good years as well as lean. Hidden in the "panic" voiced by the industry in late 2005 was a major shift on all levels of movie-making, movie exhibition, and reception. Celluloid – 35 mm film – is slowly disappearing to be replaced by digital recording, distribution, and projection. The movie-going experience is changing and will continue to change, as more and more people watch films at home on DVD, on cable, or on web-based video on demand.

The core of media that we're looking for is in a constant state of change. Everything about media is in perpetual change. The design of media, the loosely integrated relationships between the producers of media and its audiences, keeps getting rewoven as the audiences, the technologies, tastes, and culture – you and I and all the things we do, including the media we read, watch, and listen to – change. It is not very likely that, in the course of our investigation, we'll find a single, stable definition. What we will find are a few constants that will guide us through our attempts at understanding the meaning of media gained by close analysis of their history, their texts, and the ways in which we respond to them.

First, we need to consider the way we will use certain key terms. The media refers to the aggregate of profit-making, technology-driven companies *and* products that make up news delivery, radio, music, recordings, advertising, film, television, and the varieties of digital transmissions and interactions. *The New York Times*; NBC; Paramount Pictures; Rockstar, the company that makes the "Grand Theft Auto" video game; Sony, the manufacturer of PlayStation that plays GTA, as well as televisions and computers, and the company that owns a movie studio and record labels; Apple, the company that makes computers, the iPod, and distributes iTunes; TBWA/ Chiat/Day, the advertising agency that created the iPod commercials – these are all part of the media, their companies, products, and we, the consumers. Mass media is a term, sometimes used derogatorily, that refers to these companies and products when they are created and consumed by very large numbers of people. Popular culture is mass media seen from the other end. Rather than being concerned with the owners and major producers of media, popular culture embraces its products and the people who use them in a variety of ways, even those not intended by their creators. Popular culture is the *use* of media, the way it is understood, enjoyed, hated, consumed, made part of the life of an individual or the larger cultural group she belongs to. Popular culture embraces media, but it is more than the sum of media's various parts.

Popular culture can be thought of as an environment that includes media, which includes its productions – tunes, video games, Internet sites, movies – its listeners, and its artists. While this environment encompasses and informs all that we address here, it is the media themselves that will receive most attention. We can begin by considering media as a series of *texts* and *contexts*. A text is a coherent, related unit of expression, like a rock song: a formal construction of words and music, following certain conventions, communicating, mediating thought and emotion. It is recorded on a digital or analog medium, broadcast or played on CD, MP3, or iPod, and listened to. Everything involved in the making, distributing, and listening to the song constitutes its context. There is a lot of mediation going on here, beginning with the songwriter and performer, ending with the listener, and mediated by a host of technological processes on the way. We need to define, unpack or decode – a concept we'll address further on – all parts of the process in order to understand what the study of media, their texts, contexts, and cultures, entails.

Almost always, definitions raise more questions than they answer. Are blogs, which have rapidly entered the popular culture and which borrow the conventions of the diary or journalistic opinion-making, while employing the technological medium of the World Wide Web, part of mass media? How do we categorize a music mix, made up of mass-mediated works – popular music from various sources – put together to suit personal taste? If some of the tunes that make up the mix are copyrighted and have been downloaded for free from a P2P (peer-to-peer) network, do we leave the realm of mass media and popular culture and enter the world of law? How do we square the concept of the individual, artistic imagination at work in the creation of a song, a movie, or even an advertisement with the concept of commercialized mass media and mass audience in which, convention has it, individuality plays little role?

In order to begin understanding these and other questions that will come up in the course of our discussion, I want to introduce a list of core issues, somewhat broader than definitions, and central to the complexity of Media Studies. What follows is not a definitive or exhaustive list; it is difficult to discuss any one of the items without referring to the others. All of these elements will be more fully explored in the chapters that follow, but the chapters do not follow them slavishly. These elements of the media design, like the media themselves that are covered in the following chapters, move in and out of one another as they converge in ways that continually alter the design.

Threads in the Media Design

- Audience
- Art and artifact
- Culture

- Codes and genres
- Business
- Technology
- Immediacy and change
- Evaluation

Audience

All issues in the study of media are contentious. Disagreement reigns. But there may be no one issue more contentious than the nature of the media audience. The media audience must be a large one – hence the term "mass" media. But that very adjective carries a negative connotation. The thinking is based on some empirical evidence that concludes anything made to please large numbers of people must be produced and consumed indiscriminately, must be mediocre at best, and therefore must be made to appeal to what is often referred to as "the lowest common denominator." Mass media are compared to "serious" media, the works of high culture – classical music, novels, poetry, drama – which are made *by* individuals *for* individuals, who, it is assumed, are mature, educated, and actively discriminating in their taste. By comparison, mass media must pander, make itself simple and accessible to a large audience who are, presumably, uneducated, vulgar, and passive. Even more damaging, according to accepted wisdom, the mass audiences of mass media are made *worse*, coarsened, even harmed by the media.

We find this argument throughout media history, and it is part of a kind of cultural convention in which any given society is always seeing its eventual doom, while trying to pin that eventuality on some evil influence. In the US during the 1920s, jazz was said to be causing the cultural decay, particularly (and always) among the culture's young people. In the 1950s, it was comic books and rock 'n' roll. Today video games are said to create an environment of violence that causes gamers to become desensitized to violence in their daily lives. The Internet itself is said to be a dangerous field of predation and incipient violence where young people are constantly at risk.

In the past, mass media audiences were often gendered, and that itself became a cause to condemn it. Before the advent of mass media, the popular novels in the eighteenth century were written mostly by men about and for women, and therefore considered somewhat less than major literary works. Indeed, the audience for popular mass media is often thought of, derogatorily, as "feminine": passive, emotional, undiscriminating, easily swayed. The media audience is tarred with the negative stereotypes usually applied to only one gender. The result has been a persistent discourse in which the comparison of "serious" and "popular" culture, high culture and low, is voiced in the binaries of active/passive; intellectual/emotional; discriminating/indiscriminate; uplifting/vulgarizing; difficult/simple.

It is true that many media products were and still are aimed at female audiences. Magazines like *Cosmopolitan* come to mind, and there is an entire subgenre of movie melodramas that the studios called "women's pictures." Film magazines from the twenties through the sixties, as well as contemporary celebrity and gossip magazines, are aimed at women audiences. The marketing of television in the early fifties was specifically aimed at stay-at-home housewives, taking for granted their limited and limiting experiences and offering them a window on the world. Today, television programs like *Oprah* and the various *Martha Stewart* programs – indeed, much of the output of cable channels like HGTV and Lifetime – are gendered. But if these are aimed at women, then the cable network Spike TV, action movies, televized NASCAR races and all their paraphernalia, wrestling, and first-person shooter games are aimed at men. Targeting movies, television, or sports events toward one gender or another may smack of stereotyping, but is more involved with marketing, with "segmenting" the audience. It isn't the same as using gender to derogate the audience.

Derogation of the audience has always been a way to get at the media that delights an audience. But the producers of media are difficult targets to aim at. They are usually large corporate entities, not oblivious to criticism, but inured to insults. And, because the producers of media almost always argue in their own defense that all they do is give the audience what the audience wants, they deflect criticism to that audience, which therefore remains the butt of criticism or warnings about the harm being done to them.

The fact is that audiences for mass media are as varied as are the media they listen to, watch, and read. The condemnation of that audience, as well as the media that serve them, reflects a nervousness, if not snobbishness, on the part of many people who embrace high culture and fear for its demise, or indulge in popular media and are embarrassed to admit it. That fear, and the threat of a diminishing audience for traditional forms of media – classical music, drama, serious fiction, poetry, even mass media products like newspapers – plays into larger concerns of cultural coarsening and debasement.

The notion of debasement leads to another form of audience stereotyping, this time based on age, class, and race. America has always tried to fool itself into believing that it is a classless society, despite the economic realities that show a small percentage of the population owning the largest percentage of the wealth; a large underclass of poverty-stricken people of all races; and a middle class, part of which is struggling, another part reasonably well-to-do, and both of which are the major consumers of mass media. High culture has been the traditional property of the wealthy and educated, attending and supporting what we can now begin to call small-audience (as opposed to mass-audience) art. Popular art and mass media not only become the province of middle- and working-class audiences, but, in the eyes of the protectors of high culture, mark both the audience and their art as inferior.

There are even physiological markers for this, metaphors that somehow link to the way a person looks, and marks her class, depending upon the kind of entertainment she attends to. High culture and those who love it are "highbrow." "Lowbrow" applies to rock 'n' roll music and rap, and television reality shows – anything that seems vulgar, undemanding, or pandering. The terms have a slight odor of racial stereotyping about them.

Popular "mass" culture is also the province of youth. Few adults, after all, play video games; and most popular music is originated, made, and enjoyed by young people. Those who worry about lowbrow entertainment destroying the culture always aim their concerns at young people. In the 1920s, jazz was going to ruin the young, and in the 1950s, as we mentioned, comic books and then rock 'n' roll were supposed to be turning kids into juvenile delinquents. These days, video games are blamed for making their users violent. Studies are made; congressional hearings held. The culture continues more or less intact. Or disintegrating: there has never been a time when people did not think the culture was degenerating. Perhaps it always has been.

The actual result of media bashing and audience stereotyping is to turn complex issues into artificially simplified ones. This is what stereotyping of any kind always does. There may indeed be such a thing as "highbrows," individuals who entirely eschew the popular and only read serious novels and poetry and listen to classical music – "highbrow" art. There are even some people who don't own a television or a computer. Not many. Much of the culture, however, have their brows in the right place and enjoy a variety of media for an even greater variety of reasons. The culture of media is one of both acceptance and discrimination, something that small-art (as opposed mass-art) audiences would deny, but which is common practice. There are few places, few cultures, anywhere in the world that can avoid media. Whether this means villagers gathered around the community television in the Indian subcontinent, Muslim immigrants in France watching the Arab-language news channel, Al Jazeera, on satellite, a Midwestern businessman reading *USA Today*, or an entire family enjoying *American Idol*, or someone reading a criticism of it in *The New York Times* – we all live in a mediasphere. It is much more interesting to understand what our relation is to this environment than to condemn it or people who don't resist it.

Art and artifact

The word "art" has crept into our discussion, and it is another contentious issue in the study of media, and an integral part of its design, even more so as the design attempts to hide it from view.

Our contemporary notion of what constitutes art is only as old as the nineteenth century, when the Romantics fantasized the myth of the misunderstood artist, toiling alone in his garret (always "his"; though, interestingly enough, the creator of one of the most enduring and influential works of popular art, *Frankenstein*, was a woman, Mary Shelley, wife of an English Romantic poet). The artist is misunderstood and so is his art, which can never quite find an audience as sensitive and intelligent as the artist himself. That work, growing from the experience of the artist, a product of inspiration and suffering, is personal and difficult, available only to an equally sensitive audience of the few who can appreciate beauty and complexity.

I have just indulged in a bit of stereotyping myself by claiming a kind of universal image of the suffering artist producing personal, difficult works. Historical truth is different. Art began both with individuals and with community and almost always had a social, religious, instructive force behind it. No one quite knows the purpose behind prehistoric cave paintings, which are some of the earliest artifacts we have. But these representations of animals and the outline of a human hand probably had to do with hunting. Drama emerged from communal rituals. Poetry and narrative fiction began as oral presentations passed on from storyteller to storyteller – bards and minstrels – culminating in the early eighteenth century when novels were read aloud to audiences, and the late nineteenth and early twentieth centuries when, in some cultures, silent film was accompanied by a narrator in the theater telling the story. Historically, art as something difficult, belonging to the privileged, sequestered in spaces of private contemplation in libraries, museums, or concert halls, is only one notion of the art experience. Art as a shared experience, involving a give-and-take between performer and audience, is another. "Large audience" art, mass media, popular media – no matter the term we choose – is an extension of very old communal practices.

But what about the work of art itself? Is there only one way to define it? Is it unalterably different from the notion of entertainment? Art is imaginative expression: emotion, ideas, events "made up" and formed by a hand painting on canvas, a hand writing music on a sheaf of paper, a voice singing the music, a story told on television or in film. The productions of the creating eye, hand, body, or voice, all require a viewer, reader, or listener. Art is always a circuit of mediation. The creation of a work of art involves the production of a mediating form – words, paint, music, voice, images – and an interpreter. An interpreter is the reader, viewer, listener – in short, an audience. This circuit is always open. The artist and the audience, the medium of art itself, change in large ways as tastes change, as the various intellectual and ideological forces that make and remake a culture change. It changes in small ways: every act of interpretation is an act of change, again responding to large cultural pressures but also to more local pressures of individual inclination (that include many things like upbringing, education, race, gender, class), and that most indefinable of qualities, taste.

We can visualize the process of art-making and art-receiving as a mediated circuit of production: the formal object; its reception – the attending ear and eye of the audience. All of this set within yet another circuit of ideas, emotions, forms, artifacts, policies, genders, and races called "culture." We can also conceive of art objects existing on a spectrum. There is no denying that there exist difficult, challenging works of art that demand time, intelligence, and inquisitiveness on the part of an individual who seeks to appreciate them. A good poem, a complex canvas, is meant for engagement, for processing, not quick consumption. But what happens when we travel along the spectrum? Is a best-selling novel a work of art? It requires the same kind of creative, mediating, and reading process as, say, a novel by Henry James, but on a different, more immediate level. A best-seller has to be written, published, distributed, purchased, and read. The mediated object – the collection of words making up the novel – and the act of reading are different if we're looking at a Stephen King novel than they would be were we considering James Joyce's *Finnegans Wake*, a book whose last sentence is the first part of its first sentence, inviting us to read it over and over again. A popular novel may be written in such a way that the story told takes prominence over the telling of the story. We have no greater praise for a novel than to call it a page-turner. The suppression of form, making it transparent, is a major defining factor of the works of popular culture. Form recedes behind content, even though content is the product of form. Try parsing the various parts of a rap song and see how complex its formal rhythms are.

Let's extend the spectrum even further. Perhaps nothing is further from high, small-audience art than computer games. At base they violate one of high art's most fundamental principles: single authorship. Remember that our romantic view of art idealizes the artist working away in isolation. Computer games, like the movies that spawned them, like the computer programming that makes them work – like television, newspapers, and advertising – are created through collaboration. What's more, the collaboration that results in computer games creates a medium that doesn't stand alone, but needs the active participation of the user. All art requires active engagement, but computer games *respond* to user intervention and are interactive the way no other art or media form can be. Then there is the matter of an online user group of millions (for a massively multiplayer online role-playing game like *The World of Warcraft*), each of whom interact in an imaginary world. Can computer games be considered "art"? By our criteria, yes. They are products of the imagination and it takes imagination to engage with them. They are complex but, unlike traditional imaginative works, they change in response to our own imaginative input.

Computer games fill other criteria as well: they are mass produced to make a profit for their manufacturers. Their creators may think of them as art – certainly imaginative in the detail of their computer-generated graphics and elegant computer programs. Gamers? Maybe not so much. Or not consciously. Computer games don't fulfill one traditional requirement of high art, which is quiet contemplation. They are not quiet, and they are immersive and interactive rather than contemplative. Perhaps they require skill more than the refined sensibility that is sometimes called forth by high art. But the games are engaging, and engagement itself may be the key. All art, high or low, small or mass audience, must engage its audience. The means and results of the engagement may be different, the means and results of their creation may be different, but if emotions and intellect are brought into play through a mediated object, we can consider art at work.

At the same time, there should be cause for concern that by broadening the notion of art, including within it the various productions of mass media, we may simply be diluting the idea of art beyond recognition. It is already a stretch to think of a video game as artistic, and it would be a complete break if we applied the word to a reality television show or a commercial for a prescription drug. We would risk losing all credibility. However, if we maintain the traditional direction of applying the name of art only to works of high intellectual and emotional purpose, we risk perpetuating the notion of cultural debasement, that is, of condemning both the productions and the audience for mass-mediated art as somehow less intelligent, more gullible, and simply inferior to the audience and productions of high art. It will, finally, be necessary to apply some discrimination and evaluation. We might dodge the problem, for the moment, by referring to the productions of mass media as "artifacts," or just simply "works," the objects that are made for mass consumption. We can also substitute for the misleading hierarchy of "high" art over mass art by referring to "fine" or small-audience art and popular or mass-mediated art. This, however, may be semantic sleight of hand and it will not finally free us of the ways our culture leads us to think about art and continually degrade what does not seem to fit the term. It will serve for now to use all of these terms and be as clear as possible about what we are referring to.

Culture

The design of media is woven in, by, and for its culture. The meaning of culture is as complex and contentious as meanings of "art," and it too requires some shift in thinking. We usually think of culture as being the realm of high art, just as we think of someone who is smart and discriminating in taste, someone who loves high art, as "cultured." "Culture" is often the culture's way of referring to the creation and appreciation of small-audience art. The fact is that high culture, the world of serious, small-audience art, is only one part of the broader, all-inclusive set of interactions among people, the things they say, do, make, feel, believe in, buy, sell, love, and hate that make up their culture. Culture is a kind of sum total of human activity and its representations. It is made up of all the ways people see, interact, present, and represent themselves to each other. Culture is the opposite of "nature."

The natural world is made up of anything that goes on without human intervention or interpretation. Atomic and cellular movement, the electromagnetic spectrum that carries much of our media, belong to the natural world, but not the *concepts* of atom and cells, or the division of the electromagnetic spectrum into profit-making parts: these are made up by humans to describe and manipulate nature. The change of the seasons is a response to the rotation of the earth, but not our descriptions of the seasons, which are a product of meteorology and poetry. The process of evolution is a long-term, natural series of random events that cause changes in living things. The theory of evolution is human-made narration of how these changes occur, based on natural evidence.

As soon as we apply imagination and language to nature, explain it, do science on it, turn it into a discourse understood by many people, nature becomes culture. That's why evolution can become a contentious issue. That evolution occurs is beyond reasonable doubt; but the language – the discourse, the explanation and description of a process that takes place with no apparent cause, and that places organic development in the realm of genetic accident – causes discomfort within other discourses that believe in divine purpose.

It is the nature of human curiosity and our need for narrative – for stories that explain things – that we turn nature into a cultural discourse. We need to account for things we don't understand, and we create understanding by talking about things. Many of our shared stories are ancient, and some defy scientific knowledge by the very convenience of their explanations. In nature, the earth turns on its axis, exposing one part to light and the other to darkness in a predictable rotation. In culture – our culture, right now – we still say the sun rises and sets.

Imagination and knowledge mediate the unknown into the known, telling stories that enable us to comprehend the human and non-human world; in so doing they turn nature into culture. Science is only one cultural discourse. Religion is another. So is politics. So are literature, movies, and other media. All of these and more create culture: the dominant culture that speaks to our shared values; subcultures, in which various groups express themselves in different ways, often in opposition to the dominant culture; and even the apparently independent culture of the individual. Indeed, in one-to-one communication, the way we speak and gesticulate in any particular situation, the words we choose, and the references we make are in some way culturally determined – mediated. The "self" you present to a professor is not exactly the same self you present to a friend or to your parents. You choose, perhaps unconsciously, a different representational mode. What that mode is, and the very fact that you choose different modes, is culturally determined. The same goes for the mode of art and entertainment you choose, the way you use it, and the way it was created. If you choose to listen to rock 'n' roll rather than classical music; if you read blogs rather than a newspaper; if you watch reality television rather than *Law and Order*, you are making cultural choices. You might respond immediately by saying, "no, these are personal choices." But the personal is the cultural insofar as your taste is created or influenced, formed and informed by age, social interaction, education, indeed politics, as well as taste, among all the things that intermingle to create culture.

It is important always to keep in mind that culture is a mutable thing, in fact not one thing, but a variety of subcultures that move and change within the larger dominant culture that voices and affirms the values of a society. Your taste, habits, inclinations, loves, and hates are formed and informed by many things, including gender, race, and class, and religious and political beliefs (even if your political belief is disinterest in the political). All of these are the products of or responses to culture.

The producers of media artifacts – themselves parts of various subcultures, or communities, to borrow a term used by online groups – are always attempting to understand subcultures in order to produce products they will buy. Various subcultures will often contend with one another in an attempt to impress their culture on another. Lovers of grunge rock may disparage hip-hop; fans of MySpace may not share the political passions of the DailyKos blog. Media creators try to discover and create for these subcultures: they call it "segmenting" the audience – a process that includes considerations of age, gender, race, even geography; we call it taking part in the media we like. In all cases personal taste is only one part of a larger cultural context that guides us to our choices and forms our taste.

There is no better example than the culture of music. This can be roughly divided into three parts: "classical" music, whose origins are European; jazz, whose origins are African-American; and popular/rock/country/rap/, whose origins are extremely varied. There are other forms – folk music, indigenous music, music from different cultures, and so forth – but these three will serve for now. Each of these major groups can be further subdivided on sides of both the producers and consumers of music. There are composers, performers, and the audience; there are record companies, radio stations, concert managers on one side and consumers who buy records, listen to radio stations, and go to concerts, or download tunes to their iPods on the other side. Each kind of music, each mode of production, performance, and consumption is produced by and appeals to specific cultural groups, although there is a great deal of crossover. What's more, all of this tends to change from generation to generation and from one technology to another.

We will discuss recorded music in chapter 4. It is among the most complex of media forms on both the production and reception sides. But it is also the most ready example of how cultures and media interact. The history of rap, for example, shows the emergence of a form of expression from urban African-American culture into mainstream popular music. It combines not only a musical style, but a set of cultural attitudes. It involves not only music, but celebrity, notoriety, gender conflict, and a defiance of a variety of values held by the dominant culture.

We have heard much in recent years of the "culture wars," the contention between a strongly felt, Christian-driven morality and a supposedly looser, more "liberal" view of the world. Much of this battle has to do with strongly held beliefs and practices by many groups, holding different views, some of which are expressed in political choices and media such as music, movies, and television. Media become a target of the culture wars, variously condemned as too liberal, too one-sided, too full of hate or sexual innuendo; too conservative; too liberal – too something that one side considers excessive.

Historically, media have always been involved in culture wars of one variety or another because they are so intimately involved in our cultures and in self-expression. In many respects they are the most obvious expressions of our cultures. The fact is that most people get their information and entertainment, their view of themselves and the world, and often the very fashion of the clothes they wear to make a statement about themselves and their community, from television, movies, rock groups, interactions with the Internet, or computer-based games. This makes media the steered and steering current of our society.

Codes and genres

How does culture cohere when it is such a dynamic, complex entity? More particularly, how do we understand and respond to that particular aspect of culture that we are studying, the media and our relationships to it? In attempting to answer these questions, I am going to draw upon some established ideas in Media and Cultural Studies, in particular the work one of its founders, Stuart Hall.

Hall was one of the founders of Cultural Studies, the larger branch of inquiry that, along with Film Studies, contributed to the kind of Media Studies we are undertaking here: understanding media as a complex relationship between the producers and the audience of media works and the cultures that embrace them, and the close analysis of the forms those works take. We have already touched upon Hall's basic position in our discussion of "nature" versus culture, and the ways we represent the world in order to understand it. Hall discusses the fact that all of our notions of "reality," our beliefs, demands, values, and our conviction of our own individuality, along with our fears and anxieties, are mediated through language. We know the world and ourselves by the ways we address and describe each. And "language" can be a broad term, applicable to any coherent means of communication. In that broader sense, we can use the term "discourse" when we refer to ways in which meaning is made through verbal or visual expression. Language, discourse, and our ability to share its meanings all exist through a process of coding and decoding. This occurs when we express our shared beliefs and understandings in specific ways and interpret such expressions. If we use a word, some terminology, an image, or a gesture, that has some intended meaning, it is encoded. When we interpret it, we decode it either as it was meant to be or as we think it should be.

Here is an example. "I am planning to go to college." This relatively straight-forward declaration is deeply coded, and with more than a desire to better one's self. To plan to go to college implies a social and economic background out of which the expectation of a college education can grow and be made possible. The statement is therefore coded differently from "I *wish* I could go to college," and is different still from "College is a waste of time, I'm going to work," or "College is worthwhile but I have no choice but to go to work." There may be various attitudes (themselves a kind of coding) behind these statements; but they are themselves fed by cultural assumptions and economic contexts that have formed the individuals who hold them. We can decode and respond to these statements with versions of admiration ("That's great, everyone should go to college"), a kind of transference ("Yeah, that's what my parents say to me, that I should go to college"), pity ("I wish it were possible for you to go to college"), or even scorn ("Get off it, you have about as much chance of going to college …").

Let's move our coded example into college and more specific realms of mediated language, non-verbal this time, and apparently less serious: the choice of dress. The closest we get to nature in the way we dress is to protect ourselves against it. Any protective covering would serve us if all we wanted was to be physically comfortable in a given climate. But physical comfort, in our culture certainly, is the least important purpose of clothing. Clothing is coded in terms of who we believe we are and, perhaps more importantly, how we wish to be perceived by others in our subculture, how we want to be decoded. Why else would one of our most basic uniforms, blue jeans, for example, be available in such a variety of styles, some of them specifically coded by gender and even race?

Denim has been around for a long time. The cloth originated in France and was known as "serge de Nîmes." In the mid-nineteenth century, an American tailor named Jacob Davis developed the rivets and stitching for Levi Strauss's clothing company, a style that was patented and continues as the basic way of fashioning blue jeans. Jeans were originally work pants, associated with laborers and therefore marked or coded by their class. In the twentieth century, the jean code began to shift and move up the social scale, aided by the Levi Strauss company, which recoded jeans – by means of advertising – as "Western" garb, an image that migrated into Western films. Jeans became part of the myth of the West. In the 1950s, again through movies, particularly teenage rebel films like *The Wild One* (1953) and *Rebel Without a Cause* (1955), the coding shifted, and jeans became associated with adolescence and rebellion for both men and women; in fact women had already adopted jeans as work clothes during World War II. By the 1960s, jeans became the uniform of the counter-culture and the general dress of young people. Levi Strauss took full advantage of the fact and began to create variations: "pre-worn," stonewashed, stretch (for those who no longer have an adolescent waistline), and baggy – in addition to a variety of "designer jeans." The marketing and purchasing of these various styles were coded *by their wearers* with specific meanings.

Tight or baggy, tapered or straight, low cut or high, jeans have acquired an association with the groups that wear them. They are marketed for a Western look or as part of an "urban lifestyle," marked as high fashion or as somehow belonging to an outlaw culture. Marketing and "marking" are key here. Jeans and other clothing are part of a cycle of style that keeps getting coded by people who market and people who buy them, based on their decoding and recoding of the styles, creating a circulation of desire, fulfillment, and renewed desire articulated in a complex discourse in which the "natural" element of clothing – protection against the elements – is all but forgotten. Tightness, looseness, sexy, punk, cheap, expensive, gangsta are all codes not of behavior but of what we want people to think of our behavior.

This is the process of coding and decoding that works through all discourse and is particularly potent in the production and reception of media. Clothing becomes part of our cultural expression and self-expression, part of entertainment, a major element of advertising. The fit of jeans, the choice of make-up, the genre of a television show or a video game, and the assumptions of an advertisement are all coded in various ways by their producers and then decoded by each of us as we select what we want, as we interpret what we see and hear. Our mediated lives are an ongoing process of decoding messages, as we ourselves code the "messages" that we in turn send out.

Viewed this way, media are about messages being formed, sent out, received, and interpreted. A pharmaceutical company invents a pain remedy. In order to sell the medicine, it isn't sufficient simply to announce its existence. The company must create a need to go with the awareness. It creates a series of commercials that essentially communicate the idea that all of us are always in some kind of physical pain. Since that's so, there is now a pill to take care of it. A reality show asks its viewers to play along with a fantasy of events occurring as they are seen, coded so that we forget or ignore the careful editing that puts all the separate pieces together.

The coding process is clear enough: pain is universal and continual. This pill will take care of your pain. The decoding that the pharmaceutical company asks is simple: agree with the message; buy the pill. As an individual consumer, you may do just that. Alternatively you may decode the message as being irrelevant. "I don't have a pain all the time." You may decode it by applying common sense: "If I have constant pain, I ought to see a doctor." You may decode it as a joke and make fun of someone who is always complaining of pain. Something like this happened a number of years ago when a manufacturer of a medical alert device created a pathetic advertisement in which an elderly woman, having taken a fall, cried out, "I've fallen, and I can't get up." It became a national joke, full of scorn and fear of getting old and falling down.

Late in 2005, *The New York Times* ran a long article about online pornography, focusing on a young man who virtually and physically sold his body for profit through the Internet. The piece is part of a larger cultural concern about the dangerous ways the Internet is being used, but, like all such reports, it had a bit of the voyeuristic about it. It can be read (decoded) as a cautionary tale, as something to worry about, another reason to condemn the misuses of technology. It can be read to get something of a vicarious buzz. From a different perspective, the essay can also be read or decoded as a response to the ongoing distress of the news business. Given that the reporter subsequently revealed that he had actually given financial assistance to his subject, it could be read as the news influencing the news – changing it by reporting on it. But the fact is that this kind of reporting, sensational as it is, sells newspapers, and newspapers have, in general, been losing readership at a steady and alarming rate. News reporting has come under attack – by politicians who don't like what they read in the papers, and by the public, some of whom have lost faith in how the news is reported. *The New York Times* in particular suffered a number of setbacks. In 2003, a reporter named Jayson Blair was discovered to have made up the stories he was reporting. In 2005, Judith Miller, a political reporter, was jailed for refusing to name a source. The paper supported her, until it was found out that she was too close with an assistant to the Vice President, who fed her false information about the run-up to the Iraqi War. She had breached the objectivity that all reporters are supposed to practice. She left the paper in disgrace that was shared by *The Times* itself.

In the context of the most important newspaper in the United States, the "paper of record," as it's known, whose motto is "All the News That's Fit to Print," *The Times* has coded itself as dependable, solid, trustworthy. It was once called "the great gray *Times*" because of its stalwartness in straightforward reporting. In that context, a long piece on Internet pornography might seem more appropriate to a tabloid newspaper or TV news magazine – and indeed, some months later, when the subject was testifying about Internet predators, it did make the television news. It seemed somewhat inappropriate for *The Times*, even more so given the fact that the reporter wrote about how he personally intervened to help the victim. However, in light of a paper attempting to regain readership, the piece had a certain marketing logic. An attempt at self-recoding might well be appropriate in order to gain readership. Sexuality, as we will discover over and over in media, is a prime mover of audience attention. *The New York Times*, like any other media organization, must make money and a profit to survive. It will do what it feels necessary within the limits of the genre of news reporting it has created. The particular piece was done with enough sensitivity and human interest to make it attractive, all the while fitting nicely into the genre of Internet horror story, which almost always involves a child put at risk by an online predator.

We all have a general knowledge of what genres are when we classify a movie as a horror or science fiction film, a western or a thriller. Gamers understand the genres in a general sense of individual versus online community games; first-person shooter games; world simulation games. The concept of genre began in literature, was carried over to film and television, and now extends to almost any text that is defined (or coded) with a particular storyline and setting, certain kinds of characters with particular relationships to each other and the reader, and a set of narrative expectations that must be fulfilled. A genre is, in a sense, a contract. If you select a science fiction film to watch, you are, in a sense, negotiating a contract with it; you expect certain elements – a future world, space travel, aliens. Watching a news story about a disaster, you expect a concerned reporter, visuals of physical devastation, and interviews with tearful victims asking for "closure." If the science fiction film turned out to be set in the old west or the television reporter asked "who cares about the victims of this disaster?"

you would feel cheated; the expectations coded into the genre would be unfulfilled, and so would you. If the natural disaster involved no deaths, no failures in government assistance, no children buried under the rubble, you would be both relieved and (admit it) somewhat disappointed. The fact is that every kind of sensational event has developed its own genre (one meaning of "genre" is "kind"), its own discourse, description, victims, and perpetrators. Hurricane, murder, robbery, online sexual predator, and identity theft are presented as variations on a theme, like any other television show. There are even star "reporters" of catastrophe, like CNN's Anderson Cooper.

These varieties of sensationalism, wringing our hearts with pity for hapless victims, carrying us along on an emotional roller coaster, are part of an inclusive genre called melodrama, in which emotions are large, threats of danger great, and people are in distress. Melodrama subsumes a number of other genres, and we will examine its fictional forms in chapter 6.

If genres were simply repeated without change, fulfilled expectations would quickly turn to boredom and rejection. The disaster story genre on TV news is automatically varied with each new catastrophe: hurricane, mine collapse, fire. The descriptions and the urgency remain the same, but new details keep us interested. In the fictional realm, *Law and Order*, *CSI*, and the host of other police and FBI procedural dramas manage very small variations within their genres by introducing new kinds of crimes, ever more psychotic perpetrators, and, in the case of the *CSI* variants, increasingly gory depiction of wounds. If we like a genre and respond to its codes, it takes just small variations to keep the media producers and us happy. The producers like genres because the container is ready-made to be filled with somewhat varying content. We like it because it guarantees certain dependable elements in form and content each time we watch.

Genre is the container of almost everything we see and hear through media. Its varieties and variations keep us comfortable with its familiarity and excited by its difference. The ways in which genres are encoded and the ways we decode them keep the media design active and refreshed.

Business

"The last time I checked, a media company was generally defined as a business that accumulates audiences and sells access to them to marketers."
Richard Siklos, *The New York Times*, November 12, 2006

In the media design, the audience – that is, you and me – is part of the cycle of production and reception that maximizes profits by maximizing pleasure. The media are about business. That the media are a business is part of what defines them. Making money is the prime goal and a prime means for us to identify what we are studying. In order to understand the ramifications of this, we need to go back to our discussion of art and imagination and investigate another myth – another code: high art is coded as non-commercial. Poets don't write to make money. Painters express themselves regardless of how misunderstood they are. They will keep on painting even if no one buys their work. Van Gogh hardly sold a canvas during his life. The starving artist, the lonely, even mad artist, is a mainstay of our romantic image of artistic devotion. Not so for the products of the media imagination. If anyone starves, or, to use more reasonable language, if a rock band, a television show, a screenwriter, an advertisement or its copywriter; if a network or a movie studio does not make money – and not just a little money – from the results of their work, they have failed.

Is everyone in it for the money? The answer isn't simple, though simply put, the media is all about money. Consider the choice: an individual may be in love with words and music and have the imagination to create moving combinations of both. If she chooses to use this talent to write a symphony, hope for profit plays no part. Symphonic music is the epitome of high, small-audience art. If she wants to be a rock singer, she may be content to remain an amateur, play in a garage band, perhaps do some local gigs, even put songs online. But if the desire is to be well known, to reach a wide audience, a mechanism of business and profit joins with the making of art, and the designs of media begin to form.

The media are made of art and commerce with the balance tipped to the latter. Excellence is judged by profit. Media productions, from newspapers to computer games, are pieces in the circulation of capital. As we will see in the case of journalism, even relative profitability is sometimes not sufficient to prove worth. If a movie that everyone on the production end hoped would be a blockbuster doesn't make an extraordinary amount of money on its opening weekend, it is judged a failure. If a new television show does not attract viewers instantly, it is yanked from the air. The result is that talent and imagination are often sacrificed in favor of the reliable, the formulaic, the proven, producing works designed for maximum simplicity and similarity to what is already popular. Too often genres are repeated with a minimum of variation and few surprising turns on the expected. More often than not, if the goal is to reach a large audience and make a large amount of money, the desire on the part of media producers will be to make music, television, a movie, or a computer game appeal by being easily accessible and the most like other works that have already made a lot of money.

Of course, there always needs to be an original to copy. Imitating past successes means that someone, at some time, did take a chance in creating, packaging, and marketing something that was unusual, different, even challenging. If the products of media were only repetitions of each other, they would become boring beyond audience endurance. But even in the act of repetition there is an opportunity for imagination to work. Let's think again about the *Law and Order* or *CSI* shows. The formula is strict. Watch enough installments and you will know exactly when events will occur and how the characters will react: a grisly murder, an investigation of the crime scene, processing the evidence or interrogating a suspect, a few wisecracks, little hints about the characters' personal lives, solving the case or sending it to the jury. But, within the formula, small, important, and attractive variations are worked into the storyline; interesting characters appear; unique methods of murder are invented; a particularly monstrous perpetrator is created. Variation within formula is the key to genre and genre is the key to repetition in any media form. As long as the genre remains firm and the variations fresh, the program, movie, song, or video game will gain its audience.

The news, in all its forms, is an important example of genre and variations and the pressures of commerce. Reporting on, interpreting, and distributing information about local, national, and international events made up one of the earliest of media forms, a necessity for a functioning democracy. But the work of journalism from its inception has never been free in any real sense. Newspapers have always been owned by someone or, today, some corporation. The owners influence the larger genre of the paper, its political ideology, right or left, conservative or liberal. The editors determine what makes an event "news." They choose the events a reporter will cover and the kind of photographs that will represent the event. By such determination, policy is made: a national politician stating the principles she will follow if she is elected will go unnoticed unless her words are published, distributed, and analyzed in print or on the air. A politician's statement of principles may contain ideas important to maintaining a democracy fair to all of its people, or may be general and clichéd enough to be part of the genre of political speech and condensed enough to be quoted on the air.

Important and "new," banal and generic, the speech and the ideas must be distributed and, in order to be distributed, someone – an editor at a newspaper or the news bureau of a television network – must deem them newsworthy. That decision will differ from one editor or news outlet to another, and will be determined by commercial imperatives. A tabloid newspaper devoted to celebrity scandal (like the adventures of Tom Cruise we cited at the beginning of this chapter) will ignore the politician, unless he gets involved in a sexual escapade. The local news may give the politician little or no notice because this form of media is mostly involved with sensational and scary stories of murders and fires. As we'll discover, "local news" is itself a generic form, developed not locally at all, but by a few national consulting companies, who determine the format and the "look" of local news broadcasts, down to the hairstyles of and happy conversation among the newsreaders.

Who will report on the politician's speech? Certainly a serious newspaper, like *The New York Times*, *The Washington Post*, or other large-city papers. It will be mentioned, perhaps with a small sound bite on the network news and CNN. More coverage will be offered on MSNBC. These outlets are still (at least as of this writing) committed to reporting such items. But more and more "news" is just another commodity, like any other mass-mediated artifact, to be sold for a profit. This is not an entirely new phenomenon. The news services, like the Associated Press in the US and Reuters in England, were formed in the mid-nineteenth century as purveyors of news to various papers who subscribed, allowing them to save the time and money that would otherwise have to be spent maintaining a network of reporters to gather news as events happened around the world.

With the growth of television news and the decline of newspaper readership, the commodity nature of news has changed. Competition for audiences is fierce; newspapers are old news the second they are printed; sensational news – storms, crashes, murders, celebrity trials – become fodder for television, with each network or cable channel packaging the information for maximum exposure, maximum sponsorship, and maximum income.

All news outlets now have online components, themselves supported by advertising. Their selling points are based on the ability to update information almost instantly, accompanied with streaming sound and video. But, as outlets proliferate, as paper and ink newspapers fade away, the ownership of those outlets both contracts and expands. Fewer and fewer companies own more and more media outlets; more and more companies own a large variety of media, expanding rapidly into the Internet. We can rarely point to a company that is solely involved in newspapers or television or cable channels; a company whose major business is music or books. Almost all media are owned by various conglomerates who aggregate as many smaller companies as possible. The news is one business among many owned by a media conglomerate.

We can look, for example, at the Walt Disney company. The once living individual, Walt Disney, was an animator, whose films were enormously popular. He invented Mickey Mouse in 1928, formed his company in 1929, and released his first full-length animation, *Snow White and the Seven Dwarfs*, in 1937. In the early 1950s, his company built its first theme park, Disneyland, and tied it in with a series of television programs on the ABC network: *The Mickey Mouse Club*, *Disneyland*, *The Wonderful World of Disney*. Walt Disney died in 1966. The company lived on and grew. In the following decades, more and more companies were added to the Disney portfolio. The ABC network became part of the Disney company. So did the ESPN, the cable sports network. Disney owns and operates 10 local television stations and 64 radio stations, including many stations in the same city. It owns 10 cable outlets in addition to ESPN. Its movie holdings have expanded to eight subsidiaries. It owns publishing houses, record companies, its own software and game unit, sports franchises, theme parks (of course), and, for good measure, various Internet sites, including NASCAR.com.

There are other media companies that own a great deal more. The argument is that with fewer companies owning more and more smaller units, there is increasingly less chance for diversity of any kind and a greater chance of homogeneity across the media landscape. If Disney owns six radio stations in the Minneapolis-St Paul area, will it squash programming possibilities? The larger question is, how many genres of radio programming exist today in any market, under any ownership? One of Disney's Minneapolis-St Paul stations broadcasts for children; the others carry the usual varieties of rock 'n' roll. No matter who owns what, varieties of talk radio, sports, news, and religious programming, the various genres of pop, rock, and rap proliferate around the dial. Problems of diversity and diversification are quite separate from the companies that own them.

There are many forces at work and many ways to address the conglomeration of media ownership. We could concentrate on the business side, the economics, and the negative or positive results of conglomeration. The business sections of many newspapers and journals devoted to media do just that. At the same time, we could point out that ownership great and small is a constant in media. During the studio era from the 1920s through the 1950s, film production was controlled by a handful of studios where variety and innovation continued, despite the control and despite self-censorship of content. Even today, when each movie studio is a small part of a large media company, we still find variety, and occasionally something daring. The point is not simple. Yes, more creative and distribution companies owned by fewer companies does challenge variety and threaten to put the bottom line as the topmost concern. But the bottom line will not grow without creating and distributing innovative products, whether those products are newspapers, recorded music, television programs, movies, websites, or the advertisements that keep them all in business. This must happen or audiences – that is you and me– would get bored, turn elsewhere, and the companies would lose money.

There is no doubt that the business element in the media design has designs on us. They want our attention and our money. At the same time, we remain free agents, able to choose which site to go to or which song to download; which movie to watch or computer game to play. The result is an ongoing, multifaceted tension between conglomerate owners, the stockholders to which they may be beholden, the creative personnel within the various media organizations, many of whom are intent on applying imagination within the genres at their disposal, advertisers, whose money supports media productions, and the audience, always choosing among what's available and, in a way, making new things available by refusing what is already there. This complex interaction creates a complex text, a coherent meaningful structure that emerges from the media design. This text is made of the interaction of audience, the work (song, movie, television show), the producer/creator of the work, and the medium of its distribution or transmission. All play a role, all add to the complexity.

Technology

Ownership and the circulation of capital, together with the creation of media commodities to be delivered for profit, weave the commercial design of media. But radio, television, recorded sound, newspapers, and websites have to be created and distributed widely and made accessible. The creation and distribution of media is technologically driven. Technology, in its broadest sense, refers to any device or process that is the result of the practical application of science, mathematics, or engineering. The media is born of these applications and exists because of them. It can be argued that all audience art uses technology and is created and mediated by it: the composition of music in antiquity and the invention of perspective in painting in the early fifteenth century are the results of mathematical calculation. Photography is by any definition a technology-based art whose development from a chemical to a digital base follows the history of technology from the mid-nineteenth century to the present.

Though many art forms make use of technology, mass-mediated art, indeed every aspect of media, depends upon it, is founded upon it, and is defined by it. It can be argued that the creation of the media (to borrow the title of Paul Starr's important book on the subject) began in the West in the mid-fifteenth century with the invention of movable, metal type. Gutenberg, credited as the inventor of metal type (it had actually been developed earlier, in Asia, and engravers throughout Europe were working on it at the same time as Gutenberg), was an engraver and worked from his technical expertise in metallurgy to develop metal letters that could be arranged, inked, and pressed. The printing press itself grew out of agricultural technologies of wine and olive pressing. All parts of the process, the type, the press, ink, paper, have long histories that came together at this extraordinary time of the Renaissance, and all of them required the extension of the human imagination into tools that would provide for mass distribution.

Books were made by hand for centuries before the invention of type; they were created one by one, on order, and for people who could afford them. Printing made possible the production of books in large numbers for less money. The production of many copies made possible a larger readership, which increased as did literacy in the ensuing centuries. The content mediated by books changed as well, from the largely religious content during the early days of printing to works of science, philosophy, history, and literature. A fairly straight line can be drawn from the birth of the novel in the early eighteenth century to the contemporary best-seller, and it is a line that works its way through the growth of literacy and the technologies of mass production. As we will see in the next chapter, it also leads to the birth of the newspaper.

Throughout the Renaissance, from the fourteenth through the early seventeenth centuries, a combination of intellectual and mercantile energies pushed scientific inquiry while an expanding search for markets pushed technological development. Some technologies, like those of Leonardo da Vinci's designs for a flying machine, waited centuries to be translated into mechanically feasible forms. His notes on a calculating machine led the French philosopher Blaise Pascal to build one in 1642. In 1694, the German Wilhelm Leibniz refined Pascal's calculator into a more complex machine, work that set a path leading to the development of the computer in the nineteenth century, the period that saw the development of technologies that laid the ground for modern media.

The engines driving media technologies were business interests, a growing educated class, and imperialist expansions into less developed countries – all of which called for tools and, with those tools, an ability to communicate more broadly, to reach across geographical and temporal obstacles. The key technologies of the nineteenth century involved reconfigurations, *mediations* of time and space. The railroad moved physical objects – the body itself – through space, diminishing the time it took to get from one place to another. Telegraphy and telephony, each involving technologies that enhanced the rapid communication of information, transformed one physical entity into another, erasing space. Writing became electronic code – the dots and dashes of Morse code transmitted over wires – and the human voice itself became disembodied, separated from the anchor of the body. This led to radio, which in the early twentieth century became the first mass media to enter the private space of the home. Photography and motion pictures captured and represented space. The first stopped time in favor of recording space, while the second added time back, creating visual narratives that, by the early twentieth century, began to overtake the book as a medium for the culture to tell stories about itself. Recorded sound was invented in the late nineteenth century: Thomas Edison thought that movies would be a good companion medium for his company's invention of a wax cylinder that held the impression of sound vibrations.

But then he separated the two, and they remained separate until the late 1920s, the technology of the wax cylinder evolving into the music business that continues to generate music and contend with the newer technologies to distribute it.

Television, considered a foundational technology of the twentieth century, was in fact conceptualized in the mid-nineteenth century. William Urrichio, a scholar of television history, pinpoints the first ruminations about the medium in the 1870s, when Alexander Graham Bell – an inventor of telephony – and other scientists started to imagine using the telephone to broadcast live images around the world. Even earlier, in the 1840s, a fax-like technique had been developed for sending graphics by telegraph. In short, the delivery of images, and a fantasy of television, was being developed before motion pictures. Fantasy is a key word in the history of nineteenth-century technology and the birth of modern media, and the play of imagination was a useful alternative to other, more oppressive technologies of factory production in which humans were becoming functions of machines, creating wealth for some alongside a growing class of working poor. This was also the great age of imperialism, of wealthy Western countries ruling poorer Southern countries in Africa and Asia. Many of the nineteenth-century technologies were useful means of control and communication in colonized countries and between the colonies and the countries that ran them. Time and space needed to be overcome in order to keep the colonies governed. At the same time, useful technologies for control and command could also become technologies for flights of imagination.

Speculation, whimsy, and caution about what the future might bring accompanied the work of scientists and inventors. As we noted earlier, in 1818 Mary Shelley wrote *Frankenstein*, encoding within it the enduring myth of man creating man, without the bother of the normal processes of inception and birth. *Frankenstein* was the first modern telling of the robot story, of the cyborg that, once created, develops its own consciousness and threatens its creator. The narrative would nourish countless films and feed into the development of artificial intelligence as a discipline within computer science. Later in the century, H. G. Wells in England and Jules Verne in France developed what would become science fiction, which should more appropriately be called technology fiction and future fantasy, Wells imagining Martian invasion and Verne a voyage to the moon – the latter becoming an early motion picture, and the former the basis of a radio program that sent a good part of the United States into a panic.

In 1879, George du Maurier drew a cartoon for London's satirical magazine *Punch*, in which a Victorian couple in England address their daughter in "the Antipodes," the other side of the world, a colony of the mother country, fantasized as easily accessible through a picture phone (figure 1.1). The text reads in part:

EDISON'S TELEPHONOSCOPE (TRANSMITS LIGHT AS WELL AS SOUND). Every evening, before going to bed, Pater- and Materfamilias set up an electric camera-obscura over their bedroom mantel-piece, and gladden their eyes with the sight of their Children at the Antipodes, and converse gaily with them through the wire.

EDISON'S TELEPHONOSCOPE (TRANSMITS LIGHT AS WELL AS SOUND).

(*Every evening, before going to bed, Pater- and Materfamilias set up an electric camera-obscura over their bedroom mantel-piece, and gladden their eyes with the sight of their Children at the Antipodes, and converse gaily with them through the wire.*)

Paterfamilias (*in Wilton Place*). " BEATRICE, COME CLOSER, I WANT TO WHISPER." Beatrice (*from Ceylon*). " YES, PAPA DEAR."
Paterfamilias. " WHO IS THAT CHARMING YOUNG LADY PLAYING ON CHARLIE'S SIDE?"
Beatrice. " SHE'S JUST COME OVER FROM ENGLAND, PAPA. I'LL INTRODUCE YOU TO HER AS SOON AS THE GAME'S OVER!"

Figure 1.1 George Du Maurier's 1879 cartoon fantasizing television and the picture phone, from *Punch's Almanack*. Mary Evans Picture Library.

Fifteen years before the Lumière Brothers projected their movies in Paris, du Maurier picked up on the inventions of Edison and Bell and combined them with an older device, the camera obscura, in which an image of the outside world passed through a pinhole and onto the opposite side of a black box, fantasizing nothing short of a combination of wide, flat-panel television and the mobile picture phone. The world is brought into the home through visual transmission. The imagination of mass media is all but completed.

In the first half of the nineteenth century, two Britons – Augusta Ada King, Countess of Lovelace, daughter of the poet Lord Byron; and the mathematician Charles Babbage – invented machinery and programming that would eventually become the modern computer. It was a long path that started as far back as the abacus in Asia, through the seventeenth-century calculating machines invented by Blaise Pascal and Wilhelm Leibniz, and the French weaver, Joseph Jacquard, who, in the early nineteenth century invented a means to program weaving patterns on punch cards, which, in turn, ran the looms. In the 1820s, Babbage began work on his Difference Engine to calculate mathematical tables. He started to build it, but couldn't get the necessary gears machined to the right specifications. He then proposed the Analytical Engine, which would be based on Jacquard's punch cards and perform sophisticated computation. It was never built.

Partnering him, mostly through written correspondence, Ada helped theorize programming for the Analytical Engine. She wrote poetically about its mathematics:

The distinctive characteristic of the Analytical Engine, and that which has rendered it possible to endow mechanism with such extensive faculties as bid fair to make this engine the executive right-hand of abstract algebra, is the introduction into it of the principle which Jacquard devised for regulating, by means of punched cards, the most complicated patterns in the fabrication of brocaded stuffs. It is in this that the distinction between the two engines lies. Nothing of the sort exists in the Difference Engine. We may say most aptly that the Analytical Engine weaves algebraical patterns just as the Jacquard-loom weaves flowers and leaves. (Quoted in Toole, 1992: 240–61)

And she warned against thinking more of the machine than it was:

The Analytical Engine has no pretensions whatever to originate any thing. It can do whatever we know how to order it to perform. It can follow analysis; but it has no power of anticipating any analytical relations or truths. Its province is to assist us in making available what we are already acquainted with. (ibid.)

Ada not only developed the art of computer programming, and had a modern programming language named after her, but she also set up an argument about the powers of intelligent machines that is carried on to this day.

By the end of the nineteenth century, electricity was added to the computing process and computers were put to use by the US Census Bureau. By the 1940s, another Britisher, Alan Turing, used computation to crack German war codes and the US army began using computing machines to track artillery trajectories. But, in the history of technology that concerns us, the computer lagged far behind much more simple mechanical and analogue methods of capturing and transmitting sound and light waves that became the basis of media. It wasn't until the mid-1990s that digital technology, and with it the ease of both creating and moving around words, sounds, and images, forced a convergence of traditional media forms and the industrial structures at their base. That convergence will underlie everything that follows in this book, for in the design of the media the rapid movement and the control of accessibility to television, movies, music, news – to all the artifacts of the media – is what media industries and technologies are about.

Immediacy and change

It may seem curious to use "immediacy," a word that suggests a lack of mediation, to describe an important part of the media design. But the concepts of immediacy, of the instantly available and constantly new or novel, the fleeting and changeable, the here-now-and-then-replaced, are essential to our understanding of media culture. All parts of the media design, the creative and imaginative, production, distribution, and audience reception, are in constant flux, with a steady state of demand for profit and entertainment, of satisfaction of demand, of more demand, and more products.

Perhaps the best way to understand this is to go back to our comparison between small-audience "high" art and popular or mass art. A defining feature, a primary code of what we consider to be "high" art is its uniqueness and permanence. Think of a painting in a museum. Assuming it is an original, it has the presence of a unique item, the only one of its kind, bearing the marks of its creator's own hand. We look at the painting and imagine ourselves in the presence of the painter. A Shakespeare play, though it may be printed and performed many times, affects us with the presence of its importance (we are convinced by having been told so often), the beauty of its poetry, and the profundity of ideas that seem appropriate to any period. We are told that Shakespeare's plays are "universal," transcending time and cultures, unique, and always present.

This effect of uniqueness and permanence was termed "aura" by the German cultural critic Walter Benjamin. Benjamin was a member of a group of scholars, called the Frankfurt School, who devoted much of their work, first in Germany and later (except for Benjamin, who died during World War II) in the US, to the study of media. Benjamin's 1935 essay entitled "The Work of Art in the Age of Mechanical Reproduction" was destined to become one of the foundations of media studies. According to Benjamin, the original work, the sense of authorial presence, the experience that the work of art is a direct channel (or mediation) between artist and audience, radiates an aura. Once art goes through mechanical or technological reproduction that removes a sense of the creator's presence from the work created, making the reproduction one copy out of many, aura is lost. Shakespeare comes alive in each and every performance of *Hamlet*, because the universality of his words maintains their aura each time they are spoken. But every recorded performance of the Ramones' "I Wanna Be Sedated" is a copy of an original that is itself the product of a once popular group singing a song that speaks to contemporary popular culture. It is mediated, not by live, present performers, but on the radio, on a CD, an MP3, or an iTune. When the Ramones do perform it on stage, it will be as much like the recording as possible, or a tribute band will attempt to sound like the group to which they are paying tribute. A rock concert may have an "aura" of immediate excitement, but might fail as a unique presentation of enduring truths.

Think about a television sitcom. There will be about 20 or 22 new episodes each season. But each of these episodes will have the same characters, in the same setting, delivering versions of the same lines, in the same way each week. Each character will react in the same way – literally, in the sense of responding with a look or a joke that is so slightly different from the last show as to be hardly different at all. In a sense, this meets the generic qualities we talked about earlier. Every "new" episode of the sitcom will be advertised as such – "coming up, an all new episode of *My Name is Earl.*" Not partially, but *all* new. At the same time, the episode will be a reinforcement, close to a carbon copy of the previous episode, with a slightly different plot twist. Its immediacy exists not only in its newness, but also in its sameness. Genre and "aura" do not go well together, though Shakespearean comedy and tragedy do follow generic outlines. It would be more accurate to say that in high art, individual imagination aces genre, which serves as a form to be molded by the artist. In mass-mediated art genre pushes and forms individual imagination, is duplicated, reproduced, and in the process loses its aura, but, Benjamin argues, gains by being available to a greater number of people.

This quality of sameness in the productions of media has, paradoxically, a sense of movement, of progression. Small-audience high art demands interrogation, requests intellectual activity, and evokes profound emotional response. It asks us to pause, to stop and examine, and to pull away from the flow of the everyday in order to respond. The immediate response to the repetition of a rock song or a TV show secures us in its sameness, allowing us to move on with it, to consume it and move on to the next show, the next song. Immediacy and repetition build a rhythm of expectations continually met and gradually varied.

Media industries profit on meeting expectations and thrive on change. Only by promising and fulfilling a need for the new can profits continue to be made. The new can come in the form of content – a new song by a popular group; a new sitcom that just slightly varies its genre. Each new technology for creating, recording, and distributing media creates a shift in business methods and sometimes leads to the creation of new companies and even newer technologies, and occasionally new content (only rarely new genres). The stimulus for change comes from an interaction between the audience and the media business and can be quite complex. Recall the quotation about "panic in the industry" that began this chapter. The movie business is always in a state of panic, which can be traced back to its beginnings. I pointed out earlier that Edison wanted to create a visual accompaniment to a sound-recording device. For technical reasons, this marriage was not consummated and movies developed as a silent form for some 30 years. ("Silent," however, is a relative term. During projection, silent film almost always had a live piano or orchestral accompaniment.) During the late twenties, audiences began to dwindle, putting the studios in economic distress. Some studios, Warner Bros. in particular, were close to failure. In response, they rushed to complete technologies of synchronized sound they had been experimenting with for some years. The studios looked at synchronized sound as a novelty. After all, silent film had both thrived and evolved into a sophisticated form of visual storytelling. Audience response to early sound films like Warner's *The Jazz Singer* (1927) was so positive that the changeover became universal within months.

In the early 1950s, movie audiences were again dwindling, due in part to the growing popularity of television and to the fact that families were moving into suburbs not yet served by movie theaters. Again, the studios tried to meet the challenge through technological change by bringing forth various wide-screen technologies that soon permanently altered the old box-like, 3×4 ratio of the movie screen into the various wide-screen formats we see today. Television, however, maintained the 3×4 ratio and the sides were lopped off movies to format them "to fit your television." In the 1980s, MTV videos and other commercials began being filmed and shown in "letter-box" format that emulated the wide screen. In the nineties, the introduction of DVDs, large-screen television, and high definition began changing the television screen itself.

The advent of the digital has speeded up media to a pace of breathless change. Media companies are moving in all possible directions to make money through the ease of delivery made possible by digital transfer of media objects. Music, made available for free through MP3 peer-to-peer networks, is now under pressure from copyright owners, put up for sale. Apple, the computing company, never able to penetrate more than a small percentage of the computer market, has found a new niche by selling the iPod music players and charging for downloads of music. Movie and television studios and networks, coming to terms with falling attendance at theaters and viewers time-shifting television programs with their VTRs, are making films and programs available online and on mobile phones. Some movies are being released on cable and on DVD simultaneously with their release in theaters.

Convergence is the magic media word for the way the various means for delivery are coming together in ever-changing ways. There are new combinations almost daily, many of them desperate attempts to capture an audience that is itself changing rapidly. There is nothing more fluid, fleeting, or slippery as the taste for popular art. There is often nothing more amusing than watching media producers attempt to outguess its audience. Sometimes they synchronize. Pleasure occurs for the audience; money accrues to the producers. Sometimes, desire for pleasure and desire for profit just slide by each other, and the quest continues, rapidly, always on the lookout for a perfect fit that will last for a moment or produce profit for years to come.

The rapidity of change and quest for novelty has an important consequence for writing about media. Put simply, some of what you read here will be out of date by the time you read it. That's why we'll be working with general concepts, which have some permanence, and methodologies we can use to study particular media texts, which can be extrapolated to the media texts that are current when you read this. That's also why an active website accompanies this book. The permanence of printed page can be offset by the immediacy and volatility of the digital.

Evaluation

Our discussion of change in media has focused largely on media technologies and less so on the productions formed and carried by them – the content of media. We need to return to content in order to address the notion of evaluation, of judging media critically. Earlier, I indicated that it was possible to navigate away from the usual condemnations of media and its creations as simple-minded, vulgar, and unimportant. To understand media and its various productions, we need to begin from a point of understanding their complexity rather than dismissing them as commercial and crass. At the same time, there are always evaluative acts that are carried out on all levels of media-making both from within the media – including professional journalists whose job is to review its productions – and from our situation as audience. We need to consider, for example, the imponderables of taste. How do we account for the fact that I may like the kind of music that you cannot sit still for, or that the reality shows that you find amusing, I may find banal? Within the media, how does a record company's A&R (artists and repertoire) person, who listens to many singers, make a choice of whom to record; or a movie producer, who reads dozens of scripts and listens to dozens of story pitches, choose what she thinks will make a commercially successful film, again based on experience and on taste? If questioned, you will probably defend your taste quite directly: "I like their lyrics and the way the band works together." The A&R person or film producer will most likely assert the superiority of his or her taste, and the certainty of understanding "what the public wants."

There are the professional critical voices, the evaluators we turn to in order to help us make a choice. Film reviewers, for example, are everywhere: in newspapers, on television, radio, online. They form a part of the movie distribution process. While they don't work for the studios, the studios depend upon them as part of the advertising campaign for a particular film. They speak the language of immediacy – they see a film once just before it is released – and they work within a genre all their own. They summarize a film's plot, talk about its characters, and more often than not make bad jokes and a pun on the film's title. They do pan a film on occasion, usually by making fun of it. But the studios are extremely careful of this. If they have a film they know is terrible, they won't send it out for critic previews. A film critic is part of the entertainment process. No qualifications are necessary, which is why he or she will rarely address matters of film form – how the film tells its story – or where it fits in the history of the medium. Other media do better at evaluation. Music, for example, produces some outstanding critical writing in newspapers and through magazines like *Rolling Stone*. Here is Philip Kennicott, writing in *The Washington Post* in 2006 about the Three 6 Mafia rap, "It's Hard Out Here for a Pimp," which won the Academy Award for best song in the film *Hustle and Flow*:

> Witness the explosion of a new hip-hop meme into "white culture." ... Perhaps the line ["It's Hard Out Here for a Pimp"] has resonance because so much of American political discourse is about determining who is allowed to feel properly aggrieved. Is it Muslims offended about sacrilegious cartoons, or defenders of free speech seeing their high holy delimited? Daytime talk radio has essentially evolved into a vast trading floor for the commodity of complaint. And slowly we drift to a new understanding of the basic social contract: Your liberty ends where my outrage begins.
>
> A pimp complaining that "It's hard out here" has, in a single outrageous leap, passed by the issue of whether he has any right to grievance, and is demanding – so shamelessly that it's funny – all the perks and merits of someone who legitimately feels wronged.
>
> The musical setting of the line, a deliciously catchy and melodic tag, confirms the scandal. The line that the conservative Kathryn Jean Lopez and a zillion other people can't get out of their heads is essentially a melodic ending, a sequence of notes that seems to conclude a musical thought. Yet it keeps repeating, if the person who insists that it's hard out here for a pimp is continually saying, "Case closed." I'm right, end of argument ...

I quote this at length because it shows how an understanding of contemporary music demands that we also understand the culture that surrounds it. Kennicott defines how the structure of rap, its musical lines and melodic tags, create a sympathetic response, even – or especially – when its lyric could be deemed offensive by some. In fact, the starting point for Kennicott's essay highlights another kind of evaluation that occurs on the cultural and political level. The essay takes as its starting point a conservative blogger's uneasiness about the song: it is morally repugnant but catchy, nonetheless. Kennicott analyzes the song and its effect within the context of the resistance to it.

As we have seen, media have always been the target of concern from the defenders of high culture. Evaluating media for content that might be offensive is a game that has been played for as long as modern media have existed. In the United States the game usually begins with statements of outrage from religious groups that are then taken up by a government agency and finally absorbed by the media that is the object of the outrage, in the form of self-censorship. The cycle of outrage is most clearly demonstrated in the history of film censorship. Films of the early 1930s were often openly sexual without being pornographic and, with the birth of the gangster genre, increasingly violent. Catholic groups took issue especially with the sexual content of films, but also with the glorification of gangster violence. Their pressures resulted in the formation of an internal censorship unit, called the Hays Office, after one of its directors. From the early thirties through the fifties, almost every movie script went to the Hays Office to be vetted for objectionable material, which, according to the Hays Code guidelines, included anything from sex outside of marriage that went unpunished to merely showing a married couple sleeping in the same bed, as well as any criminal activity that did not end in the capture and prosecution of the criminal.

The result was another game that went on inside of this process. Screenwriters would write in the most outrageous, most raunchy material possible, hoping that it would act as a diversion for the censorship board. The board would fall upon this material while other, more subtle, sexual references passed by unnoticed. The game had a positive effect on the imagination of film-makers and viewers. Sexuality and violence would be played out subtly, indirectly; the viewer would be called upon to imagine the unseen.

The Hays Code remained intact until the late fifties, when a number of films, most famously Alfred Hitchcock's *Psycho* (1960), began to render it useless; in time it was retooled by the Motion Picture Association of America, a powerful industry group. You see the results to this day in the rating system that begins every film and most television programming. The rating system allows the studios to police themselves and control output, essentially limiting what film-makers can do by threatening to give a film a restrictive rating. It allows them to control the audience as well, basically creating smaller, younger audience or a larger, more adult audience by means of the rating given to a film.

Censorship proclaims itself as an act of protection, but too often reveals itself as an exercise in resentment and power. The Hays Office is history, as are the senate hearings of the 1950s that sought the causes of juvenile delinquency in comic books and rock 'n' roll. But there remain various groups who watch for changes in the moral barometers of the culture at large and blame the media for causing the change. Some of these evaluate media as a measure of cultural collapse; others as purveyors of immorality. The first group wring their hands about the coarsening of taste and blame the media. The second narrow their focus, going after sexual and violent content of music, television, film, and games, insisting that exposure to such content will some-how infect the culture and that their vigilance will help inoculate the culture against the infection.

Aimed often at the "liberal media," sometimes tinged with anti-Semitism (as in the occasional, outrageous, and false claims about the Jewish-owned media), this criticism as censorship claims to speak for a segment of the culture that finds itself offended by sex and violence in media and believes it must protect everyone from the cause of this offense. The aggrieved group sets itself against the producers of the offensive material, creating a set of oppositions and promising to force change, often through boycotts or, because they rarely do have a profound influence on media producers, on distribution outlets. So, for example, WalMart – a huge market for media products – may not carry DVDs of films, CDs of music, or games deemed to be offensive by watchdog groups. Occasionally a network may pull a show, or an advertiser its commercials, if the offended group complains enough.

This "us against them" opposition to media is largely the symbolic flexing of moral and economic muscle. Such organized opposition refuses to recognize the reality that individuals are perfectly free to choose what to buy and watch or listen to. It may in fact recognize that parental control is not easy, yet rather than educate the means to gain that control, it bypasses it by attempting to remove the thing it wants controlled.

Sometimes the government will step in, particularly to support groups that support these groups. The infamous half-time event during the 2004 Super Bowl game, during which singer Justin Timberlake exposed singer Janet Jackson's breast, resulted in the Federal Communications Commission levying a $550,000 fine on Viacom, the company that owned CBS at the time (later a court found the fine excessive). The event was vulgar enough in itself, though only a bit more vulgar than much of television often is. Despite claims that it was an "accident," media observers saw it as a rather transparent attempt on the part of CBS to test the limits of sexual display. Conservative morality groups in their turn tested their powers to punish such displays. The FCC's decision to side with them, and ratchet up its censorship powers over all network programming, led to greater caution on the part of broadcasters. Caution, as always, plays out in areas of sexual content; rarely in violence, which, on television, has grown incrementally during the ensuing years, especially as the FCC keeps raising its fines in response to continued agitation by groups who are themselves agitated by what they see on television.

The varieties of media criticism, from movie reviewers to political or religious pressure groups to the MPAA, are almost exclusively involved with content. A movie reviewer discusses a film's plot, the MPAA gives an R rating for sexual content, and a conservative watchdog group will decry the sexual innuendo of *Desperate Housewives*, while describing the content in detail on their website. What is left out is the determining factor of content, the *form* that creates content. If we look again at the article on the rap song quoted earlier, or the following discussion of a computer game, we understand that content alone does not explain our response to media:

> The prince's internal conflict is given tangible form when his blood is infected by the Sands of Time, which causes him on occasion to turn into the powerful Dark Prince, a savage, primal creature. The Dark Prince can easily slay demons, and must do so to replenish the sand that keeps him alive. He must also speed through the game's elaborate obstacle courses to reach safety before his sand runs out, and the player is likely to die repeatedly in the attempt. This is exciting, but sometimes more frustrating than fun. (Herold, 2005)

Imagination, emotional and physical engagement, mark the relationship between a gamer and the game.

The cultural analyses of "It's Hard Out Here for a Pimp" and the above poetic description of *The Prince of Persia: The Two Thrones* express an understanding of what happens when we evaluate media as a formal construct in which we, as participants, play a part. Content doesn't exist by itself but is determined by form, which includes the internal structure of a song or television show as well as the larger external structures of production and distribution. When we consider a computer game, for example, we would need to go beyond concerns that its violent content will desensitize its players to violence in the "real" world and instead try to analyze how it situates a player either as a first-person participant or part of a large, online community. We would need to analyze the quality of the graphics and the intricacies of the inter-action between player and game. We would need to understand that form responds to the desire of the player and that the player can influence the form of a game.

The communities become part of the total structure of gaming that we need to study in order to understand and evaluate gaming as a practice, a part of the media complex, its art, business, and its audience. The notion of form as primary object of study, with an emphasis on the fact that the media audience is part of the media text, and that text is intricately connected with the cultures that surround and infiltrate it, make up the design of media studies.

Conclusion

One important aspect of that cultural surround must be mentioned, because the design lives within it and we live within it, and that is the concept of *modernity*. Modernity is not part of the media design; it is what designs the media. It is not a thing, not something out there, but rather a state of culture, of a society, of the way people think about their world and their place in it. Modernity is a state of uncer-tainty, where we can no longer rely on external or even internal events to provide us with a secure and coherent environment. Modernity is change, which may be its only constant. It is the attempt to comprehend the universe, which physicists tell us is simultaneously infinite and finite; and life, which evolutionary biology theorizes comes from perhaps four basic gene sets. Modernity is a state in which we may turn to religion to provide us with the balance and anchor we do not find elsewhere, or to computer games or rock 'n' roll to focus our emotions and intellect. It is the cynicism of the media, working imagination in the service of commerce, and the desire of the audience to be entertained, distracted, and to create a community on MySpace. Modernity is the lack of a secure mooring. And it is the media – beginning with telephony, movies, radio, and televison, and now with computers – that allow us to be unmoored, to travel without moving, to maintain virtual relationships with friends, to carry our imaginations beyond our place and even our time. These are the beginnings and ends of the media design, and are influenced by the business structure in which they thrive together with the entire cultural surround in which they and we live.

References

The epigraph from the *The New York Times* is at: <http://www.nytimes.com/2005/11/09/movies/09cruise.html>.

Art and Artifact

Codes and genres
The classic text on encoding and decoding is Stuart Hall, "Encoding/Decoding," in *Media and Cultural Studies*, 2nd edn, ed. Meenakashi Gigi Durham and Douglas M. Kellner (Malden, MA, and Oxford: Blackwell, 2005), pp. 163–73.

Fashion
Blue Jeans: "Levi Strauss — The History of Blue Jeans": <http://inventors.about.com/library/inventors/bllevi.htm>; "About LS&Co./Invention of Levi's 501 Jeans," <http://www.levistrauss.com/about/history/jeans.htm>.

"American Denim: Blue Jeans and Their Multiple Layers of Meaning": <http://www.latech.edu/tech/liberal-arts/geography/courses/290/290lects/gordon.htm>.

For more on the discourse of fashion, see Stuart Engel, "Marketing Everyday Life: The Postmodern Commodity Aesthetic of Abercrombie & Fitch," *Advertising & Society Review* 5/4 (2004); <http://muse.jhu.edu/journals/advertising_and_society_review/v005/5.3engel.html>.

Journalism
The New York Times article on online pornography is from Kurt Eichenwald, "Through His Webcam, a Boy Joins a Sordid Online World," *The New York Times* (December 19, 2005); <http://www.nytimes.com/2005/12/19/national/19kids.ready.html>.

An article on the genre of disaster reporting is Jack Schaffer, "Disaster by Numbers: If the Earthquake Doesn't Kill You, the Clichés Will," *Slate* (June 1, 2006); <http://www.slate.com/id/2142768/>.

Games
On games, see Paul Young, "Film Genre Theory and Contemporary Media: Description, Interpretation, Intermediality," in *The Oxford Handbook of Film and Media Studies*, ed. Robert Kolker (New York: Oxford University Press, 2007), pp. 224–59.

John Leland, "The Gamer as Artiste," *The New York Times* (December 4, 2005), C1.

Technology

Material on early television is from William Urrichio, "Old Media as New Media: Television," *The New Media Book*, ed. Dan Harries (London: British Film Institute, 2002), pp. 219–30.

Material on Babbage and Lovelace comes from: <http://www-groups.dcs.st-and.ac.uk/~history/Mathematicians/Babbage.html>; and: <http://ei.cs.vt.edu/~history/Babbage.html>.

The quotation from Ada comes from Betty Alexandra Toole, *Ada, The Enchantress of Numbers* (Mill Valley, CA: Strawberry Press, 1992), pp. 240–61, and can be found at: <http://www.agnesscott.edu/lriddle/women/ada-love.htm>.

A good reference book is Paul Starr's *The Creation of the Media: Political Origins of Modern Communications* (New York: Basic Books, 2004).

Immediacy and Change

Walter Benjamin's essay, "The Work of Art in the Age of Mechanical Reproduction," can be found in *Illuminations*, ed. Hanna Arendt, trans., Harry Zohn (New York: Schocken Books, 1968), pp. 217–51.

On copyright, see William W. Fisher, III. "iTunes: How Copyright, Contract, and Technology Shape the Business of Digital Media. A Case Study": <http://cyber.law.harvard.edu/media/uploads/53/GreenPaperiTunes041004.pdf>.

Evaluation

The quotation from Philip Kennicott comes from "Picking Up the Lyric but Missing the Beat," *Washington Post* (March 7, 2006; <http://www.washingtonpost.com/wp-dyn/content/article/2006/03/06/AR2006030601856.html>.

On censorship, see Jon Lewis, *Hollywood v. Hardcore: How the Struggle over Censorship Saved the Modern Film Industry* (New York: New York University Press, 2000).

The quotation on video games is from Charles Herold, "Confronting the Demon Within, and Other Good Fun," *The New York Times* (December 24, 2005; <http://www.nytimes.com/2005/12/24/sports/othersports/24vide.html>.

CHAPTER TWO
From Broadsheet to Broadband:
The News

Were it left to me to decide whether we should have a government without newspapers, or newspapers without a government, I should not hesitate a moment to prefer the latter.

Thomas Jefferson, 1787

The obligation of the press is to take the government seriously when it makes a request not to publish. Is the motive mainly political? How important are the national security concerns? And how do those concerns balance against the public's right to know?

"Fit and Unfit to Print," *Wall Street Journal*, June 30, 2006

When we think of journalism, the concept of objective reporting comes to mind. This chapter examines that concept and considers the varieties and genres of journalism across all media, from print to Internet.

Permanence, Portability, and the Public: A Brief History of Print Media

Long before writing came into being, human societies had developed languages with which to communicate. The spoken word can communicate many things – stories, jokes, feelings; the telling of recent events – but it is ephemeral, an immediate mediation that lasts only as long as the speaker and listener recall the communication. The development of writing made the mediation permanent. Writing becomes an important, permanent medium for the reporting, recording, and explanation of events, of thinking, of deeds done or imagined. It creates history. We begin to understand what old cultures were about as soon as we find their words, or at least images – pictographs or hieroglyphs – that suggest extended communication. We can trace such markings as far back as the Ice Age. We find early writing on tortoise shells in China some 8,600 years ago. But it is generally accepted that the earliest example of extended writing occurred in what is now southern Iraq around 3300 BCE, with a fully formed alphabet occurring in Palestine in the seventeenth–sixteenth centuries BCE. The development and spread of writing moved swiftly through the Middle East into Egypt, where the medium that received the impression of the alphabet, papyrus, the early form of paper, was invented.

The invention of paper (and ink) is a milestone of early technology because language gains permanence when it is written down. Further, writing spreads throughout a culture when it can be moved around from place to place. Clay tablets and stone tokens might serve for account ledgers that are among the earliest permanent markings we have, but information, ideas, and the expression of imagination need to circulate in order to reach people.

Papyrus, made from plant fibers, was an early portable medium, and can be dated around 3000 BCE. Rag-based paper, closer to what we have now, came to the West from China around AD 105 and moved through the Middle East and into Europe by 610. But paper was only one part of the developing media. It was, in effect and in physical fact, the base technology, a portable surface on which writing could be placed. But in order for the written word to gain wider circulation, the writing itself had to undergo a change. Handwritten manuscripts were time-consuming to make and limited in their distribution. In the European Middle Ages, they were written almost exclusively in Latin and were theological in content, produced mainly by monks in sections of a monastery known as scriptoria. They were produced, many beautifully illustrated and illuminated, on order, for other monks, for wealthy nobility, and for not-so-wealthy scholars – the members of the population who could read.

The majority of the population in the Middle Ages was poor and illiterate. Even if ordinary people had access to manuscripts, they could not read them. Average citizens received news by word of mouth, informally by means of social contact in the market or tavern, and formally from a town crier or a herald sent from their feudal lord to inform them of such events as an impending battle, a rise in taxation, or the death of a member of the ruling class. Literacy expanded during the Renaissance. The development of political, economic, and religious cultures during the thirteenth to sixteenth centuries recognized that more widespread literacy might be a virtue and a source of profit rather than a threat. But the uses of literacy depended on the availability of material to read, which itself depended on a growing use of the vernacular in communications – French, Italian, German, English, for example; the languages of the people – rather than Latin, the language of the religious and learned classes. The rise of literacy depended as well on another technological advance, the result of a series of convergences: the development of movable type, of suitable paper to receive the impression made by the type, of ink to make the impression visible on the paper, of a mechanism to press the inked type onto the paper – the portable, distributable printed word. The convergence of these technologies began in Asia and moved through the Middle East into Europe where Johannes Gutenberg printed his famous Bible in the mid-1450s, and William Caxton printed a history of Troy, the first English book, in 1474, and in 1476 the first poem was printed in English, Geoffrey Chaucer's *Canterbury Tales*.

The public sphere

The development and deployment of books, and the increasing growth of literacy from this convergence of technologies is a complex tale of further technological change, of politics, and religion. It involves the evolution of a middle class with the means and the leisure to read and a quest for knowledge; of governments that began modifying and loosening their ties to religion and gradually (very gradually) started looking to the people to support the ruling classes. It depended on the formation of a mercantile, capitalist, system that fostered the circulation of goods, money, and information.

Politics, business, and information go hand in hand in the development of a public sphere, an important concept in the development of media. Paul Starr defines the concept as "the sphere of openly accessible information and communication about matters of general and social concern." We can go beyond this and think of the public sphere in the contexts of mediation we have been developing. The private sphere might be considered as the interior life of the individual and its extensions into the domestic sphere of family. This is a largely imagined space, because it pretends that there can be such a thing as life cut off from the outside, from economics, politics, and the cultures they create. The private sphere may be seen as a product of ignorance of the external world, or the construction of an idea of independence and self-sufficiency. As literacy grew and communications became part of the lifeblood of commerce (note that "commerce" shares a common root with "communication" and "community"), politics, and class, the boundaries between private and public began to blur, or, more accurately, to flow into one another. The history of media parallels, even perhaps creates, the convergence of private and public, so that, today, simply turning on a television set or logging on to the Internet makes you part of the public sphere, a participant in the external world.

In the sixteenth and seventeenth centuries, the impoverished working classes were trapped in something less than a sphere and more like a cycle, where labor and economic survival made for a constricted world; while the burgeoning middle mercantile and property-owning classes began creating a world where public and private intertwined, where business, art, intellectual activity, politics, and religion intersected, and where the printed word increasingly acted as the medium – in the form of books, pamphlets, or broadsheets. At the same time, the oral tradition was maintained as members of a largely illiterate working class would pause in the streets to hear the news or popular novels of the time read aloud to them from the latest broadsheet – a single-page publication, containing some of the latest news and opinion. The news as we know it today is born from this early circulation of information. By the early

1700s, readers in England and in the American colonies could buy not only broadsheets but also news pamphlets, "news books," and newspapers. Print media, in something of the form we are still familiar with, was born.

"Information"

Degrees of information

Journalism – communicating news about ongoing events via printed words and images – is the earliest example of media aimed at a large audience and created for profit. But what constitutes journalism; what is "the news"? To investigate some of the givens of journalism, the attitudes it embodies and that we, as consumers, embrace, we need to examine the ideologies and the realities of journalism. Today, we are told that journalism is based on the notion of "objectivity," or freedom from bias or prejudice. Journalism carries with it the promise, indeed the premise, of objective reporting; it is supposed to deliver a narrative of facts, "the first draft of history" as the cliché tells us. But in practice journalism is part of the media design: it is commercially driven; it seeks a large audience; it is powered – from the invention of print to the Internet – by technological innovation; and, by definition, it seeks novelty, the new, the contemporary. As a narrative of fact or of sensation, the news is a mediation of contemporary events through conventions evolving from its beginnings, filtered through the imagination of an individual reporter or the political position of the medium's editor or owner. To understand more fully the place of news and journalism within the media design, and in particular how the mediations of journalism have been extended by broadcast and digital means, we need to look at these basic and difficult questions: What is news? What is information? Where does it come from? For whom is it meant? How should it be consumed?

"News" is the result of reporting recent or ongoing events in the world or the nation, political and economic, involving warfare, scientific breakthroughs, disasters both natural and manmade, health, politics, criminal activity and corruption. Events alone, however, do not constitute news. Events and the people who create or are engaged in them become news when they are reported and when such reporting is mediated by the editorial perspective of the news organization. As in all communication, the mediation is not completed until an audience – a reader or viewer – completes it. The ideal of unbiased objectivity is, in many ways, a feel-good myth that journalists like to nourish. Nothing in this process is neutral. News or "information" of any kind is always interpreted, by the reporter, the reporting, or the reader who assents or disagrees with the reporting. The broader concept of "information" is an even trickier term because it implies a neutral collection of facts that are carried by various media from a source to an audience. But again, no media are neutral, no information is neutral, and a narration – even a simple listing – of "facts" will always involve interpretations.

Objectivity and interpretation were in contention from the earliest days of broadsheets and newspapers. It was common practice for printers to be required to have a government license – meaning, in effect, that material opposing the government could not be published. One of the first English newspaper publishers, Thomas Archer, was imprisoned in 1621 for not having such a license. The situation did not improve when journalism came to America. The first colonial newspapers attempted to avoid political news and wrote mostly about foreign affairs. But political material did get published, and indeed arrests were made of publishers who challenged the government in America's pre-revolutionary days. John Peter Zenger, publisher of the *New York Weekly Journal*, was jailed in 1734 for his paper's support of merchants opposing the colonial governor. Zenger continued to edit the paper from jail and sued the colonial government.

The Zenger incident serves as an example of the age-old dichotomy between government concerns about libel and sedition on the one hand, and citizens' right to free expression on the other. The idea of a free and unfettered press was deeply impressed in the ideology of American capitalism. In the remarkable year of 1787, when the new nation established its Constitution – supported by a series of newspaper articles we know as *The Federalist Papers* – the first amendment established, in one sentence, freedom of speech and freedom of the press. In the early days of the Republic, Congress backed up this freedom by giving newspapers preferential mailing rates. However, only eleven years later in 1798, as newspapers quickly became increasingly politicized, the United States government enacted the Alien and Sedition Acts. Once again, publishers on the wrong political side were jailed. As we will see, the jailing of news people occurs to this day.

This brief history indicates how sensitive newspaper people, readers, and the government are to "information." Then, as now, confronting the news and the idea of objective reporting really comes down to the question of how we interpret what we read. Something as simple as a weather report in the newspaper (or on a television news program) would seem to qualify as unbiased information – science, in fact, since meteorology is based on collections of data, which are observed and used as predictors of climate behavior. But, as often as not, the weather is presented as a threat – "big changes" are predicted, but only revealed after the commercial break. Even minor fluctuations are given value judgments: clouds are bad; sunshine is good. The weather is turned into a kind of melodrama, intertwined with disaster.

What happens with news that involves more complex issues that touch society's core cultural values? In 1925, the infamous trial of John Scopes, a Tennessee high school biology teacher, pitted the teaching of evolution against the religious fundamentalist belief that God created the world and its creatures within six days at a relatively recent date. The trial, complete with teams of high-profile lawyers on both sides, anti-evolution demonstrators, lemonade stands, chimpanzee sideshows, a live radio broadcast, and a gaggle of reporters from the nation's most prominent newspapers, was the 1920s version of a media circus – an event whose media coverage over-shadowed the "news" and became a story in itself. With the rise of Christian fundamentalism since the 1980s, the emotional debate over evolution has begun again. Scientists agree that the facts of evolution are, simply, incontrovertible – beyond controversy. The science of evolution constitutes one kind of information, based upon careful observation. Yet reporting about recent discussions of evolution routinely includes equal time for the "other side." Is this an appropriate practice of "fair and balanced" reporting, allowing the audience to make its own decision, or is it a lost opportunity to present a scientific truth in the face of superstition? Put more broadly: does objective reporting necessarily entail giving equal coverage to opposing viewpoints, even if one side is based on observable facts and the other based on emotion? Is the simple fact of controversy sufficient to demand coverage of all sides?

In November of 2006, as the war in Iraq was spiraling into increasingly widespread violence, some news organizations made an interesting decision. Until that time, "sectarian violence" had been the journalist's cliché used to describe the daily shootings and bombings carried out by Shia and Sunni against each other. The US government, with a huge stake in maintaining its diminishing authority, refused to name this struggle, which had already claimed thousands of lives on all sides. Finally, in November 2006, the National Broadcasting Company – specifically Matt Lauer on the popular *Today* show – and then the McClatchy Company, owners of a number of newspapers across the country, began referring to the events as a civil war. The government, however, continued to avoid the term until March, 2007, when a Pentagon quarterly report stated that some of the violence in Iraq could be described as a civil war.

What happens when the press – or in this case a morning news and entertainment television show – ceases to be "objective," and reporting suddenly become policy-making? Instead of "information," were these news outlets making news by changing the discourse? Or were they reporting facts that the government chose to ignore? One reason the US government refused to use the term "civil war" was because acknowledging it would take away justification for intervention by American troops – in a civil war, there are no enemies for foreign troops to take arms against, unless they are protecting one side against the other. Therefore, the change in terminology by these news organizations indicated, in effect, that they were taking a stand, alongside the majority of the American people, against the US involvement in the war.

"Information" and "objectivity" are vehicles that can be coded to mean almost anything, from an eyewitness report describing the breathtaking devastation of a Middle-Eastern conflict; to an alleged reporter, who is actually a spokesperson for a government initiative, providing "information" that is anything but neutral about the policy she or he has been hired to promote; to a pharmaceutical company's advertisement for a new medication; to advice on how to survive a hurricane or a terrorist attack. "Information" becomes the lubricant for the news media, meaningful and meaningless enough to allow something to slide by without attention needing to be paid, signifying simply "something about something," just relevant-seeming enough to grab attention.

"News," on the other hand, still carries a connotative charge, a sense of something happening; it carries a sense of excitement – "we bring you breaking news!" But, like so many others, the word has been co-opted. An advertiser can claim to be bringing you "news" of an important new product. A publicity agent will offer "news" of a celebrity's impending marriage or divorce or entry into rehab. Despite the fact that, when you open a newspaper in the morning or turn on the network news in the evening, or go to any number of websites, you expect to read, see, and hear about what has recently happened in the world, the news you get may not be the news you need or any news at all.

William Randolph Hearst and Joseph Pulitzer proved this when they started modern journalism in the decades following the Civil War. Instead of being mouthpieces for political parties and their operatives, they were profit centers for strong and politically opinionated businessmen. As a result, Hearst and Pulitzer developed their product by selecting, reporting, in some instances creating, news in ways they hoped would increase circulation and in turn their income. The concept of freedom of expression formalized itself into the politics and economics of expression, two functions basic to the media design.

Hearst and Pulitzer strove to outdo each other, buying newspapers across the country and competing by attempting to make their papers more and more sensational. Crime and political misdeeds were their specialty. They not only reported the news, they tried to make it. Most infamously, the Hearst and Pulitzer papers stirred up war fever by playing upon a growing revolution of Cuban nationals against their Spanish colonial rulers, creating a surge for war against Spain. When a US warship, *The Maine*, blew up while in port at Havana, Hearst and Pulitzer decided it was the result of an attack by the Spanish and therefore further inflamed public and political opinion until the President, William McKinley, found no option but to go to war against Spain, in Cuba and the Philippines. Hearst had sent the painter Frederic Remington to Cuba, along with his reporters. Remington cabled Hearst, "Everything is quiet. There is no trouble here. There will be no war. I wish to come home." Hearst responded: "Please remain. You furnish the pictures, and I'll furnish the war."

Pulitzer's papers ran a comic strip with a strange-looking character named, after the color of clothes he wore, "The Yellow Kid." It was so popular that Hearst recruited the artist away from Pulitzer, who, although helpless to keep the cartoonist, kept the character, having it drawn by someone else. This character lent its name to the kind of jingoist, populist, rabble-rousing news-making that both publishers practiced: yellow journalism (figures 2.1 and 2.2).

"Yellow journalism" was not about providing information to a public eager to expand their understanding of the world. It was, rather, about creating a public that would buy the news, incorporating it into patterns of sensation and excitement, *making* a readership by turning news reporting into a variety of narratives about crime or war. The process created in its turn not only financial but also political power for the owners of large newspapers. They controlled editorial content, and by creating a readership, were moved to attempt to sway them. It was a feedback loop. As the readership grew, advertising grew, and so power and influence increased.

This self-fulfilling cycle drives most media. The media producer imagines the audience he or she wants, creates a product he or she believes will attract that audience, and when the audience appears, keeps feeding it what seemed attractive to it in the first place. The process – the feedback loop – is, of course, more complex than this

Figure 2.1 Contemporary cartoon of Joseph Pulitzer. North Wind Picture Archives/Alamy.

simple theorem. Much planning goes into determining the desired audience, which might not always manifest itself in ways that the media producer imagined. But when the process is successful, riches accrue to the media producer in the form of profits, and to the audience in the form of pleasure or – in the case of much journalism – titillation. In the world of nineteenth-century American newspapers, the pattern involved establishing as much dominance of the market for news as was possible, and cultivating an audience by constructing and presenting the news in a sensational manner that would guarantee a positive response by that audience. Newspapers became monopolies while the news they reported or created quickly became generic, with stories about politics, war, murder, and corruption following conventional patterns of exposure, condemnation, and graphic detail. CNN proves this now whenever they give air time to the latest celebrity trial or mass shooting. Yellow journalism thrives when the *New York Post* blares front page headlines of a celebrity drug bust, and even when *The New York Times* investigates child pornography, though with a modicum of responsibility; it exists when the NBC "news" program,

Figure 2.2 Cartoon of Joseph Pulitzer and William Randolph Hearst. Courtesy of the Library of Congress (LC-USZC4-3800).

Dateline, joins the ranks of sensationalism with its "To Catch a Predator" series in which online sex offenders are lured in front of the camera by actors portraying their alleged victims.

Mediating the World

As we will do time and again in this book, we return to the concept of mediation. You and I want the news to tell us something about the world, about politics, entertainment, technology, or sports that we didn't know before. The news should be our most trustworthy mediation of the world, reporting, explaining, delivering to us information we would not otherwise be able to access. But to the media who "do" the news, it is one commodity among others. This is what Hearst and Pulitzer understood. To make money, newspapers must be sold; to sell them, the public had to be made excited enough to desire them. You and I rarely have direct contact with events beyond our personal interactions. Even if we do – say we take part in a political demonstration or attend a big sporting event – we are aware only of our own experiences. To know more, to get context and detail, requires not only wider coverage, more eyes and ears on the event, but also more expertise, more insight. Journalism at its base is about a reporter being in a place where events are occurring, or talking to an informed source, and knowing how to interpret events, knowing whom to ask for assistance in the interpretation, owning the ability to express what she has learned, and even expressing an opinion or personal impression.

As in any other media operation in our society, the news has an economic imperative. Reporters in the field need the support of an organization that will pay them, gather and edit their work, and publish it. The earliest American newspapers were basically one-person operations, reprinting news of Europe, arguing domestic politics. But, as journalism turned into a large-scale business operation, more and more people were needed to supply and interpret the facts. During the nineteenth century, news organizations took advantage of emerging technologies and used the telegraph as a means of rapidly gathering information – as did the government itself during the Civil War. Central news-gathering companies, such as the Associated Press and United Press International in the United States, Reuters in England, and Agence-France Presse were formed in the nineteenth century to feed information to the newspapers that subscribed to them. Many of these agencies still exist, often providing the initial facts of a story.

As the news business grew and expanded, initial facts ceased to be the central issue. Power and influence might be used to convince a frightened public that a war was necessary, or to convince a curious one that the latest celebrity trial or sensational murder is important, but this is not the same as creating an informed public – which is the job of responsible journalism such as the "muckraking" investigative journalism carried on in the nineteenth century in the face of Hearst and Pulitzer. Curiously, responsible journalism might not even involve the public at all, if we recognize that the media audience is not an undifferentiated mass, but rather is made up of individuals, each one capable of taste and choice. Hysteria is the opposite of reason. It is also the opposite of individual thought. The screaming headlines and feverish rabble-rousing of yellow journalism are so self-contained that there needn't be an audience made up of individuals who want a war or some other desperate action, or who have less than a passing interest in who killed whom. The audience becomes part of the narrative created by the newspapers. There are individuals who pay attention to the news and there is the audience desired by the tellers of the news, an audience that the newspaper hopes to create. The more that desired audience is realized by means of people paying for the newspaper, the more the paper will continue to provide sensation. But when that self-perpetuating cycle begins to come apart, as it does from time to time, journalism fragments and changes, as does its audience.

Regional and nationwide

Early on, in the colonial period, newspapers served large and varied constituencies (relative, of course, to the population at the time). For example, *Freedom's Journal*, the first African-American owned and operated paper, addressed former slaves and anti-slavery forces in the North from 1827 to 1830. It began a long tradition of newspapers addressed to and by minorities, groups whose voice is only sometimes heard in the mainstream media. In the post-civil war period, newspapers developed as local voices, while some rose to national prominence. What is important to note – in the face of today's growing news monopolies – is that almost all newspapers originated locally, and most had their city as part of their names: *The Richmond Times-Dispatch*; *The New Orleans Picayune*; *The Miami Herald*. Until the 1960s, every major city had a number of newspapers, publishing in the morning and the evening. Twentieth-century readers had no national newspaper until *USA Today* began publication in 1982, although the national business paper, *The Wall Street Journal*, had been publishing since the late nineteenth century.

Today, some local newspapers, like *The Washington Post* and *The New York Times*, have become national due to the extent and quality of their coverage. Others, like the *New York Post* and the New York *Daily News*, remain tabloids in the yellow journalism tradition, though without the influence enjoyed by tabloids in the days of Hearst and Pulitzer. Most papers still have a strong political slant in their editorials, though the political spectrum in most papers is fairly narrow, between center right and center left. Almost all newspapers continue the traditions of their origins and endorse local and national political candidates at election time.

Technologies of distribution

Radio, arriving in the American home in the 1920s, was an immediate agent of change. The coming of media into the domestic space shifted the culture in major ways. Instead of having to go out and buy a paper, bring it back and take time to read it, the news – however reduced in detail and depth – was now within earshot, inside the home, and it did not require a reader to sit still in one place. At the same time, movie theaters began presenting a newsreel – a short film of major events – along with the feature film program. The public could get news without buying or reading a paper.

As a result, newspaper circulation began a long decline that continues to this day. Old press empires crumbled, while new ones formed. Once television arrived in the late 1940s, the downward spiral of newspaper print circulation accelerated. By mid-century, newspapers – especially evening editions – began going out of business. The decline of this particular segment of readership was partly the result of the availability of evening network news, but also reflected the growing workload placed on families. There was simply less and less time available to read a newspaper in the evening.

Growing outlets for the news, changing demographics and reading habits, changed the newspaper. So did the growth of media empires that differed from the models set in the nineteenth century by Hearst and Pulitzer. Many newspapers became the holdings of large corporations. *The Los Angeles Times*, long owned by the politically powerful Chandler family, is now the property of the Tribune Company, one of many newspapers and television stations they control. The news magazine empire of Henry Luce – *Time*, *Sports Illustrated*, and *Life*, once the premier source of photojournalism – is now part of the Time Warner entertainment conglomerate. Some newspaper corporations themselves began buying other "properties." There still are "media barons," most especially Rupert Murdoch. His News Corporation owns the tabloid *New York Post* as well as the Fox News Channel and MySpace.com, and also the very staid *Times* of London, not to mention more than 100 other papers and broadcast outlets around the world. His 5-billion-dollar acquisition of *The Wall Street Journal* made headlines in 2007. Unlike their forebears, the power of these owners is more economic than editorial. Newspapers no longer have the power to whip up a war frenzy, though they still can misinform the public by not investigating why a war is being fought. All of them, even those in reasonably good economic shape, are subject to stock-market pressures. As part of corporate portfolios, they need to show not only a profit, but also the promise of stock growth. If they don't, they are downsized and reporters are fired.

Journalism as political heroism and martyrdom

Newspapers are reduced in numbers and in influence, their circulation has dropped, but they are hardly relics, and they still play an important role in the public sphere. In the early 1970s, the potent reporting of *The Washington Post* and *The New York Times* was influential in the fall of President Richard M. Nixon. More recently, in the summer of 2005, a *New York Times* journalist, Judith Miller, went to jail for 85 days for refusing to disclose her sources to a federal grand jury investigating a Bush administration information leak. Protecting sources is the most common reason given by journalists who refuse information to authorities. If they name sources, they fear that others will be unwilling to provide them with insights and information in the future. The fact that reporters need sources to provide information is an indication that this information still has potency.

The Judith Miller case involved the uncovering of a CIA operative, the wife of dip-lomat Joseph C. Wilson. Wilson was sent to Africa to discover whether the former head of Iraq, Saddam Hussein, was buying uranium ore to build nuclear devices. Saddam was not doing this, and Wilson wrote an article in the *The New York Times* denouncing this particular lie that the government was using to create support for the war. In retaliation, an unnamed source in the Bush administration leaked information to the press that blew the CIA cover of Wilson's wife, Valerie Plame.

Judith Miller was involved in this messy scandal. Her jailing initially made her a journalist hero. Subsequently, however, it was discovered that she was not a very objective reporter, and, in fact, something of a mouthpiece for the administration. Her power within *The Times* was partially responsible for her newspaper *not* present-ing the most rounded story about the allegations of Iraq having "weapons of mass destruction" that led to the Iraq War. Miller was fired from the paper. One govern-ment official involved in the scandal was found guilty of perjury.

This was a different story from the one some 30 years earlier when, at the height of the Vietnam War and the heyday of the Nixon administration, both *The New York Times* and *The Washington Post* published material that hastened the end of both. In 1971, *The Times* published what were called "The Pentagon Papers." Consisting of classified material from a RAND Corporation and the Defense Department, these top secret documents, which revealed the extent of governmental misinformation about the war, were released to the press by military analyst Daniel Ellsberg. The government sued to stop publication, an injunction that was overturned by the Supreme Court.

In 1973 (by which time Nixon had won re-election to his second term), two report-ers for *The Washington Post*, Bob Woodward and Carl Bernstein, began exposing the paranoia of the Nixon presidency and traced the creation and execution of the infa-mous Watergate burglary, in which the administration hired people to break into Democratic National headquarters. The Pentagon Papers and Watergate scandals led to Nixon's impeachment, resignation, and eventual pardon. Woodward and Bernstein were widely regarded as heroes; their book about the Watergate investigation, *All the President's Men*, was turned into a popular movie (directed by Alan Pakula, 1976). (See figure 2.3.)

Much of the Watergate inside information came from an anonymous source who came to be called (after a character in an infamous pornographic movie) "Deep Throat." Woodward and Bernstein were steadfast in refusing to name this source, and speculation about his identity continued until 2005, when a former FBI deputy direc-tor revealed that he was Deep Throat. The interest in the revelation attested to the staying power of this story and the notoriety of the reporting some 30 years earlier.

In the early summer of 2006, *The New York Times*, *The Los Angeles Times*, and *The Wall Street Journal* all reported on an example of the Bush administration's spying operations on civilians as part of the "war on terrorism." A previous revelation had exposed widespread telephone wire-tapping; this time, it was bank records that were being examined. The response of the government was swift and hard, some conserva-tive politicians accusing *The Times* of traitorous behavior. The *Wall Street Journal*,

Figure 2.3 Journalists as heroes. Robert Redford and Dustin Hoffman as Bob Woodward and Carl Bernstein, *The Washington Post*'s Watergate reporters in *All the President's Men* (dir. Alan J. Pakula, 1976). *All the President's Men* © Warner Bros., 1976.

whose editorial page is conservative, attacked itself, blasting its own reporting of the operation! Both the *Journal* and *The Times* published editorials, one condemning, the other defending its right to inform the public. These varying, conflicting views on the responsibility of the press echo across the history of journalism and, more than anything else, indicate the vitality of news reporting.

I spoke earlier about the narrative that is created when news mediates its audience – creating a cycle of presentation and response in which all parties, owners, reporters, editors, and readers, join. The news offers what it believes its readers want; its readers assent by buying the paper (or reading it online, or watching the news on television). In some instances, the outbursts of bold investigative reporters create a particular kind of narrative, a melodrama of heroic commitment, of suffering bravely for their profession, fighting the government, going to jail. Despite, or in face of, declining numbers of newspapers and declining numbers of readers, the crusading journalist remains something of a cultural celebrity, even a hero.

As far back as the 1920s, the newspaperman was mythologized as a semi-heroic, roughneck sleuth. One of his earliest incarnations was in the 1928 play, *The Front Page*, written by Ben Hecht (who started his writing career as a Chicago reporter) and Charles MacArthur. It was made into a film no less than three times. But the most famous movie reporter is Thompson, the eyes and ears of the audience in Orson Welles's *Citizen Kane*, the most famous fictional newpaper owner. Throughout the film, Thompson is seen in profile, the surrogate for our own curiosity, trying to put together the pieces of an insoluble puzzle – the character of the fictional newspaper tycoon, Charles Foster Kane, who is based on the real tycoon, William Randolph Hearst. These fictional reporters have had their imitators in "real" life: New York reporters Jimmy Breslin and Pete Hamill, and the Chicago columnist Mike Royko, even Norman Mailer, the late novelist who sometimes did journalism, attempted to imitate the tough, grizzled, hard-drinking reporters depicted in the movies.

The end of journalism

The romanticized myth of the reporter-detective that began in the mid-1920s is fading from both the cultural imagination and the newsroom itself. In the place of respected journalism and respect for journalism, we too often find widespread cynicism on the part of reporters and lack of respect for journalism on the part of their audience. This turnaround has been due to scandals, such as the Judith Miller affair, as well as the discovery in recent years of some reporters who made up stories they claimed as fact. A prime example is Jayson Blair, a young *New York Times* reporter who was forced to resign in May 2003 after a reporter for the *San Antonio Express-News* accused him – rightly, it turned out – of plagiarizing an article she had written. Further investigation by a *Times*-appointed committee found that Blair had fabricated information in dozens of stories he had written for *The Times* in the months prior to the San Antonio incident.

More damage still has been caused when the government is found to subvert the practice of journalism by planting "reporters" and stories that promote its own programs while masquerading as fact. A most bizarre example was the appearance at White House press briefings in 2004 of a "reporter" named "Jeff Gannon," who asked easy questions of a presidential press secretary who had ready answers. The White House press pool is made up of carefully chosen, usually seasoned newspersons, who are investigated by the FBI before being given a press pass. But it turned out that "Jeff Gannon" was not a reporter, but someone named James Dale Guckert, a gay man who ran an online escort service, featuring provocative pictures of himself. How this person gained access to a notoriously homophobic administration remains a mystery to this day. What is not a mystery is that "Jeff Gannon" is still online, writing a right-wing blog.

The Gannon story may be bizarre, but is perhaps less pernicious than other manipulations of the press performed by the government. Again in 2004, the administration paid a conservative columnist, Armstrong Williams, more than $200,000 to promote its education program in his columns and cable television appearance. The promotions were not announced as such; nor were the "video press releases" created by the Education Department and offered as news to various outlets. The videos were narrated by someone who pretended to be a reporter. Both activities were declared illegal by the Government Accountability Office.

The issue in cases like these is less a matter of "journalistic objectivity," or even of government manipulation of the news, than it is of the implied contract of trust between news reporting and its audience. The news is meant to be based on events that actually occurred, and that is our expectation. Political commentary is meant to be based on a trusted writer's careful reading of events based upon a point of view that is clearly stated or implied. When fiction is played as fact, or news turns out to be based not on an interpretation of events but a creation of them, then the media design, and our place in it, turns into a blind maze. "Objectivity" is, as we have seen, a position taken and a goal rather than a probability; but fictionalizing the news or politicizing it without announcing it as such removes ideological certainty as well as journalistic credibility. We need to stress that the phrase "journalistic credibility" is itself a cultural construct, coded with our own desire to trust and be secure that what we read, see, and hear is what it appears to be. We would like to believe that there is a "truth" out there that can be mediated in ways, told to us as a "story," that we can understand, easily grasp, and trust.

Taking sides

Politics and journalism, as we have seen, are always tightly linked, the latter being the expressive voice of the former. Politics can be the enemy of journalism as well. A case history of this can be seen in the ascendancy of right-wing politics and culture that began under President Reagan in the 1980s. Partly driving this ascendancy was an ongoing attack on and attempt to discredit the news media as being "biased" in favor of the left. To understand this, we need to look again at the reigning myth of journalism, its dominant code of objectivity. Objectivity is coded as an impossible transparency in the reporting of news, in which the reporter and her editor are simple mediators of information, untainted by opinion, politics, or personality.

The problem is that the code of objectivity is impossible to decode as intended. Every newspaper, every reporter, every television news producer, and every member of the news audience has his or her ideological skew. Some newspapers try to contain their ideological perspective in their editorial and op-ed pages, where the work of guest columnists or regular political feature writers appear. Some papers publish both liberal and conservative columnists. Network news broadcasts attempt objectivity by having at least two points of view of any given political story. But despite balanced editorial opinion, despite reportage that gives "both sides of the story," and despite attempts to present facts as neutrally as possible, the *de*coding of the news, the way we receive it, will be determined by our own ideological and cultural position. We are told that, with objective reporting, it is up to us to make up our minds. But our minds are made up of a number of conflicting ideas and emotions, determined by personality, upbringing, and the culture we inhabit. The making up our minds is rarely a matter of picking one point of view over another in a news story, but of where we choose to situate ourselves in the news narrative, right or left, willing to parse the narrative elements, to see through obvious, or not so obvious, falsehoods.

Photojournalism: the power of the image

Few things are more immediate in emotional impact and so fraught with ideological baggage as the photographic image. The image has been an important element of news reporting since the nineteenth century, growing in influence as technologies of visual reproduction allowed more and more visual detail to be printed. Photojournalism is manifested in the still images appearing in newspapers and magazines, the newsreels that accompanied movies before the advent of television, on television itself, and now online. Its power is such that our strongest memories of historic events, especially those of great cultural trauma, are contained not in the written narrative, but in the visual image that accompanies or substitutes for it. On such occasions, it is the image rather than the written narrative that carries the emotive and intellectual force of a story and carries a charge that changes the way we think. The image may have more power to move us than the written word.

The code of the real   The photographic image carries the strongest of codes – the code of realism. Starting from the clichés, "seeing is believing," and moving through the trust we have that what is present in the image was present when the image was taken, we are acculturated into the belief that images do not lie. But images are no less difficult to manipulate than prose. They are representations, mediations of the thing itself, and therefore open to all kinds of interventions: recreating an event for the camera, composing the image to emphasize and dramatize the parts of an event, cropping a photograph so that part of an image that might mitigate the force of the photograph itself is left out. Manipulation can occur on the editorial side as well. If a newspaper has a low opinion of a political leader, the photography editor may well choose the least flattering close-up of him or her.

Perhaps the best way to explain the phenomenon is that photojournalism carries "the reality effect," the illusion, even the feeling of certainty that what we see is what must have been. The reality effect is no more critical than in the photojournalism done during wartime. There are many facts of war – any war – and many fictions. The facts all cluster around sacrifice and death. War is about killing more soldiers on one side than are getting killed on the other. There is also the fact of distance. A relatively few of us, certainly in the United States, have experienced war directly. We depend entirely on journalism to give us a clear understanding of events, of the killing – a fact the government understands and attempts to manipulate by controlling journalists' access to the battlefield or to images of dead soldiers, as well as to official strategies and policies regarding a war.

Wartime images are therefore important in communicating the experiences of war, critical to an understanding of what the effects of a war "really" are, and, at the same time, critical to the government in building up the patriotic fervor necessary to allow the government to continue prosecuting a war. As early as 1855, during the Crimean War that was waged by the British against the Russians, a photographer, Roger Fenton, was commissioned by the British royalty, through a London print shop, to take pictures. All of them were staged, and none of them showed the extraordinary carnage of this war. A few years later, Mathew Brady and a corps of traveling photographers he supervised set out to document the American Civil War with their cameras. Officers and soldiers, alongside battlefields and the dead became memorialized. One Brady photographer, Timothy O'Sullivan, published "Harvest of Death," an image made in 1863, in a book, *Photographic Sketch Book of the War* (1865–1866). The image is faked to the extent that bodies as well as cannonballs were moved and posed for greatest effect. (See figures 2.4 and 2.5.)

Two of the most famous war photographs of the twentieth century are both under contention regarding their authenticity. They prove better than most that authenticity finally lies within the image itself and the response to it far more than what may have existed in front of the camera lens. As mediations of death and victory in war, these

Figure 2.4 A staged photograph from the Crimean War by Roger Fenton (1855). Courtesy of the Library of Congress (LC-USZC4-9174).

Figure 2.5 Timothy O'Sullivan's 1863 photograph of the bodies of Federal soldiers. From *Gardner's Photographic Sketch Book of the War* (1865–6). Courtesy of the Library of Congress (LC-DIG-ppmsca-12558).

photographs gather and express emotion by their own form, by the *performance* of the image and the reception of that performance by the viewer.

Joseph Rosenthal's image of the raising of the flag on Mount Suribachi, on Iwo Jima, was taken in February, 1945, for the Associated Press news service. Everything in this picture, but most especially the dynamics of its composition – the eager energy of the soldiers pushing up the flag, signaling exertion, will, and triumph, with the American flag at the apex of the effort – are irresistibly triumphant. The image has appeared in many venues; there is a monument in Washington based on the photograph; Clint Eastwood made the 2006 film *Flags of Our Fathers*, relating the history of the photograph and the soldiers in it.

Yet, since the photograph was first published, accusations have swirled that Rosenthal staged it. Eyewitnesses agree that Rosenthal arrived after marines had already raised a flag on the peak; Rosenthal's photo captures the raising of a second, larger flag. Rosenthal contends that he did nothing to pose or direct the marines, and that he never hid the fact that this was the second flag to be raised. Two marine photographers, one shooting still photos and the other shooting motion picture footage, were present. Yet Rosenthal's detractors insist that the picture is too perfect to have happened spontaneously. The question, in this case, is whether it matters or not? Is the "reality effect" and the energy of victory that is the image itself more important than how the image was constructed? (See figure 2.6.)

The war image is highly charged by the immediate contact it makes with the event it portrays. Nothing is more immediate than death on the battlefield. "Loyalist Militiaman at the Moment of Death, Cerro Muriano, September 5, 1936" (figure 2.7) is almost as famous as the raising of the flag at Iwo Jima. It was taken by Robert Capa during the Spanish Civil War, a bitter struggle between left- and right-wing forces that was an immediate antecedent of World War II. It was published, among other places, in Henry Luce's *Life* magazine. Its immediacy – the impression of an event that is *un*mediated – is expressed through the dynamic composition of the shot and the expressive right-to-left movement; the sense of the shot soldier almost blown out of the frame is so vivid that it takes a moment to realize that it is a photograph of death happening. Attempts have been made to prove it fake, though all evidence confirms this is an image of something terrible happening taken at the moment of its occurrence.

The image that results in action   Images like those of Rosenthal and Capa (who went on to join Magnum – a collective of photojournalists, currently in partnership with the online magazine *Slate* – and who lost his life in a landmine explosion while photographing in Vietnam) document and memorialize the violence and victories of wartime. They communicate immediate events and then come to stand for, indeed symbolize, the wider emotions of war, in effect transcending their moment. Other examples of photojournalism, both still and moving images, are so powerful that they enter the cultural psyche and become part of the cultural memory. Lee Harvey Oswald getting shot in a Dallas jail, caught on live TV; troops burning down a hut with a cigarette lighter during the Vietnam War; "smart" bombs finding their targets in the first Gulf War; Airplanes penetrating the World Trade Center – these images are

Figure 2.6 Joseph Rosenthal's photograph of the raising of the flag at Iwo Jima, February, 1945. PA Photos/AP.

interwoven with personal memories and together create a kind of communal recall of the most anxious kind.

Some images are so powerful that they provoke action. The history of the modern civil rights movement has been well documented in print journalism, from the desegregation of the armed forces in the late 1940s, through Brown vs. Board of Education in 1954, and the Montgomery, Alabama bus boycott in 1955, through the march on Washington in 1963, and the signing of the Civil Rights Act in 1964. But one could argue that images of police dogs attacking people had as powerful an influence as all the words and editorials that addressed the movement (figure 2.8). Indeed, an Associated Press image is said to have moved President John F. Kennedy to take positive action. More recently, the appalling photographs of American soldiers torturing

Figure 2.7 Robert Capa's "Loyalist Militiaman at the Moment of Death, Cerro Muriano, September 5, 1936". ROBERT CAPA © 2001 By Cornell Capa/ Magnum Photos.

Figure 2.8 Bill Hudson's photograph of the dog attack on civil rights marchers, Birmingham, Alabama, 1963. This image is said to have changed John F. Kennedy's mind and helped bring him to action on the side of the civil rights movement. PA Photos/AP.

Iraqi prisoners in the Abu Ghraib prison pressed readers and viewers to understand that there were still other facets of civil rights, that oppression and humiliation can be inflicted anywhere when balances of power become disrupted.

The Abu Ghraib photographs represent an extension of news media beyond the traditional boundaries of print. They were not taken by professional news photographers, but by the very people perpetrating the abuse. They appeared not only in newspapers, but also on television and online, transmitted instantaneously. It could well be argued that this very immediacy, the instantaneous transmission of disturbing images that are then shown over and over again, creates an unexpected narrative not of emotions pushing us into action, but of pain and violence to which we can respond only with helplessness. News was once a matter of choice; it is now something that we can only avoid by actively ducking for cover. We become part of journalism's narrative almost against our will.

The news beyond the paper

The history of the image in journalism is intertwined with the movement of journalism itself from print to other media. Photographs in newspapers were common by the latter half of the nineteenth century. Newsreels – cinematic documentations of current events – started as early as film itself, around 1895. William McKinley was the first president to be filmed. William Randolph Hearst himself got into the film business shortly after the turn of the twentieth century and began making newsreels through various film studios, before settling in with MGM. Henry Luce, whose *Time* and *Life* Magazines were major alternatives to the daily papers, started what was the most famous "newsreel," *The March of Time*. The quotation marks are important, because the weekly *March of Time* films combined actual newsreel footage with re-enactments and unashamedly staged scenes, all encapsulated by a booming "voice of god" narrator who lent a portentous air to the proceedings, creating not so much a sense of communication as domination of the viewer. Facts are fictionalized; fictions presented as fact. Not unlike tabloid journalism.

Newsreels presented a kind of temporal problem for the delivery of news. They suffered from time constraints, the necessity to choose and condense stories – not unlike similar problems that continue to plague network news. Because newsreels depended on celluloid that had to be delivered from the news source to the studio, then developed, edited, and distributed to theaters, they were "new" in name only, their news dated by the time they were exhibited. And newsreels required active seeking out by their audience, who had to go to a movie theater to see them. Of course, many, many people went to the movies on a regular basis, and newsreels were part of a double bill of feature films, along with cartoons, a short subject, and coming attractions that entertained movie-goers on nights out. In major cities, there were even a few movie theaters that showed only newsreels – something of a forerunner of the 24/7 cable news networks. Still, like buying a newspaper – which also suffers from a delay between the news event and the event reported – something like an act of will was involved to seek out the news. This was no longer necessary with radio.

Radio and politics We will examine the early history of radio in detail in chapter 4. For our purposes here we need only recognize that news reporting, in however abbreviated a form, quickly became a standard part of the radio broadcasting schedule in the 1920s. As the major networks consolidated their power, they formed their own news-gathering and reporting bureaus. So did the United States government, especially as represented by Franklin Delano Roosevelt, President from 1933 until his death in 1945. While earlier presidents made some desultory use of new media, Roosevelt embraced it. He not only cultivated the political reporters from various newspapers, but he also directly embraced his audience through a series of regular broadcasts called "Fireside Chats." He made himself the center of the news and in so doing created a political personality and started the relationship, sometimes friendly, sometimes contentious, between non-print media and the political process.

It is just here that we find a further expansion of the concept of news, which develops as an extension of the power of the early news barons, like Hearst and Pulitzer, but occurs at the other end of the spectrum, where the news happens. Roosevelt closed the media loop, and altered the narrative in which the news solicits an audience by catering to its presumed desires. By cutting around journalism, going directly – as directly as an electronic medium and a politician who was a consummate performer could – to his audience, Roosevelt created a narrative of trust and connection. Through an economic depression and a world war, Roosevelt merged political influence with news in ways the press barons could only dream about. In fact, he negated journalism by turning politics into immediate discourse that left journalism itself behind. It was as if mediation disappeared behind the kindly, paternal voice of assurance that Roosevelt projected. More importantly still, he turned politics and, inevitably, broadcast journalism into a cult of personality, a process that was completed not by another politician, but by a "real" journalist, Edward R. Murrow.

Edward R. Murrow and broadcast journalism Roosevelt was a politician who created his persona on the radio. Murrow was perhaps the first media journalist who never worked in print and who created a persona in radio and then television that, like Roosevelt's, transcended the person himself and became a cultural icon. Murrow was put to work by William S. Paley, who built CBS into a viable competitor to the then-dominant radio network, NBC. Sent to London before the US entered World War II, Murrow produced broadcasts during the German bombings of that city that helped to transform the image of the gruff, bullying journalist from the "Front Page" movies into an engaged and poetic, sympathetic, and authoritative voice. The Germans supplied the war, Murrow the prose pictures. This is Murrow, sonorous, somewhat sadly, deeply involved and simultaneously above it all, reporting in August, 1944:

> This is London. These doodle bugs come over, sounding like a couple of dissatisfied washing machines hurtling through the air. They come at every hour of the day or night. Living here is like being under unobserved artillery fire.

The other night one of them hit a hospital. Hit it smack on the roof. Most of the nurses were sleeping downstairs, but one of the maids, a 30-year-old, sallow, squint-eyed individual, was sleeping on the top floor. These doodles explode on impact and have very little penetrating power. This one went off when it hit the roof. A few minutes later, before the dust had settled, a doctor friend of mine was making a round of the wards. There he found the maid, pretty well bespattered with glass. She was the only casualty … she said to the doctor, "I'm so ashamed. I should have been sleeping downstairs, but I wasn't, and now I am the only one to be hurt. And what will the hospital think of me, being such a nuisance and all."

When Murrow returned from Europe, he did not get involved in day-to-day news casting at CBS, though he was central to its operations, if only as a symbol of seriousness. Others of his original group – Eric Severeid, Charles Collingwood, Howard K. Smith – took up that job. Murrow joined with a producer, Fred Friendly, and together they created a series of radio and, later, television documentaries and commentaries. Murrow's 1954 television broadcast attacking Joseph McCarthy, the senator whose name is synonymous with the vicious and mindless red-baiting of the 1950s, is regarded as a monument of journalistic bravery. It was re-created and celebrated as recently as 2005, in a film whose title came from Murrow's sign-off line, *Good Night and Good Luck*. Murrow's 1960 documentary, *Harvest of Shame*, about the exploitation of migrant workers, transcends its subject – still a rankling issue in American politics and culture – becoming something of the bad conscience of television reporting, which today is less willing to take upon itself the muckraking job of exposing serious social issues.

But the trajectory of Murrow's career through the 1950s is prophetic of what happened to television journalism. As with radio, we will discuss television in depth in a later chapter. For our purposes here, we need only note that television rapidly took over from radio and further eroded newspaper readership. Television's delivery of the news grew through the fifties, expanding from 15- to 30-minute broadcasts in the early sixties. But, as the network's power grew, William Paley, Murrow's one-time mentor, wanted his network to enter the commercial mainstream. Murrow's career changed. He began to do more and more celebrity interviews and televized visits to famous people's homes, pointing the way to the kind of frivolous reporting that would overtake much of broadcast news in a few decades.

By the end of the 1950s, Murrow's career was over, largely because, as a widely recognized, independent, figure, he clashed with the corporate image of CBS. This is an interesting paradox inherent in broadcast news: networks and cable television want a recognizable "face" associated with their broadcasts, someone with whom the viewer can feel comfortable and have confidence. But, as corporate entities, they can't have that face be associated with anything but the broadcast and the company that runs it. Murrow was too much an independent; too ready to take up controversial issues.

The years immediately following the Murrow decades saw television journalism grow with a certain earnestness and a seeming desire to emulate the seriousness of print. The networks – NBC and CBS in particular– seemed to be operating with good faith. They spent money on foreign news bureaus and attempted not only through their nightly news broadcasts, but also through documentaries and specials, to provide a similar sweep of news and information as newspapers and news magazines. They both exposed the political world to the public and became, in turn, the tool of politicians. That difficult interplay of independence from the public and the newsmakers, while simultaneously dependent upon both – as well as corporate sponsorship – created pressures the networks could hardly bear.

Television and politics   Television first witnessed the presidential nominating conventions in 1948. In 1968, with passions against the Vietnam War running high, and protestors taking to the streets, it became a participant when the Democratic nominating convention turned violent and reporters were pummeled by security guards and the Chicago police. This was a tumultuous time, and the culture at large was at odds with itself, with people both for and against the war loudly, sometimes violently, voicing their feelings. The images of reporters getting roughed up (one of them was CBS's Dan Rather) had a powerful effect. This was a different form of photojournalism – the television cameras capturing an attack on their own people. The images added to a growing concern of a government out of control.

It didn't take long for the political parties to understand that this kind of image did them no good and that they could better use television as much as, and finally more than, television used them. The 1968 convention was the last in which television got the better of the politicians. After that, the Democratic and Republican parties began using their conventions as political and ideological spectacle. They used their airtime to show off and make speeches. By the 1990s, as television outlets expanded and audiences became harder to target and maintain, the networks stopped doing "gavel to gavel" coverage and broadcast convention highlights only. Politicians, meanwhile, discovered that they could market themselves on television with as much success as any other commodity. Instead of news, politics became a product. We will examine this further in chapter 3.

Politicians, political news, and television have played a kind of cat-and-mouse game with one another. Two events during the 1950s marked the unpredictable three-way interaction between television, politics, and their audience. In 1952, when Richard M. Nixon was running as Dwight Eisenhower's Vice President, he was accused of taking bribes. Eisenhower was ready to dump him. Nixon took to television and, with his wife sitting smiling to one side, delivered a speech in which he denied the charges, enumerating his income and expenses in embarrassing detail. He referred to his wife's "respectable Republican cloth coat," and offered that the only political gift he received was his daughters' dog, Checkers. (This was an attempt to hook into cultural memory of Roosevelt's more famous dog, Falla.) In his extraordinary film, *Nixon* (1995), Oliver Stone re-creates and summarizes the speech: "It was shameless, it was manipulative, it was a huge success." Nixon and Eisenhower went on to win the election. Nixon went further and became President in 1968. In 1974, the Watergate scandal exposed by *The Washington Post* and *The New York Times*, with impeachment hearings held daily on television, Nixon resigned in disgrace.

Beginning in April, 1954, one month after CBS broadcast Edward R. Murrow's exposé of the red-baiting senator, Joseph McCarthy, the American Broadcasting

Corporation (ABC) and the DuMont network (which would, decades later, morph into Fox) broadcast the hearings that McCarthy's committee held to reveal "Communists" in the army. These hearings were actually an attempt on the part of McCarthy to get back at the army, who had accused his assistant, Roy Cohn, of pressuring the military to give special treatment to a friend of Cohn's. McCarthy's ability to force the army to appear for hearings was a mark of the power he created by exploiting fears of "Communist infiltration." But, at the same time, attempting to embarrass the army on television exposed the crudeness of his behavior and offered, at long last, an excuse for so many politicians who hated McCarthy, but feared him, to begin to bring him down.

The televized hearings exposed McCarthy visually and aurally. His loutish appearance and strange whiny voice didn't quite fit his monstrous reputation and only helped expose his strange and threatening demeanor. The hearings also allowed another voice to be heard that proved stronger than Edward R. Murrow's because it was, until that point, unknown, unassuming, and filled with quiet and righteous indignation. During the hearings, as was his method, McCarthy went on the attack, this time accusing an assistant of the army's counsel of having once belonged to a Communist organization. The counsel, a meek, elderly New England lawyer, Joseph Welch, struck back in defense not only of his assistant, but also on behalf of much of the public who had had enough: "Have you no sense of decency, sir," he asked of McCarthy, "at long last? Have you left no sense of decency?" That was it. That December, the Senate voted to censure McCarthy. In two years, he was dead. (See figure 2.9.)

Figure 2.9 Senator Joseph McCarthy, with his colleague, Roy Cohn, during the Army–McCarthy Hearings, 1954. From the film *Point of Order* (dir. Emil de Antonio, 1964). Point Films © 1964.

These events indicate the rather tenuous position television placed itself in during its formative years. More than print journalism, it was and is always careful about the lengths it can go to investigate and expose, while, at the same time, when it *does* choose to expose, or – in the case of the army–McCarthy hearings, or the televized candidates' debates in 1960, where a sweaty Richard Nixon came off badly against John F. Kennedy, or the Watergate hearings – mediate events, it can create surges in public opinion. But that is precisely the problem. As commercial entities, network and most cable television outlets must win viewers in order to please advertisers. Newspapers have to keep their advertisers happy as well, but these are held at a greater distance from editorial content than are televisions sponsors. The television viewer, meanwhile, plays a somewhat passive role in all of this. Dependent on what the news shows and how it shows it – how it mediates it – the viewer can only decode what he or she is given. It is perhaps quite accidental that the Richard Nixon of the Checkers speech came off well, while the same Richard Nixon of the presidential candidates' debates came off poorly. An argument could be made that the same "cameras" were gazing at both, in the sense that the television news apparatus and the purposes of broadcasting a news event had not changed. But the interpretation – the individual and cultural perceptions of each of these two political individuals – had. Perhaps viewers of political news on television are not that passive after all. As with all media, viewers are influenced and interpret in a complex interaction of cultural demand and personal response.

The 1950s and 1960s were the great shakedown periods that allowed television and its viewers to figure out how best to work out the tenuous balance between representation and perception, to balance news reporting, public service (mandated by the Federal Communications Commission, which is meant to oversee the airways, but largely acts as a facilitator for the purchase of broadcast licenses and a censor), and investigation. The news became more personalized as it became more immediate. The *face* – the way newsmakers looked and sounded – became an important part of the narrative of delivery and reception of the news.

Television discovered early on that, when it came to news, it was a matter of personality. Edward R. Murrow may not have lasted in television because his personality was too strong, too independent of the network that carried him. Walter Cronkite, who anchored the CBS evening news for 20 years, was a personality able to create that tender and tenuous relationship with viewers. He was "trusted." His credibility was based as much on his continued presence as on his ability to report the news. He used it well. The tears he shed when he reported the assassination of President John Kennedy in 1963, and his quiet but determined editorializing against the Vietnam War, were both affecting and effective. News in the living room became linked to the personality delivering it.

In the years during and following Cronkite, other anchors on the three networks – Dan Rather on CBS; Chet Huntley and David Brinkley, John Chancellor, Tom Brokaw on NBC; Peter Jennings on ABC – each served various audiences who accepted them as a dependable presence in what passed as television journalism: short "stories" with little detail, along with a growing emphasis on personal, emotional matters: health, survival, and "sacrifice." The news, as in the days of yellow journalism, becomes melodrama with the anchor leading a personable cast of characters whose story may dominate the news they report. The death from lung cancer of ABC anchor Peter Jennings in 2005 provoked a public sense of loss, as did the death of NBC's *Meet the Press* anchor, Tim Russert, in 2008. Jenning's replacement, Bob Woodruff (a member of an anchor team that ABC set up to attract younger viewers), became news when he was badly injured by a roadside bomb near Baghdad. Dan Rather, who took over from Walter Cronkite, continually stirred up discussion and even discomfort when he reported from Afghanistan wearing native costume, when he wore a sweater on the air, or when he signed off with the word "courage."

When Rather resigned in 2005 (under circumstances we will discuss further on), his interim successor was Bob Schieffer, a member of the generation following Edward R. Murrow. Schieffer appealed to the older viewers who make up the majority of the network news audience. In an attempt to broaden that appeal, CBS installed Katie Couric, who was well known to TV audiences as co-anchor of the morning *Today* show. Hiring her for the *CBS Evening News* was an important event, a move to break the male-only presence of TV news anchors. In her first years as anchor, Couric failed to pull in more viewers, though whether this is the result of a gender-biased perception that privileges the "authority" of a male voice, or whether Couric is simply without authority regardless of gender is not clear.

The TV news narrative   Earlier, we spoke of the narrative created when newspapers offer sensational headlines and stories that attempt to create readership. Network news attempts a different kind of narrative in which the viewer carries on a kind of silent dialogue with the news anchor. Whatever constitutes "trust" – a sense of confidence; a combination of gravity and some sense of humor; perhaps a touch of skepticism – speaks to viewers who respond with loyalty. This, of course, has absolutely nothing to do with the quality of reporting, the amount of attention and detail given to a particular story, or to the ability on the side of the news gathering and reporting organization or on the side of the viewer to discriminate between news and sensationalism. This is why our relationship to the person reading the news on the air has, ultimately, little to do with what that person is reading and everything to do with how we respond to the person him- or herself. Personalizing the news leads us away from its content; but, at the same time, our argument is always that content is a product of form.

The stories told by yellow journalism, its screaming, vulgar headlines, its hysterical appeal to immediate emotional response, or the more refined, but no less emotional stories told us by *and of* an older male presence reading the news in our homes are part of the same story. This story is in addition to, or in place of, the actual news being delivered, and its subject is the delivery itself, the mediation of world and local events that determines the ways we understand them and ourselves in relation to the world.

Local television news   As the networks developed their nightly news broadcasts, so did the affiliated and network owned and operated television stations across the country.

While we will examine details of television in chapter 5, it is important to note here that local TV news was initially an opportunity for community service, for enlightening localities about events important to the community, even a point of cohesion, of bringing members of a community together – not unlike local newspapers. It also began, and continues, as an opportunity for local operators to make money from advertising revenue. The local news is a profit center, the biggest source of advertising revenue for local station owners. Like the networks, local news developed personalities that became well known and even trusted within the communities they served. For many years, anchors and format presented the atmosphere of their locality.

But in the 1970s and 1980s, changes took place that made the local news less a site of community news and information than a kind of melodrama of crime and weather. Two things were at work. One was the desire of local operators to increase profit by increasing viewership and therefore advertising revenue. Therefore, local operators seek to maximize profits by packaging what they think is the most palatable news program. At the same time, local operations have been bought up by big media companies. If not owned and operated by the networks themselves, many are owned and operated by companies that own a number of stations across the country. All of this has led to homogenization of local news formats in the interests of maximum control of production.

One result is the desire to maximize profits by minimizing expense and to create a production style that maintains uniformity across operations. Reporters and investigations are expensive – as the networks have also discovered. One way to cut the expense is to buy pre-packaged news, produced by the national owners of the local outlets or by independent production companies. This is especially important as local outlets try to increase their profits by extending news broadcasts to as much as 90 minutes in localities that do not have enough local news to fill that time. Another is to hire consultants to prepare the production of the news broadcast itself, which results in newscasters and newscasts in one locality looking and sounding identical to newscasters in another part of the country, carefully dressed and combed, drained of almost all individuality. When it was discovered that audiences might respond well if the news readers were friendly to each other, they began chatting and joking on air. The result is that local peculiarities and regional uniqueness give way to a unified look and presentation that makes the local global – or at least national. The viewer and the "news team" share a friendly gaze and a happy smile. Meanwhile, the "news" that's delivered is sensation-driven, following the cynical directive "if it bleeds, it leads." The melodramas of crimes, fires, car wrecks, and bad weather take precedence over the arguably more important issues of local politics and public service.

I said that the local news creates a kind of melodrama. The continuous reporting of robberies, homicides, home invasions, rapes, car crashes, combined with weather reports (each local outlet attempting to outdo one another with the latest meteorological technology that can pinpoint the weather "right down to your neighborhood"), while always promising or threatening "big changes," all work to create a narrative of threat and fear. Melodrama is a genre that addresses the very fragile state of daily life, so fragile that it can break open in violent emotional outbursts caused by unexpected events. The local news assumes that its viewers are uneasy – about their domestic lives, their economic state, the uncertainties of the world at large – and takes that unease as the norm that it can excite by reporting on unsettling events.

The old yellow journalism attempted to engineer shock and outrage. By continually presenting local violence and threats, most of which have little if any bearing on the lives of individual viewers, local news implies a terribly dangerous world, a world best avoided. It engineers fear. But, in order to work, melodrama has to re-create, at the end, a state of fragile equilibrium. The local news does this by implication, that in order to survive the dangers out there, it is best to stay in here, within the smiling gaze and happy chatter of the newscasters. Although they may look grim for a moment when they report the latest armed robbery or warn of the upcoming thunderstorm, at the end of every broadcast they smile at us and at each other, pass pleasantries, and suggest that our safety is within their gaze. Stay at home and watch your local station. You will be kept up to date on all the latest horror stories and be safe. If you must go out, take the news along on podcasts or cell phones and never be far from stories of disaster.

Since the patterns, the look, the narrative of local news became set by the 1980s, its format has changed very little. With few exceptions, the news of one city looks more or less the same as another: light on politics and policy; heavy on crime and catastrophe. All smiles. One wonders what William Randolph Hearst and Joseph Pulitzer might have thought.

Public Broadcasting

Television may be floundering in its attempts at the serious reporting of news that is meaningful, as well as politically, historically, and culturally relevant. But there is a radio network that is very much responsible for picking up these responsibilities.

We will discuss the founding of public radio in more detail in chapter 4, and point out here that the United States is one of the very few industrialized nations without a government-funded broadcasting service (the US does support the Voice of America and other services for overseas transmission of propaganda). The Corporation for Public Broadcasting, of which National Public Radio (NPR) is the radio and Public Broadcasting System (PBS) the television arm, was set up in part to correct this omission and to provide broadcasting services to remote localities too unprofitable for commercial radio stations. It should be noted that, although public broadcasting does not depend on advertising revenues to the extent commercial broadcasters do, it accepts private donations from corporations and individuals, grant money from various non-government foundations, and airs "underwriting spots" that are very much like commercials. Local stations are free to accept "underwriting" (read sponsorship) at will.

PBS, more visible and more expensive (given that it is television), is particularly careful about how it presents news and information. Its daily news program, *The News Hour with Jim Lehrer*, makes a concerted effort to present equal sides to any politically charged story. *Frontline* does occasional investigations of pressing issues: one installment, "The Dark Side," examined Vice President Dick Cheney's role in the run-up to the Iraq War and the subsequent failure to find the weapons of mass destruction whose existence were used to justify the invasion. *Frontline* has also produced an important, in-depth study of the news media and its responsibilities.

But it is NPR that carries the burden of news and information. With a huge private endowment, NPR has one of the largest budgets for news programming in the country. Largely freed of government interference, but still cautious of charges of bias, NPR offers a wide range of programming, anchored by *Morning Edition* and the late afternoon *All Things Considered*. These programs present headlines and more in-depth analyses of both hard news and "magazine" stories. The latter include science and nature pieces, book and film reviews, occasional pieces about celebrity, always something on music – in short, each show is like a talking version of a well-edited, serious newspaper. During the rest of the broadcast day, NPR and its subsidiaries offer to member stations a range of news and information programs, many of them in call-in format. Eschewing the rant of many AM radio call-in shows, NPR's call-in hosts (for example Diane Rehm or Neal Conan) are serious, calm, and respectful; guests are authors, politicians, experts in many fields, who participate in an ongoing dialogue with hosts and callers. NPR programming fulfills that narrative we have been discussing in which the news, its producers, and its audience speak to one another in ways that give some vitality to the tired cliché about offering the news audience enough information so that its members can make up their own minds – and change them when more information is offered.

New news media

As vital as it is, NPR's audience is very small, though growing steadily. This is in marked contrast to the continually falling viewership for network news broadcasts and readership of newspapers. Accelerating this decline, since the late 1990s, news audiences have been offered new media forms that have changed the ways news is delivered and received. The very design of the news has been radically altered. In order to understand what has happened to news media since the 1980s, we need to rephrase some important questions we have asked about the news and its audience: who is the audience; what do they – we – want from the news; how do we want it delivered? Is the news another form of entertainment; a way to be stimulated by reading or hearing about outrageous events, catastrophes, and celebrity crimes; in other words, a means to acquire vicarious experience of death and deprivation, and other forms of sensation? Does the news remain the means to be an informed citizen?

The front page As we have seen, newspapers have served all of these audiences. The yellow press and the tabloids serve up sensation and gossip. Tabloids devote their front page to screaming headlines. On Monday, June 2, 2008, the *New York Post*, a tabloid owned by a contemporary press and media baron, Rupert Murdoch, ran a headline about a drug bust of a no-longer very famous celebrity, Tatum O'Neal. The function of this newspaper is clear from its design: loud, immediate, trivial. The tabloid genre, established by the yellow press, is coded for immediate sensation and minimum import. But, unlike local television news, which aims to scare its audience, the *New York Post* often invites its readers to laugh. It is overtly entertaining, even silly. It makes little pretense of mediating serious news and can be quite self-conscious, even tongue-in-cheek about it. Other tabloids may take themselves seriously, and may even have some serious reporting on their inside pages, but they want readers to be entertained, to be deflected from news about the complexity of the world.

Compare this to the front page of *The New York Times* on the same day. The bold visual (the images are in color: cheap technology that permitted daily newspapers to print full-color images only became available in the mid-1990s) takes the place of the main headline that might otherwise be placed in the upper-left section of the page. It is touching rather than sensational, and deals with the ongoing concern about the way the US government treats foreign prisoners, in this case in Baghdad. The rest of the page provides a series of choices of stories whose importance – according to the editorial decisions made at *The Times*, with the most important news "above the fold" and the rest below – can be determined by the reader herself. No mention is made of a celebrity drug bust. As the "newspaper of record," *The Times* is known for offering a minimum of a sensation and a maximum of authoritative information. (See figures 2.10 and 2.11.)

Up to the minute-24/7   Look at any newspaper, any day, anywhere in the world, and you will see variations of this kind of reportage and layout: serious or sensational; local and/or national; brief and simple or carefully written with much detail; large format with headlines and story, or all headlines, as sensational as possible. One thing will mark them all. They are static. Once printed, the paper becomes its own permanent record. A century ago, there were many more newspapers than there are now, which allowed a variety of formats and news. Morning and evening editions of newspapers were common. A few still publish regional editions today, but, by and large, once a paper is printed and distributed, it is done for the day. News broadcasting on the radio, on television, and now on the Internet constitutes a radical change to this state of static publication. Not only do these media reach a larger audience and – in the case of radio and television – demand somewhat less attention than print, they most importantly allow for up-to-the-minute news reports. Once printed, a newspaper is not only static, it is no longer news – at least as defined as the stable record of an ongoing series of events.

In the early days of broadcast news, regular radio and television broadcasts might be interrupted by "special bulletins" of what editors like to call "breaking news." In some cases the interruption was warranted – the shooting of President Kennedy in 1963 is an example – more often, these bulletins were simply alarmist. Whether or not they announced a true emergency, they definitely broke viewers' concentration on the "regular program already in progress." In the 1970s, some local AM radio stations went to an all-news format. This provided an active stream of news available to the various localities where the stations were received. By the early 1980s, the state of broadcast journalism began its most radical change in a process that continues to this day and is still redefining how the media inform us and we it.

Figure 2.10 *The New York Times* front page, June 2, 2008. Courtesy of *The New York Times*.

Figure 2.11 *The New York Post* printed page, June 2, 2008. Courtesy of *The New York Post*.

Ted Turner, an Atlanta businessman, began one of the first major cable operations in the United States in the late 1970s. In 1980, he launched CNN, the Cable News Network. All news, all the time on television. Its popularity grew slowly but steadily (as did cable as a whole during the eighties), and it built its reputation by having many reporters in the field, both in the US and abroad, and bringing late-breaking stories immediately. This, just during the period when network news organizations were cutting back on reporters and bureaus, and newspaper readership continued in decline.

The turning point came with the first Gulf War that began in January, 1991. All news media covered the run-up to this war, the rationale for which was Iraq's incursion into Kuwait. President George H. W. Bush had issued an ultimatum that Iraq must be out of Kuwait by a certain date or else the US would attack. But, as the deadline approached, network news tended to lag behind with precise information and a timeline. At the same time, there was, for those who had followed CNN's growth, an almost instinctual move to turn to them – and the instinct proved correct. They had reporters and cameras on the ground – and on the roof – and broadcast the first images of American bombs falling on Baghdad. Later, both CNN and the networks broadcast official US military footage that made the bombing of Iraq look like a video game, reducing the seriousness of the enterprise, allowing viewers and reader to believe that the first Gulf War was an easy win. The entire episode became a narrative of American triumphalism, with journalism telling us a story that was fully engaged with the dominant view of the war held by the government and by many people who tried to come to terms with the event.

The end of news

For more than a decade following this war, CNN became a kind of visual equivalent of the old news wire services such as AP and Reuters, providing ongoing, apparently reliable reporting. Turner created an international news channel and a headline channel to accompany CNN. Then, in 1995, he sold all his holdings, all his cable networks, and his film libraries to Time Warner, itself a conglomerate made up of the old Luce news magazine empire and the Warner Bros. film studios. At the same time, other all-news cable networks appeared. The pressures of providing news on a 24-hour, seven-days-a-week basis began to take their toll. Beginning with the trial of O. J. Simpson in 1996, CNN started to move into round-the-clock coverage of events that were somewhat akin to the *New York Post*'s fascination with flamboyant celebrities. News as diversion, or, in the newly minted media term, "infotainment," a phenomenon that goes as far back as the yellow journalism of Hearst and Pulitzer: a presentation as news of something that is indeed happening out in the world – a celebrity trial, a natural or man-made disaster – and that may have some importance, but whose relevance is small to begin with and diminishes with the amount of time and attention given to it. Such coverage is more about diversion than information, of making important events that have little or no importance in themselves. The latest murder, a movie star's new child or visit to rehab, or the last big storm (unless the destruction has large social consequences) actually removes our attention from relevant information.

Two cable networks were formed to compete with CNN by creating their own 24-hour cable news services: NBC joined with Microsoft to create MSNBC, and Rupert Murdoch (owner of the *New York Post* and the Fox network, among other media) launched the Fox News Channel, an outlet for largely conservative opinion. The three foundation networks, CBS, NBC, and ABC, maintained their basic news format – an early morning news and entertainment show, the nightly news half-hour, and time allowed in the late afternoon for local news by the affiliates – and continued to cut down or out their various overseas and national bureaus. Reporting shifted focus from "hard" news – politics, social policy, international news – to "soft," with stories about health, animals, the weather, and celebrities. Their news magazines, most famously *60 Minutes* (whose long-time producer, Don Hewitt, worked with Edward R. Murrow in the early period of television news), gradually covered more and more soft stories, so that today we have reached the point where some of these programs, ranging from ABC's *20/20* to *Entertainment Tonight*, mimic the best and worst of tabloid journalism. In sum, the networks tried and tried, with little success, to keep up with the changing demographics of their viewers and meet their cable competition.

The news online

What we have been noting is a kind of rise and fall of journalism as well as a shift of responsibilities between media. Broadcast news is not in such good shape these days because it cannot decide what constitutes its audience, Meanwhile, National Public Radio is revitalizing the public sphere by allowing an intelligent interaction with its listeners, who are responding in relatively great numbers. But NPR is only one part of the public sphere. The advent of the Internet has turned the news media inside out and changed not only the delivery of the news, but its very creation and production. The Internet has made journalism available to anyone with an ISP address; it has made print and network journalism teeter on the brink of obsolescence; and made everyone a potential news commentator. By the late 1990s, most newspaper publishers understood that they could take advantage of the Internet to put up online versions of their papers that would have the advantage both of being available to much broader audience than the print edition and would be dynamic instead of static. It could be updated at a moment's notice.

Compare the front page of the print edition of *The New York Times* for June 2, 2008, with the web edition that same morning. This is only a small portion of *The Times*'s home page, but it is enough to indicate the difference from the print version The photograph of the Iraqi jail is different from the one in the print addition, as is the lead. The latest news is about the surgery that Senator Edward Kennedy underwent for a brain tumor. There is a second lead about an attack on the Danish Embassy in Pakistan. The paper's various sections – which have multimedia inserts, including videos and aural reports – are presented on the left. Unlike the front page of the print edition, the online home page carries advertising, as do all of the linked pages. Some of the links call up intrusive full-screen ads. The panel on the right of the screen includes advertising and links to the paper's well-regarded op-ed columnists. At first glance, the web edition looks very much like the print version. But there is a wealth of content and a variety of ways to get to it, which, in addition to its constant updating, and the ability to search past issues, make it a very different version of the paper (figure 2.12).

A great deal of thought goes into creating a newspaper's home page to allow the maximum ease of navigation on the part of the reader and to create a viable, screen alternative to the ease of turning the pages of a print edition. But even more important is the ability to keep the newspaper timely. Pull up the home page of *The New York Times* and keep an eye on it: you will notice it updates itself every few minutes, "pushing" new content into your browser. The immediacy and timeliness of news delivery allow anyone online to keep up with events almost as they happen. But, more crucially, it benefits from the accessibility of an enormous variety of journalism. Almost every newspaper in the world is available online, from the British tabloids (which

Figure 2.12 *The New York Times* web page, June 2, 2008. Courtesy of *The New York Times*

make the *New York Post* look tame) to the Middle-Eastern news service Al Jazeera. All network, local, and cable outlets have an online presence, often placing more information online than is broadcast, and frequently extending their service to RSS ("Really Simple Syndication") feeds that allow regular updates on users' computers and go beyond the Web to broadcast news to cell phones.

Blogosphere

The burden on the news audience has never been greater than it is today. Beyond the almost overwhelming amount of continually updated news online is the opportunity for the reader of the news to become a producer of news. Admittedly, the tradition of reader input in print journalism is quite old: the "Letters to the Editor" section of almost every newspaper allowed readers to voice opinions, and the introduction of the op-ed page allowed for more extended opinion pieces. But a newspaper's editors decide which letters the editor is to print, and usually reserves the op-ed page for experts or professionals in the field the essay addresses. The reader – and later the listener and the viewer – is still primarily on the silent end of the news narrative. Then came the Internet and the blog.

Even before the Internet, networked computing allowed for two-way communication (we will talk about this in more detail in chapter 7). Blogging emerged from a combination of available technologies, including bulletin boards, listservs, instant messaging, and email. What sets blogging apart is the graphic design that makes blogs readable and, most of all, easy to use as a publishing vehicle. But, more than any of these, a blog is a public, open forum to be read by anyone who can find a particular blog, and, in most instances, open to receive responses from its readers. The narrative has changed; the blog becomes everyone's journal, everyone's opinion, and some people's news-making machine.

In an incredibly short time, blogs have become the media for personal diaries and for political opinion: there are literally millions of them, and their numbers grow. They have become a way for journalists to express opinions beyond what they say in print, and for others to become journalists if only in their blogs. Blogs have become a means for non-journalists to influence the news and, beyond that, political events themselves. They are emerging as a means of corporate communication and public relations, with companies such as Wal-Mart that used blogs to overcome public criticism of their operation – criticism fueled in part by other blogs. A contributor to the "Wal-Mart Facts" blog on August 31, 2006, writes:

> With the anniversary of Hurricane Katrina upon us, I wanted to express my appreciation for what the company [Wal-Mart] did for me during that time last year. I was in Louisiana for the storm. Born and raised outside of New Orleans, I lost my home to Katrina. I was working at Distribution Center 6048 at the time and as traumatic as the whole catastrophe was, the good people at my DC supported me.

Wal-Mart's self-serving may not fool too many people. More serious is the political and media influence of bloggers, and sometimes their ability to get as close as possible to events the mainstream media (as bloggers dismissively call print and broadcast journalism) can't quite handle. In November of 2005, many cities in France erupted in racial violence. African and Middle-Eastern families, who had been brought into France as laborers, have long been the targets of a fairly widespread racial hatred; the adolescent children of these families are particularly hard hit in terms of unemployment and lack of educational opportunities. They expressed their frustration and outrage by taking to the streets and destroying property. These events were widely reported, as such "riots" often are, with some background of the cause of the violence, but more emphasis on the destruction itself. A Swiss magazine, *L'Hebdo*, decided to send reporters of various specialties into the Paris suburb of Bondy during and after the events to create a blog. The result was a very different kind of personal diary – written by professional journalists, it chronicled not the events of an individual's life, but that of a community, a social and racial class and, by extension, a society. Similarly, many blogs from both sides of the border blossomed during the bombing of Lebanon by Israel in July and August of 2006.

The extraordinary political power of bloggers came to the fore in a major political scandal of 2005–6, which involved payments to members of Congress by a lobbyist named Jack Abramoff. Lobbying on behalf of Indian tribes that wished to build gambling casinos, Abramoff was revealed to have played the tribes against one another, insulting them while manipulating votes for or against them among the politicians to whom he made payments. All of Abramoff's political contributions – and, it turned out, bribes – went to Republicans, though some contributions from the tribes he represented went to Democrats as well. On January 22, 2006, Deborah Howell, Ombudsman for the *Washington Post*, reviewing that paper's detailed coverage and investigation of Abramoff's tangled finances and influence peddling, wrote that Abramoff "had made substantial campaign contributions to both major parties."

An Ombudsman, or "public editor," is present at many newspapers as a neutral arbiter. When the *Post*'s Ombudsman made this statement, she inadvertently squeezed a trigger that set off a charge among readers of a paper that, given its location and reputation, is a major source for political news. The charge came from the left: it was simply not true that Abramoff made contributions to the Democrats. Readers-turned-bloggers flocked to the online edition of the *Post*, which has its own moderated and edited blog space, together with links to other blogs. There the response to Howell's erroneous attempt to be evenhanded was so severe, so angry, that it forced an equally severe response from the *Post*, which deleted all postings and shut down the blog, claiming the responses were vituperative, vulgar, and so numerous that the editors couldn't keep up. Typical of the comments was this:

> It is time for [Howell] to be reassigned to a position in which she can be either nakedly partisan by her own declaration, or where she can do much less damage to the paper of record. Its time for the Post to grow some blass [sic] and take on the legislature and the adminstration for the many crimes the [sic] have committed and continue to commit in the absence of direct and continuous public scrutiny. If the Post envisions itself as the primary paper portal for clothing advertisements for the residents of Washington DC than [sic] it is on the right track. If it is attempting to be paper of record of [sic] for the nation it is failing terribly.
>
> The nation has a need for a NEWSPAPER. If the Post will not fill its roll [sic] it will be replaces [sic] by those who wish to do this job. Many are doing it for free currently in the blogsphere, largely because the Post and the NY Times and others have been MIA for the last 6 years. Change or be replaced.
> Posted by: patience | Jan 15, 2006 10:33:20 PM |

"Change or be replaced." The *Post* couldn't change the minds of its bloggers, so it shut down the blog, which was almost immediately replaced by someone on Blogspot, a web space for creating blogs, under the address "wapolies.blogspot.com." Deborah Howell admitted her error in her *Post* column on January 22 (the fact was that Abramoff did not directly contribute money to Democrats as he did to Republicans, but directed the tribes he represented to do so) and expressed surprise at the tone and the number of blogged responses she received. The *Post* reopened its blog and returned some of the original postings – those it deemed acceptable. But by this time bloggers had not merely made news – by correcting a factual error – they had also become news by bringing a major newspaper to heel.

The political right is no less active in using blogs to their advantage. The response to CBS news anchor Dan Rather's report on President Bush's military service record is an example of a concerted blogging effort that resulted in the shake-up of an entire news organization. On September 8, 2004 – less than two months before the presidential election – Rather reported on the *60 Minutes* TV news magazine that CBS had obtained memos criticizing the Texas Air National Guard performance of George H. W. Bush in 1972–3. Conservative bloggers sprang into action, calling the documents fakes. After nearly two weeks of publicly discounting these skeptics, CBS began to lend credence to experts who questioned the memos' authenticity. On September 22, CBS announced it was forming an independent review panel to investigate the matter. The panel's report, released in January of 2005 (two months after the election), found fault with many of CBS's procedures, centered upon the failure to authenticate the documents. CBS apologized to viewers, terminated one top executive, and demanded the resignations of others. Dan Rather had, in the meantime, announced that he would retire as CBS's evening news anchor in March 2005 and stay on as a *60 Minutes* correspondent; this he did until June of 2006, when he left the organization entirely. At the time of this writing, litigation over the affair was still going on.

These are just two examples of the steady stream of political discourse maintained by bloggers across the political spectrum, sometimes nasty, often influential, and occasionally beyond the bounds of acceptable behavior. In May, 2007, CBS shut down access to bloggers who wished to comment on presidential candidate Barack Obama. So many of the comments were so violently racist, CBS felt that, in this instance, censorship was the most reasonable policy. One result of blog power is that news media are now immediately accountable. But the question is, responsible to whom? As we pointed out, newspapers have always had a "Letters to the Editor" section, where readers could express their opinions, but, as we noted, such letters are always subject to editorial selection. The *Post* tried to moderate and edit its incoming messages during the Howell affair, but wound up having to shut the blog down as did CBS. Blogs are about *not* being edited. They are about instant self-publication of any opinion. Those Swiss reporters blogging in a Paris suburb may have been making journalism, as are, for example, mainstream reporters in Iraq. The emphasis is on "reporter," presumably a professional trained in gathering, understanding, and expressing their understanding of events as objectively as possible. There are certainly professional reporters and commentators writing thoughtful, responsible blogs; there is even a blogspace for newspaper editors. A few bloggers have become media celebrities in their own right, like Marcos Moulitsas Zúniga of the left-wing *Daily Kos* or Michelle Malkin, who writes a blog on the right. But many of the blogs that are currently influencing news reporting are the work of amateurs offering little more than opinions at best – or, at worst, rants. Theirs is the voice of what author Howard Rhinegold calls "smart mobs" (or, in more accepting language, "citizen journalists"), lacking the modicum of reasoning that should go into informed journalism.

Perhaps I risk sounding too conventional, even nervous, about the way partisan voices can influence mainstream media. It is certainly arguable that the MSM – to use the abbreviation of bloggers – need shaking up; that they, like every corporate element of the media design, easily grow complacent and unwilling to act with investigative vigor, or simply fearful that if they investigate or even report with too much depth, if they uncover too much, readers on one political side or the other will take offense and not watch the broadcast or buy the paper. There is no doubt that bloggers get in front of the news. There is also no doubt that they are too often themselves the news itself, forming a reflexive loop in which their influence outweighs the importance of events and the reporting of them.

When the news works: Hurricane Katrina

Robert MacNeil, an old broadcast journalist, who helped create the PBS *Newshour*, wrote that much news reporting, and television news in particular, "acts as the cheering section for the side that has already won." Rarely is broadcast news in front of a story; too often it churns around the same story over and over without casting much light. However, in those rare instances when it does take a lead, its power is extraordinary. It happened many years ago when television news, along with print media, began exposing the hopelessness of the Vietnam War. It happened again in 2005 with the natural and human catastrophe of Hurricane Katrina.

News reporting, like most other media productions, falls into generic patterns. News stories are determined by their content – politics, warfare, medicine and health, business and economics, entertainment – and by the language used to create the narratives that give form to the content. The natural disaster story is among the most common and exciting genres for news reporting and its audience – especially for an audience not immediately affected by the catastrophe. The language of ruin and death, of inconvenience and loss of a home, of personal suffering and heroic deeds guarantees participation in that large narrative we have been discussing, the circulation of news and response, of report and audience, of the voices that speak the news to us and to which we respond with our attention and assent.

When the generic boundaries are breached by an event that cannot be contained within the usual discursive patterns that news reportage automatically falls into, interesting things happen, new language may be developed, with a new way of addressing power, and perhaps a larger narrative of social interaction and the awareness of injustices can form.

Storm warnings   Knowledge of New Orleans' vulnerability to flooding was as old as the city itself. It is built below sea level. The inadequacy of its levee system to stand up to a large storm surge was as clearly known as it was ignored. The degradation of the salt marshes that served to protect the city from the Gulf of Mexico was also well known. Flooding in previous storms had proven that the city's poor, African-American community was concentrated in those sections most vulnerable to flooding should the levees give way. Weather forecasters had analyzed and predicted a renewed cycle of numerous, strong hurricanes prior to the 2005 season. During the summer of 2005, the seawater temperature of the Gulf of Mexico was reported to have reached 95 degrees, the result, many scientists agreed, of global warming, and the precursor of heavy rainfall.

In July of 2004, the Federal Emergency Management Agency (FEMA) concluded a hurricane simulation and issued a detailed report and news release that predicted breached levees and massive damage should a category 3 storm hit New Orleans, complete with suggestions on how to deal with sheltering and caring for the people affected. During the same year, the government cut funds to US Army Corps of Engineers, who are charged with maintaining the levees. In the days before Hurricane Katrina made landfall, the White House received detailed information about probable outcomes. In March, 2006, the Associated Press acquired and distributed a tape recording, made the day before it hit, of an impassive President Bush and then head of FEMA, Michael Brown, listening to dire warnings about the hurricane's potential effects. In short, what happened to New Orleans on August 29, and the days following, should have been no surprise to anyone who was paying attention. It was news, but the cause of the news was not the result of unknown or unavailable information.

When the levees broke The news itself was somewhat slow in coming. We are never more fully reminded of the fragility of communication and the technology that produces it than when a disaster hits a locality and electric power and access are cut off. The earliest news reports on August 30, the day after Katrina reached the coast, remarked that the eye of the storm had veered away from a direct hit on the city. That was technically true, but by later in the day the breaching of the levees and resulting flooding were revealed, and in the days following the terrifying images of the Superdome filled with desperate people, of bloated bodies floating in the streets, and, perhaps most importantly, the awareness that the most seriously affected by the storm were the city's poor, African-American population, seemingly abandoned by everyone, challenged the public perception of their own safety and the government's ability to preserve it.

We should be careful about romanticizing the role of the press in Katrina coverage. Not all of it was positive. Some commentators in print and online allowed their racism to bloom without editing. There was, in fact, a barely contained racism in some of the early reports by the mainstream media of looting and gunfire in the city, and of bizarre violence inside the Superdome. Almost all of this later proved to be based on rumor, exaggerated, or downright false. At the same time, we cannot downplay the degree to which the news *led* the response to the storm and its aftermath. The *New Orleans Times-Picayune*, unable to print their paper, continued with online editions. The cable networks – as they do with any natural disaster – went around the clock with hurricane news. There were, from September to December of 2005, over a million blogs about the event.

The press speaks to power But the press, cable, and network news went further than simply report. They confronted government mishandling of the disaster; they questioned authority; they played upon the personalities of their anchors, allowing them to push the news beyond reporting the outrage of New Orleans residents into venting their very own outrage. At times reportage simply revealed, juxtaposing, for example, the President's comment to his FEMA director, Michael Brown – "Brownie, you're doing a heck of a job" – with Brown's own statements revealing his ignorance of the proportions of the disaster. At other times, reportage confronted. These are the words of Anderson Cooper, CNN's fashionable young anchor of *Anderson Cooper 360*, interviewing Senator Mary Landrieu of Louisiana on September 1, four days after the hurricane made landfall. The Senator was thanking the government for aid. Cooper interrupted:

> Excuse me, Senator, I'm sorry for interrupting, I haven't heard that because for the last four days I've been seeing dead bodies in the streets here.... And to listen to politicians thanking each other and complimenting each other, you know, I gotta tell you there are

a lotta people here who are very upset and very angry and very frustrated and when they hear politicians … you know, thanking one another, it just, you know, kind of cuts them the wrong way right now, 'cause literally there was a body on the streets of this town yesterday … being eaten by rats because this woman had been laying in the streets for forty eight hours and there is [sic] not enough facilities to take her up. Do you get the anger that is out here?

Cooper's and CNN's star rose after his Katrina reporting, and his seven o'clock news program was moved to the more prime time of ten. He was accused, by some, of grandstanding. At the moment of the broadcast, he was expressing a national frustration.

To their credit, the news media have not allowed the Katrina story to die. On the air, and in his blog, NBC news anchor Brian Williams insisted on almost daily reports on the aftermath of the hurricane and a government that continues to react poorly. The result of all this is an interesting example of an ongoing, open-ended media text. There is a series of events: first the hurricane, an act of nature that may have been exacerbated by human activity or the lack thereof, and whose potential for damage had already been mediated by scientific study and advanced warning. Next, the flooding of New Orleans, an event that was predicted and ignored until it was too late. This is followed by another flood, a human flood of poor African-Americans, the heart of the city of New Orleans, abandoned and subsequently "rescued" by being relocated to shelters and temporary housing as far away as Michigan. These events are mediated by a babble of images and voices trying to mediate, ameliorate, exploit, or evade the event, creating a discourse that mixes information, criticism, shock, and sentimentality. It is a discourse that ignites issues of racism, of the way we think of and treat the poor, of governmental cynicism and ineptitude that the news rarely confronts so directly. The discourse places its audience in a peculiarly uncomfortable position. There are so many voices to attend to, and so many hard realities to face, that it is tempting to turn away and move past the din.

Breaking news

Finding one's way is the key issue when dealing with the news media. All of its mediations, all of its outlets, all of its voices – including our own – create a huge, unfinished narrative told from multiple points of view. We can slip into any one, driven by our own personal, cultural, ideologically determined choice. We can also avoid all of it and treat it as so much background noise. Or we can create our own narrative of the world and its meaning to us, by reading, viewing, and listening to the wealth of often contradictory information available in print, on the air, and online. We can become our own mediators, attending to and judging, being skeptical, and, above all, being attentive.

References

The quotation from Thomas Jefferson is contained in a letter dated 16 January, 1787.
The quotation "Fit and Unfit to Print" is from *Wall Street Journal* (June 30, 2006); <http://www.opinionjournal.com/editorial/feature.html?id=110008585>.

Permanence, Portability, and the Public: History

Early communication

Among the many sources for the history of early communication is David Crowley and Paul Heyer (eds), *Communication in History: Technology, Culture, Society*, 4th edn. (Boston: Allyn and Bacon, 2003).

Print

An excellent, detailed history of the book is Lucien Febvre and Paul Victor's *The Coming of the Book: The Impact of Printing 1450–1800*, trans. David Garard (London: Verso, 1997).

The public sphere

The definition of the public sphere comes from Paul Starr, *The Creation of the Media: Political Origins of Modern Communications* (New York: Basic Books, 2004), p. 24.

Journalism

A brief history of journalism can be found in Michael Schudson and Susan E. Tifft, "American Journalism in Historical Perspective," *The Press*, ed. Geneva Overholser and Kathleen Hall Jamieson (New York: Oxford University Press, 2005), pp. 17–47; and in Starr's *The Creation of the Media*, cited above. The Federalist Papers can be found on the Library of Congress's website: <http://thomas.loc.gov/home/histdox/fedpapers. html>. A British site offers a good history of journalism at: <http://www.spartacus. schoolnet.co.uk>.

Important sites for information about journalism: *The State of the News Media*: *Annual Report on American Journalism*: <http://www.stateofthenewsmedia.org>; The PEW Research Center for the People and the Press: <http://people-press.org/>.

Information on muckraking journalism is in Schudson and Tifft, pp. 23–4.

A readable history of twentieth-century news media is David Halbertam's, *The Powers That Be* (Urbana and Chicago: University of Illinois Press, 2000). See also the detailed reports of the "Project for Excellence in Journalism," <http://www.stateofthenewsmedia.org>.

Technologies of distribution

The best source for who owns what is the *Columbia Journalism Review*: <http://www.cjr.org/ tools/owners/>.

Journalism as Political Heroism and Martyrdom

Judith Miller

The New York Times's own summary of events is by Don Van Natta, Jr, Adam Liptak, and Clifford J. Levy, "The Miller Case: A Notebook, a Cause, a Jail Cell and a Deal," *The New York Times* (October 16, 2005); <http://www.nytimes.com/2005/10/16/national/16leak.html>.

Photojournalism

History of photojournalism online: <http://www.dartcenter.org/>.

The reality effect

The term belongs to the French critic, Roland Barthes, who used it in an essay of the same name in *The Rustle of Language*, trans. Richard Howard (New York: Hill and Wang,

1986), pp 141–8. See also Barthes's book on photography, *Camera Lucida: Reflections on Photography*, trans. Richard Howard (New York: Hill and Wang, 1981).

Crimean and Civil War photos

Many images are located at the Library of Congress site: <http://www.loc.gov>. Information on these pictures comes from Jeannene M. Przyblyski, "Loss of Light: The Long Shadow of Photography in the Digital Age," in *The Oxford Handbook of Film and Media Studies*, ed. Robert Kolker (New York: Oxford University Press, 2007), pp. 158–86.

Iwo Jima

A visual history of the photograph can be found at: <http://www.iwojima.com/>. A discussion of the controversy is at the Associated Press website: <http://www.ap.org/pages/about/pulitzer/rosenthal.html>.

Capa's fallen soldier

A discussion of the authenticity of the photograph is at: <http://www.pbs.org/wnet/americanmasters/database/capa_r.html>.

McKinley

An important discussion of the early newsreels of President McKinley is Jonathan Auerbach's "McKinley at Home: How Early American Cinema Made News," *American Quarterly* 51/4 (December 1999): 797–832.

Newsreels

An online timeline of newsreel history is at: <http://history.sandiego.edu/gen/filmnotes/newsreel.html>.

Edward R. Murrow

The relationship between Murrow and CBS is well told by David Halberstam in *The Powers That Be* (Urbana: University of Illinois Press, 2000), pp. 134–57. You can hear recordings of Roosevelt and Murrow on the website of the University of Missouri, Kansas City: < http://library.umkc.edu/spec-col/ww2/dday/voices.htm#1>.

Nixon's Checker's speech

A video of the speech is at: <http://www.americanrhetoric.com/speeches/richardnixoncheckers.html>.

Army–McCarthy Hearings

Emile D'Antonio's *Point of Order* (1964) is an excellent documentary, made up of footage of the hearings. It is available on DVD. Excerpts of the exchange with Joseph Welsh can be found at: <http://www.americanrhetoric.com/speeches/welch-mccarthy.html>.

The end of news

The phrase comes from an important article by Michael Massing, "The End of News?," *The New York Review of Books* 52/19 (December 1, 2005). It can be found online at: <www.nybooks.com>.

The News Online

Blogosphere
Figures for blog usage are from: <http://www.cyberjournalist.net/news/003674.php>.
Blog for journalists: <http://www.editorsweblog.org>.

French uprisings
Bruno Giussani, "A First Blog of the First Draft of History," *The New York Times* (January 30,
    2006); <http://www.nytimes.com/2006/01/30/technology/30riots.html>.

Abramoff scandal
Deborah Howell, "Getting the Story on Jack Abramoff," *Washington Post* (January 15, 2006);
    <http://www.washingtonpost.com/wp-dyn/content/article/2006/01/14/
    AR2006011400859.html>.
The blog entry for the Deborah Howell controversy can be found at: <http://blog.washington
    post.com/washpostblog/2006/01/new_blog_maryland_moment.html>.

Dan Rather
For a discussion of the Rather–*60 Minutes* affair, see Corey Pein, "Blog-Gate," *Columbia
    Journalism Review* (2005): <http://www.cjr.org/issues/2005/1/pein-blog.asp>.

Report on the CBS blog shutdown
Katharine Q. Selve, "Muzzling All to Hush a Few," *The New York Times* (May 8, 2007):
    <http://thecaucus.blogs.nytimes.com/2007/05/08/muzzling-all-to-hush-a-few/>.

Smart mobs
Howard Rhinegold, *Smart Mobs: The Next Social Revolution* (Cambridge, MA: Perseus Books,
    2002).

When the News Works: Hurricane Katrina

Robert MacNeil
The quotation, about news as "the cheering section for the side that has already won," is from
    Halberstam, *The Powers That Be*. pp. 138–9.

The genre of disaster
Jack Schaffer, "Disaster by Numbers: If the Earthquake Doesn't Kill You, the Clichés Will,"
    Slate (June 1, 2006): <http://www.slate.com/id/2142768/>.
FEMA Report on simulated hurricane: <http://www.fema.gov/news/newsrelease.fema?id=
    13051>.
Summary of pre-Katrina information can be found in Sidney Blumenthal, "No One Can Say
    They Didn't See it Coming," *Salon*: <http://dir.salon.com/story/opinion/blumen-
    thal/2005/08/31/disaster_preparation/index.html>.
Summary of Katrina blogs: <http://www.bloggersblog.com/hurricanekatrina/>.
Transcript of Anderson Cooper interview: <http://transcripts.cnn.com/TRANSCRIPTS/
    0509/01/acd.01.html>.

CHAPTER THREE
The Pitch:
Advertising

Is it possible to engineer desire?

Television commercial for Lexus

None of the popular media we are discussing is free of advertising. Commercials appear in, next to, in between the news, television, movies, radio, and websites. Advertising is a medium itself, even as it mediates other media content, with its own conventions and genres, and a complex methodology for influencing its audience.

Advertising and Modernity

The lubricant of media

Each year, much of the pre-game news reporting for the Super Bowl is not about the sportsmanship but about the commercials. People, presumably, watch the Super Bowl as much for the commercials as for the football. Why? Because at a cost to advertisers of around $2.6 million for a 30-second spot aimed at reaching an audience of about 144 million (figures for 2007's Super Bowl XLI) – a good number of them in the coveted 18–49-year-old male market, the group most likely to spend money – the ads are assumed to be the most creative that advertising agencies can manage. Perhaps. The fact is that they turn out to be only commercials, with all the silliness and artfulness, the crassness and imagination that go into most other commercials. More interesting is the phenomenon of news reports that keep reminding us how interesting these commercials are: these news reports constitute free commercials for the Super

Bowl commercials. This is an advertising executive's dream come true, and an indication of the pervasiveness of advertising throughout the media. In fact, we can go further: Advertising is the lubricant of media. It supports, infiltrates, controls and finally makes possible all aspects of media and, in a very real sense, many aspects of our lives. Much of the world is awash in advertising. It is the medium through, with, and on which the media must pass. It is the media's medium.

Because it is so pervasive, advertising has become part of the background noise of our lives. Perhaps we pay attention to commercials during the Super Bowl; sometimes an ad will catch our eye and even persuade us to buy something. But it is doubtful that we consider advertising in an aesthetic, philosophical, or even critical light. But the fact is that advertising is a medium through which we can view and understand the modern world. For one thing, advertising provides us with a history of the way technology *looks*. The history of advertising is a history of modern design, and we will return to this shortly. But there is another point. In its very ability to move us, to change our minds, and to fashion an image about ourselves that we might want to buy into, advertising is linked to the processes of modernity that we addressed in chapter 1.

The job of modern advertising is to alter the stable relationship of the individual self and its world and make us want what we never thought we needed. As sure as the railroad contracted physical space and the telephone and radio contracted virtual space by allowing the immediacy of the voice to substitute for the reality of distance; just as movies created a virtual narrative space into which the viewer could emotionally wander; so advertising reconfigured the individual as part of a web of consumption, coaxing eye and ear into spaces of promised fulfillment. Jackson Lears wrote that advertising is "the promise of magical self-transformation through the ritual of purchase" (Lears, 139). The emphasis is on transformation, moving us from one state of mind to another, challenging our security, and creating desire.

Advertising as text in context

The transformation is not only of our minds but of the very economic structure of our society. By moving us to buy, advertising creates the circulation of capital that is a foundation of the media design. Advertising – advertisers hope – will inform and entertain us in a variety of ways, all to the end of having us purchase a product or service. When we buy, we help create profit for the company that is advertising, making them richer, allowing them to advertise more. The more successful the advertisement is, the more money the advertiser makes, and the more the company will advertise, thereby supporting the medium that carries ads: newspapers, magazines, radio shows, television programs, websites, movies, billboards, Nascar drivers, T-shirts, baseball caps. Our money helps support advertisers, who in turn support various media. Advertising is visible, whenever we turn on a television set, and invisible, every time we click a link on a commercial website. Advertising is indeed the lubricant in this process, allowing media to flourish by providing the cash it needs. But it is also a text in itself, actually a complex series of texts, with its own conventions, codes, genres, and stories to tell, with audiences to reach and create.

Advertising is a combination of art, psychology, and social engineering. It calls upon the graphic arts, storytelling, the rhetorics of persuasion, and various processes of deceit. Advertising brings every methodology it can muster to bear on one thing: creating desire in its audience – desire to purchase the product being sold – or at least regard it in a positive light. But try as they may, advertisers cannot account for every individual, for all the vicissitudes and varieties of gender, race, age, economic situation, education, and taste. Therefore they attempt, through the most thorough research possible, to fashion their ads based on the best guess of the best possible audience, trying to *create* that audience in the process of creating desire in it. Advertisers study demographics (what makes up the target audience, where they live and how they can be sorted) based on many factors, including age, income, gender, and ethnicity; they form focus groups, where a representative assemblage of consumers are asked their opinions about a product; they place cookies – tiny files placed by an advertiser on a user's computer to track the user's browsing and shopping patterns; they analyze all kinds of consumer behavior through quantitative and behavioral research. In short, advertisers try to target their audience and fashion ads that will hit that target and will do everything they can to make it happen. To the degree that someone who does not know us *can* know us, we are each known. Known as individuals and as a member of a group that coheres by a number of external factors: age, gender, race, income, education, past and current buying habits. Advertising leaves as little as possible to chance.

The ad campaign that results from all this work can be targeted to a specific medium – television, a newspaper or magazine, on a local or national basis – or, it can take place across the media with space ads placed in magazines and newspapers; 20-, 30-, or 60-second spots for television; banners or pop-ups for websites; product placement in television shows and movies. The campaign may be blatant or subtle; as loud and irritating as a screaming TV spot for a local car dealer; or as subtle, attractive, and sensual as a magazine advertisement for a clothing or cosmetic manufacturer.

Early advertising in the US

Although advertising is a sign of modernity, it actually can be traced back to the earliest history. It is as old as mercantilism itself, perhaps going back as far as the Babylonians in 3000 BCE, when merchants announced their goods in the streets, or, later, when the Romans wrote ads on the walls. Renaissance artists would often paint likenesses of their patrons – the rich businessmen who supported the arts – at the foot of the cross of a crucifixion scene as a means of thanking them, advertising their generosity in hopes that more would be forthcoming. Much closer in time and to home, in 1729 Benjamin Franklin began classified advertising, complete with woodcut illustrations, in his newspaper, the *Pennsylvania Gazette*. Classified advertisements have been the bedrock of a major source of income for newspapers since Franklin's time, and can be considered part of the news itself, providing information of availability of everything from jobs to houses to dates. Newspaper display ads for local merchants offer a timeliness – such as an announcement of a three-day sale – unavailable in most other media, even the Internet. On the downside, newspapers are sometimes beholden to their advertisers, occasionally censoring coverage of news that might offend them. More recently, newspapers have lost revenue (classified ads are a major source of newspaper income) due to stand-alone online classifieds, like Craigslist.

The first American ad agency – that is, a company whose job is to advertise other companies and their products – was opened in Philadelphia in 1841. In 1850, one of the first celebrity advertisers, P. T. Barnum, promoted a national tour for the Swedish soprano Jenny Lind, stirring up so much interest that a crowd of 40,000 gathered to watch her arrival in New York. Before the advent of electronic media, and beyond newspapers, advertising in the nineteenth century took advantage of all available outlets – almost anything legible, from trading cards to billboards to catalogues. The latter, particularly in the form of the Montgomery-Ward and the Sears Roebuck catalogues, expanded the range of consumption from metropolitan areas into the rural. A century ago, the Sears catalogue offered such variety that one could purchase by mail a pair of boots, a dress, a refrigerator, a buggy, or the pre-cut and fitted materials, complete with blueprints, to build a house. Mail order catalogues were a kind of pre-Internet database of domestic items, a virtual department store, working – even as Internet shopping does now – through the post office to deliver the physical goods. (See figure 3.1.)

Commercial radio

Radio provided the first electronic medium for advertising and opened up not only a new carrier for commercials, but also new forms in which an advertisement could be created. Radio began as a public service, commercial free. But, in 1922, someone went in front of a microphone on New York station WEAF to sell apartment co-ops and the obvious became immediately clear: radio was a means to reach a large audience that was present and receptive, already listening to the radio and who did not have to buy a newspaper or open their mail. Soon, dramatic or comic narratives were created, music was added to the verbal pitch, the entertainers in a radio show would deliver the commercials themselves, resulting in advertising by indirection, advertising as entertainment tucked into the other entertainment, with the program carrying the commercial. But indirection is a slippery concept in advertising. Subtle or blatant, entertaining or simply shouting the message, the advertiser's point is always to deliver a message to buy; or to create a mood, the result of which is to make the audience buy (or, at the very least, desire or approve of) a product, a person, or an institution.

Radio advertising was important for the development and expansion of radio itself, turning it into a commercial medium, and moving it rapidly from public service to entertainment for profit. It was equally important as a means of refining the methodologies of advertising, of integrating it tightly with programmatic material so that the shows being advertised became the vehicles or media of advertising. A radio show was often sponsored – paid for and developed – by one company, and so in its very presentation was announced as its property: "The Lux Radio Theater," for example, was named after a soap. "The Chase and Sanborn Hour" was named after a coffee.

Figure 3.1
Advertisement for the opening of Sears' first retail store, *Chicago Tribune*, February 1, 1925. Courtesy of Sears Holdings Archives.

Both products were advertised by the J. Walter Thompson agency, one of the oldest in the United States.

Advertisers controlled not only the content, but also the very lifespan of a radio program, helping fashion it to achieve the largest possible audience and canceling it – by removing their sponsorship – if the audience shrank. The advertiser enveloped program, schedule, and audience. Selling and entertaining became seamless, with the listener moving within its flow.

Television adopted this model early on, but the television networks soon chafed under the external control of companies and their agencies. By the mid-fifties they began to go to the "magazine" format of advertising, in which companies bought airtime rather than entire programs. Despite this attempt at distancing themselves, commercial time and costs were and remain determined by ratings. The higher the ratings for a show, the more it costs to advertise on it. We will discuss the interaction of television programming and commercials in chapter 5. What is important to note is that advertising defines radio and television media – its content, its economics, and the way we, as audience, interact with them.

Advertising and Design

The visual field

As creative as its advertisers might be in the new medium, radio remained limited to sound, voice, and music. But advertising at its most potent exists as an object for the eye, telling a story through sight, asking us to see the product and, by seeing, under-stand why it is so important for us to have it. The advertising image, still or moving, is always a kind of narrative: it tells a story that proposes first of all a lack – something is missing or wrong with our lives, our appearance, our smell, our form of transporta-tion, our health, our social or sexual life – and then offers a way to fill that lack with a product or service that will make the bad better and fill the empty place in our life. This narrative can, of course, take the conventional form of a little dramatic story, of the kind most familiar from television commercials. But the "story" can be perfectly static: it can exist in the very design of an ad, the way its figures are posed; the way colors are used; the way the eye is asked to move around the image. The advertising image can work by connotation, suggestion, or allusion.

Early on, this visual structure was often straightforward and presentational. The nineteenth-century Sears catalogue presented a kind of visual database, filled with page after page of straightforward images, frontal, *there* for the shopper to choose from. This kind of advertising had its equivalent in very early motion pictures, in which the subject, the small drama, or visual event was presented frontally; uncompli-cated, a cinema of attractions. Early advertising was a simple presentation of some-thing attractive (according to the styles of the day), calling on the eye directly, attracting it to the product. This is not to say that early advertising was not embel-lished. Recall the fact that modern advertising is a part of the greater movement of modernity, refocusing the eye and self, moving it beyond a stable place to a place of imagination and desire. The product must be attractive, even seductive – it must *move* the viewer.

As a product of modernity, advertising was constituted by the space-altering, identity-shifting technologies of the nineteenth century that de-centered the modern world, broke down barriers, expanded the reach of perception and the imagination, and created unease about the secure location of the self in the world. But advertising is also a refuge from modernity, using design to offer escape from a world that seems to be moving too fast for comfort, diminishing the place and function of the individual in the process. In this dual role, using the aesthetics of modernity and depending on a sense of the shifting subject, the desire of an individual to change, to be contemporary, while at the same time playing on the fears of modernity, advertising triumphed. Advertising destabilizes the subject by making people unhappy with their current state. It offers to restore stability through the benefits of its product.

Modernism is the aesthetic response to modernity and is most evident in the painting style called abstract expressionism. Modernism promotes form over content, or, more accurately, insists that "reality" exists *in* the form of the work. Painting, for example, can represent a bowl of fruit; but a bowl of fruit is not what painting is about, which is color, light, shadow, shape on a two-dimensional canvas. Abstract painters evoke the forms of painting, not what painting can represent.

Advertising is essentially about representing *more* than the product itself. It seeks to reorient the subject, the individual, in a world of products that will help the consumer feel secure in an unstable universe, while at the same time making the consumer feel she is part of modernity. Advertising is, above all else, a kind of progressive holding action – creating an illusion of moving forward even as it satisfies desires for security. And like modernist art, advertising, especially in its design, locates us in the formal expression of a desired object. Although its aim is to draw our attention to a desirable product, the means of creating desire lies in the visual and narrative form of the ad itself. Drawing upon the decorative and fine arts of the moment, with the narrative structures of movies, advertisements become a means of expression that often enough exist on their own terms, regardless of what they are selling.

Art nouveau   Late in the nineteenth century, there began an important reciprocal interplay between advertising and various movements in the visual arts. The art nouveau movement, which started in England and moved to the United States, was in fact a *reaction* to modernity, an attempt to call upon earlier forms of art, invoking lavish design. It went hand in hand with the arts and crafts movement, whose proponents included William Morris and Gustav Stickley, and which sought to counter the growth of factory production with handmade craftsmanship. When adopted by advertisers, however, art nouveau produced a number of changes in the ways advertising and its products were represented. As a fine art and decorative style, art nouveau evoked the European Middle Ages as well as Asian art forms. Its sensuous lines and warm colors were meant, in part, to counter the hard lines of factories and machinery. It attempted as well to soften the clutter that was so much a part of ornate Victorian decoration, and to introduce a gentle eroticism into a somewhat repressive society. The art nouveau style occurred in painting, illustrations, interior decoration, advertisements, and even in typography. As an advertising style, it supplemented those straightforward, functional ads that were the norm at the time. Its emphasis was on elegance, emphasizing form as a means to seduce the eye. It pressed the erotic component that has always been, and increasingly continues to be, a major component of

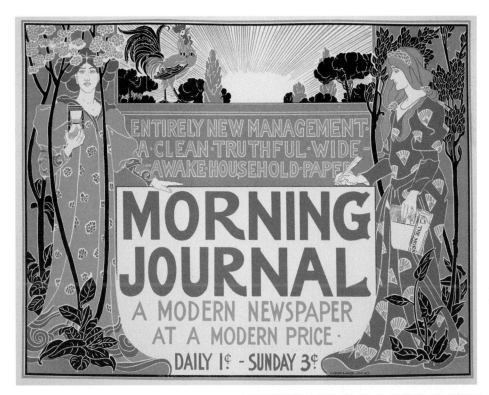

Figure 3.2   Art nouveau poster designed by Louis John Rhead (1857–1926) advertising the *Morning Journal*. Private collection/the Stapleton Collection/the Bridgeman Art Library.

advertising form and content. (See figures 3.2 and 3.3.)

Art nouveau was meant to be a movement away from modernity, an illusion of a sensuous, curvilinear world that could be sequestered, hidden away from the hard realities of technology and manufacture. As an advertising tool, it offered this illusion as a means of fulfillment and pleasure – two of the fundamental promises of all advertising and linked to the process of changing identity that was a part of modernity. But this decorative separation from the modern world was short-lived, and art nouveau soon morphed into a new set of design principles more in sync with industry and with the movements in the larger world of art. By the late 1920s, art, industry, and advertising met in a style that was to determine the "look" of the twentieth century: art

Figure 3.3   This poster for the 1933 Chicago World's Fair shows a transition from art nouveau to art deco design. Copyright © Swim Ink 2, LLC/ CORBIS.

deco. This style was to merge so tightly with advertising that it would become a metaphor for all that the modern world had to offer.

Art deco Art deco is geometric, almost diagrammatic in its forms, drawing not on styles from the past, but on contemporary movements toward abstraction in the fine arts, new architectural styles emerging in Europe, and engineering practices. It joined industrial design and advertising through the concept of "streamlining." Originally an engineering term, by the late 1920s "streamlining" came to signify clean lines, uninhibited movement, minimal ornamentation – in short, the design of progress, of the modern, the new, and the forward-looking. Terry Smith writes, "one part of streamlining's visual message was the promise of smooth sailing through the elimination of friction; its aim was to sweep through resistance of all kinds. It strove to be the visual surface of the irresistible tide of modernity itself …" (Smith, 379). Art deco would influence the design of steamships, house and office exteriors and interiors – New York's Chrysler Building is a major example – and even the packaging of consumer products.

Perhaps the most iconic of all art deco designs, the one that is the clearest metaphor of clean lines, speed, and forward motion is Henry Dreyfuss's Railroad Engine, the *20th Century Limited*. Keep in mind that the railroad was one of the nineteenth century's most important technologies, shrinking distances, and changing personal geography by allowing people to move easily from one place to another. But the railroad had always been associated with heavy industry and the filth of coal-fire soot and smoke. Creating a railroad engine whose design defied the very industrial stuff of modern technology was, in an important sense, a realization of advertising's essence – a machine of desire, calling on its audience's craving to cut through obstacles and achieve a goal. Streamlining was idea and image, a visual struggle against the economic stagnation of Depression-era America. Art deco industrial design is sometimes referred to as "depression moderne"; it promised forward movement and progress, the overcoming of any obstacle. In the face of the very real economic obstacles of the time, it offered the visual fantasy of shapes that cut through all resistance.

The extent to which this design has impressed the cultural imagination and, more specifically, the advertising imagination, can be seen in a 2003 magazine advertisement for Mercedes-Benz. One of the essential elements of car advertisements is creating a fantasy of unrestricted motion, a distraction from the realities of slow-moving traffic. To that end, these ads frequently associate their product with free, unimpeded speed, most often with airplanes. But this particular Mercedes ad, calling upon cultural memory not only of high-speed train travel, but also of its 1930s symbol, is an indication of art deco's lasting influence, and the embedding of the concept of streamlining into the modern consciousness (figure 3.4).

Advertising, design, and culture

Advertising has always been an imitator, drawing upon visual and narrative techniques in the other arts in order to create a contemporary look and feel. From time to time,

Figure 3.4 This advertisement for Mercedes-Benz compares its car with the streamlined design of the Twentieth Century Limited. Courtesy of Mercedes-Benz.

painters and photographers would lend their talents to advertising campaigns. This was especially true in the 1920s and 1930s when the streamlined forms of art deco design became a visual metaphor for the modern world.

There were many designers, beside Henry Dreyfuss, who made a visual mark on advertising and modern design. Raymond Loewy also designed locomotives, and, throughout a career that lasted until 1986, he brought the principles of streamlining to an enormous range of objects and products, large and small, that influenced the look of the modern world: airplanes, the Lucky Strike cigarette pack, household furniture and appliances, a perfectly streamlined pencil sharpener, the redesigned 1916 Coke bottle. In addition, he created logos for the US Postal Service and the Exxon and Shell oil companies. Logos are the visual "signs" that companies or institutions choose to represent themselves and their products; they are, in a sense, the mediator between the products and the company and are meant to communicate visually, instantly, and memorably as much as possible about what the company stands for. Loewy's work was part of a large-scale process of integrating commercial products and the imagination of individual consumers into a streamlined flow of modernity (figure 3.5).

Product and industrial design is only one part of advertising, but it is the most visible. It influences the very ways in which our world is expressed and the ways in which we perceive the world, and becomes a part of the daily *mise en scène* – the visual space – of our lives. The very fact that a contemporary Mercedes-Benz ad can call up the history of design from as far back as the 1930s attests to the power of these visual forms. The interaction of art and commerce was never as strong again as it was in the thirties, though the mutual influence of art on advertising, and advertising on art, continues.

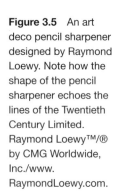

Figure 3.5 An art deco pencil sharpener designed by Raymond Loewy. Note how the shape of the pencil sharpener echoes the lines of the Twentieth Century Limited. Raymond Loewy™/® by CMG Worldwide, Inc./www. RaymondLoewy.com.

The pop art movement of the 1960s, for example, took advertising as a subject, asking us to see what happens when the ordinary becomes focused as an object of attention. The rapid cutting and abbreviated narratives that are a mark of television commercials influenced the style of music videos and they, in turn, influenced movies, which came back again as a further influence on advertising. Designers still work to create a visual image of their product which, along with various advertising campaigns, results in what advertisers call "branding," a complex of product, the images created to represent it, and consumer response that results not only in instant recognition, of, for example, Coca-Cola, but also associations of pleasure and satisfaction. "Branding" is the collection and merging of all aspects of the product, its advertising, and the desire of the audience into something that transcends all of these into something like a self-contained object of desire.

The real thing

But it is just here that the clash with modernity occurs. Advertising draws upon images of modernity; it speaks the language of progress and improvement. Raymond Loewy said that the Coke bottle was a perfect example of modern design, and then went on to streamline it even further. Anything perfect can be made more perfect. Advertising depends upon making things more perfect. Coca-Cola has advertised itself as "the real thing" and wants the whole world to sing its praises – and the world follows suit. But in the mid-1980s Coke announced that it was changing its formula (no doubt a publicity gimmick to boost brand recognition in the face of falling market share). Coke drinkers complained bitterly; they thought that the real thing was real enough. Coca-Cola's headquarters was besieged with angry phone calls and letters. The company proceeded to reinvent the old Coke as "Coca-Cola Classic", giving the name "New Coke" (and, later, "Coke II") to the new formula.

It is rare for consumers to take such an active role in product development, and we always need to be skeptical when a company seems to be bowing to consumer desires, since it is the producer of a product who usually takes the active lead in creating audience desire. The main thing that companies want from their consumers is for them to purchase the product. To do that, they must sell not only a sense of modernity and progress, but also of stability and recognition. This is the major work of encoding advertisements with elements of the contemporary, the future, and the past, which, taken together, must be decoded by consumers as fulfillment. Tomorrow and yesterday must be today.

Contemporary advertising

This is the core contradiction: while making use of the aesthetic techniques of modernism, addressing all of the issues of modernity – streamlined forms, the visual equivalents of movement and progression – advertising is finally not about the future, but about the constant maintenance of a core, conservative point of rest, comfort, control, and security in the present. To demonstrate this, I want to make a leap into contemporary television commercials – to, in effect, streamline our movement from past to present.

Unlike radio, television was a commercial medium from its start, and the techniques developed in other areas of advertising were immediately brought to bear in the TV commercial. From direct pitches, with a spokesperson standing in front of a product, extolling its virtues; to catchy music and subtle imagery; to condensed, heavily encoded narratives, offering a dramatic situation in which a character is shown diminished and lacking until the product is purchased, television commercials have become the most artful form of contemporary advertising. They not only continue the metaphor of streamlining in their content – promising easy passage into a better life – but they are streamlined in their form, the best of them constructed to deliver their message quickly, sharply, and with maximum effect.

"Someday is today"   A typical example can be found in a television commercial for Verizon, one of the giant companies that is narrowing the field of ownership of telecommunications (which includes cell phone, broadband Internet, cable, and corporate communications). This particular Verizon commercial has interesting generic characteristics. Its market is primarily that of businesses, not individuals. But, shown across the television spectrum in prime time, it was meant to impress on all viewers the company's progressive technological edge, modern, yet somehow domestic and comfortable. The ad plays on an advertising convention, promising something will happen "someday" and concluding that "someday is today." In the voice-over, Kiefer Sutherland, the actor most famous as Jack Bauer in the Fox series *24*, presents a number of technology communication scenarios and problems, tagging each with the comment "someday…." "Someday someone will put together one truly seamless global to global wireless network…." The visuals take the form of an interesting montage, photographed in brilliant color with state-of-the-art digital effects. We see a woman blowing soap bubbles, an African-American man with a child in hand, businessmen talking, tracking shots of meetings, a wide-angle shot of a woman walking

Figure 3.6

Figure 3.7

Figure 3.8

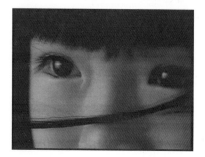

Figure 3.9

Figures 3.6–9 Verizon's "Someday is Today" commercial creates complex-visuals of work and family.

through a bank of computer servers. There are split images; images in negative; a man balances on a chair in the office, a woman does a jig, a man does a handspring, another rides a swing between skyscrapers. The script, as in so many corporate advertisements, emphasizes the *people* behind the product and promises that "at Verizon, we never stop working for you" (figures 3.6–3.9).

Visually, and in its voice-over, the commercial touches upon the need for technological innovation and the concern that this need will not be met. But it encodes itself with an anxiety *that is already solved* and, like most ads, invites a question from the would-be customer – "how am I going to get by?" – with the answer already built in. This time, the question is meant to be asked by businessmen. The ad's taglines, "Someday is Today" and "we never stop working for you," answer the question and, through the antics of the business people shown throughout the commercial, indicates that the anxieties have been taken care of. Decode the commercial the way it asks you to do, and you will understand that a company need only purchase services from Verizon and technology that we only dreamed about is available right now, along with solutions to all the business problems we've been worrying about, and provided by people who will work closely with you and make you happy. End of anxiety; return to a point of comfort.

Fifty-three seconds of swiftly stated hope and fulfillment, the commercial encompasses the entire world and all ages in the service of business. It becomes something of a compendium of modern advertising techniques. Shown during prime time – between the hours of 8 and 11 – and in alternation with another Verizon ad that uses "That Works" instead of "Some Day" as its tagline, it encourages not only businessmen but everyone to feel good about Verizon (the merger of Verizon with another telecommunication company, MCI, was in part the reason for the advertisement). Given the ubiquity of cell phones, and the enormous amount of advertising dollars spent by various cell phone service providers, it doesn't hurt Verizon, who also heavily advertise their consumer products, to let everyone know that they bring seamless networking to the business world as well. The use of Kiefer Sutherland's voice is part of the process of creating good will in a wider audience. At the time of its appearance, Sutherland was an extremely popular television star, and, even though the commercial doesn't identify him (commercials rarely, if ever, identify their voice-over narrators), anyone familiar with *24* would recognize his voice. During the run of these commercials, Kiefer Sutherland fan sites were buzzing with the news of his doing a voice-over, proof of the fact that the commercial was aimed at more than the business community.

Visual excess   Visually, the Verizon ad makes use of many elements of contemporary televisual techniques, especially what critic John Caldwell calls the televisual "excessive style": a use of color, of camera movements, angles, unusual lenses, and digital composition that spill beyond the message. The style *seems* more than the message calls for – recall what we said about the form of an ad being as important as its content. After all, Kiefer Sutherland could simply read the copy over a few simple images of people using computers and telephones in their office. But this "spilling beyond" is part of most advertising, because most advertising is not simply about a selling a product but about selling need, fulfillment, and goodwill, while entertaining the consumer into the bargain. Why does Verizon's ad agency begin this ad with soap bubbles or end it with the tight close-up on the eyes of an Asian child with a wisp of hair across her face? Why a wide-angle shot craning down on an African-American father and child? Why the digitally composed image of a businessman riding a swing between skyscrapers? The latter image, along with others of businessmen and women enjoying their lives amidst computers, use a visual shorthand – richly colored, swiftly moving – to signify the essential point that Verizon business wireless helps make work carefree. They are fantasy images, excessively coded beyond the realm of daily office drudgery, but at the same time carrying forward, or perhaps leaving a residue of the commercial's basic point. The decoding process allows us to understand that we won't be swinging through the skyscrapers, but may be happy enough with the company's services and free of the worry that the office network will go down.

The images of children are further spillover, further excess. The happy child hand-in-hand with his smiling parent, combined with the sweet face of an Asian child that ends the commercial, suggest a healthy multiculturalism – a racial inclusiveness that, since the 1980s, many advertisers have recognized as important in order to appeal to as broad an audience as possible – and a sense of domesticity counter to the workplace, to the worldwide scope of the product being sold. Today's marketplace is global and, if a product can promise to make global communication possible, so much the better. But the children's faces, the bubble-blowing, alongside the adults doing handstands and swinging in the canyons of the city suggest that the product will make work child's play and, more subtly still, will bring a childlike enthusiasm into the workplace. Verizon business wireless turns the workplace into a playground.

Excessive streamlining

This excess would seem to contradict our streamlining metaphor. Why would an advertiser go to such costly ends to transmit these messages in a style in excess of the core message to be communicated? Some advertisers believe in the simple direct sell (this is particularly true of commercials for local car dealerships): explain what the product does, sing a song about it, even yell about, and get it over with. But even more advertisers understand that a sell works best when it is embedded in and delivered by a striking and attractive vehicle. In an important sense, Verizon and other advertisers are selling *awareness* as much as they are selling a product. Even more, they are selling advertising itself. By creating an excessive style, they are demanding that you, the audience, pay attention to the fact of advertising. You may never have need of Verizon business services, but you will – from the advertisers' perspective – always have need of advertising. Success, therefore, is measured by how your attention is gained, how the advertisement has streamlined itself into your consciousness, and how well it has cut through the clutter of all the other advertising that bombards you.

Advertising as Mirror

Cosmo

The Verizon ad is an example of using indirection to direct our attention, creating a visual style in excess of what the ad is selling. I want to look for a moment at another kind of attention-getting ad, this in the form of static images in magazines, specifically *Cosmopolitan*. *Cosmo* is aimed at a specific audience of young women in their late teens to mid-thirties, an age group much coveted by advertisers. It carries earnest articles about sexual behavior, fashion, and self-help – a collection of "how to's" and how not to. Article titles may include items such as "What is Sex Like for *Him?*," or "His Secret Pleasure Zone (Map Included!)." The pages may carry photo essays on "shirtless guys." Some of *Cosmo*'s articles and advice on sexuality border on soft-core pornography, which is certainly part of their attraction. There is a mix of playfulness and earnestness that makes the magazine a reflection of its readers: a young woman opening *Cosmo* is supposed to see an image of herself and her life.

The advertisements *Cosmo* carries incorporate the act of reflection that drives the magazine as a whole. They are carefully photographed and designed, with high production values. They inevitably display a female model, posed and lit, situated in a *mise en scène* (the composition of the space inhabited by the figure, made up of the way the figure is framed and lit, and including the objects within the frame) that highlights her beauty, as enhanced by the product. An advertisement for Bebe clothing offers a particularly straightforward example. (See, in particular, examples of Bebe fashions on their website, <http://www.bebe.com>). A line of clothing will be especially sexualized, the image presenting the female figure in a provocative posture to set off the clothing. Aimed entirely at a female readership, presenting, as almost all advertisements do, a fantasy of fulfillment, with an explicit if unstated promise – "wear this item or this brand and you will be attractive" – these ads are coded as a kind of mirror of desire. Sometimes the model in a fashion or cosmetic ad will look to one side, informally, even coyly, inviting the viewer's gaze; some ads will have the model looking directly at the camera so that the image is almost literally a reflection of fulfilled desire.

The figure in a Bebe ad, while more or less fully dressed (the company is, after all, selling clothes), may be lounging or stretched against a background the color of which repeats or complements the clothes she wears. She may wear sunglasses, even if indoors. Despite the way she is posed, the figure seems always ready to move, and appears open to the gaze of ... well, whom? This is the question of so many of the fashion, accessory, and cosmetic ads in *Cosmo* magazine and elsewhere. Who is the model looking at? Who is looking at her? As a kind of fantasy mirror, the primary gaze is that of the female reader, but there is another, implied, gaze: that of the desiring man. The *Cosmo* reader looks at the ad and sees, presumably, what she would like to look like; or, more accurately, sees an experiential surrogate for herself, decoding the image – "I could feel this attractive, this seductive, if I wore these clothes." But in the process of decoding, the reader also imagines someone looking at her through the surrogate in the ad: the model herself. The sexual attraction becomes imaginatively transferred and is meant to empower the female viewer. The majority of the advertisements in *Cosmo* not only put the model, but also, by transference, the person looking at the ad, in a dominant position. The model's gaze (figure 3.10) communicates directly to the female reader, giving her a knowing assurance of control, and suggesting a community involving the model, the reader, the brand, the magazine, and other fashionable and attractive women. The mirror effect reflects not merely the individual, but, by communicating a fashion style, suggests that the consumer, purchasing that look, will become one of a number of attractive individuals. There are few examples in the media in which the woman is allowed to imagine such power.

Fashion and the body

The *Cosmo* ads are a subset of fashion promotion, which is a genre unto itself and responsible for an enormous part of the advertising universe. Clothing, jewelry, or cosmetic products, the act of modeling itself, the way the fashion audience is addressed, the entire coded structure of fashion is aimed at presenting an unattainable ideal expressed through unattainable bodies, in seductive or aggressive poses of the kind that would draw stares of disbelief, if not downright fright, if enacted in daily life. Fashion has been justly condemned as presenting an impossibly thin body image, which, some fear, creates an alienation from one's own body (which, in the case of the vast majority of women, could not possibly look like that of a model) or,

Figure 3.10 The model's gaze at the reader becomes a fantasy mirror of desire. Getty Images/Frazer Harrison.

Figure 3.11 Ordinary Bodies. A European billboard for Dove's Campaign for Real Beauty. Olaf Kowalzik/ Alamy.

worse, the development of eating disorders as young women attempt to attain the fantasy body style of a fashion model.

The Anglo-Dutch company Unilever, which makes a variety of products from food to soap, has created an advertising campaign for their Dove soap and cosmetics products that attempts to cash in on this fear. They call the campaign "Real Beauty" (figure 3.11). Through worldwide print and television ads, interactive billboards in cities around the world, on YouTube, and on its website – all of which solicit funds for a "uniquely me" program to foster self-esteem and positive body image in school-age girls and older women – Dove is carving out a niche that it hopes will gather women who do not see their reflection in the mirror of conventional ad campaigns. Dove hopes its advertisements will be decoded as the expression of a caring, concerned voice, advocating for women who do not measure up to the fantasy standards of high-fashion beauty. Since that includes almost every woman, the market potential is enormous. The campaign has been a success for Unilever, but perhaps not a big enough success to create a change across the fashion and cosmetic universe.

The magic mirror effect of fashion advertising, reflecting a perfect body and promising a perfect sexuality, are unique to its genre. It is too much of a fairy-tale narrative to be told elsewhere. It may be used to sell clothing and cosmetics, but its main product is the positing of an unrealizable ideal. Yet the ideal is too lovely a fantasy to give up. The Dove campaign, seemingly open-hearted in its invitation to women with non-fashion model bodies and faces, but cynical in its desire to sell to this audience – all the women in the world – may make it a great deal of money. So far it is unique in its genre. Fairy tales are more potent than reality.

Apart from the fantasy world of high fashion, most advertising moves between a narrower spectrum of perfect and less-than-perfect. The usual channel is amelioration, making things better rather than perfect. Perfection is always an ideal, but most advertisers know just how far they can reach, just how tall a tale about perfection they are able to tell. The narratives must be in the realm of the possible, offering the solution to a problem by reaching for and promising a state of "well-being" rather than an unattainable ideal. After all, if every product were as unattainable as the image of the fashion model – the impossible image in the mirror – nothing would be sold. How, then, do advertisers sell well-being, a state of ease with self and world, of pleasure with ourselves and comfort among others? First, we need to be sold on the fact, made to believe the fact, that our current state is not so good, and that we need to attain a better one. Then we have to be convinced that the product will make that state better, will streamline us into a more comfortable, a more perfected state of mind and body.

"Ask Your Doctor if it's Right for You"

All pain all the time

Fashion aims at the perfect exterior body, but aims too high, to a body nobody can have. A healthy body, however, should be in the realm of the possible for anyone. Most of us are healthy, though subject to the usual aches and pains that are biologically inescapable. Some of us are sick, though sickness has a far-ranging latitude of possibilities. Is a headache being sick? A sore muscle? The flu? Is it the same degree of sickness as diabetes, HIV-AIDS, cancer? Pharmaceutical companies and the agencies they hire to sell their products often try to blur the line between ordinary and serious. Some manufacturers of analgesics (pain relievers) create commercials in which characters talk about "my headache pain" or "my pain" in general, creating the notion, much desired by the pill manufacturer, that we are all in some kind of physical pain most of the time and need their pill to make it go away. Advil has run ads showing a man involved in various activities, each one with its attendant pain: tennis, bicycling, yoga. "Every new pain a different pain reliever," he complains. "But not any more. Today I'm all Advil ... Who knows what's going to hurt next?" He looks at his wife in a contorted yoga pose; the camera zooms in and he gives a sort of disbelieving, long-suffering smile. "But at least I'm ready." The not-so-subtle suggestion that the man's wife is a source of his pain is typical of commercials, in which one or another member of a couple is the source of the problem the product can solve.

Medicine and the government   This imagined/created state of constant physical discomfort has been exploited from the time modern advertising began. The growth of "patent medicines," "nostrums" – now called over-the-counter medications – paralleled the growth of advertising; they have always moved in tandem, often skirted legalities, and have always been a source of income. By the late nineteenth century, patent medicine manufacturers threatened to withdraw their advertising from newspapers if their products were made illegal, thereby silencing journalists who might otherwise have investigated their efficacy. In 1906, the US government enacted the Pure Food and Drug Act. This oversight policy came partly in response to the revelation of unsanitary conditions in the meat-packing industry in Sinclair Lewis's muckraking novel *The Jungle*. The Pure Food and Drug Act was also a response to the American Medical Association's creation of a voluntary drug-approval program, which was itself a response to exposés of medical frauds in a series of magazine articles. As a means of better enforcing the policy, the government created a department, the Food and Drug Administration (FDA), in 1927. But it was not until 1938, during the administration of Franklin Roosevelt, that a full set of laws and restrictions were put into place to protect the public from unsafe medicines; and not until 1962 that drug manufacturers had to prove that their prescription medicines actually did something without seriously harming the patient. To this day, there are no stringent laws for over-the-counter medications.

This history is important in order to understand the long dance that has been going on between pharmaceutical companies, government regulators, and the consumers of medicines. "Patent" medicines – overseen by the Federal Trade Commission – continue to be advertised without much restriction. They range from the widely consumed products of large pharmaceutical companies (such as Advil, manufactured by Wyeth, a company that makes a variety of prescription medications) to the obviously fake diet pills hawked on daytime and late-night television and cable news channels that are regularly pulled when the Federal Trade Commission finds them ineffective, but that manage to quickly reappear under different names. But it is in the realm of ads for prescription drugs that advertising becomes a complex, sometimes painful, and sometimes deadly, business. (See figure 3.12).

Figure 3.12 An early advertisement for Carter's Little Liver Pills, a patent medicine that was proved to have no benefit at all. Wellcome Trust Medical Photographic Library.

You may have a disease and not know it Historically and legally, the mediator between patient and medication is the doctor. The "selling" of drugs was (and to a great extent still is) the job of sales representatives, hired by the drug companies, who visit doctors, tell them about their company's products, and give the doctors samples that they, in turn, give to their patients. The samples would, the drug companies hope, lead to a prescription. Drug companies historically showed restraint in advertising, partly because they did not want their products to be compared to patent medicine or their ads compared to the hucksterism of over-the-counter drug advertisements. This began to change in the early 1980s when the drug companies started direct-to-consumer ads.

By 1997, public advertising of prescription drugs had proliferated to the point that the FDA had to legislate certain standards for prescription drug ads. The commercial was required to state what the drug was intended to do. It was also required to warn viewers of the drug's possible side effects – the point being that all prescription drugs (and, for that matter, any drug that is at all effective) will alter body chemistry and therefore not merely alleviate certain symptoms, but also produce side effects that could be harmful. There was another side effect of the advertising, one desired by the pharmaceutical companies: the growth of the drug companies themselves, who got busy buying each other out, merging to form even bigger, more powerful, corporations. They began to use that power to influence public policy, to lobby politicians, and to turn themselves into major profit centers.

What had once been an intimate mediation between patient and doctor became, in a matter of a few years, a mass-mediated barrage of magazine and television advertising, whose main purpose was to turn as much of the public as possible into patients who would be their own advocates for medications that the advertisements told them they needed. The drug companies – "big Pharma," as their critics call them – insist that they are informing the public of new cures while justifying high profits in terms of the money required to research them. Their critics say they are interfering with the doctor–patient relationship, creating a need where none existed, and lining their pockets in the process. As some companies have found out to their detriment, some of their "cures," made popular through advertising, are killers.

When we analyze pharmaceutical ads, we find that almost every one follows a very few basic patterns: they identify a health problem, convince the reader or viewer that he or she has it (and may not even be aware of having it), present the curative drug, give the list of side effects in such a fashion that they can be glossed over by the consumer, and end, inevitably, by asking the audience to check with their doctor to see if the drug "is right for you." The consumer is asked to become a kind of surrogate for the drug salesperson, talking the doctor into prescribing something. The doctor is put in a position of explaining to the patient that the medication is not "right" for him or her, or yielding to the wisdom of the advertisement. In short, drug advertising, television commercials for drugs in particular, create multiple narratives: they tell a story about liberation from pain and affliction, using graphic-heavy imagery and actors pretending to be doctors, all in the service of creating another narrative, this time between the patient and the doctor in which the former tries to convince the latter what is best.

Side effects The FDA mandates that all prescription drug ads must mention their side effects. Every drug has them; every patient needs to be evaluated for them. A patient who is fully aware of side effects may question the doctor very closely about any medication; therefore, every advertiser must find a way to reduce the visibility of side effects in order not to frighten or confuse the viewer. In magazine ads, drug companies tend to print a full-page summary of a drug's use and side effects in type so small as to be illegible, using language, complete with chemical formulae, often too scientific for the lay reader. The information is similar to what is provided to doctors or that comes packaged with a bottle of the medicine. In TV ads, there must be an alternative to small type. According to the FDA's ruling, television ads need only mention *major* side effects. The drug companies and their ad agencies have determined that mentioning three side effects is about the limit before the viewer becomes confused or scared off. The commercials make it all the easier to swallow by hiding the warnings in plain sight. (In the wake of some recent prescription drug scandals, the list of side effects has become somewhat longer.)

We can see the process at work in the advertising for a class of drugs called statins, useful in reducing LDL cholesterol that can clog arteries. Many drug companies manufacture a version of a statin drug, and they all work more or less the same way. The job of advertising is to discriminate between what tiny variations may exist between the various drugs, and to overcome consumer advocate complaints that statins may cause toxicity and that one statin in particular, Bayer Pharmaceutical's Baycol, was withdrawn because it caused fatal side effects in some people. Here is an example of how it is done. Astra Zeneca is among the largest drug companies. Its statin is called Crestor, and its advertising has been fairly straightforward. Its magazine and television ads were based on a simple metaphor of downward motion. Crestor lowers cholesterol; therefore, "lower" becomes the design principal. A magazine ad shows a large, luminous arrow, pointing downward, with information printed on each side, under the universal drug ad line, "Ask your doctor...." On the next page is densely printed medical information about the drug and its potential problems.

A television ad for the drug also employs the downward metaphor, with actor Mandy Patinkin (who once played a doctor on TV) stepping down a long spiral staircase with decreasing cholesterol numbers on each step. Patinkin's commentary is straightforward and matter-of-fact. "Getting high cholesterol down is important." Cut to closer shot: "For some people it's even more important." It is not made clear who constitutes "some people" because it is implied that the viewer may be one of the some and should find out. He congratulates the viewer for following good diet and exercise. But then, as he continues down the steps, he hypothesizes: "You've tried just about everything, but now medical information comes along that suggests you may need to get that bad cholesterol even lower," and a small text appears citing a medical study. Cut to close-up: "now what do you do?" The question is planted and hopefully some anxiety is raised. We are told about Crestor and to ask our doctor "if it's right for you." The graphic of the downward arrow appears, along with a promise that the drug can lower cholesterol by 52 percent. (The ad does not explain 52 percent of what, and this vague use of percentages is common across the advertising spectrum.) A small text at the bottom of the screen says that results may vary. The side effects – "Crestor's not for everyone ..." – are announced in a fairly straightforward manner: liver disease, muscle cramps, not for pregnant women. But the pick-up line after the warning, "Do you still need to get your cholesterol lower?" follows without a beat, so that the initial question about need almost cancels out the warnings.

A key point to note is that sound is almost as important as image in television commercials. Not only does music set the tone, but also the very sound of the voice-over and the way it is edited adds to the effect. Sound is edited just as the image is. Typically, a sound editor will digitally remove pauses in a commercial voice-over so that the delivery is rapid, if not quite breathless. Presumably, if the narration doesn't sound halting, the viewer will not have time to pause and ask questions. The rapid elision between the warning and the provocation – "Do you still need …?" – is typical and allows any possible concern that might be raised by hearing of side effects to be cancelled out by the immediate restatement of what is hoped to be the greater concern about high cholesterol.

As such things go, Astra Zeneca's Crestor ad was fairly responsible, and their website presents a rich amount of additional information. Other statin ads are somewhat more diversionary. Vytorin is a statin combined with another drug that is supposed to block cholesterol absorption as well lower blood cholesterol. It is manufactured by Merck, though the company name does not usually appear in the television ad and is in very small type on the drug's web page. We'll see why in a bit. The pitch for this medicine is that high cholesterol can come not only from bad eating habits and insufficient exercise, but also as an inherited trait from your relatives. Perhaps so, but, taking this as its premise, the ad works by removing the onus of lowering cholesterol from the viewer and transferring it first to the viewer's family and then to the benefits of the product. After all, you can't do anything about your genes. The visuals are a series of diptychs showing nice food on the left and persons – of various races and genders – on the right. They are dressed to look something like the food. The side-effects warning is pronounced over the same visuals and the same background music so that they maintain uninterrupted visual attention that can easily distract from the message. Happily, the ad does mention the recommended way to lower cholesterol, a healthy diet, a few times.

What makes Vytorin special is its combination with another drug, Zetia. Not to miss a marketing opportunity, Merck also manufactures Zetia as a stand-alone drug. One television ad for Zetia involved a small dramatic narrative of a group of medical students walking along busily with their teacher in a mock question-and-answer session about cholesterol-lowering agents. Of course, Zetia is the drug they choose. The side-effects warning is performed as part of the give and take, all but lost in the drama of medical students and their professor heading off – to lunch. Which gives them the opportunity to add the common-sense tag of eating correctly and getting exercise.

These few examples give no real indication of the amount of advertising for prescription and non-prescription drugs that floods television. Because they are marketed for older Americans, who are more likely to be ill than younger ones, they tend to be concentrated on the network evening news broadcasts, whose audience fits the drug makers' demographic. On some days, usually weekends, almost all commercials on the evening news are drug ads. No opportunity is lost to promise better health or to simply promote themselves, even when they make serious, deadly, errors.

A drug manufacturer is quite likely to invent a product and then invent a problem the drug can cure (a game not restricted to drug manufacturers alone). The Novartis drug company sells Zelnorm, a laxative. Originally, its ads were aimed at women only; later it broadened its market to men as well. Its ad shows people with words like "chronic constipation" written on their stomachs, and urges not to let your doctor tell you simply to take any laxative, but to push him to prescribe the product. "If I don't bring it up, you bring it up," an actor playing a doctor tells the viewer in its commercial. Zelnorm's website even offers a checklist that will help you twist your doctor's arm. Unfortunately for Novartis, the arm-twisting did not work. The FDA ordered the drug withdrawn because it might cause cardiovascular problems.

Sometimes an ad won't mention a drug at all. The Eli Lilly Company has run a spot about depression, a serious and treatable disease. It is a responsible advertisement, highlighting symptoms and directing the viewer to the company's website. Sometimes the problem and the drug are so trivial that the commercial has to convince the viewer that the problem exists. Restasis increases tear production for a problem called "chronic dry eye." One commercial states "you can have chronic dry eye without knowing it." But when a person is in real pain, he or she does knows it, and when a promise of relief is offered, it will be taken, which can get drug manufacturers into trouble.

Can advertising kill?

Such was the case with the marketing and prescribing of "cox-2 inhibitor" drugs developed for the relief of arthritis, a disease that afflicts about 15 percent of the US population and nearly half of all elderly people. It is incurable. Only its primary symptom, joint pain, can be relieved – by anti-inflammatory drugs, all of which carry a risk of stomach bleeding. New arthritis pain relievers, with a huge profit potential, apparently more safe than earlier medicines, were marketed under a variety of names, the best-known and soon the most infamous being Merck's Vioxx. Vioxx and its competitors were found "safe and effective," the two touchstones for approval by the Food and Drug Administration. However, there quickly emerged a specific risk concerning Vioxx and its relatives. They cause cardiovascular problems – heart attacks – even a year after patients *stop* taking the drug. Evidence seems to prove that Merck knew this before launching its $161 million marketing campaign. Before Vioxx was recalled, 20 million people were taking the drug; 88,000 of them had heart attacks, and 38,000 died.

Merck withdrew the drug in the fall of 2004, before the FDA forced it to do so, and at one point the company was fighting some 27,000 lawsuits. On the bottom right of Merck's web page (<www.merck.com>) is a link to information on its recalled product, mostly touting the lawsuits it has won to date. On television, it often runs ads that speak about the company's responsibility. On ads for its other products, like Vytorin, the company name is barely visible. Finally, in the fall of 2007, Merck agreed to a $4.85 billion settlement for all outstanding suits.

Never to miss a selling opportunity, a manufacturer of an over-the-counter pain reliever, Tylenol, ran television ads early in 2006 in which its "Director of Sales" looks the viewer in the eye, and warns that taking extra doses of pain relievers does not make the pain go away. Falling into the genre of the "honest" ad, the Tylenol spot joins the Dove "real beauty" campaign in promoting straight talk as a selling point, inferring that its unnamed competition is dishonest. If Merck got into trouble, there is no reason why the manufacturer of Tylenol could not profit by proving how responsible it is in comparison.

It is tempting to blame advertising for the Merck-Vioxx affair, but it seems that even doctors were unaware that the company knew about the danger of its product and therefore they could not counter their patients' requests for the drug. More broadly, to blame advertising for anything would seem to disregard a simple fact: people do not have to pay attention to it. This is an optimistic view, certainly, but its validity is proven by the lengths to which advertisers go to bypass or neutralize rational responses. The streamlining of the message that allows it to slip past a person's reason is too effective. The fact that the "Director of Sales" for the manufacturer of Tylenol has to use a commercial telling us *not* to throw a lot of pain relievers at a headache, after so many other ads have told us differently, indicates that even the companies that make products are afraid not merely of lawsuits, but of the likelihood that too many people will believe what they say and do things that will make lawsuits possible.

The result of all of this is something manufacturers and their advertising agencies dread and work very hard to overcome: consumer and even political resistance. Despite the torrent of pharmaceutical ads, sales of prescription drugs are down. Even drugs for "erectile dysfunction" – Viagra, Levitra, and Cialis – the subject of many embarrassing ads and floods of email spam, have fallen. Advertisers always depend on sexuality to sell products. Drugs that promised – to men, at least – increased potency seemed like a sure thing, and they were for a time until the novelty wore off, and until there were reports that the drugs could cause vision problems (thereby eliding the pill with the old joke about going blind). The reputation of the drug companies has fallen very low for a variety of reasons, ranging from their carelessness about selling dangerous products to their carelessness in being so closely involved with politics. In some cases, states are intervening in an attempt to lower drug costs, sending in "unsales" teams to educate doctors about generic and over-the-counter alternatives to heavily advertised brands. The only response the drug companies seem capable of is to continue telling us about the diseases we have that they in turn can cure. Pfizer, a drug company that makes another cox-2 inhibitor, Celebrex, linked to heart attacks but not withdrawn from the market, has tried to begin advertising again.

Ask your doctor if this is right for you.

Political Advertising

The landscape of desire

The question is whether it is possible to streamline advertising so that it slips past our capacity to decode messages in any way other than how the advertiser wants us to. Is it possible to so carefully craft the process of integrating us into the message of an advertisement that it completely overcomes resistance with the promise of fulfillment and relief? Would pharmaceutical companies spend millions of dollars to sell their medicines if they didn't believe this to be true? Advertisers of all kinds of products study our behavior, our habits (and not only our buying habits), and our weak points in order to find an entry that will bypass reason and play upon emotion, hoping to be sure that we decode their message into a stimulus that will make us part with our money.

Most advertising speaks to the fear of lacking something – health in the case of the pharmaceuticals – and our desire to look, feel, and live better than we do now. There are darker emotions that advertisers play upon, deeper emotions of fear and anxiety, feelings of resentment and discontent, even hatred. These darker emotions are the target of the most complex kind of advertising, a form that moves from the private to the public sphere and affects more of us more deeply than a drug with serious side effects: political advertising.

The circulation of political power

Commercial advertising is about the circulation of capital: products and services promoted and sold in order to make a profit for their manufacturers so that they can make more products and services, advertise them, make a profit, and continue the cycle. Political advertising is about the circulation of ideology: beliefs that we hold about ourselves, our lives, our community, our country – ideas, images, *feelings* aroused by broad and often conflicting concepts such as freedom, religion, opportunity, class, race, gender, responsibility, morality itself – and the attendant anxieties that occur if we are led to believe these ideas and feelings are under attack. Political advertising embodies ideology, figuratively when we are urged to vote for or against a law or proposition concerning an issue that we believe in; or literally in the body of someone who wants to be elected to carry out our ideas and feelings within local, state, or national government. Political advertising attempts to sell us another person's power to act on behalf of our beliefs.

The ideal – indeed the ideology – of a liberal democracy is that we freely elect our officials, rationally judging their ability to carry out our beliefs and our political needs, comparing, evaluating, deciding, then casting our vote. The reality is somewhat different. Free choice is an undependable variable; ideas, beliefs, feelings are vague, subject to change and to manipulation. Politics and politicians need to be more certain about the outcomes of voting. Politicians need to be able to quantify, to know voter habits and psychology so that they can, in effect, manufacture a personality for themselves that embodies what the voters want; they need as well to attempt to create the ideal voter, the collective personality that will cast a vote for them instead of the opposition. They need to advertise.

Discussing political news in chapter 2, we noted how two politicians, Franklin Delano Roosevelt and Richard Milhous Nixon, used broadcast media to create personality and to manage voter perceptions. Roosevelt developed the image of the president as patriarch, lofty but warm, thoughtful, and understanding, accessible by means of his voice, through the "fireside chats" he broadcast regularly; he cast himself as a man for, if not of, the people. Nixon was not so successful. His frowning demeanor and peremptory tone of voice, and his heavy, sometimes sweaty jowls, as well as the suggestion of paranoia in many of his remarks, created unease in viewers. The contrast was particularly marked when Nixon debated a young and vigorous John F. Kennedy on television in the 1960 presidential campaign.

Political advertising and its use of the media to cultivate personality pre-date Nixon and Roosevelt by many decades. William McKinley appeared as a candidate in an 1896 newsreel, marking not only the first political figure to be filmed, but, by being so mediated, initiating a major shift from information provided by newspapers to information supplied visually, a shift that by the mid-twentieth century would change the political media design. McKinley remained enmeshed with the media throughout his presidency, sending the US into the Spanish–American War that was so well advertised in the yellow journalism of the time; the same war that made Theodore Roosevelt and his "Rough Riders" famous. When McKinley was assassinated in 1901 (his funeral widely viewed on film), Theodore Roosevelt became President, and he used the press to cultivate an image of a rugged man of the people.

Cartooning the presidency

Politicians using media to foster, affirm, or manufacture an image constitute a history of increasing sophistication, growing professionalism, and nastiness. By the early 1950s, and the presidential candidacy of the World War II hero General Dwight David Eisenhower, politicians and their parties had begun to employ advertising agencies and public relation firms to take as much uncertainty out of the electoral process as possible. As in all other advertising, research and manipulation played increasingly powerful roles in convincing the public that one candidate was either better or worse than another. As with any other product, political advertising attempts to create desire for a product – in this case, the candidate – and fear about what would happen if he or she were not elected.

Eisenhower's campaign hired professional advertisers to create a variety of spots. Roy Disney (Walt's brother) drew animated cartoons celebrating "Ike," as Eisenhower was popularly known. For another series of ads, entitled "Eisenhower Answers America," the candidate was filmed as if he were fielding questions about his policies. In fact, his answers were filmed at one place and time and, at another, various people were filmed asking the questions. An African-American man queries, "General, the Democrats are telling me I never had it so good. Can that be true?" Eisenhower growls, "When America is billions in debt, when prices are doubled and taxes break our back, and we are still fighting in Korea? It's tragic and it's time for a change."

All of the spots in the "Eisenhower Answers America" campaign use the most basic, even primitive, cinematic editing techniques (figures 3.13 and 3.14): a character in one shot looks in a particular direction and the candidate in the next shot looks in the

Figure 3.13

Figure 3.14

Figures 3.13–14
"Eisenhower Answers
America." Ike's answers
were pre-recorded. Then
people were found to ask
the questions.

direction of the first. It appears as if they are talking to each other. The example given here contains all those elements that will become standard in political advertising: creating an illusion of concern and providing a non-answer is by now generic, as is talking about the opposition in dismissive tones (though these early ads are somewhat mild by today's standards). Back in the 1950s, the choice of an African-American to pretend to ask a question of the candidate was particularly canny. The outgoing president, Harry Truman, had desegregated the armed forces in 1948, and set in motion a number of proposals that began the civil rights movement. The Supreme Court was poised to hear arguments on the legality of the "separate but equal" doctrine of school segregation. The Southern wing of the Democrats ("Dixiecrats") was brutally racist and had broken from the party over the race issue. The Republicans – still thinking of themselves as the party of Lincoln – attempted to court the African-American vote. However, Eisenhower's response does not touch on issues of civil rights, but offers a perfectly generic response: too much debt, too many taxes, war. A tragic situation. The overstatement is typical, as are the generalities that blame the Democrats without having to name them.

Rosser Reeves, the advertising executive who developed the campaign, defined what he was doing. "This new way of campaigning, in essence is a new use of what advertising men know as 'spots' .... The humble radio or TV spot can deliver more listeners for less money than any other form of advertising." He made it clear that Eisenhower's responses should touch on "just three problems: Corruption in government; high prices and high taxes; war!" It was all scripted, all predetermined to "deliver more listeners for less money." The candidacy was packaged, and the packaging helped Eisenhower get elected.

Engineering fear in a daisy

Fear is the other side of desire. Advertisers want you to desire their product, even if they have to scare you into doing it. Pharmaceutical advertisements are based on a narrative of fear of disease and a promise of relief. Political campaigners were well ahead of the pill-makers. In 1964, Lyndon Baines Johnson was running for president against Barry Goldwater, an early figure in the neo-conservative movement. It was a difficult moment in American history. John Fitzgerald Kennedy had been assassinated a year earlier, leaving his Vice President, Johnson, to assume the presidency for the rest of his term. America's participation in the Vietnam War was surging and growing more unpopular. Johnson was more liberal than Kennedy, particularly in matters of civil rights. In the conventional position taken by conservatives, Goldwater was campaigning for a reduced role for government and – ominously, given the build-up in Vietnam – a strong military stance against Communism. In his acceptance speech at the convention that nominated him, Goldwater pronounced one of the more infamous of political statements: "extremism in the defense of liberty is no vice and … moderation in the pursuit of justice is no virtue."

Johnson's campaign played upon the anxieties created by Goldwater's statement and created a television commercial that became as infamous as Goldwater's own statement. The campaign hired the advertising agency of Doyle, Dane, and Bernbach, and they produced the "Daisy" spot (figures 3.15–3.17). The camera zooms in to a little girl in a field pulling the petals off a daisy and counting, haltingly, "2, 3, 4, 5, 7, 6, 6, 8, 9 ...." As she removes all the petals, a strong, echoing voice-over is heard doing a more serious, less confused countdown. The camera moves closer; the girl looks up. The camera zooms quickly to her eye as the countdown nears zero. On the count, as her eye fills the screen, there is a cut to a nuclear explosion. Johnson's voice is heard: "These are the stakes: to make a world in which all of God's children can live or to go into the dark. We must either love each other or we must die." Over a title card, a deep voice intones, "Vote for President Johnson on November 3rd. The stakes are too high."

The ad caused such an uproar that it was pulled after one airing. However, the media aided the campaign by showing the commercial as part of its national news broadcasts

Figure 3.15

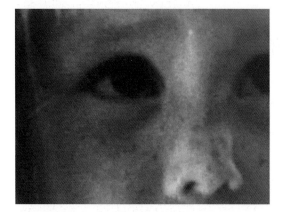

Figure 3.16

Figure 3.17

Figures 3.15–17 Images from the Lyndon Johnson Daisy ad. Shown only once, it had devastating effect.

covering the election. Johnson won the election by a landslide. The "Daisy" ad was an important moment in the growing sophistication of campaign advertising, an example of creating a metaphor of fear and distrust without directly mentioning issues or even the name of the candidate targeted by the ad. A visual narrative of innocence destroyed by nuclear war borne of the opposition candidate's extremism proved to be irresistible.

Willie Horton

Despite its limited exposure at the time, the "Daisy" ad set a pattern that became more rigid and more single- (and simple-) minded in following election years. Ads became more dependent on images to deflect viewers from the complicated problems a candidate would need to deal with once in office, moving the voter instead into a place either of mindless dread or mindless optimism. No campaign was more brutal in its single-mindedness than the "Willie Horton" ads run by George H. W. Bush against Michael Dukakis in the 1988 campaign for President.

Dukakis was governor of Massachusetts, a state that had a policy of allowing prisoners out for weekend furloughs. One of them, Willie Horton, kidnapped a couple, raped the woman, and stabbed the man while out on furlough. The Bush ad pinned this act of violence directly on Dukakis, who, of course, had nothing to do with it. The images were simple: a bright photograph of Bush; a darker photograph of Dukakis; an even darker one of Horton (figures 3.18–3.21). The subtitles and voice-over are sarcastic. "Bush Supports the Death Penalty." Dukakis, we are told, opposes it. The voice-over tells the Willie Horton story and indicates that Dukakis personally allowed the convict out to rape and murder, ending with a sarcastic tag: "Weekend Prison Passes/Dukakis On Crime." The ad ends with the image of Dukakis, which, by association with the preceding information and the subtitle, makes him look even more stupid than he does in exactly the same image that starts the ad. The language of indictment, no matter how false, colors our perception of the candidate. This is exactly the hoped-for result.

The Bush campaign accompanied this with an ad that further streamlined the visual narrative, encoding it so tightly that there is no apparent way out. "The revolving door" commercial is in black and white. It begins with images of a prison tower and guards at a wall, then dissolves to staged images of "prisoners" going through a revolving door. The image is the metaphor is the message. Dukakis is soft on crime. Elect him and rapists and murders will be in and out of jail and get you. Dukakis was not elected. He could not overcome the imagery. When he tried, arranging a photo opportunity for which he dressed in army gear and rode in a tank, he looked ridiculous. The "tough on crime" message never became a major part of the Bush administration. Its latent racism was permitted to simmer.

Figure 3.18

Morning in America

Not all political ads are negative. Jimmy Carter, running for president in 1977, and seeking to rebuild the office from the ruins left by Richard Nixon, offered change and hope. When Carter ran for re-election in 1981, his opponent was Ronald Reagan, well known to voters as a movie actor. Reagan's ads promising "morning in America" proved irresistible, forming a kind of inverted streamlining. The Carter presidency was facing complex problems that were prophetic of the world to come: American hostages held by the revolutionary (and at the same time repressive) Iranian government, an oil embargo that led to shortages at the pump. During his presidency, Carter turned from the image of the innocent well-meaning guy from the South to the brooding modernist, telling the public to conserve energy, and warning them about cultural malaise. What Carter learned, and many advertising executives already knew, was that in the world of politics, dark realism sells nothing without the promise of an easy cure.

Figure 3.19

Reagan promised a return to a brighter, simpler time. In the same breath, he offered an image of toughness, especially against our old "enemy," the Soviet Union. He offered the way forward *and* backward: he would slash through the dark realities of a complex world and return America to its unquestionably simple role as world leader. Like the model in a *Cosmo* ad, Reagan was formed into the image the culture wished to see of itself. But rather than a perfect beauty, Reagan's image was manly, tough, folksy, a threat to our enemies, a protector of ourselves, our friend in office, though without Franklin Roosevelt's intelligence and charm.

Figure 3.20

Political advertising online

In the years since Reagan, laws have been passed that put campaign advertising into the hands of organizations that act as surrogates for the candidates, thereby relieving the candidates of economic and moral responsibility. Political advertising has grown uglier, much of it turning

Figure 3.21

Figures 3.18–21 The Willie Horton ad. This blatantly racist political ad. helped defeat Michael Dukakis.

into assassination of the character of the opponent with misrepresentations so painful and exaggerated that they can barely be defended without making the victim appear simply defensive. This mode continues in the move of the political into the Internet. While every candidate has a website, often an important tool for grass-roots – as opposed to corporate – fundraising, the Internet also affords special interest groups even more open space for their attacks. The explosion of political blogs provides a forum for a variety of political views, but also provides an unedited, sometimes uninformed, space for ever more concentrated political poison. Even individuals, making use of social networks like YouTube, are making their own political ads, attacking candidates, perhaps just for the fun of it.

This mode of political attack – often called the politics of personal destruction – is an evolution of a basic advertising tactic, an integral part of the encoding of advertising that works by humiliation. Commercial after commercial portrays a husband humiliated for being just too stupid – unable, for example, to get the right car insurance – or a wife inadequate in her house cleaning. Humiliation is a simple, basic technique to make one person look bad and another look better because he or she knows more. In commercial advertising, humiliation is often lighthearted and humorous: the stupidity of one character makes the other look smarter because she uses the product. Humiliation in political advertising is much more serious: it is used to destroy a reputation and, by contrast, affirm the righteousness of the opponent. In either case, the viewer is asked to make an absurdly simple comparison. Who would choose the loser? Who would believe someone who is discredited? Who would not want to be smarter? Unfortunately, the consumer is rarely the winner; the choices made on the basis of advertising are rarely the right ones. Within the media design, the consumer may only act as a kind of pass through. He or she may buy the product (or vote for the candidate) and be no smarter as a result. The advertiser wins by taking the consumer's money or getting the vote. The political humiliation ads attack the opposition as incompetent, wrong-headed, as being against morality or defense; and suggests that the voter would be stupid to vote for him and smarter to vote for his opponent. The political advertiser looks at the consumer as a vote; the commercial advertiser sees her as a dispenser of cash. Whether the objective is profit or winning an election, the energies of advertising serve to diminish the media consumer, making him or her a means toward an end, integrating the individual into the world of the advertisement.

The Consumer as Tool in the Time of Convergence

Eyeballs

When we read a well-argued newspaper article about a candidate, we are presented with an array of facts. But a political ad discrediting a candidate's war record, or a commercial for a cholesterol-lowering drug, turns the viewer into a kind of binary switch. Respond positively: vote for the other candidate; ask the doctor if it's right for you. Respond negatively: don't do either and possibly suffer the consequences – a candidate who is "out of the mainstream," or a heart attack from high cholesterol. Advertisers of all stripes work to maximize a positive decoding of the message.

In this period of convergence, advertising is undergoing some revision. "Eyeballs" – the synecdoche advertisers use to refer to our attention, especially for television and Internet ads – are wandering. With media outlets shifting and coming together in new ways, the Internet having become the latest site of commerce, and digital television recorders allowing viewers to skip commercials entirely (just as we can simply turn the page to avoid an ad in a magazine or newspaper), advertisers now have to find new methods, or refresh old ones, to get our attention. Internet advertisers are becoming especially inventive in using technology to grab attention.

Dot-com, a brief history

In the last chapter of this book, we will examine the history of the Internet in some detail. Let us note here that, in its beginnings in the early 1990s, the Internet, including the World Wide Web – that portion of the Internet that works through text, images, and hyperlinks – was a non-commercial medium, supported in the United States by the National Science Foundation and by universities. Advertising, especially by large corporations, was slow in coming and followed the lead of Internet users. It's not that commercial organizations were ignorant of the potential for Internet advertising. The assigning of commercial domain names, those addresses that end in ".com," began in the mid-1980s. But among the earliest institutions to sign on were universities – Carnegie Mellon, Purdue, Rice, UCLA – which used the .edu domain common to all educational institutions. The .com domain names were first taken mostly by computer technology, communications, and military supply companies, who knew early on about the Internet's users and potential. Companies like IBM, Intel, Bell-Atlantic, Boeing, Lockheed, and Apple were online in short order. Among the few pioneers, outside of technology companies, was Time Warner, the media company formed by joining the old movie studio, Warner Bros., Henry Luce's old news magazine empire, and the cable outlets of Turner Broadcasting. Time Warner established an early search site called "Pathfinder" in 1994 and began to include advertising. Meanwhile, the National Center for Supercomputing Applications at the University of Illinois (which, in 1993, had developed Mosaic, the first web browser) began to solicit advertisers to its site. Mosaic ultimately morphed into a commercial browser, Netscape, which in turn became Mozilla and, finally, Firefox, a competitor to Microsoft's Internet Explorer. Microsoft, the company that made its fortune in computer software, took some time to realize the importance of the Web.

In 1996, America Online (AOL) adopted Netscape, buying it outright in 1998. AOL, which had its start in the pre-Web Internet bulletin boards of the 1980s, became one of the first paid subscriber portals into the Internet and, of course, was commercial to its core. The circle was completed when AOL purchased Time Warner in 1999 in a widely publicized convergence, creating a clash of old and new media companies that did not allow the combination to survive as commercially viable partners.

It is important to consider the links among all of these elements – the Web, the browsers used to access it, and the companies who attempt to own them – when we seek to understand the changes advertising is going through. Many companies followed Time Warner into web advertising during the mid-1990s, and, as web usage grew and grew, by the end of the twentieth century what was once the dream of a free and open community became more an owned and sponsored one. The Internet became a new frontier for companies to expand into. But they did it carelessly and the initial rush of individuals and companies to make money from Internet businesses and advertising ended in financial collapse and an economic recession in the early 2000s. The return to financial stability required a rethinking of how the Internet could be used to commercial advantage and clever calculations on how to use advertising on this most public of media.

Online design

Even as corporations began flocking to the Internet, there was and remains a great deal of uncertainty about how to reach their audience and what kinds of advertising will best work in a medium that is still thought of as open, accessible to anyone, and owned by its users. The Internet is indeed the most public of the mass media; it appears to be unmediated, and with it individuals can express themselves in ways that would have been impossible through the old media forms. But the corporate world is uncomfortable with such freedom; it makes it difficult for them to know who you are and what they can sell you. Traditional media developed methods to measure their audience: ticket sales; Nielsen diaries, in which television audiences recorded their viewing habits; surveys; demographic breakdowns based on sales; focus groups made up of a cross-section of individuals who would comment on television shows, on movies, and on advertisements themselves – all to help advertisers target their products. The Web and its users were initially hard to measure and attract. Just how advertising should appear online was a matter of trial and error. Not only does the overall design of a site have to be attractive, but ease of use, finding the right links, and moving smoothly through the site are also important. But even site design is not enough. Users have to get to the site, have to know, among the approximately 50 million (and growing) sites out there, just where the advertiser wants them to go. (See figures 3.22 and 3.23.)

Spam   Of course, not all online advertising is well designed and well researched. The crudest and cheapest method of reaching consumers is through email. The result is spam, email messages containing advertising, created mostly by small entrepreneurs, many of whom are simply out to defraud people by selling anything from stocks, to prescription medications, to pornography. Spam is the opposite of streamlined advertising. It depends only on the ability of the spammer to send out as many emails as possible, while masking their source. The persistence of spam remains something of mystery because, despite the fact that most people regard it as a nuisance, and despite the various technological barriers set up to prevent it from coming through, spam

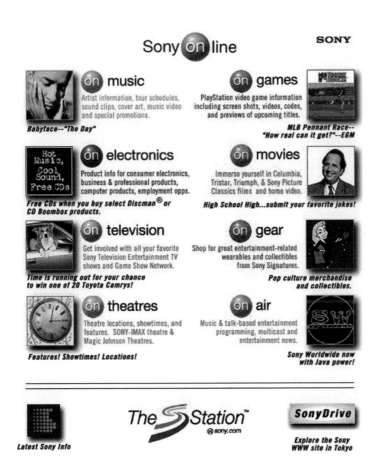

Figure 3.22 Web design before and after. Sony's website in 1996.

continues and, apparently, works – though one can only wonder who the people are who buy goods and services from such a source.

Perhaps spam only proves what all advertisers believe, that there is an audience for anything, and that people want to be offered something, even if it is a fake stock tip or a discount drug. But spam is too unfocused, too crude, too hit and miss to have much appeal compared to the email promotions that legitimate merchants send to those consumers who select to be notified about products and sales. The more sophisticated design and interactive capabilities of the Web offer the chance not only to attract users to a site, but also to make immediate contact with potential consumers and actively guide and form their buying habits. Using new technologies, advertisers can take much guesswork out of the process of finding customers and, in ways previously unavailable in older media, lead them in the directions they want them to follow.

Online ads in context Online advertisers use a number of techniques in their attempts to reach exactly the audience they want. One, called contextual advertising, delivers ads that are related to the content of a particular website you are on, or a specific

Figure 3.23
"Sonystyle" today. Blocky, awkward design gives way to a streamlined, attractive web page, rich in graphics if not easy to navigate.

search you are making. Another attempts to understand your behavior – based upon tracking the websites you visit – and to lead you to ads for the appropriate products. In conventional print advertising, ads are often placed that are relevant to the content of a particular kind of magazine or article, or even a section of a newspaper. *Cosmopolitan*, as we've seen, contains ads for clothing, jewelry, and cosmetics that are relevant to its target audience. The local news section of a paper or the local news television broadcast will contain ads for local businesses.

Online, the techniques used to place ads in the context of the main content of a site, or relevant to the kinds of content that a user might be searching for, are much more intriguing. If I Google "behavioral advertising" or "contextual advertising," I get hundreds of thousands of hits. On the right side of the first page of results, under the rubric "Sponsored Links," are links for advertising companies that offer, according to one of them, "Content specific ads … Reach your perfect audience now!" One link is for WiseGeek.com, offering a "Free and Straightforward Guide to **Contextual Advertising**." The last two words are in bold face, clearly demonstrating that the search engines picked up my search terms – "contextual" and "advertising" – and fed in links to companies that pay to advertise on Google, and are specifically targeted to the context of my query.

Clicking on WiseGeek.com provides me with a concise definition of what I am looking for: "Contextual advertising is advertising that relates directly to the content of the webpage on which it is served – it is advertising that is *in context* with its environment." It further informs me that Internet contextual advertising began with the implementation of cookies, those tiny files deposited on your hard drive whenever you visit a web page, which keep track of your searching and send back information on you and your Internet usage. There are also four more paid ads for agencies that will help maximize my profits by placing ads on appropriate websites, and an ad for Google itself.

We can try a more common search. If I search on "computers," I get over 564,000,000 hits. On the top of the first search page are highlighted links for HP, Dell, and Toshiba, who paid for their results to come up first. Along the right side of the page are other sponsored links for computer sales, contextually related to my main search. (Be aware that, with the passing of time, and the volatility of the Internet, the links that come up will have changed. What are you finding now when you do these searches?)

Behavioral advertising is a little more troubling because of the detailed information it gathers about users. It, too, is based on older advertising practices that attempt to predict what consumers will buy based on their habits of searching, or what they have already bought, or what the search engines and databases predict they might buy. Online, behavioral advertising makes use of cookies and the record of visits to particular websites to create a database of user buying habits. As Claria, a major Internet advertising company, clearly stated: "Behavioral marketing … rejects the conventional wisdom that the Internet shopper is somehow 'elusive.' Quite the contrary, no shopper provides more information about his or her preferences than the online shopper, and behavioral marketing targets those preferences." Combined with other techniques that define your online behavior with increasing sophistication and detail, companies can profile you down to the time of day you opened a particular site, what you've purchased, and, based on that, what you are likely to purchase.

Refining the Advertising Narrative

Identity

We've spoken about the grand narrative of advertising: its story of desire and fulfillment, its promise of moving you easily (even if you have to be humiliated first), through a world of obstacles and needs – improving your health and personal appearance, finding the automobile or cell phone that best expresses your personality, selecting the prescription drug or political candidate that is "right for you." If, for us, advertising is a narrative of desire fulfilled, for the advertiser, it is a quest narrative: a quest to find us, catalogue us, and create those desires only they can fulfill. As audience, we are their object of desire, and they must streamline their techniques in order to capture first your attention and then your money.

Every time you visit a commercial website – and even the most personal social networking sites like MySpace or YouTube – you become deeply entwined with commercial interests. Every time you make a search; every time you shop and enter your name, home address, phone number, email address, credit card number on a website; every time a website deposits a cookie in the "temp" file on your hard disk; you are marked, captured, put in a database; thereby satisfying the advertiser's quest. We have all been scared by the threat of "identity theft." But the reality is that our "identities" – the marketable part of them, at least – are already "stolen." (The fact that any information, even the most personal, that we may put on a social networking site is available to anyone is an issue we will discuss further in chapter 7.) Our marketable identities make up part of the great media design; a melodrama, if you will, in which desire is identified as need for a product, and need is calculated down to a mouse click. It's all quite harmless – unless the databases get stolen and our marketable selves are used to empty our bank accounts. Otherwise, despite all their efforts, we remain pretty much in control of our roles in the drama. Unfortunately, that fact continues to drive advertisers to greater lengths in their efforts to become masters of the tale.

At the outset, I stated that advertising is the lubricant of the media. In fact, advertising and media work seamlessly together and lubricate, or streamline, each other. In the face of an audience that keeps fragmenting and a media design that keeps shifting, forcing media companies and advertisers to keep searching for a format that will recapture an audience that is moving away from television, away from newspapers, and away from movie theaters, advertisers feel compelled to collect more information about us, just as newspaper publishers, television networks, and film studios are searching for various ways they can make money on their products now that so much attention has shifted to the Internet.

Product placement

One way companies are hedging their bets is by simply forcing advertising everywhere. Online, this takes the form of pop-up ads or in the contextual advertising that pushes advertisements onto the results of a search. In older media, advertisers do not leave things to chance either. Rather than wait for a commercial break in a television show, or lose all opportunities because of the lack of commercial breaks in movies, advertisers simply place their products *within* the narrative. A narrative inside a narrative. The process of "product placement" ("brand integration," as it is known professionally), is relatively simple. Film and television producers work in concert with advertising agencies to get products seen and mentioned as part of the film or TV show. Money almost always changes hands, though some companies will be pleased just to have their product shown. The result is that, if a brand name is seen or mentioned, it is not an accident. If the "integration" is successful, the viewer may simply absorb the product with the narrative of the program or film, barely aware that yet another narrative, the push to buy a product, is being told.

The process is nothing new; it is as old as the media that survive by advertising We see it in the integration of commercial products as prizes in the game shows of radio and early TV. Today's quiz shows continue this tradition, presenting mini advertisements as they describe the prizes offered to contestants. We have already noted how, in early television, sponsors owned the shows and would have the stars present advertisements. Sports teams use sponsors' names and logos on every piece of equipment and clothing. Mark Burnett, the creator of the major "reality" shows, made deals with car companies, offering Pontiac cars as a prize on *Survivor*. Similarly, Oprah Winfrey gave away Pontiacs to her audience, turning her show into one great commercial.

The more subtle form of product placement attempts to ingrate the advertisement silently. Almost everyone can recall ET's love of Reeses Pieces in Steven Spielberg's film *ET* (1981). More subtle still is the appearance of a seemingly everyday object in the narrative. The hero will drive a car, but the choice of car is not accidental. Chrysler cars figured prominently in a Harrison Ford movie, *Firewall* (Richard Craine, 2006), and in a hand-in-glove arrangement, Chrysler television commercials and its website advertised the movie.

With the technologies of digital insertion, the product no longer needs to be present at the time of production, allowing for greater flexibility as well as geographical specificity. On televised sports events, advertisers can digitally insert billboards around the playing field, permitting local and national advertisers to display their products. On sitcoms, a product can be virtually placed on the set, a fine opportunity for advertisers to reap the benefits of syndication. If a sitcom runs for a number of years, and the old shows are sold off, or syndicated, to local television channels, virtual product placement allows new advertisers to place images of their products – a box of cookies, for example – to take advantage of the context of the new market.

As an example of product placement, I want to point to a film called *The Weather Man* (Gore Verbinski, 2005). Nicholas Cage plays the title character, David Spritz, in what is surprisingly (for Hollywood) a gentle film, at once both serious and funny, about a man who barely succeeds in life and feels – like the junk food people on the street throw at him – disposable. Junk food is a theme and a sponsor. McDonald's, KFC, and Wendy's all get equal time, whether in the dialogue or in the way the shots themselves are composed in order to include references to various fast food restaurants. The film contains less obvious product placement as well. David Spritz drives a Volvo, and indeed the Ford Motor Company (who owns Volvo) advertised the fact on its website, tying their advertising in with the film. Product placement, in this film, becomes theme and parody, part of the narrative, a cultural reference, and as integrated into the cinematic world of the character as corporate images are in the world that constitutes our daily lives. (See figures 3.24 and 3.25.)

The consumer inside the culture of advertising

No form of entertainment is immune. Just look at a Nascar race, a big, loud canvas of advertising that covers every car, every driver. And that, I think, is the point. After all, why should entertainment be only an escape? Advertisers think it shouldn't be. The producers of film and television think it shouldn't be. They do not want us to escape

Figure 3.24 Product placement in the movie *The Weather Man* (dir. Gore Verbinski, 2005). *The Weather Man* ©Paramount, 2005.

Figure 3.25 This is not a commercial break, but a scene in the former CBS comedy, *King of Queens*. The product placement is so extreme and obvious that it becomes a joke for those who know what's going on. *The King of Queens* © Sony Pictures Television and CBS Productions.

the provocation of ads and their potential to make us buy a product, along with their ability to place us into the story of desire and fulfillment. But how do we square this all but universal commercial environment with the idea that we, as media consumers, are free to decode, unpack, and read advertising according to our needs? Advertisers always seem to be one step ahead of our needs. Their work is sensitive to the culture, to subcultures, to race and class. The Dove campaign mentioned earlier consciously embraces difference, attempting to appeal to all women who know that their image is not reflected back to them from the faces and figures of models in cosmetic ads.

Glaxo Smith Kline, the pharmaceutical company, exploited Black History Month by running a self-promoting ad in which an African-American, supposedly a research scientist for the company, spoke about how difficult it was finding new drugs. (The decoded message being "that's why we charge so much.") The fact is, the turmoil over race and gender has become fodder for ad companies, who have played up the role of women, and have used people of color in order to make their advertisements appeal to a wider audience – or a narrower one. Advertisers will target specific races, even specific gender orientations, in order to get their message across.

Advertisers strive to stay just ahead of the culture and its subcultures, but when they fall behind, they throw the full force of imagination and technological prowess into the work of catching up, as in the case of Internet advertising, where they now track our every mouse click. Their space ads and commercials are often the origination of visual ideas that turn up later in movies, and the narrative and technological advances in film-making influence advertising in their turn. Advertisers will use everything in their arsenal to immerse us in their work and *prevent* us from decoding it in any other way than the way they intended, even if they move in odd directions. There is, for example, an increasing use of violence in commercials used to get our attention. A commercial for a cell-phone company has one person knock out another by throwing a phone at his head! In other commercials, people fall or crash their cars. Showing people getting hurt seems to be the latest way advertisers try to get our attention.

Unlike the rest of the media it supports and infiltrates, advertising allows a very limited amount of negotiation. We are perfectly free to do a few things when confronting advertising: we can enjoy a clever ad; we can laugh with it or at it; we can purchase whatever the advertisement is selling; we can ignore it, and if enough of us do, the ad will disappear and perhaps the product will too. But ads are increasingly difficult to ignore.

While businesses and corporations insist that advertising is meant to inform the public about new products, we learn little of value from ads. News informs; advertising persuades. Cinematic and televisual narratives provide emotion; they tell us stories about the way we live, or would like to live, or would hate to; music moves us. Advertising moves us only in the direction of purchase. But, as we have seen, the orchestration of the movement, the amount of creativity – however cynical – that goes into an advertising campaign is worthy of attention not only to keep us aware of the purpose of advertising, but also to understand the amount of cultural (as well as corporate) capital that is at stake.

Almost any advertisement you can think of works by incorporating an understanding and exploitation of cultural attitudes, practices, and beliefs. It expresses these through elements of design, and through dramatic or comic narratives that are artful if not artistic. Advertising is one of capitalism's essential narratives – part of its story and much of its defense. Inasmuch as we live in capitalism and are an element of its narrative – our lives as commodities – we need continually to decode advertising, understanding how it plays upon our fears, desires, sexuality, or self-esteem. We need to be aware of how advertising attempts to persuade us to see ourselves in the world in particular ways, and how advertising itself sees us in a world that it seems to envelope.

References

Advertising and Modernity

Super Bowl commercials
These can be found on YouTube.

Jackson Lears
The quotation comes from his book *Fables of Abundance: A Cultural History of Advertising in America* (New York: Basic Books, 1994), p. 139.

Overviews
William M. O'Barr's "What is Advertising?", and "A Brief History of Advertising in America," *Advertising & Society* 6/3 (2005), present a useful survey with many images: <http://muse.jhu.edu/journals/advertising_and_society_review/v006/6.3unit01.html>; and <http://muse.jhu.edu/journals/advertising_and_society_review/v006/6.3unit02.html>.
The best sites for the history of advertising are: Duke University's "Emergence of Advertising in America: 1850–1920": <http://scriptorium.lib.duke.edu/eaa/>; and Ad*Access: <http://scriptorium.lib.duke.edu/adaccess/>.
See also "The Museum of Public Relations": < http://www.prmuseum.com/>.
Information on ancient advertising is from Stanley J. Baran, *Introduction to Mass Communication*, 4th edn. (Boston: McGraw-Hill, 2006), p. 378.
For an excellent study of the contemporary state of advertising, see Ken Auletta, "The New Pitch: Do Ads Still Work?," *The New Yorker* (March 28, 2005); <http://www.newyorker.com/archive/2005/03/28/050328fa_fact>. See also Raymond Williams, "Advertising: The Magic System," in *Problems in Materialism and Culture* (London: Verso, 1980), pp. 170–95.

Commercial radio
The best source is Erik Barnouw, *A Tower in Babel: A History of Broadcasting*, vol.1 (New York: Oxford University Press, 1966).

Advertising and design
The concept of cinema of attractions is borrowed from Tom Gunning's "Cinema of Attractions: Early Film, Its Spectator and the Avant-Garde," in *Early Cinema: Space-Frame-Narrative*, ed. Thomas Elsaesser and Adam Barker (British Film Institute, 1989), pp. 56–62.

Art nouveau
Information on art nouveau comes from Laurie Schneider Adams, *Art across Time* (New York: McGraw-Hill, pp. 858–9. A good site for art nouveau images is: <http://www.arts-crafts.com/archive/archive.shtml>.

Art Deco

See Justin De Syllas, "Streamform," *Architectural Association Quarterly* 1/2 (April, 1969): 32–43.

Terry Smith's *Making the Modern: Industry, Art, and Design in America* (Chicago and London: University of Chicago Press, 1993) is an excellent study of how art and commerce influenced one another in the 1920s and 1930s. The quotation on streamlining is on p. 379. See also Patricia Johnston, *Real Fantasies: Edward Steichen's Advertising Photography* (Berkeley and Los Angeles: University of California Press, 1997).

"Excessive style"

See John Caldwell, *Televisuality: Style, Crisis, and Authority in American Television* (New Brunswick, NJ: Rutgers University Press, 1995).

Advertising as mirror

For a discussion of how one advertiser consciously set out to create a community of fashion, see Stephen M. Engel, "Marketing Everyday Life: The Postmodern Commodity Aesthetic of Abercrombie & Fitch," *Advertising & Society* Review 5 (2004): <http://muse.jhu.edu/journals/advertising_and_society_review/v005/5.3engel.html>.

"Ask Your Doctor if it's Right for You"

Medicine and the government

A brief online summary of regulation is at: <http://www.pbs.org/now/science/drugads.html>.

For further detail, see the Federal Drug Administration website: <http://www.fda.gov>. See also: <http://www.medicalconsumers.org/pages/HOWTOREADADRUGAD.html>.

You may have a disease and not know it

Shankar Vedantam and Marc Kaufman, "Doctors Influenced by Mention of Drug Ads: Offbeat Study Finds Familiar Brand Name Can Evoke Diagnosis," *Washington Post* (Wednesday, April 27, 2005); <http://www.washingtonpost.com/wp-dyn/content/article/2005/04/26/AR2005042601624.html>.

Side effects

The magazine ad for Crestor is found in *Time* (February 13, 2006).

See also the Kaiser Foundation report on drug advertising: <http://www.kff.org/rxdrugs/loader.cfm?url=/commonspot/security/getfile.cfm&PageID=14372>.

Can advertising kill?

The Vioxx scandal has been widely reported. Some of the most thorough information is on the NPR website: <http://www.npr.org>.

Alex Berenson, "Pfizer Boldly Advertising Celebrex Again," *The New York Times* (April, 28, 2006); <http://www.nytimes.com/2006/04/28/business/media/28cnd-celebrex.html>.

Rich Thomaselli, "Glaxo Drafts Employees to Polish Industry Image: New Strategy Makes Entire Sales Force a National PR Machine," *Advertising Age* (December 4, 2005); <http://

adage.com/article?article_id=48590&search_phrase=Glaxo+Drafts+Employees+tTo+Polish+Industry+Image%3A>.

Political Advertising

The standard work on the subject is Kathleen Jamieson's *Packaging the Presidency: A History and Criticism of Presidential Campaign Advertising*, 3rd edn (New York: Oxford University Press, 1996).

Cartooning the presidency
An enormous archive of television political ads is available at: <http://livingroomcandidate.movingimage.us/>.

The quotation from Rosser Reeves is from: <http://www.pbs.org/30secondcandidate/from_idea_to_ad/collection>. This site contains a wealth of information about political advertising.

Dot-com
An archive of old Internet sites is at: <http://www.archive.org>.

Online ads in context
For a history of product placement, see Jay Newell, Charles T. Salmon, and Susan Chang, "The Hidden History of Product Placement," *Journal of Broadcasting and Electronic Media* 50/4 (December, 2006): 575–94.

For the quotation from Claria, see: <http://www.adage.com/MarketingIntel/pdf/ClariaBehaviorialBasics.pdf>.

Product placement
Lorne Manly, "On Television, Brands Go From Props to Stars," *The New York Times* (October 2, 2005); <http://www.nytimes.com/2005/10/02/business/yourmoney/02place.html>.

Sharon Waxman, "Hollywood Unions Object to Product Placement on TV," *The New York Times* (November 14, 2005); <http://www.nytimes.com/2005/11/14/business/14guild.html>.

Sam Lubell, "Virtual Ads a New Reality on TV Shows," *International Herald Tribune* (January 10, 2006); <http://www.iht.com/articles/2006/01/01/ business/digital.php>.

CHAPTER FOUR

Music in Every Room:
Radio and Recorded Music

*Few inventions evoke such nostalgia, such deeply personal and vivid memories,
such a sense of loss and regret.*

Susan J. Douglas, *Listening In* (1999: 8)

Radio began as the medium of assimilation, drawing the culture together, addressing its diversity. Today, it constitutes our cultural and emotional memory, surviving, despite being superseded by new media technologies. This chapter examines the history and culture of radio, weaving it with the history of recorded sound, for the two are closely linked, and emphasizing how closely radio and the music it delivers follow the history of race in American culture.

The Coming of Radio

On the air, in the home

In this book we have, so far, examined two very different genres of media, each of whose history goes hand in hand. Journalism and advertising came of age together in the nineteenth century. Both have their origins in a much more distant past, and each have different, though inseparable, functions – one to inform, and one to sell. While the aim of journalism is to inform us about the world, advertising informs us about how to spend our money. Advertising is cash centered: all of its modes and genres, and all of its creative work, are focused on getting our approval, stoking our desire in order to part us from our money. Journalism is supported by advertising – all media are, which is why we can think of advertising as the media's medium. Journalism's content is expressed in various media – on paper, on radio and television, online – and, like advertising, journalism has a number of subgenres: information about world events, entertainment, political commentary, and disasters. Journalism advertises itself as an objective, even transparent, medium, and we have examined how the very notion of "objectivity" is itself an ideology that needs decoding.

Radio has no such stated ideology, no rationalized set of conventions, but it too works through a kind of transparency. Like journalism, it is a medium through which other forms of expression, other genres, and journalism itself, can pass. But unlike journalism, which expresses itself through a variety of media, radio is one medium only. Whether we listen to over-the-air broadcasts on a box at home, or stream it through our computer, or listen to satellite radio in the car, or listen through earphones on the street, it is constituted, on the technological level, as a delivery medium. Radio is first and foremost a transmission technology and can be defined by the fact that it provides a channel for other media that can be *listened to*. But since these "other media" are, when carried by radio, always in the form of sound, and since sound itself, not to mention what it conveys, is not a neutral thing, radio needs to be examined not only as a technology, but also as a cultural form with a defined history. Radio needs to be understood through the ways we listen and what we listen to – music especially.

We also need to understand *where* we listen to it. Movies were developed at about the same time as radio and recorded sound. Thomas Edison, who was one among many early developers of moving pictures, first began thinking about film as an accompaniment to his sound-recording devices. To see a movie one had to leave home. However, purchase a record or a radio set, place it in the home, and the sound is there, in the domestic space. The public sphere becomes enveloped within the private. The home is made the medium through which a world of sound passes.

Telegraphy and telephony

Historically, radio is part of the wave of late nineteenth-century technologies that reconfigured space by separating sound and image from their human source. Telegraphy, telephony, recorded sound, radio, television, and film were technologies of disembodiment, negating distance, removing the need for proximity between individuals, making direct contact possible, but without the actual presence of bodies. Each of these inventions introduced a kind of virtuality not only by distancing a source (someone on the phone or a musician in a studio) from an audience (a person on the other end of the line or a person listening to a recording on a player or the radio), but also by making the medium itself largely invisible. Each of these technologies functions by using technology to substitute imagination for presence. People on either end of the telephone are invisible to each other, but their voice and all they express are present. An image on a movie screen is only a play of light – there is literally nothing there – but complex emotions and intricate characterizations can be created nonetheless. A voice on the radio can be anywhere, or, if it is recorded, nowhere but on a disc or tape when transmitted. When we add music to the mix, we find that the process of broadcasting recorded music involves multiple mediations, from recording studio to disc (or, today, to digital file), from disc to broadcast, from broadcast to reception at home, in a car, or on the street.

Electronic reproduction   The virtuality of these media is important from another technological perspective, the refinement of analog reproduction that allowed for long-distance transmission. Print, the original format of journalism, is a direct, analog process. Type is molded into the form of letters, then set to create words, sentences, and pages, inked, pressed on paper, read and interpreted by the reader. The mechanics are now very sophisticated, and typesetting is done largely by computer. But the direct contact of type to paper, and the mechanical reproduction and distribution of the paper remains the same as it was hundreds of years ago. The recording of an old analog LP is an equally mechanical, analog process: the vibrations of sound waves are physically pressed into a plastic medium, and then translated back into sound waves by an amplifier, a loudspeaker, or a pair of earphones. Similarly for the pre-digital image-making processes of photography or motion pictures: light, reflected from a face or a landscape, will alter the composition of a chemical compound laid over a strip of celluloid. When the chemical is developed, the alterations show up as light and dark images that represent the original subject. The sound and image technologies of the nineteenth century were all analog, but also were aiming at a wider disbursement. They depended upon the barely tangible physics of sound and the electromagnetic spectrum. Instead of pressing sound onto a plastic material, telephone transmission could be broadcast, along phone lines, or, in the case of radio, over the air to be delivered on a receiver. The physical intermediary is thereby removed.

These transformations permitted the separation from the point of origination to the point of reception that allowed the new technologies to evolve into mass media. This separation was physical – telephony removed the need for proximity in the act of communication from one person to another – and imaginative, as film allowed the development of a new form of visual storytelling that worked by eliding time and space before a viewer's eyes. As an aural medium, radio worked not by creating images directly, but by suggesting them, using sound to provoke thought and emotion, transferring the act of image-making to the imagination of the individual listener, making radio a portable medium in many senses of the term. Its only physical tether is the source of sound.

Radio is an open-ended experience. The news, political commentary, comedy, drama, and music that it carries have to be completed by the listener at the place of reception. Radio and visual media are different from print in that they do not allow for real-time rumination. Reading a newspaper can be a leisurely activity; the paper can be picked up and put down; items can be skipped. Listening to radio is a job of quick interpretation, fast decoding, and rapid image-making. At the same time, radio can act as a kind of aural wallpaper, providing a background, existing *there* as part of our environment, a soundtrack for our daily life. As an object requiring attention, or as a soundtrack, the qualities of listening made it, from the start, an indispensable part of the experience of modernity.

Early inventors   Radio began as a technology in search of a purpose, emerging from the minds and hands of engineers, inventors, and amateurs, who were working and playing with new ways of putting electricity to use to transmit sound. In the 1840s, Samuel F. B. Morse developed a code made up of simple electrical pulses of two lengths – referred to as dots and dashes – that could be transmitted over wire to convey information. It was put to wide use during the Civil War and continued in use by ships at sea until the end of the twentieth century, when satellite and broadband communications rendered it unnecessary. Morse code provided a language for specialists and a tool for inventors to further explore transmission of sound over the air.

In 1876, Alexander Graham Bell patented the broadcasting of voice and music over telegraph wires, leading the way for a number of inventors to begin solving the problems of radio frequencies, their amplification, and the ability to send them over long distances. In the process, they combined telephone and telegraph technologies, untethering them from lines and discovering the means to broadcast voice and music over the airwaves. The solution to wireless broadcasting depended on technologies of amplification and distribution. The vacuum tube, the physics and mathematics of electromagnetic frequencies all played a role. Various individuals, of various nationalities, tuned the process literally and figuratively – an Indian, Jagadish Chandra Bose; an Italian, Guglielmo Marconi (both worked on developing wireless telegraph); a Canadian, Reginald Fessenden (he transmitted voice and music at the turn of the twentieth century); the Austro-Hungarian Nikola Tesla (he perfected high frequency electronic transmission); and an American, Lee de Forest (who invented the vacuum tube, now almost obsolete, though still used in television sets and computer monitors that employ cathode ray displays).

War, sailboats, and hams

People in government, in business, and professional sports quickly saw the value of radio communication. Events during the Civil War were telegraphed; later in the nineteenth century the Americas Cup sailboat race was reported by Marconi's wireless; commercial shipping used wireless communications between ships at sea. Radio and telegraphy communications played an important role during World War I, and revolutionaries in Russia used radio for political ends in 1917. Outside of these specific uses, beyond (perhaps underneath) the growing understanding of how important radio transmission was to communicate information, there was the work of amateur engineers and hobbyists (predominantly young men) who worked to perfect the technology through the early 1920s.

Radio as a source of play remains to this day, even as the Internet takes over as the medium of one-to-one and one-to-many communication. As a relatively simple technology, with relatively inexpensive equipment, amateur radio – ham radio, as it's called – provides a peculiar kind of community, based upon some specialized knowledge. Ham radio operators have to know Morse code; it is still a requirement of the Federal Communications Commission in order to receive a license. They have to know the basics of radio technology. Beyond that, ham radio provides a global club-house and a local means of emergency communication – ham radio was very effective during Hurricane Katrina in 2005, when other forms of transmission failed. While it may no longer be the source of invention, its continued existence carries an originating mark of radio as a personal medium, one of active engagement and invention, a technology close to home. It has its analog today in software enthusiasts (again mostly male and mostly solitary) who create various kinds of shareware for computers and social networking sites.

Domesticating radio

Taking radio out of the hands of hobbyists and the military and putting it into the home took some time. At the end of World War I there was a very brief move, on the part of the navy, which had made much use of radio during the war, to continue its use as a government-run monopoly. Had this occurred, the US, like just about every other country in the world, might have had a government-run broadcasting system. The British Broadcasting Corporation (BBC), England's great state-run, but largely independent, broadcast organization, was created in 1922. An equivalent body did not come into being in the US. As we will see, the Federal Communications Commission was eventually set up to license broadcasting and manage the broadcast spectrum – the electromagnetic frequencies used to broadcast radio, television, mobile phone, and other over-the-air transmissions – but the only directly government-run broadcasting operations in the US were the overseas propaganda stations, like the Voice of America, that were developed during World War II.

The start of commercial radio   Instead of the government overseeing the development of radio, the gradual development of small, independent stations began before World War I. After the war, large corporations – American Telephone and Telegraph (ATT), the Radio Corporation of America (RCA), General Electric, Westinghouse – began aggregating power, positioning themselves to own as much of the airwaves, and, equally important, as much as possible of the equipment that transmitted over the airwaves and received those transmissions. In 1920, events converged in a way that initiated commercial radio and immediately defined some of its basic functions – broadcasting news and selling things.

The Westinghouse Corporation began the manufacture of radio receivers, but needed content as a means to sell them. At the time, a trained amateur operator, Frank Conrad, who worked for Westinghouse, was experimenting with radio in Pittsburgh, Pennsylvania. On election day, 1920, with the backing of Westinghouse and a license from the US Department of Commerce, he set up the first commercial radio station, KDKA, which proceeded to broadcast election results to its listeners. Two years later, at WEAF, a station in New York, a sponsor paid $50.00 to have commercial announcements made, selling apartment co-ops in Queens. The design of the medium was set: information for sale. What remained was further consolidation, the development of radio networks, the working out of a relationship between broadcasters and the government, and the creation of content and an audience.

FCC, RCA, CBS, ABC Radio developed with minimal assistance from the US government. Yet, despite being privately held and commercially driven, radio (and other telecommunications) are public, in the sense that their transmissions go out over the airwaves into people's homes. The "airwaves" themselves – actually that portion of the electromagnetic spectrum that carries radio and other communications – need overseeing. The spectrum is limited, and in any locality only one frequency can be used by a given broadcaster. It was and is unlikely that the growing number of competitors for this real estate would amicably or selflessly divide it amongst themselves. Although the Radio Act of 1912 had been an early governmental attempt to address these issues, it soon became clear that more supervision was needed. In 1927, the government established the Federal Radio Communications Commission (FRC) to oversee the public side of telecommunications; it was superseded in 1934 by the Federal Communications Commission (FCC), which still exists today. Its job is to license broadcasters, set technical standards, and manage the spectrum. Its history has been largely that of a politically driven body, working in the service of broadcasters and other interests rather than the public good. It is responsible for the current state of telecommunications in which a relatively few media companies own many radio and television stations.

The government could barely keep up with broadcasting's rapid growth. By the late 1920s, two of the large broadcasting companies, the National Broadcasting Company (a subsidiary of RCA) and the Columbia Broadcasting Company (CBS), were formed and dominated the airwaves. Major figures who would fashion broadcasting's future came to power. David Sarnoff, an immigrant from Belarus, who worked for American Marconi Telegraph Company, and who rose to prominence when he telegraphed news of the sinking *Titanic* in 1912, went on to be the powerful director of RCA for many years. With the assistance of General Electric and Westinghouse, he helped develop a business that manufactured both the hardware for broadcasting and the content and programming to feed it. William S. Paley, son of a Russian immigrant cigar salesman, used funds from his father's business to purchase CBS and develop it into one of the dominant broadcasting networks of the twentieth century. Paley would be responsible for bringing Edward R. Murrow to radio and fashioning the standard for broadcast news. Both men worked hard at creating a dominant, commercial medium.

The third network, the American Broadcasting Company, came into existence much later. It resulted from action taken by the FCC in its attempt to break up the growing monopoly of RCA. NBC was first split into two networks, NBC Red and Blue. The "Red" network was largely commercial, devoted to music and entertainment. The "Blue" network made some attempt at educational broadcasting. In 1943 it was sold to Edward Noble, owner of Life Savers candy and the Rexall drugstore chain, and became the basis of ABC. The domination of the networks, first in radio, then in television, was set and it continues – despite changes in ownership and inroads by cable, broadband Internet, and Tivo – until this day.

Recorded Music

Early recording technology

A listener to radio in the 1920s would have heard a far richer variety of programming than that available today: comedy, drama, horror and mystery, romance, quiz and variety shows, a lecture, and a great deal of music. Music was a foundation for all commercial radio programming and has now become identified with it. Early radio, however, preferred live to recorded music, partly because of the prestige of having musicians performing in the studio and because of various regulations that discouraged the playing of recordings.

Even though most of the music on early radio was live, it is important to note the technological affinity between radio and recorded sound. Thomas Edison's technicians developed sound recording along with their work on motion picture photography and projection. The two technologies were severed from one another – one reason offered is that the inventors could not create sufficient amplification to enable the sound, recorded on wax cylinders, to be played along with the projected images – and each went their own way until the late 1920s.

The recording and distribution of music developed quickly and independently of either film or radio, despite a very limited technology. In its earliest, pre-electric phase, the music source, a singer or an entire orchestra, would be placed in front of a horn that would funnel the sound vibrations to a needle that vibrated in response to the sound, leaving an impression of the vibration on a wax cylinder or disc. Playback would reverse the process. The result, even when sound recording became electrified, using similar amplification techniques to those of radio, was a very limited frequency range. The limitations of frequency reproduction were extreme. Despite this, radio became a mediator for music and a means of selling it: performers and songs heard on the radio could be purchased on records.

Early recorded music and race

Fidelity of sound was not an issue in the early period of radio and recorded music, and did not become one until after World War II when "high fidelity" recording and the FM radio band made quality reproduction of music a possibility. Accessibility was. The early popularity of the novelty of recorded music was every bit as expressive of a desire for entertainment in the home as was radio. The joining of the two was inevitable. Early recorded music drew from many places: from vaudeville, the variety show format that thrived on the stage from the nineteenth through the middle of the twentieth centuries; from popular song; from classical music and opera in particular. There was also an especially important influence of African-American music that manifested itself in a number of styles, informing and finally transforming music in records and on the air.

Blacking up   "Blacking up," the tradition of a performer smearing his face with burnt cork, was done across the board: white singers imitated African-Americans, and black singers too would put on a "black" face and mock themselves, as if looking in a double mirror. The origin of blacking up lay in the minstrel shows put on by white performers that originally made fun of slaves. But the masquerade evolved into vaudeville, and reached its peak in the performances of the entertainers Eddie Cantor and Al Jolson, the latter bringing his blackface act across media as sound reunited with film in the 1927 film *The Jazz Singer*. Blackface was a racist tradition, born of mockery and perhaps masking a sense of guilt. When it was put on by African-American performers, largely out of a need to appeal to a white audience, it may have been done as a form of mockery, not merely of themselves, but of the white performers who were mocking them. It was all a complex move of exploitation, assimilation, and role-playing, phenomena that would mark the history of radio and recording in direct and symbolic ways.

African-American musicals were performed by white vaudeville artists; this music was enormously popular and eventually found its way to records and radio. No less popular, though repellent by today's standards, was "coon music," sung by white singers doing grotesque parodies of African-Americans, and by African-American singers doing grotesque parodies of themselves in songs like "Der'll be wahm coons a prancing" or "My Darktown Gal," along with even more appalling titles. As just one example, the African-American vaudeville star Bert Williams teamed up with another African-American comic, George Walker, to put on blackface and bill themselves as "Two Real Coons." To us, this is an abhorrent expression of inverse racism, and seems especially strange when absorbed by the very culture it is aimed to make fun of. At the time, when racism was even more deeply ingrained in the majority culture, such an act was understood, if not accepted, as a rather brutal matter of course, and in many ways it was necessary for African-American performers to adopt and accommodate in order to thrive from their work. Accommodation is not easy to understand and less easy to accomplish until we understand an entertainment regime where one's livelihood is weighed in the balance of self-deprecation.

Perhaps when viewed from the perspective of "foundation," the history of black music and its performers can be better understood. The musical expression of African-Americans after the Civil War and through the 1920s, even when distorted by white performers, can be seen as laying the ground and providing the lifeblood of twentieth-century forms from jazz to rock to rap. The blues and ragtime, early forms of jazz created by black musicians, became popular in white culture, which despite prejudice, or in the face of it, took full advantage of it. As an example, the extremely successful Jewish composer Irving Berlin was writing ragtime songs by the 1920s. Black musicians continued their invention, even as white musicians softened it, making it more "palatable" for white audiences. The forms evolved into the great varieties of swing, modern jazz, and rock 'n' roll; and even into the music of "high" culture, as when George Gershwin's *Rhapsody in Blue* and *Porgy and Bess* moved jazz-based music into the concert and opera halls. We can trace this pattern repeatedly as one African-American musical style after another developed over the course of the twentieth century.

The successes and failures of black performers in white America are as curious as they are varied. An African-American concert singer, Matilda Sissieretta Joyner, underscores this point. Joyner went under the stage name of "the Black Patti" (after the then famous operatic soprano, Adelina Patti) and fought against strong racist pressures to forge a career in opera and popular music. Her popularity and name recognition was such that an African-American A&R man (A&R stands for Artists and Repertoire, the person responsible for choosing and recording performers), J. Mayo "Ink" Williams, named a record label after her in the late 1920s. Despite the fact that it was a short-lived venture, it was an indication of the growing presence of African-Americans in the music business; one that would grow until it entered the mainstream many decades later, even though it meant that African-Americans could be further stereotyped as talented entertainers.

This small example of the formation of a record label based on the work of a well-known singer emphasizes the close relationship between performance, recording, and broadcasting in the early 1920s. As recorded music became more and more the norm on radio from the 1940s on, this relationship grew more intense. Record sales, the "charts" of hits published by *Billboard* and *Variety* magazines; royalties; kick-backs; payments made by record companies to get their tunes played on the air (known as "payola"), all made radio and recorded sound inseparable and symbiotic. And as so often happens in media culture, economics assisted art. The tight integration of recording and radio assisted the assimilation of African-American music into the mainstream.

Jazz and moral outrage   The processes of exposure made it possible for African-American music to reach audiences wider than the musicians might have found on their own, and it provided a means for minorities and their work to enter the world of popular culture, including radio. But it did not come easily. As more people, and especially youngsters, began listening to jazz, and as jazz became more popular on records and on the air, conservative voices were raising alarms.

In 1921, the music chairwoman of the General Federation of Women's Clubs wrote: "Jazz disorganizes all regular laws and order; it stimulates to extreme deed, to a breaking away from all rules and conventions, and its influence is wholly bad." In the same year an educator wrote: "We have seen the effect of jazz music on our young pupils. It makes them act in a restless and rowdy manner" (quoted by Hilmes, 1997: 47–8). Change the language slightly, bring it up to date, and we hear it again in the fearful comments made about rock 'n' roll in the 1950s, rap in the 1990s; or, in a different medium entirely, computer games and social networking sites in the 2000s.

The language of fear of the unknown and the different is always mixed with the desire to control, and both are an inseparable part of the discourse of mass-mediated art.

In the case of music, racism may be the dominant note, but it contributes to a general fear that young people will be sent into some kind of lawless, uncontrollable state by being exposed to music – a fear that continues to be heard throughout the history of media. The voices of outrage and control rarely, if ever, put an end to the music they fear, and the outcome is always some kind of assimilation. Like minstrel songs and ragtime before it, jazz evolved and became a dominant musical form, especially from the 1930s throughout the 1950s, played by white and African-American musicians. As they would throughout the history of modern popular music, African-Americans provided the imagination and creativity that kept it vital. The music could not be controlled, no more than its audience could be, despite attempts to blame and contain it.

Racism and Assimilation

Amos 'n' Andy

Music was not the only form of entertainment in which African-Americans became the foils, the bad conscience, the source of ridicule, and inspiration. Blackface was performed in one of the most popular, most controversial radio (and, briefly, television) programs in the medium's history. Amos and Andy were African-American characters, naive, foolish, always getting into trouble, always speaking in a ridiculous parody of black dialect, and never quite understanding their place in the urban world. Amos and Andy were played by Charles Correll and Freeman Gosden, white performers, putting on an exaggerated white man's idea of black dialect – black voice, if you will – developing what would become, from its start in the mid-1920s, the longest-running radio show.

That *Amos 'n' Andy* played upon stereotypes is beyond argument. Here is an example of dialogue, quoted by Michele Hilmes, from a broadcast during the election year of 1928:

AMOS: I don't know either to be a Democrat or a Republican.
ANDY: Well, where wha' your ancestors?
AMOS: My aun' didn' have no sisters.
ANDY: No, no, your ancestor, your … never min'. … Listen, Coolidge is a Republican an' fo' de' las' fo' years or so he's done had Hoover locked up waitin' to put him in office.
AMOS: What you mean he done had Hoover locked up?
ANDY: Well, I was readin' in de paper right after Hoover was nomulated dat Coolidge was gettin' ready to take Hoover out of de cabinet.

(Quoted in Hilmes, 1997: 91)

Audience response to this kind of comedy was overwhelmingly positive and ambiguous at the same time. The popularity of the program – so popular that Gosden and Correll took it on the road, performing live in blackface – speaks to the desire to ridicule and laugh at minorities. But, at the same time, racism, even overt racism, can be cloaked in a certain geniality. There was nothing especially malicious about *Amos 'n' Andy*. The program certainly did not represent African-Americans as threatening characters in the ways that film and television have sometimes portrayed them. Just the opposite; they were depicted as foolish. But, at the same time, their unthreatening, bumbling manner was an element that made them attractive. The characters were harmless, so it was harmless to laugh at and with them. This is not an excuse for the program, but an attempt to understand its enormous popularity, and a way to understand that popularity in and of itself is not merely a cause for blanket condemnation.

The history of *Amos 'n' Andy* parallels that of African-American music – a mixture of entertainment, imagination, racism, and assimilation. As we discussed earlier, the blackface minstrel show tradition had been a popular form of entertainment since post-Civil War days. In *Amos 'n' Andy*, as in minstrel shows, white performers mediated the culture's low opinion of African-Americans by ridiculing them; black performers ridiculed themselves and the white audience by exaggerating the exaggeration. Blackface (or "black voice") was an act of mediation – an act of condescension, exaggeration, a process of distancing, of giving comfort to the feeling of majority superiority – and a way of addressing racial fear and ridicule. At the same time, blackface and minstrelsy addressed a peculiar level of comfort across the racial spectrum, which may account for the diversity of opinion within the African-American community itself regarding *Amos 'n' Andy*. Many members of that community were entertained, despite the ongoing and, until the 1950s, unsuccessful struggle of the NAACP to have it taken off the air. (See figure 4.1.)

The fact that people were entertained by *Amos 'n' Andy* does not excuse the show's content, though it does go a small way in allowing us to understand how large-audience media work. Racism is a form of comfort: it allows a culture to feel comfortable with its sense of superiority. But security is also a comfort. Minority audience members may feel comfortable enough to accept stereotypes for what they are, and may even be amused by the portrayal of characters lower in the socioeconomic scale than they are. *Amos 'n' Andy* told a story about the movement of African-Americans up from the South, attempting, comically, to assimilate themselves into Northern, urban culture. Despite the racial stereotyping, the story was told with humor, and with some warmth. The title characters run a taxicab business. Another character, Kingfish, leader of the community lodge, "The Mystic Knights of the Sea," is always scheming to get rich. They were all, in turn, foolish and hopeful, even while talking in idiotic dialect.

As I said, the NAACP argued to have *Amos 'n' Andy* removed from the air from its very beginning. It did not meet with success until the early 1950s, when the show crossed over to television and the characters were, of necessity, played by African-American actors (see figure 5.6). Black comic characters played by black actors put a new cast on the program. This was perhaps no less racist, but less confrontational, in the sense that it did not attempt to mock African-Americans by having them played by Caucasians. But for some in the African-American community, the show may have been a means to judge their own distance from the stereotypes and to understand race

Figure 4.1 This publicity photo adequately expresses the illusion of the popular Amos 'n' Andy radio show. Freeman Gosden and Charles Correll are reflected back from their blackface personae, Amos 'n' Andy. Correll Family Collection.

and class. Margo Jefferson, writing in *The New York Times* in 1994 about the television version of *Amos 'n' Andy*, recalls:

> One day at school I was chatting with a classmate, and we started recounting the last episode of "Amos 'n' Andy." Nothing seemed more natural than that he would slip into a rendition of one of Kingfish's famous exclamations. It may have been "I'se regusted!" or "Holy mackerel!" (basso voice quavering, eyes turned heavenward); perhaps he stroked his chin and intoned, "Well, now, Sapphire .... " In any case, as soon as the words came out of his mouth, I stopped enjoying myself. I smiled weakly and hurried the conversation on. But because he was white and I was black, all sorts of other things had suddenly attached themselves to Amos, Andy, Lightning and Kingfish: charged talk about "equality" and "prejudice," about what holds "us" back and how "they" like to think we behave.
>
> I tell the story because it told me something about comedy in a nation that is not a melting pot or a mosaic but one big ethnic variety show stuffed full of mixed dialects, mixed manners, and mixed motives.... Comedy is about our needs, our place in the world, and how we cooperate or collide with people just as obsessed with their own needs and place.

"One big ethnic variety show ...." Without dismissing its racism, it still is possible to imagine *Amos 'n' Andy* as part of the great process of negotiation, separation, and assimilation in American culture, a process in which radio played so important a part from the 1920s through the 1940s. *Amos 'n' Andy* was not the only dialect show on the air nor was it the only one that spoke to attempts at assimilation. At about the same time that *Amos 'n' Andy* rose to popularity, *The Rise of the Goldbergs*, a comedy about a Jewish family in New York, appeared and itself had a long run, eventually, like *Amos 'n' Andy*, winding up on television. *The Life of Riley* presented comedy about Irish-Americans, and in the late 1940s *Life With Luigi* addressed Italian-Americans. It, too, came under attack for stereotyping. These shows were *used* by their audience – or, more correctly, audiences – independently of the ethnic groups they pretended to represent, and at the same time they were used by the producers of media to establish a pattern: a set number of characters, each one of whom had identifiable and repeated traits in the way he or she talked and reacted to situations, which themselves were repeated with small variations in show after show. In *Amos 'n' Andy*, Kingfish would always dependably attempt a get-rich-quick scheme, and fail; in *The Goldbergs*, Molly, the family matriarch, would always supply a voice of homespun reason. The format eventually became the TV genre known as situation comedy.

The importance of these shows lies as much in the form of their transmission and reception as it does in their racial stereotyping or their attempts at ethnic integration. The overriding point is that radio infiltrated the homes and the lives of a majority of Americans, confirming their prejudices or affirming the uniqueness of their own race and class, separating, leveling, and assimilating simultaneously. Radio offered permission and means for the imagination to move outward. Like the African-American music that influenced and was absorbed by popular musical forms throughout the 1930s through the present moment, radio and its ethnic programs infiltrated the culture, expanding consciousness even as the culture as a whole contracted and became more homogeneous, and poor. Radio grew to maturity at a time when the American economy was contracting into the Great Depression that began in the late 1920s and its popularity lasted throughout World War II and through the 1940s. Radio offered permission and means for the imagination to move outward even as realities of daily life pressed in. Radio played as important a role in cultural survival as it did in cultural integration.

Diversity and negotiation

Ethnic and racial comedy represented only a part of the programming in radio's first decades. There was much high-mindedness on the part of early broadcasters, and classical music, serious drama, even lectures, constituted a great deal of what was on the air. When NBC – a network created to supply programming for the radios sold by its parent, RCA – debuted in 1926, its first programs included symphonic music, opera, popular songs, and comedy. An installment of *Amos 'n' Andy* might have a classical musician as a guest. The first decade of radio might promote stereotypes; but, as a medium, it was hard itself to be stereotyped.

The diversity of early radio programming came partly out of a democratic spirit, the desire to offer as much to as many people as possible, and to cover the spectrum of taste with the maximum of choice. It also came from a desire to cover and garner as large an audience as possible. All media exist within a dialectic of abundance and narrowness of programming, an attempt to balance a great deal of choice while aiming at specific or wide audiences. This is part of the process of negotiation we have discussed, in which programmers offer and audiences choose what they will (in the case of radio) listen to.

The process of negotiation, which is contained within the encoding/decoding model we have been following, is central to media studies. We see it operating in the broad appeal of *Amos 'n' Andy*: the media consumer does not accept or decode everything she sees and hears according to the way the media producer wants her to. Broadly speaking, a listener (or a viewer, or someone surfing the Web) *negotiates*, according to her taste, her class or race, her education – the totality of her personal and cultural context – what she will make of a mass-mediated event.

Let's look again at Margo Jefferson's comments about her response to the television version of *Amos 'n' Andy*:

> Comedy is such a mixture of empathy and superiority, identification and alienation. Belonging to the type of the educated Negro, I found Lightning [a character on *Amos 'n' Andy*] provocatively unlike me (which let me laugh at him) and yet oddly like me (which let me laugh with him). For one thing, we were both cross-eyed. For another thing, which had precious little to do with race, I was a child, and his was the comedy of regression: broad, slow gestures; grimaces and double takes; sounds that broke language into vowels, syllables and tones. Besides, what child undergoing socialization doesn't know exactly what it feels like to get caught, literally or metaphorically, in a garbage can and to try desperately to get out before the adults find you? Oh, me .... (Jefferson, *The New York Times*, 1994)

Jefferson analyzes the negotiating points she makes in regard to the show; she understands what works for her and what doesn't. She surprises herself – "Oh, me" – and is delighted to be surprised. She has negotiated her location within the complex contradictions of the show and her responses to it.

When we think of the early history and development of radio, "negotiation" becomes a broader concept, a complex interaction of the listener within an expanding media space in which a variety of sounds and voices, genres – comedies, serious and popular music, news, and regional programming – contended for attention. A listener living on the Midwestern plains not only got news about local farming conditions, but also heard voices and sounds from the city. Like the Sears catalogue before it, urban space, this time by means of sound, entered the rural. Throughout the country, sounds of regional and ethnic dialects were heard and, no matter whether genuine or not, sense had to be made of them. Members of an enormous, anonymous audience had to individualize themselves through the choices they made. The producers of those voices had then to recognize those choices and program accordingly.

Some early radio voices provided a point of negotiation that worked against assimilation and for exclusion. Radio was immediately attractive to the evangelical voice, enabling many preachers to reach a large audience. One of these, Father Charles

Coughlin, an early religious broadcaster, moved to the far, exclusionary right, playing upon the despair and resentment fostered by the deprivations of the Great Depression to voice anti-Semitic, anti-Communist, pro-Nazi sentiments. When his divisive voice was silenced by CBS, he responded by buying time on other stations. His popularity continued until the government, the National Association of Broadcasters, and the Catholic Church worked to silence him when the country entered World War II.

Coughlin's popularity, like that of recent right-wing radio voices (which we will examine later), indicates the health of the negotiation process. Some of the *results* of that process may not be healthy, but its dynamism, and ultimate self-correction, is. All in all, in its first decades, radio was too heterogeneous, too diverse to be taken over by a single voice. Radio was a force of modernity; it spoke to difference and offered itself as a point of cultural cohesion at the same time. Out of its fragments, the sheer variety of its offerings, colliding and mingling with the much greater variety of its listeners, a web of cultures was formed, still heterogeneous, never homogenized or of one voice, but connected, if only through the shared experience of listening to the imaginary worlds of sound.

War of the worlds

Modernity is always about fragments, cohering or ricocheting; it involves subjectivity, the ways in which we understand our identity. It is about contingency – events occurring as if by chance, unexpected, even unwanted. Radio allows an expansion of identity through its aural spaces and cohesion through its simultaneity – many people listening at the same time. But cohesion is a fragile thing and can be broken. The aural imagination can take on a life of its own, nourished by voices and sounds that are themselves fragmented, evocative, playing into anxieties that are always a product of modernity.

On the night before Halloween, October 30, 1938, thousands of people fled their homes in fear of an invasion from Mars. The invasion was the creation of a radio narrative based on H. G. Wells's novel *War of the Worlds*, created and performed by Orson Welles, one of the most imaginative artists of the twentieth century. (Welles is best known for his 1941 film, *Citizen Kane*; in the thirties he was active in New York theater and radio and, after *Kane*, continued to be an important and influential figure in film and other media.) The phenomenon of *War of the Worlds* was the result of a number of events coming together serendipitously and, ultimately, comically. The program was part of a series of radio adaptations of literary works performed by Welles and his Mercury Theater Company on the CBS network. In this instance, Welles did more than simply adapt, he turned radio itself, and its ability to broadcast news bulletins, into the very form of the dramatization. Rather than doing a straightforward, dramatic reading from a script, Welles fragmented the performance, creating the illusion of a musical program that was being interrupted by "breaking news."

The news bulletin was a standard feature of network broadcasting and was carried over to television; it continued to exist into the 1970s. Breaking the continuity of regular programming, it would grip the listener with an adrenaline rush of startling information. (Audiences dislike having programming interrupted, which is why the news bulletin largely disappeared from both radio and television in the 1970s.) News bulletins in the late 1930s would have been especially troubling, because there was military conflict in Europe that, within a few years, would erupt into World War II. Welles's imitation of interrupted programming sounded like the real thing – unless, of course, the listener had tuned in to the beginning of the program where the usual announcements and introductions took place. But not everyone was listening at the beginning. Opposite the Mercury Theater broadcast was the most popular program of the time, a ventriloquist act turned into a radio series, Edgar Bergen and his dummy, Charlie McCarthy. Many listeners may have been switching back and forth between the two shows, and, in the process, getting caught short by the imitation news-bulletin format of the first part of Welles's broadcast.

As Welles delivered one "bulletin" after another, conveying the idea that a space-ship from Mars had landed in New Jersey, war anxiety, station surfing, and his radio show imitating radio all converged to cause panic – people actually took to the streets, attempting to flee the invasion. Was this a result of naivety or gullibility, or was it partly the response to a relatively new medium? Media audiences are rarely as naive as media critics give them credit for being and, by 1938, radio was all but universal in people's homes and hardly a novelty. I think *War of the Worlds* was an example of assimilation working in reverse. Various media and various times have spurred various kinds of action, though perhaps none has gotten people out of their houses in panic. In this case, listeners, so assimilated into the rhythms of broadcasting – its generic patterns of sound, narrative, news, and entertainment – were at the same time anxious about the world situation. Something in the negotiation process slipped; imagination became tinged with panic; people believed in what they *thought* they heard; and what they knew was going on in the world at the time. They got scared. So did Welles, who had no idea, until near the end of his broadcast, that he had created something close to a nationwide panic.

Ventriloquism of the imagination

We need to pause for a moment to consider the fact that, at the time of Welles's broadcast, many people were tuned into a ventriloquist act: Edgar Bergen and Charlie McCarthy. Listening to a ventriloquist on the radio? Radio scholar Michele Hilmes points out an interesting paradox that is at play when we think about radio. It involves the interplay of visual stimuli and imagination. *Watching* a ventriloquist depends upon willfully imagining that a voice is thrown into a wooden doll. One is aware of the illusion even while entertaining it and being entertained by it. *Listening* to a ventriloquist requires the double imagining of hearing the illusion of a voice being thrown. The same kind of imagination was involved in listening to *Amos 'n' Andy*, which depended upon an audience hearing "blackness" in the voices "thrown" by two white performers. *War of the Worlds* was an unintended act of ventriloquism, using the fragments of radio voices to throw a scare, believable enough to put people on the road.

We might expand this concept to encompass the entire universe of radio and recorded sound, which deliver disembodied voices to an invisible audience, who in turn re-imagine what or who may embody the voices and sounds. While I don't think that this accounts for the assimilation processes we have discussed, it did permit the listener a wide latitude of interpretation and an ability to become comfortable (or, in the case of *War of the Worlds*, uncomfortable) with the otherwise disembodied sounds emanating from the radio.

Radio in World War II and the Age of Television

Radio in wartime

By the 1940s, radio was all but universal. It was a round-the-clock companion, and its audience was fully measured and gendered, with shows aimed at young, old, male, and female. Daytime programming appealed to homemakers with soap operas, those open-ended melodramas about romance and sacrifice, their stories moving slowly across weeks, months, and years. The soaps were constructed to appeal to women working in the home. Male audiences were served by broadcasts of sports, where the ability to describe a baseball game became so well articulated, so able to communicate visual experience, that sportscasters could re-create a game in the studio with only the recorded roar of the crowd and sound of a bat hitting a ball needed to simulate a virtual event. In the evening hours, dramas, comedy, and concerts of popular and classical music were the rule. Radio and the movie business were closely intermingled. Movie stars appeared on radio variety shows and it was a matter of course that a movie would be adapted as a radio drama – the visual absorbed into the aural: movies for the ear.

World War II initialized many changes, most especially in journalism. In chapter 2, we discussed a particular radio newsman, Edward R. Murrow, whose reports from London communicated a war to a nation still uncertain about its role. Murrow was one of many newscasters, who, when the US did enter the war, provided information and commentary. During the war, President Franklin Delano Roosevelt used radio to disseminate patriotic propaganda, rallying the country, using the communal power of the medium to create not so much assimilation as cohesion, to make the audience of one mind about the war and the country's part in it.

This was also the time of American radio's expansion abroad. Armed Forces Radio was set up specifically to entertain and inform US troops stationed overseas. The Voice of America was created by the Office of War Information, a propaganda unit of the government, broadcasting over short-wave, largely inaccessible to American audiences. The VOA provided optimistic programming in a variety of languages about America's role in the war. Later, along with its CIA-funded sister stations, Radio Free Europe and Radio Liberty, VOA reached the peak of its influence during the Cold War, attempting to infiltrate Soviet states with programs in praise of American democracy.

It continues to function as the closest thing to a government broadcasting service, with television outlets and a website. It bears the stamp of the political party in power.

Post-war changes in radio and recorded sound

In order to understand the changes radio went through after World War II, we need to think about new technologies of sound and its transmission, as well as shifting media economies. The rise of television ended radio's media ownership of the domestic sphere. A number of radio stars – mostly comedians – took their programs over to television, for a while often playing both media at the same time. The networks shifted their focus, their time, and money on the new medium. Network control of radio gave way, gradually, to the local stations that were now becoming more independent.

The movement of audiences from radio to television was part of a broader change in post-war culture, in which audiences were growing younger, tastes were shifting dramatically, and music, especially, was reflecting it all. Music is among the most potent forces in shaping and expressing a culture, and, as both changed, radio changed.

Sound technologies

Technologies of sound recording and reproduction in the post-World War II period had an important influence on the changes taking place in broadcasting and listening habits. Before the war, music was available in only a few sonically constrained forms: radio was broadcast over the AM band, which has a restricted frequency range, full of static, and very dependent on the proximity of the receiver to the radio station. There were stations that broadcast only during the day while others – "clear channel" stations – could, on a clear night, be heard hundreds, sometimes thousands, of miles away. Listeners were limited by which stations they could receive, and by the repertoire those stations chose to play. Recordings, in contrast, allowed the listener free choice of what to listen to and when, but they had other drawbacks: they were made on hard rubber discs turning at 78 revolutions per minute, their sound quality was limited, and they were subject to snaps and crackles resulting from marks on their fragile surface.

Various technologies opened the sonic space. Tape recording, developed during the war, allowed for greater flexibility and increased frequency range during the recording process. Recording in stereo opened up the musical space, giving depth and clarity to the sound. The ability to press records at playback lower speeds, 45 and 33⅓ rpm, made the increased clarity and range available on playback. As always, good technology led to changes in concept and imagination. Recordings at lower speeds allowed for more music to be made available on disc. A 33⅓ rpm long-playing record (LP) could hold almost an hour's worth of music. The first beneficiary of this was classical music: one album could now carry a complete symphony. But the longer form of the LP also provided popular music producers an opportunity to provide a suite of music from a singer or group and, eventually, the development of albums that presented a coherent musical theme. The work of The Beatles in the late 1960s (the themed album *Sergeant Pepper's Lonely Hearts Club Band*, for example) and The Who in the early 1970s (the rock opera *Tommy*) was an end product of the extended time available on the long-playing record.

Paralleling the improvements to recording technologies was the advent of frequency-modulated (FM) radio, which uses different frequencies and different methods for carrying sound on those frequencies. FM, which had existed since radio began, did not achieve prominence until after World War II, when the FCC began issuing new rules and licenses. FM has less of a geographical reach than AM, but a much broader frequency range within that reach. It is static-free and able to carry two channels of sound, making stereo broadcasting possible. In the 1950s, most amplitude-modulated (AM) stations simply broadcast the same programs on their FM band. By the 1960s, simulcasting was on the wane, and stereo broadcasting the norm. FM stations proliferated as separate broadcasting entities. Meanwhile, in the mid-1950s, transistors replaced vacuum tubes, making radios smaller and portable.

The result of all these changes was the growth of a culture of sound, with "high fidelity," or "hi-fi," becoming a catchphrase to sell new radios, phonograph players, and records just as "high definition," or "HDTV," is becoming the growing norm for new television technologies today. The aural spaces where radio and music took place changed as well. Radio became portable; the listening space could be moved from the home or the car to the streets themselves. Music became the constant companion. Technologies converged and with them popular music changed. The result of that change was a new culture of music, of listening, of response, and, finally, of radio itself.

African-American Influence and the Culture of Rock

The changes in the cultures of music, radio, and listening have, as they did in the earlier days of radio, much to do with race. To understand this, we need some historical and cultural background. The end of World War II ushered in a long period of economic expansion in the United States and an equally long period of political repression and cultural anxiety. America was victorious in the war, but the revelations of the genocide committed by the Nazis on European Jews, the use of the atom bomb to end the war in Asia, and the politically expedient anti-Communist crusade at home that began almost as soon as the war ended all conspired to create a general atmosphere of uncertainty and fear. Large demographic changes took place during and after the war. With so many men in the military, women entered the workforce in large numbers, achieved economic freedom, and then were urged to give it up and return to domestic life when the war ended. There was increased migration of African-Americans from the rural South to the urban North. Black soldiers had served with distinction in a segregated army during the war. By presidential order, that segregation was officially ended after the war, marking the first step in the long, painful process of the civil rights movement that continues to this day.

The strains and anxieties produced by these events were manifest in many places in American life, but were not always detrimental. War's end created new energies in the culture; young people asserted themselves, and their tastes influenced the popular arts. The influence of black culture continued and strengthened over the post-war years.

Norman Mailer's "The White Negro"

One stream of influence flowed from the post-war jazz scene. Bebop, also known as modern jazz, was developed by young African-American musicians Charlie Parker, Dizzy Gillespie, and Miles Davis, among many others from the mid-forties on. The form depended upon improvisations played within complex rhythmic patterns. It was a sophisticated style that demanded listening rather than dancing. The audience for bop and "modern jazz" was always relatively small, reaching its peak during the 1950s. Much more influential than the music itself was the culture of hipness and cool, an attitude of liberated sexuality and calm, an ironic understanding of one's uncertain place in the world, which was part of the aura of modern jazz and the African-American subculture that informed it. It reflected as well the anxieties of the post-war world and, as such, moved into larger intellectual subcultures of the 1950s. This culture of Black hipness detached itself from the music that helped spawn it, and spread into the youth cultures and *their* music that developed in the 1950s. An expression of this culture of hipness can be found in an influential essay of 1957, called "The White Negro," by the novelist Norman Mailer:

> A stench of fear has come out of every pore of American life, and we suffer from a collective failure of nerve. The only courage, with rare exceptions, that we have been witness to, has been the isolated courage of isolated people.
>
> It is on this bleak scene that a phenomenon has appeared: the American existentialist – the hipster, the man who knows that if our collective condition is to live with instant death by atomic war, relatively quick death by the State ..., or with a slow death by conformity with every creative and rebellious instinct stifled .... [I]f the fate of twentieth-century man is to live with death from adolescence to premature senescence, why then the only life-giving answer is to accept the terms of death, to live with death as immediate danger, to divorce oneself from society, to exist without roots, to set out on that uncharted journey with the rebellious imperatives of the self. ... The unstated essence of Hip, its psychopathic brilliance, quivers with the knowledge that new kinds of victories increase one's power for new kinds of perception. ... One is Hip or one is Square. ... (1992: 337–58)

I quote this at some length because it so clearly articulates the strain of rebellion that was burrowing under the constrained and contained culture of the 1950s, and because, like the writing of the Beat novelists and poets – Jack Kerouac and Allan Ginsberg, among others – it has the rhythm of the jazz that emerges from

African-American culture and whose spirit informs its ideas. It contains the kernel of rebellion that is so much a part of the new musical forms being developed. Mailer prophesies not only the youth rebellion of the 1960s, but also the music that came to accompany it.

Mainstream popular music

Hip and cool emerged from jazz, but jazz was not the musical form that would flourish among the teenage cool. Even during its peak in the 1950s, modern jazz, as a musical form, never reached a very large audience or moved far from its urban roots. It was played on some radio stations and in a few hip nightclubs, but existed – outside of nightclubs – on important new record labels like Verve, Blue Note, and Atlantic. Some of these labels would soon be carrying another strain of African-American music that would enter the popular mainstream and change it permanently.

After World War II, popular music was represented largely by white singers performing songs written by a stable of composers in what was popularly known as "Tin Pan Alley." Originally a district of New York City where the sound of songwriters pounding on pianos resembled the banging of pans, by the mid-twentieth century Tin Pan Alley was less a place then a state of musical mind. Its composers produced music broadly melodic, extremely romantic, and sung by the likes of Frank Sinatra, Patti Page, Tony Bennett, or Nat King Cole and Johnny Mathis (two major African-American performers in the mainstream of 1950s pop). It was ubiquitous. Movies, radio, television, and recordings carried a sound that was rich, smoothly rhythmic, but – with the exception of the influence of jazz and blues on a few performers – definitely "square" as opposed to "hip." This was the music that dominated the charts and was played across the radio dial. As more and more stations became all music, all the time, Tin Pan Alley pop was the music everyone listened to.

African-American radio and DJs in black voice

As always in media, economics are a primary agent of change, and the change to all-music format came about as radio station managers realized that playing records proved the least expensive means of providing content. Airing music involved submitted playlists and paying royalties, but these costs were modest compared to the financial investment that other radio formats required.

But equally important, and more interesting in the movement to all-music radio, is the influence of African-American music, and its medium, African-American radio. This has a long history. Jack L. Cooper, an African-American DJ, created *The All-Negro Hour* in Chicago in 1929. By 1937, Cooper was playing records on the air, becoming one of the first disc jockeys *and* the first African-American disc jockey. The blues singer B. B. King briefly had the role of DJ in Memphis in 1948. By the late 1940s, there were, across the country, some 200 radio stations aimed at African-American listeners. Another wave of assimilation was about to begin.

Alan Freed　African-American music received widespread distribution because of these stations. A bit later, another kind of transfer of African-American culture occurred when the hip patter of black disc jockeys began to be imitated by white DJs. In a peculiar repetition of the blackface/blacktalk of the *Amos 'n' Andy* days, some white disc jockeys tried to sound African-American. Wolfman Jack is probably the best known because of his role in George Lucas's 1973 film, *American Graffiti*. But before Wolfman, back in the early 1950s, there was a figure who combined hipness, African-American music, and a prophetic understanding of the emerging cultures of radio that would ultimately turn it upside down: Alan Freed, a "white negro," the man who, arguably, invented rock 'n' roll. Freed was a disc jockey who became the conduit of rhythm and blues into the white world. The music he played had been around for years on the stations aimed at black audiences. In the business, African-American musical styles were known collectively as "race" music – a kinder term than "coon music," the phrase used back in the early part of the century. It was rhythm and blues (a term coined by record producer Jerry Wexler), a powerful blend of blues, New Orleans jazz, gospel, and African folk influences, that came to be called "rock 'n' roll" when it crossed over to white audiences just before Freed came on the scene. He would argue that he invented the name.

When Freed began broadcasting – first in Cleveland and then in New York – his love of the music and his energy in presenting it was infectious. Freed would take requests from listeners, play records, pound on a phone book, and howl like a dog. In fact, he called himself "Moon Dog" until a New York street person and musician of the same name threatened to sue. He produced concerts where a range of African-American talent – The Platters, LaVerne Baker, Chuck Berry, Bo Diddley, Sam the Man Taylor, Fats Domino, Little Richard – played for large, mostly white audiences. He brought rhythm and blues into the white world in the face of a backlash as strong as that which occurred against jazz in the 1920s. The backlash was, in part, racist. The original R&B musicians were black. However, as white performers entered the scene, as Bill Haley, Jerry Lee Lewis, Buddy Holly, and, most important, Elvis Presley, further popularized the music, adults rebelled against its overt sexual energy– against energy itself. (See figures 4.2 and 4.3.)

Rock 'n' roll and civil rights

In the decade after World War II, American culture became increasingly nervous and suspicious of the activities of its young people, worried – just as conservative adults had been in the 1920s – that somehow they were getting out of control. Congressional hearings were held on a phenomenon called "juvenile delinquency," a phrase that was used as a catchall to describe a general post-war uneasiness and restlessness among teenagers. From comic books to music, all the entertainments of young people came into question, and the racial element of rock 'n' roll was a cause for particular worry among those made nervous by popular culture. Their worry was reflected in movies, such as *The Wild One* (Laszlo Benedek, 1953), in which Marlon Brando plays a member of a motor-cycle gang, or *Rebel Without a Cause* (Nicholas Ray, 1955), with

Figure 4.2 Publicity photo of Alan Freed, the disc jockey who, arguably, invented rock 'n' roll in the mid-1950s. Bettmann/CORBIS.

James Dean as a misunderstood young man. *Blackboard Jungle* (Richard Brooks, 1955) presented teenagers acting up to the sound of Bill Haley's "Rock Around the Clock." Despite (or because of) its association with delinquent youth, rock 'n' roll and its listeners grew in numbers and spread rapidly. Black musicians, as they had been throughout the history of popular music in the twentieth century, were again influential and their music assimilated.

But there was an important difference from the 1920s. The birth of rock 'n' roll in the early 1950s paralleled one of the most important social and cultural processes

Figure 4.3 The heyday of rock 'n' roll. New Orleans singer Fats Domino from the film *The Girl Can't Help It* (dir. Frank Tashlin, 1956). *The Girl Can't Help It* © 20th Century Fox, 1956.

of the post-war world: the civil rights movement. Historically, the movement had its origins shortly after World War II in the 1948 desegregation of the army and the landmark Brown vs. Board of Education case in 1954. These were just the beginnings of a series of events such as the Montgomery bus boycott in 1955, the integration of Little Rock's Central High School in 1957 and the University of Mississippi in 1962, and the murder of three white civil rights workers in Mississippi in 1964. The demoralizing and brutal treatment of African-Americans was challenged throughout the 1950s and 1960s, culminating in the passage of the Civil Rights Acts of 1964 and 1968.

Early rock 'n' roll did not directly influence the civil rights movement, though it could be argued that the movement influenced the development of rock 'n' roll and the assimilation of black music into the white mainstream. Early rock was a symptom of profound shifts in the culture's racial attitudes, marking a split in generations, a new activism among young people, and a continuing acceptance of African-American influences in music. Parents may have been outraged, but their children were forming a bond with a new musical form. Negative reaction only helped the music become even more popular.

Rock 'n' roll went through rapid changes through the decade of the 1950s. A process of assimilation began when, as we noted earlier, a number of white singers variously mixed blues, rhythm and blues, and country and western genres, and folk music, in short, borrowing heavily from a variety of African-American and white musical sources. This was a fertile period of invention. The African-American roots of rock produced a diverse growth, with various styles that continued to evolve, eventually pushing out older forms of popular music before becoming part of a larger protest movement that had its roots in civil rights.

This musical assimilation provided yet another wrinkle in the cultural and ethnic dynamics of rock 'n' roll. Among the most prolific of rock 'n' roll songwriters were two Jewish composers, Jerry Leiber and Mike Stoller. They wrote "Hound Dog," recorded first by a black performer, Big Mama Thornton, and then covered by Elvis Presley – a song that helped catapult him to fame. They went on to write "Jailhouse Rock" and some twenty other songs for Presley. They wrote "On Broadway" for The Drifters, "Yakety Yak" for The Coasters; and "Kansas City," recorded by almost every singer during the 1960s and 1970s.

Black and white in the culture of rock

The cross-fertilization of musical styles did not, ultimately, benefit African-American performers, who were largely left behind the ascendancy of the white singers who borrowed from them. So were the songwriters from the world of Tin Pan Alley, as more performers began writing their own songs. At the same time, the music being produced began to weave itself inseparably into a new culture of rebellion and change.

Broad generalizations have to be made with caution, so these are cautious generalizations: the 1950s can be understood as a decade of containment on both the political, cultural, and individual level. The culture as a whole was anxious and wary of modernity in any of its forms. Threats real and imagined; a politics of repression; children defying the conservative values of their parents; the struggles over civil rights symptomatic of major changes roiling beneath the surface of a culture that wanted to present itself as placid – all generated a sense of change and the fears that always accompany it. The birth of a new music indicated that many energies were at work that might not be immediately visible on the cultural surface, but that would prove to have long-term effects. By the late 1950s, the energies of the first wave of rock 'n' roll pushed against the culture's conservative fears. The culture changed; music changed; and radio changed. The changes converged in powerful ways.

After being battered by Cold War, anti-Communist hysteria, many people were ready for some new energy, signaled by the election of the youngest man ever to be elected president, John F. Kennedy. While Kennedy was not a very progressive figure (recall that it allegedly took news photos of police brutality against African-American protestors in the South to push him to pursue civil rights legislation more vigorously), his very youth seemed to create an aura of possibilities. Because of this, his assassination in 1963 was a huge blow. The assassinations that followed – Kennedy's brother Robert in 1968, and the two towering figures of the civil rights movement, Malcolm X in 1965 and Martin Luther King in 1968 – came as abrasive shocks for the growing movement toward social and political change in the country, a movement that began to emerge in the rock 'n' roll generation of the 1950s. The Vietnam War – hugely unpopular – continued that abrasion. From the Kennedy era through its end in the early 1970s, the war escalated while the voices opposing its mindless brutality grew progressively stronger. Music served as either a balm to the abrasion or a rebellious edge. Whether tripping out or marching in a demonstration, rock 'n' roll became background and foreground to a generation of change.

Rock's continuing evolution

A number of elements contributed to the changes that occurred in popular music during the sixties. One was the enormous influence of music from England, spearheaded by The Beatles and known as the "British invasion"; by 1965 the US pop charts were dominated by groups like The Rolling Stones, The Yardbirds, The Who, The Kinks, and The Animals, to name just a few. The various nuances of British invasion sound developed out of American rhythm and blues, as well as musical styles native to Britain. In the United States, American folk music entered into the mix of styles that had already enriched rock 'n' roll. Bob Dylan's early songs, for example, were influenced by folksinger Woody Guthrie, who was himself part of a tradition of triumphant socialism that rang through Depression-era America in the 1930s. To the disinherited and poor, Guthrie sang "This land is your land, this land is my land." In the early sixties, Dylan, perhaps less sure than Guthrie, would prophesy more vaguely that the answer was blowing in the wind.

Music was now speaking directly to and about the spirit of the times, with energy, delight, and anger. It was varied and *usable*: The Beatles' early gentleness appealed to younger audiences, while The Rolling Stones seemed angrier, rougher, and more attuned to a revolutionary spirit. Dylan sang from a place of restlessness, his lyrics often surreal, and always provocative; Paul Simon and Art Garfunkel's lyrics came from a place of urban angst which they managed to blend with ineffable melodic tenderness. The African-American influence continued to provide musical energy through Soul and Motown – the latter an example of how the work of a single producer-songwriter, Berry Gordy, could create an entire genre of music.

It is important to note that the subjective embrace of rock by its audience, the passionate attachment to the music, was not unique. Before rock fans there were the flappers of the 1920s, who frantically danced the Charleston and, later, bobby soxers – teenagers who swooned to performances by Frank Sinatra and other crooners in the 1940s. Music of any style creates passion. That is its purpose. The rock phenomenon, especially in the late sixties and early seventies, added politics to passion; the music became a surrogate voice, or, more accurately, a medium of expression – for the artists who made it; the record companies and radio stations that recorded and played it; and most importantly for those who listened.

Listener and music became reflections of each other and, from the 1960s on, the varieties of rock and popular music continued to represent the varieties of cultures. The rapid evolution of rap, another example of African-American musical influence first identified in the 1980s, is an example. A voice of black experience, sometimes violent in its imagery, often inventive in its wordplay, always sophisticated in its use of sampling – using small pieces of pre-recorded sound to act as background – rap has entered the mainstream. Like the other African-American-influenced styles before it, rap is sometimes co-opted, tamed, and used for commercial exploitation; but its essential forms continue to evolve.

Rock and radio

By the early 1970s, rock, in its various forms, superseded almost all other forms of popular music, and the playing of rock almost superseded all other forms of radio. I noted earlier that, as the attention of the public and broadcasters shifted more and more to television and away from radio, the original radio networks ceded greater control to local stations, many of which, a few decades later, became in turn the properties of large media companies. As FM stereo attracted more listeners, stations began using its superior sound to broadcast more music. With important exceptions, radio became a jukebox, and variety was manufactured by the styles and genres of music featured by any given stations – soft rock and hard; oldies (further subdivided by decade); urban (a catch-all for music by and for African-Americans); disco; punk; garage; heavy metal; country and western; world music; rap; jazz; classical; and so on. Such fragmentation is as much an indication of the ways in which record producers and radio programmers attempt to differentiate themselves as it is of a segmented audience or of musical styles themselves. As we have seen, all media attempt to find a specific, dependable audience, and attempt to define it down to its pocketbooks. Listeners, meanwhile, expand their tastes. They may not segment themselves to as fine a granularity as record producers and station managers, but they avail themselves of the array of choices this segmentation provides. The result is an enormous amount of variation, often based on small differences.

The varieties of rock completely changed the business of music and radio. In the end, the medium that was an instrument of assimilation, serving and bringing together a diverse culture, was now fragmenting, and its power to bring groups together was heading in other directions, as was the music it was playing. With the exception of religious broadcasts and some all-news stations, all music, all the time was very much the rule throughout the 1960s and 1970s. Other forms emerged in the 1980s, and with them came attacks on the powers of assimilation.

Radio and the Spoken Word

The age of the singer-songwriter has now passed. No longer a chorus for political action (though rap is still a strong voice of an angry cultural and racial minority), radio remains the background music for our lives, while other forms of discourse have come into play that continue to make radio a force – no longer of assimilation, and too often of anger and division.

Radio never completely gave up on the spoken word. Disc jockeys often created well-defined personalities who played their voices along with records – as the stories of Alan Freed and Wolfman Jack attest. In the late 1950s and 1960s, a New York radio performer, Jean Shepherd (best known outside of radio as the writer/narrator of the 1983 film *A Christmas Story*), used the medium as kind of free-form expression of stories, observations, reminiscences, improvisations. His was a night-time voice, talking along with a jazz background, conjuring not images, but a rhythm of talk, memory, and the city.

Shepherd's was a voice of intellectual embrace and emotional energy. Other vocal rhythms, counterpoints played between a host in the studio and listeners calling in by phone, began as far back as the 1930s, and gathered speed as DJs took on-air requests for tunes, reaching their height of popularity in the 1990s. Most radio is now all-music, but the parts that remain all-talk have a large cultural presence, a dedicated listenership, and, in some instances, a great deal of influence.

Censorship and shock-jocks

Like sixties rock, talk-radio today is a peculiarly cultural and political phenomenon, though unlike its musical counterpart, strikingly marked by gender – the hosts and the callers are almost exclusively male. The so-called "shock-jocks" are sometime or one-time disc jockeys, who now spend their airtime talking, making crude jokes, and attempting to be as vulgar as possible. Theirs is a kind of locker-room humor that appeals to the bad boy in everyone. Don Imus and Howard Stern are the major players. They depend on the instant satisfaction of impolite language, racial slurs, ridiculously sexist attitudes toward women, leavened with some occasional political commentary. Imus and Stern can be looked upon as transgressive voices, pushing the envelope of the culturally acceptable – the *media* acceptable.

There is an interesting history to this. Radio and television (as well as movies) are media of the public sphere and have always been pressured both by regulatory bodies – the FCC in the case of radio and television – religious groups, and, always, by their sponsors, to constrain themselves within the never quite determined and always expanding boundaries of public taste. Censorship is the general term, no matter where it comes from. Pushing against the bounds of censorship is always the artist's prerogative. Out of the clash comes invention – or nonsense. Exactly what "public taste" is can't be well defined. As one Supreme Court justice said about pornography, "I know it when I see it."

When dealing with a large audience, the only absolute certainty is that someone will be offended by something said or done on the air. The tendency, then, is to say nothing that might offend anyone. The result can be a level of media discourse so bland that it exists in a kind of alternate discursive universe from the one we all inhabit. Few of us never curse or let slip an unkind or unseemly remark regarding a person's gender or race, or voice a strong political opinion. But the legal limits about what could or could not be said on the air were implicit through most of radio's history and made explicit in the 1970s.

The seven filthy words   The comic George Carlin tested the limits of on-air free speech in 1973, when he recorded two comedy albums discussing a list of seven words that could not be said on the air. Carlin was arrested and charged with obscenity in 1972 when he performed a routine on this theme at Milwaukee's Summerfest. WBAI, a listener-supported station in New York run by The Pacifica foundation, played one of the albums that contained the transgressive words. The Pacifica Foundation and its stations were founded on principles of free speech and expression for stations that were presumably unrestrained by sponsorship. Listeners would pay to support the stations – much as they do now for Public Television or National Public Radio. The FCC did not agree that listener support meant that Pacifica's airways were open to any speech and took exception to the broadcast of dirty words. They ruled against WBAI's right to broadcast them. The case went to the Supreme Court in 1978; the radio station lost. The ruling is interesting enough to be quoted at length because it incorporates many of the ideas of the public and private spheres that have concerned us throughout our discussion:

FEDERAL COMMUNICATIONS COMMISSION v. PACIFICA FOUNDA-TION ET AL. SUPREME COURT OF THE UNITED STATES 438 U.S. 726 July 3, 1978, Decided

MR. JUSTICE STEVENS delivered the opinion of the Court (Parts I, II, III, and IV–C) and an opinion in which THE CHIEF JUSTICE and MR. JUSTICE REHNQUIST joined (Parts IV–A and IV–B).

This case requires that we decide whether the Federal Communications Commission has any power to regulate a radio broadcast that is indecent but not obscene.

A satiric humorist named George Carlin recorded a 12-minute monologue entitled "Filthy Words" before a live audience in a California theater. He began by referring to his thoughts about "the words you couldn't say on the public, ah, airwaves, um, the ones you definitely wouldn't say, ever." He proceeded to list those words and repeat them over and over again in a variety of colloquialisms. The transcript of the recording, which is appended to this opinion, indicates frequent laughter from the audience. At about 2 o'clock in the afternoon on Tuesday, October 30, 1973, a New York radio station, owned by respondent Pacifica Foundation, broadcast the "Filthy Words" monologue. A few weeks later a man, who stated that he had heard the broadcast while driving with his young son, wrote a letter complaining to the Commission. He stated that, although he could perhaps understand the "record's being sold for private use, I certainly cannot understand the broadcast of same over the air that, supposedly, you control." ... The question in this case is whether a broadcast of patently offensive words dealing with sex and excretion may be regulated because of its content. ... [T]he broadcast media have established a uniquely pervasive presence in the lives of all Americans. Patently offensive, indecent material presented over the airwaves confronts the citizen, not only in public, but also in the privacy of the home, where the individual's right to be left alone plainly outweighs the First Amendment rights of an intruder. ... Pacifica's broadcast could have enlarged a child's vocabulary in an instant. ...

The Court's ruling against Pacifica went on to stress that it was limited, that it did not have the force of censoring "an occasional expletive ...," nor did it have any say over a monologue given in front of a live audience (this in distinction to the censorship by local authorities of an earlier comic, Lenny Bruce, whose work in the 1950s and early 1960s brought down the wrath of the New York police and the authorities that licensed nightclubs). The Court's main concern was the early hour in which the routine was aired and that it came at a time when children could be listening.

The Supreme Court's judgment attempted to strike a balance between what it understood as the media's "uniquely pervasive presence in the lives of all Americans" and the privileged place of the private sphere, where the individual had a "right to be left alone." The suggestion is that media are as intrusive as they are pervasive and that individuals need protection from the intruder. The ruling seems to sidestep the reality that individuals have the power to turn off or avoid material they find offensive. It is that sidestep that allows censorship to thrive on the one hand and challenges to be made by the media on the other.

During the first decade of the twenty-first century, the Federal Communications Commission, when it was not busy selling off the electromagnetic spectrum, and especially when it was driven by political forces worried about the state of the private sphere, returned as a censorious body. Under pressure from various right-wing groups, responding in part to the infamous Janet Jackson "wardrobe malfunction" at Super Bowl XXXVIII, the FCC enacted the Broadcast Decency Enforcement Act of 2005, which allows it to levy a fine of $325,000 to $3 million for any on-air incident it deems inappropriate. The result has put broadcasters in an uncomfortable position of not knowing what might result in a fine, and, at the same time, has provided license for some broadcasters and audiences to see how far the boundaries might be pushed.

Imus and Stern

In the 1970s, George Carlin was obviously testing the waters. His routine did not so much incorporate the forbidden words, as talk about them. He was, in effect, doing media criticism. Imus and Stern, however, make the filthy words part of their discourse, beckoning and embracing anyone who would be tickled or outraged by vulgarity, racism, and sexism. Imus occasionally takes a political stand. Stern simply revels in vulgarity. For example, the two performers have a "feud." Feuding is an old radio shtick in which personalities pretend to hate each other, allowing for verbal fireworks and putdown humor. Here is what the Stern/Imus feud sounded like. This is a transcript from Imus's CNBC television show, as reported in the *New York Post* in 2003:

> Stern: Hey, stupid bitch, you want me to talk about your daughter and what went on between her and Linden?
> Imus: Yeah.
> Stern: And Al Rosenberg? ...
> Imus: Yeah.
> Stern: Whose bitch?
> Imus: Why don't you just keep your mouth shut, OK, punk?
> –Imus then hung up on Stern, prompting the self-styled King of All Media to snarl, "Pussy. What happened, Pussy? Whose bitch now? Yeah, play a song, stupid ass. He can't even be a man. What a woman ... Nice showdown, douche bag."
> Imus later recapped: "That was Howard Stern. You know what's interesting about him? It's just so easy to get him upset. What a whiny little bitch."'

Regular listeners to Imus and Stern may agree that this is a fairly mild interchange, but it is representative of their general schoolboy silliness and talking dirty for the sake of talking dirty. And, while Imus makes some claim to political discourse, occasionally interviewing politicians or even supporting them, in the end Stern is the more political figure. For better or worse, he actively battled the FCC for the right to say even the most ridiculously vulgar things on the air. He lost. More and more stations and sponsors cancelled his program as the FCC became increasingly conservative and censorious. In 2006 Stern finally moved to non-commercial satellite radio, a new version of radio that is outside of FCC governance. This was not a move based totally on taking a stand against censorship. He was paid $500 million to help him stand firm. In 2007, after making an egregious racial slur, Imus was simply removed from the airwaves – briefly.

Stern and Imus are a joke, even when they are not especially funny. Their most interesting work is using radio as an expression of transgressive speech – using the public or, in Stern's case, "private" airwaves to say things that are barely permissible in non-media public. With their words, radio becomes *anti*-radio. They invert its norms; their listeners are put in a steady state of hope for something more outrageously vulgar to be said in the next breath. The power of assimilation becomes an act of defining and segmenting an audience. For Howard Stern and satellite radio, it is an act that is defining new broadcast technologies.

Hate radio

Stern's politics are those of a grown-up child's daring the powerful to stop him from acting up and acting out. Within the context of media political cultures, he may actually be a beneficial force in loosening up conservative restrictions. Perhaps somewhat less beneficial are the conservative talk-show hosts that have proliferated on local and national radio since the 1980s. These shows target what they define as "liberalism" and indulge in a raucous politics of resentment and anger.

Although conservative talk-radio can trace its ancestry back to Father Coughlin in the 1930s, a number of contemporary events made its proliferation possible. Until the 1980s, there was an FCC ruling that insisted on a balance of political opinion broadcast by any one station. If any one political opinion was broadcast, it had to be matched by an opposing opinion. It was called the Fairness Doctrine and was in place from 1949 in order to keep radio programming from becoming a voice for any one particular party. In the 1980s, Congress attempted to encode the doctrine as law. Ronald Reagan, whose presidency was key in the conservative revival, vetoed the legislation, effectively ending the mandate for "fair and balanced" broadcasting. With the end of the Fairness Doctrine, stations were no longer responsible for giving equal time to opposing voices.

During the same period, the FCC removed regulations that limited the number of media outlets a company could own. The result, continuing to this day, is that more and more media are owned by fewer and fewer companies. A company like Clear Channel, which owns 1,200 stations nationwide, can syndicate a program originating from a local station and give it immediate national exposure. A media company with large holdings and a particular political leaning was now free to give it a broad voice, and many of those voices were from the right.

The rise of neo-conservatism and the presidency of Ronald Reagan was the overriding factor that made possible the relaxation of broadcast rules and regulations and the rise of right-wing discourse. Neo-conservatism is a complex set of ideologies that grew from a wholesale distrust of liberal government that came about, in part, as a response to the cultural upheaval that we spoke about in relation to sixties rock music. The youth rebellion of the 1960s frightened many people. The 1970s seemed, to them, a decade of lost power. The US lost the very war in Vietnam that the 1960s counter-culture rebelled against. The fall of President Richard Nixon brought about a wholesale distrust of government that, for some, seemed to reach its peak in the presidency of Jimmy Carter (1977–81), who complained of a "cultural malaise" in America and appeared helpless in face of Islamic militancy abroad. In the home, the women's movement and the push for an Equal Rights Amendment aggravated, for some, a perceived loss of potency and the presumed male right to power. These complex responses to what seemed to be a loss of agency in the family, the community, the nation, and the world are given a simple voice in right-wing talk-radio, which often focuses on some unsavory aspects of racism and xenophobia, anti-feminism, and a generalized male-centered belligerency, along with resentment. Right-wing talk-radio appeared to address the aggrieved and give them voice. Talk-radio hosts, from Rush Limbaugh on, were following in the footsteps of Father Charles Coughlin, the radio preacher of the 1930s we spoke about earlier, who railed against government, Communism, and Jews. In fact, Susan Douglas writes that Limbaugh was, to the early 1990s, what Father Coughlin was to early 1930s: "a radio orator who many people feel gave voice to what they really felt but hadn't yet put into words."

The difference is that Limbaugh, G. Gordon Liddy, Oliver North, Sean Hannity, Neal Boortz, and a host of others have dropped the anti-Semitism, find it difficult to locate a Communist enemy, and have substituted women, environmentalists, and, most especially, "Liberals," and "the liberal media" as their enemies. By inviting callers to phone in, they successfully create a closed universe where the only discourse allowed is complaint and resentment voiced within carefully contained and agreed upon frames of reference. This is a very close assimilation of true believers and the on-air individuals who give them voice; at the same time, it is an act of segregation, blocking off the believers from an alternative – what the broadcasters and their listeners would call "liberal" – perspective.

We can see how that discourse operates in this transcription of a rant by Neal Boortz, a talk-show host based in Atlanta, Georgia. In April, 2006, the country was engaged in a round of discussion about immigration, bringing outbursts of concern for jobs and, regrettably, of racism aimed at Hispanics crossing the Mexican border for work. Here are some of Boortz's comments in response to a caller. Boortz is very much a Limbaugh imitator; listeners who know them both will recognize the similarity in their speech rhythms:

> The 11 or 12 million illegals in this country are not going anywhere. They are staying right here.… If you think the … United Nation's Human Rights Commission screamed when we force fed Gitmo prisoners, who were trying to kill themselves through starvation, calling that torture, then you just stand back and you listen to the howling … that would follow as sure as night follows day or Bill Clinton follows flatbellies [this word is indecipherable] the howling that will erupt with category five force when we try to send these criminals back across the Mexican-American border. The United Nations and the Euroweenies, who have their own immigration problem with their own M word – it's Muslims for them – they will start screaming about human rights violations like you've never heard them screaming before. They are not going to be shipped back.… First of all, where will we store 11 million Hispanics waiting to be shipped back to [here he names Latin American countries, using an exaggerated Spanish accent] …? I know [the caller says 'Superdome'] … Superdome! Exactly or the Astrodome in Houston. That's where we'll put 'em. We've got practice.…

Throughout our discussion, we have talked a great deal about genres, the convention-limited variations on themes and their expression that make up much of media content and enable them to contain and code their own complex structures and reproduce material in familiar forms. Genres enable us, as audience, to decode meaning according to the recognizable patterns of a genre, or sometimes against them. It is remarkable how quickly right-wing talk-radio has become generic, so tightly coded that Boortz can telegraph an enormous amount of instantly recognized code in about 165 words. His subject is immigration, a complex issue involving international relations, the appropriate treatment of people, economics, and fear on all sides. Within that discussion are embedded references to our torture of Muslim prisoners in Guantánamo, insulting remarks about the UN, Europe, Latin Americans, and Muslims, the obligatory right-wing whack at Bill Clinton, a reference to Hurricane Katrina, and a climax that seems to connect to the most racist underpinnings of post-hurricane commentary that we have already noted in our discussion of journalism in chapter 2. We have practice rounding up people we don't like, Boortz says – we did it with the poor in the Superdome after Katrina. All of this is cemented within an isolationist stance that would be easily recognizable to anyone listening to right-wing commentary as far back as the 1930s and earlier.

Not to be outdone, Rush Limbaugh offered the following diatribe on his show on June 7, 2006. The occasion was a speech by Mark Malloch Brown, Deputy Secretary General of the United Nations, condemning the US for threatening to withhold its UN dues:

> So Mark Malloch Brown is saying the reason that the United Nations is unrecognized for its greatness and its value, the reason that it's not recognized for its true benefit to world peace and blah, blah, blah, blah, is because of me and Fox News poisoning your minds. What's new? This is just another pointy-headed, elitist liberal saying you're a bunch of mind numbed robots and you can't make up your own minds about things. The United Nations has not changed. It's still the bar scene in the first Star Wars movie. It's nothing but the vast majority of its members being tinhorn dictators and other, you know, little rug rats that are given legitimacy. …

"Pointy-headed liberal" is a phrase taken straight from the anti-Communist days of McCarthyite 1950s. Rug rats, the derogatory term for children, is applied to a community of diplomats. More pointedly, the bar scene in *Star Wars* is meant to be a celebration of cosmic diversity. Rush turns it into a potentially racist allusion. And, just to be sure we get it, his website for the day's broadcast includes a Photoshopped mock-up of caricatures.

The music and radio of the 1960s served as an emotionally integral companion to progressive, positive social action. It was a movement for change and assimilation. The words of too much of talk-radio provide a support for discrimination, an illusion of action against a world that seems to its listeners to be getting away from them, to be incomprehensible, and, above all, unmanageably complex and diverse. Discomfort with complexity and ambiguity can lead to its opposite: comfort with oversimplification, stereotyping, and the creation of an enemy. "Liberalism" takes the place of 1950s Communism as an ideological enemy. This is radio acting against its old role as a unifier of a diverse culture, creating instead a protected world, where everyone is a "ditto head," and host and callers permit nothing but the vociferous reinforcement of a limited and unhappy world view.

Public radio

There are responses to right-wing radio. Air America, an outspoken liberal broadcasting service, has an online stream and limited on-air distribution. But the network that most strongly upholds the standard of objective journalism and responsible talk is National Public Radio, the closest the US has to state-sponsored broadcasting. NPR consistently attempts to execute some of what radio has always done so well: to act as an intelligent voice in the public sphere, providing news and entertainment, allowing a variety of views to be heard, and refraining from calling names.

NPR began as a frequency allocation demonstrating again how, in the media, technology pushes content. When radio broadcasting began in earnest in the 1920s, there was a strong urge to make it as much as possible an educational and cultural (in the sense of "high" artistic culture) medium. This urge was squelched when radio quickly turned commercial, but was revived again with the advent of FM broadcasting in the late 1940s. The FCC reserved the lower end of the FM spectrum for non-commercial, educational broadcasting. Use of the non-commercial band was sporadic and without organization until Pacifica, a loose network of FM stations, was formed in the late forties. Along with programming classical music, jazz, lectures, poetry readings, and, increasingly through the years, progressive political commentary, the Pacifica stations created a model of listener support. Instead of advertising, they asked listeners to "subscribe" to the stations, and to that end they instituted fund drives. Pacifica remained a "niche" broadcasting outlet, never gaining a very large audience, and, by the 1990s, it was torn by internal political battles.

Meanwhile, in 1967, the idea of a community of non-commercial stations was taken up again when the government created the Corporation for Public Broadcasting. CPB was set up as a public entity, funded by the government, and charged with administering funds for the Public Broadcasting Service (PBS), its television arm, and for National Public Radio. Since its inception in 1970, NPR has managed a successful and politically smart structure of diverse network programming and autonomous local stations, sometimes owned by universities (many of these, as well as other local educational radio stations, existed before NPR). Many NPR outlets are the only local stations available in rural areas, which gives the network some political clout. Conservatives, who see NPR as left of center because it investigates issues in depth and does not skirt complexity, and who do not believe that the government should support broadcasting, regularly threaten the network's funding. However, each time they threaten funding, they are reminded by their constituents that the broadcast services provided by NPR's local stations are often the only ones available in their area. The funding threats are withdrawn.

Politics and funding are a continuous part of the background noise of NPR, though that noise has been muffled since Joan Kroc, the widow of the man who invented McDonald's, bequeathed the network a $230 million dollar gift. So endowed, the news-gathering apparatus of NPR is now as good or better than any radio and many television news operations. Despite the grant, and despite the fact that there is increasing support from local and national corporate contributors (who are acknowledged in sponsorship announcements), local NPR stations maintain their biannual fundraising marathons, which helps their budget, but, even more, furthers the culture of community involvement.

More important is the fact that NPR and its affiliates deliver a depth and breadth of programming that keeps the radio tradition vital. It is centered on news and information, particularly through its two flagship programs, *Morning Edition* and *All Things Considered*; but also includes many call-in shows, music of various styles, comedy, even variety programs – with songs, jokes, and skits – like *A Prairie Home Companion*. The spectrum of its coverage is probing and respectful. And, even though its news operation has become more mainstream as it has become more established, it is still richer in the detail of its coverage than other news outlets. The amount of time that most NPR stations devote to news – two hours in the morning and afternoon, hourly news roundups and public affairs call-in shows in between – allows for coverage akin to that of a major newspaper. It is a range that offers analysis and opinion, sometimes counter to the prevailing political ideologies of the moment, but more often in the cultural mainstream. In sum, NPR is something of a reflection in miniature of what radio used to do: it presents a variety of genres and formats, inspires and evokes – and sometimes provokes – through the medium of sound.

Yet, in terms of its audience, NPR falls far short of reflecting the time when radio was ubiquitous American culture in the 1930s and 1940s: a large number of people – perhaps most people – listened regularly, often to the same programs in ways that created listener communities. Today, radio audiences are fragmented and divided by class and education. Listeners to right-wing talk-radio are likely to regard NPR with disdain as part of the "liberal media." NPR listeners may regard talk-radio with equivalent disdain as lowbrow propaganda, or possibly fear it as a font of verbal abuse. Others choose to divide their time among the dozens of music stations around the dial, allowing radio to provide the background music to their lives.

Radio and New Media

Online and on satellite

Like all media, radio has moved online. Within recent years, almost every radio station has instituted a website where a listener can hear a live stream of programming. Many stations, including those in the NPR network, podcast their programs as well. There are even radio "stations," like RadioParadise.com, that exist only online. There is also satellite radio, which sends signals that a listener can receive while traveling all over a broad geographical area such as the continental US. XM Radio, one of the first satellite services (the other being Sirius Radio – the two are now merged), has a free online service. At some sites, a listener can create his or her own playlist of songs. (We will have more to say about new radio technologies in chapter 7, "Digital Spaces".)

But this move to the Internet or satellite has hardly changed the medium. Because radio is a medium in the most basic sense – it carries content – where it is located or by what means it is broadcast does not essentially change that content. Delivering news and information, organizing tunes into a genre – urban contemporary, country and western, pop, classic rock, contemporary rock, classical, jazz, contemporary jazz, delivering dirty stories, Howard Stern style, or the rant of conservative hosts, remain radio's current practice. Although it may no longer be mediating a culture into a diverse and cohesive listening public, it still provides the comforts or incitements of words and music in a mobile environment.

Radio communities today

While it no longer addresses the nation the way it did for the World War II generation, radio still emerges from time to time as a community-making phenomenon. For example, as the Hispanic population increases in the United States, radio, newspapers, and television have emerged as their mediated voice across the country. Urban areas are served by a variety of Spanish-speaking media, and even small localities, like rural Minnesota, have radio stations bringing Hispanic news and entertainment. Spanish radio's communal power helped to organize hundreds of thousands of people to participate in a "national day of action for immigration justice" in April of 2006. It is even more important to understand that stations like these are serving a population that has not yet made a wholesale move to the Internet, and who find programming in general, and encouraging voices in particular, a means not only to connect with each other, but also to enable political action.

Alternatively, a radio station can exist simply as a means to serve a micro-community otherwise completely cut off from the world. Inmates on death row in the Louisiana State Penitentiary near Baton Rouge have a Christian-based radio station. The prison DJs play a variety of music – weighted heavily toward Cajun swamp pop and always monitored for violent content – take requests, and provide a discussion group for Muslim inmates. Like radio anywhere, the prison radio station provides not merely an escape – an imaginary movement outward, beyond one's physical circumstances – but also a corresponding move inward, by acting as a medium for the collective voices of the inmates. In a fragmented media world, even the smallest, most unlikely, medium can have positive effects.

The political and the personal

The politics of media is a subject at work throughout the pages of this book. Every time we address the ability of media to move people, to influence opinion or actions, we are touching on politics, which, whether in service of a candidate or party, an ideology, or simply swaying opinion, has everything to do with power.

Radio, like most media, has been a voice of the powerful, using power to speak to the powerless. But even in the days of its majority, when Franklin Delano Roosevelt used his "fireside chats" to harness the nation into a solid ideological, wartime front, radio also provided countervailing voices on many sides of the political spectrum. The days of its majority long past, radio is still providing a political voice, for the disaffected, the disenfranchised, the disgruntled, or for those still hungry to understand the world. As an essentially passive medium – even when a program invites call-ins – radio allows disembodied voices to crawl into our attention, to stimulate us with news, or soothe with music, infuriating us with outrageous opinion, urging us to action. This is considerable power.

Susan Douglas writes:

> Even today, in the age of TV and the Internet, Americans have learned to turn to radio to alter or sustain particular emotional states: to elevate their moods (classic rock, oldies), to soothe themselves (classical, soft rock, smooth jazz) to become outraged (talk and shock). Some modes of listening have helped constitute generational identities, others a sense of nationhood, still other, subcultural opposition to and rebellion against that construction of nationhood. Most modes of listening generate a strong feeling of belonging. Even as mere background noise, radio provides people with a sense of security that silence does not, which is why they actively turn to it, even if they aren't actively listening. (1999: 8)

It is precisely this sense of sustaining emotion even in a state of passive listening that makes radio a continuous presence and continuing contender despite its status as an "old" medium. As I write this, National Public Radio's *Morning Edition* is streaming on my computer. I barely hear it, and it doesn't respond to me at all, but it is there, and it acts as a connection.

References

The Coming of Radio

The standard histories of radio, and the sources for much of the material in this chapter, are Eric Barnouw, *A History of Broadcasting in the United States*, 3 vols. (New York: Oxford University Press, 1966–70); and Michele Hilmes, *Radio Voices: American Broadcasting, 1922–1952* (Minneapolis: University of Minneapolis Press, 1997).

Early inventors
The gender specific attraction of early radio is discussed by Kristen Harring, "The 'Freer Men' of Ham Radio: How a Technical Hobby Provided Social and Spatial Distance," *Technology and Culture* 44/4 (2003): 734–61.

FCC, RCA, CBS, ABC
Brief histories of the networks and their founders, along with other material on broadcasting, can be found at the site of the Museum of Broadcast Communications: <http://www.museum.tv>.

A chart of the FCC's electromagnetic "real estate" can be found at: <http://www.ntia.doc.gov/osmhome/allochrt.pdf>.

Recorded Music

A standard history is Russell and David Sanjek, *Pennies From Heaven: The American Popular Music Business in the Twentieth Century* (New York: Da Capo Press, 1996).

Early recording technology
See Mark Katz, *Capturing Sound: How Technology Has Changed Music* (Berkeley, Los Angeles, and London: University of California Press, 2005); and Brian Regal, *Radio: The Life Story of a Technology* (Westport, CT: Greenwood Press, 2005).

Early recorded music and race
For an excellent discussion of race in early twentieth-century music, as well as examples of the music itself, see: <http://www.ischool.berkeley.edu/~mkduggan/neh.html>.

Blacking up
See Michael Rogin, *Blackface, White Noise: Jewish Immigrants in the Hollywood Melting Pot* (Berkeley and Los Angeles: University of California Press, 1966).

Jazz and moral outrage
The quotations about jazz are from Hilmes, *Radio Voices,* cited above, pp. 47 and 48.

Amos 'n' Andy
Dialogue is quoted by Hilmes, *Radio Voices,* p. 91. See also Melvyn Patrick Ely, *The Adventures of* Amos 'n' Andy: *A Social History of an American Phenomenon* (Charlottesville and London: University of Virginia Press, 1991). Much of the information for the discussion of the program comes from Ely's excellent book and Hilmes's in-depth analysis. The quote from Margo Jefferson is from "Television View; Seducified by a Minstrel Show," *The New York Times* (May 22, 1994); <http://query.nytimes.com/gst/fullpage.html?res=9901E2DF1438F931A15756C0A962958260>. Hilmes also quotes from Jefferson's essay.

Diversity and Negotiation

A history of Father Coughlin is at: <http://www.spartacus.schoolnet.co.uk/USAcoughlinE.htm>.

Ventriloquism of the imagination
Hilmes talks about ventriloquism and radio in *Radio Voices,* p. 87.

Sound technologies
See Katz, *Capturing Sound;* and Regal, *Radio: The Life Story of a Technology,* cited above.

Norman Mailer

"The White Negro" appears in *Advertisements for Myself* (Cambridge, MA, and London: Harvard University Press: 1992), pp. 337–58.

African-American radio

Information on early DJs is from Hilmes, *Radio Voices*, p. 272.

Information on Jerry Wexler and rhythm and blues is in Bruce Weber, "R&B Impresario, is Dead at 91," *The New York Times* (August 15, 2008): <http://www.nytimes.com/2008/08/16/arts/music/16wexler.html>.

Rock 'n' roll and civil rights

On the fears about "juvenile delinquency," see James Gilbert, *A Cycle of Outrage: America's Reaction to the Juvenile Delinquent in the 1950s* (New York: Oxford University Press, 1986). A good history of rock and the cultures it thrived in is Paul Friedlander, *Rock and Roll: A Social History* (Boulder, CO: Westview Press, 1996). On Lieber and Stoller, see Jeffrey Melnick, "Tin Pan Alley and the Black-Jewish Nation," *American Popular Music* (Amherst, MA: University of Massachusetts Press, 2001), pp. 29–45.

Radio and the Spoken Word

Censorship and shock jocks

"I know it when I see it" was a statement on pornography made by Supreme Court Justice Potter Stewart in an opinion in the obscenity case, Jacobellis v. Ohio in 1964.

The seven filthy words

The complete court ruling is at: <http://www.law.umkc.edu/faculty/projects/ftrials/conlaw/pacifica.html>. A transcript of Carlin's routine, including the forbidden words, can be found at: <http://www.law.umkc.edu/faculty/projects/ftrials/conlaw/filthywords.html>.

Imus and Stern

The feud is quoted in "Stern and Imus in Gutter-Fest," *New York Post* (December 5, 2003).

Hate radio

On the Fairness Doctrine, see Patricia Aufderheide, "After the Fairness Doctrine: Controversial Broadcast Programming and the Public Interest," *Journal of Communication* 40/3 (summer, 1990): 47–72; Susan J. Douglas, "Letting the Boys be Boys: Talk Radio, Male Hysteria, and Political Discourse in the 1980s," *Radio Reader: Essays in the Cultural History of Radio*, ed. Michele Hilmes and Jason Lovigilo (New York and London: Routledge, 2002), pp. 485–504.

The transcript from Neil Boortz comes from a recording of the broadcast at: <http://radio.about.com/b/a/256821.htm>.

The transcript of Limbaugh's comments are at: <http://www.rushlimbaugh.com/home/eibessential/war_on_terror/who_cares_what_pointy_headed_un_elitists_say.html>.

Public Radio

Sue Schardt and the Christian Science Monitor Publishing Company, "Public Radio: A Short History," <http://www.wsvh.org/pubradiohist.htm>.

Radio Communities Today

Annie Baxter, "Spanish-language station reaches out to rural Hispanic population," <http://news.minnesota.publicradio.org/features/2004/03/18_baxtera_latinoradio/>.

N.C. Aizenman, "Immigration Debate Wakes A 'Sleeping Latino Giant,'" *Washington Post* (April 6, 2006); <http://www.washingtonpost.com/wp-dyn/content/article/2006/04/05/AR2006040502543.html>.

Lia Miller, "To Marshal Immigrant Forces, Start at Ethnic Radio Stations," *The New York Times* (April 10, 2006); <http://www.nytimes.com/2006/04/10/business/media/10radio.html>.

Paul Von Zielbauer, "Spinning Hope on Incarceration Station; Radio Coming to You Live on Death Row at Angola," *The New York Times* (April 12, 2006); <http://www.nytimes.com/2006/04/12/arts/12radi.html>.

The political and the personal

The quotation is from Susan Douglas, *Listening in: Radio and the American Imagination, from Amos 'n' Andy and Edward R. Murrow to Wolfman Jack and Howard Stern* (New York: New York Times Books, 1999), p. 8.

CHAPTER FIVE
Watching TV

DANNY: *Don't worry, Mom, I know all about cannibalism. I saw it on TV.*
JACK: *See. It's okay. He saw it on the television.*

From Stanley Kubrick's *The Shining* (1971)

When we ask what's on television, we are inquiring about a complex array of genres – news, comedy, drama; parody and satire; music and variety – in a medium that continues to evolve. Television is the expression of a desire for a shared place in the private sphere where we can enter a flow of programming from the superficial to the profound, from the personal to the political, and sometimes the vulgar. Through analysis of particular shows and digressions on history, genres, and politics, we will discover the various ways in which television asks us to respond.

From the moment of its appearance as a home appliance in the late 1940s to the present, and despite all possible competition for our leisure (and working) time, television is our prime source of news and entertainment. The time we spend watching it, or at least having a set on somewhere in our vicinity, grows yearly, according to the annual Nielsen surveys. Its technical evolution from a low-resolution, black-and-white image to high-definition color that rivals the look of film is a tribute to continuing technical improvement. The programming we see in high or low definition is a tribute to the way genres can be packaged and repackaged – the ways in which conventions, once begun and accepted, are repeated with variations over and over. Television is a cultural marker of our desire for the comfort of the familiar in the guise of the new.

A Brief History of Television

We usually think of television as a recent invention, following on the heels of radio, sometime in the early 1950s. In fact, the idea of transmitting images over the air is as old as the idea of transmitting sound. The technologies were not far behind, and television – almost as we know it – has been around at least since the 1930s.

Nineteenth-century technologies of imagination

Television was *imagined* before it was invented. The technologies of sound recording and the moving image, of telephony, long-distance broadcasting, and image transmission were developed almost simultaneously in the mid- to late nineteenth century. Thomas Edison's company concentrated on recording sound and the moving image. By creating a *record* of sound and light waves they established an asynchronous means of distribution: image and sound could be recorded, reproduced, and then physically transported to distribution and exhibition points (Nickelodeons, and then movie theaters for film; the home for recordings and, eventually, radio) where an audience would gather to view the movie, or a household gather to listen to a recording.

Inventors of live transmission of sound and voice – telegraph, telephone, and radio – were also thinking about images, even before the technologies for image transmission were available. The ancestor of the fax, for example, was developed in the 1850s. By 1877, Alexander Graham Bell was developing ways to send images long distance. Other inventors and writers were imagining means for the synchronous transmission of images, of seeing as well as talking across space, *negating* space, mediating the body. In chapter 1, we looked at the remarkable 1879 cartoon by George du Maurier, showing a British couple sitting at home, talking to, and seeing, their daughter in the far East (figure 1.1). Colonialism – the rule of countries by foreign powers – was an important political aspect in the imagination of the nineteenth century that drove technologies. The ability to see people in those countries would have been a useful part of governing them from afar. *Usefulness* always drives invention at some point; tinkering and fantasizing in turn drives utility.

Television on radio's heels

Imagination became fact early in the twentieth century. During the 1920s, radio was saturating the marketplace and entering every home. Experimentation in image broadcasting proceeded in earnest. David Sarnoff, head of RCA, was active in financing inventors and licensing technologies – and thereby ensuring that his company would own and produce as much of the hardware (radio and television sets) and software (the programming) as possible. At the 1939 New York World's Fair, Sarnoff demonstrated analog television in a form close to the way we know it today – or at least have known it until recently: the image transmitted over the electromagnetic spectrum and reproduced by means of a cathode-ray tube scanning a fluorescent surface.

World War II put a temporary halt to the development of television in the United States, but production of television shows and television receivers accelerated dramatically once the war was over. By 1948, the Federal Communications Commission had instituted a freeze on licenses for new stations while it figured out how to process the avalanche of applications on file and allocate the electromagnetic spectrum. This timeout was extended to 1952, due to the outbreak of the Korean War. The results of "the freeze," as it's known in television history, had long-lasting repercussions. Sarnoff used the time to corner as much of the market as possible for RCA television sets. Various standards for color television were devised, although it was another decade before color sets were widely available to consumers. During the freeze, the FCC saved a portion of the UHF band for educational television, a move that made public broadcasting possible. In short, this period allowed for a shaping of the television broadcast spectrum as well as the spectrum of ownership and programming that covers television to this day.

Television would be a commercial medium and stay that way. The model had been set by radio, and because all media operate by imitation, radio dictated what was seen on television. After all, radio had gone through a long shakedown period before the commercial network model emerged as the dominant form. The major radio networks – NBC, CBS, and ABC – were well in place by the end of World War II, and the varieties of programming and the audiences who listened to them were equally well established. The initial urge on the part of broadcasters was to simply slide the business and programming models from radio to television. They tended to ignore the specific differences of the two media.

Attempts to elide the radio broadcasting model into television could not, of course, hide essential differences. "Hide" is an operative term: television revealed what radio could not show – the moving image. Radio provoked the listener to create the imaginative space supplied by voice and music alone. Television provided the images to represent that space. Television was at the same time more and less than its predecessor. It opened the visual field but also constricted the imagination. It created an imaginative space, but took away from the domestic space and limited mobility within that space. Television needs to be looked at, consuming any attention that is directly paid to it. Listening to radio allows a great amount of mobility. One can even take radio outside and on the road; to watch television, you need to be in one place and relatively immobile. At the moment of its introduction, TV therefore changed the way people attended to media and changed the very configurations of the domestic space where media were located.

The woman's window on the world   Television fitted well within the cultural trajectory of post-World War II America, which emphasized the stability of the family, the suburban home, and the woman who should stay there and raise a family while the father was out making a living. Technology and ideology joined in the conservative effort to lock down the culture after the upheavals of the World War II. Early advertising for television sets were markedly gendered: TV was marketed for women, offering them a window on the world, a companion for the dull hours of daytime domesticity, a machine to create stability during the forced togetherness of evening time. Television offered to open the world while effectively closing it down. It promised to make up for the drudgery of the homemaker, but it demanded the gaze of the entire family. Even though it was offered as an empowerment for women, the power it gave them was the captivity of home and children. Hopefully, the entire family would be as rooted to the "window on the world" at night as mother was during the day. A window, of course, frames what we see and frames off what we can't. Television's "window on the world" tightly controls what we see. (See figures 5.1 and 5.2.)

Feminizing early television was a successful ploy that helped to move it rapidly into the home (and this contrasts well with the male-dominated tinkering that marked early radio). Once it got into the home, its offer of visual pleasure, of *seeing* what was once only heard, of providing a domestic, more intimate, version of the cinema, and diverting attention away from the pressures of domesticity, its growth and popularity were unstoppable. In 1950, 9 percent of American households had a television set; by 1954, 55.7 percent; by 1962, 90 percent. Saturation occurred by the end of the 1950s – everyone who could own a set, who could afford one, and who lived where a TV signal could be received, had one. All growth figures from the early 1960s on are about owning multiple sets in one household.

Early television programming

What did people see on early television? There was a large-scale transfer of programming to TV from radio. The enormously popular radio program *Amos 'n' Andy* first appeared as a television series in 1951, and was, in fact, one of TV's first situation comedies, a genre that would become a television mainstay and which we will examine in detail later on. Famous radio comedians, like Jack Benny and Bob Hope, had new lives on television. So did musicians like Lawrence Welk, Dinah Shore, and the singing cowboy, Roy Rogers; children's heroes like the Lone Ranger and Sky King; and early newscasters like Lowell Thomas and John Cameron Swayze. Quiz programs were brought over from radio to television and thrived until they were proved to be fraudulent. And, as we will see, original dramatic programming thrived in television's early years. There were Westerns and courtroom dramas, police procedurals, and private detective series. Situation comedies abounded, with one, *I Love Lucy*, retaining its popularity decades after its production.

Variety shows – with comics, singers, jugglers, acrobats, musicians, ventriloquists – presented in a vaudeville format that, historically, preceded radio, thrived during the 1950s and beyond. Arthur Godfrey's popular radio variety show made the transition to television with great success. The most successful vaudeville-style variety show host was Ed Sullivan, who from 1948 to 1971 presented a Sunday night variety show that served as a platform to introduce new talent to the public. Elvis Presley appeared,

THE SPHERE—January 17, 1953

Figure 5.1 Early advertisements for television sets pictured them as the center of the home and the cause of domestic tranquility. Mary Evans Picture Library.

though photographed from the waist up to censor out his famous gyrating hips. Later, The Beatles were on Sullivan's show, their music all but drowned out by hysterically shrieking fans.

Milton Berle worked in a variety show format on *The Texaco Star Theater* and helped to introduce sketch comedy on it (figure 5.3). But his show was mainly about Berle himself: the slapstick Berle getting hit with a giant powder puff, the cross-dressing Berle appearing as an outlandish woman, Berle taking pratfalls, or Berle grabbing a guest by the teeth. This was television as hilarious narcissism, the comic body displayed on a shadowy picture tube. The program was so popular in the early 1950s that people stopped everything to watch it; if they didn't have a television set, they would go and stand in front of an appliance store to watch Uncle Miltie on the display TVs in the window.

Figure 5.2   This still is from the film *All That Heaven Allows* (dir. Douglas Sirk, 1955), in which a lonely widow is given a television set by her children to keep her company. In its early days, TV was sold as a woman's home companion. This image indicates that the companion remained the woman at home alone. *All That Heaven Allows* © Universal, 1955

Sid Caesar's *Your Show of Shows* was another early example of sketch comedy, which remains a vital comic format, living on in *Saturday Night Live*. Caesar was an energetic comic, able to play off a talented ensemble group of fellow comedians. He and his producers also knew the value of talented writers, with people such as Mel Brooks, Neil Simon, and Woody Allen as part of his writing team. (See figure 5.4.)

Sid Caesar's comedy, though original to television, still had its roots in radio – verbal comedy with the addition of visual gags. In contrast, Ernie Kovacs was not only a television original, he was and remains one of the few comics who make full use of the form of television – its small screen, the electronic image that could be pulled and distorted, the spatial coordinates that could be altered to create a gag. One of Kovacs's funniest scenes was an anti-gravity routine in which the comic would sit at a table and pour a bottle of milk that would come out at an angle and miss the glass. The trick was simple: build the set at an angle and place the camera at the same angle, and adjust the whole image so that the angle was not noticeable. Lindsay Pack accurately noted that, for Kovacs, television was a toy to be played for all the tricks he could pull out of it. Few comics have made the medium the message in the manner that Kovacs did. Fewer still have depended as much on the intelligence and attentiveness of the viewer as Kovacs and Caesar. (See figure 5.5.)

Ethnicity and comedy   The fact of visual presence – the presence of the image – made a literal transfer from radio to television impossible. This was nowhere more true than in the case of *Amos 'n' Andy*. Radio's white performers in blackface would have been unacceptable on television, so *Amos 'n' Andy* was given a new television cast made up of talented African-American actors (figure 5.6).

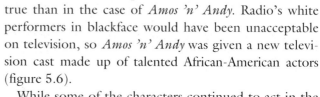

While some of the characters continued to act in the same buffoonish ways as their black-voice, radio predecessors, the program was a good-natured, if exaggerated, often funny representation of a minority reaching for middle-class status. Stereotypes remained – particularly in the character of the conniving and always bumbling Kingfish – and the controversies the show had caused on radio continued undiminished. Moreover,

Figure 5.3   Milton Berle clowns around with Dean Martin and Jerry Lewis in a 1950s television show. Milton Berle © Sagebrush Enterpises, Inc., 1989.

this was the 1950s, when the civil rights movement was beginning to build. The NAACP fought hard for the cancellation of the show. Though their voice was not unanimous and did not represent all of the African-American community, it prevailed. Television then as now was intensely sensitive to any offense programming might cause that would, in turn, make advertisers turn away. *Amos 'n' Andy* was pulled in 1953. It lived into the 1960s in syndication (the arrangement by which a series is purchased to be shown on local television stations), and can be seen still on DVD.

Amos 'n' Andy was not the only show that relied upon stereotypes for its entertainment value. Other ethnic comedies – *The Goldbergs, Life With Luigi, The Life of Riley, I Remember Mama* (which began life as a movie) – lived on through the 1950s. These were warmly sentimental comedies, continuing the radio tradition of assimilation, and marked with a kind of innocent nostalgia for some imagined "good old days" fitted in with a necessity for integration into a new society. *The Goldbergs* and *I Remember Mama* were notable for their foregrounding of a strong matriarchal figure. *The Goldbergs* was created

Figure 5.4 Sid Caesar as one of his characters, the Professor, the world's greatest authority. The "interviewer" is Carl Reiner. Sid Caesar © Sidvid, 2000.

by its star, Molly Berg, one of the few women with executive power in early television. None of the shows lasted long past the 1950s, when memories of the immigrant past faded from much of the culture. *The Goldbergs* ended shortly after the family moved to the suburbs, their assimilation complete.

Live television and the "golden age" Much television in its first decade – comedies, variety, and drama – was "live." It was transmitted as it was being performed in front of the camera. The effect was somewhat akin to radio in the sense that listeners and performers enjoyed a synchronic experience, a connection of immediacy: what was seen and heard was happening at the moment of production and reception.

In the years since the 1950s, some nostalgia has grown around a fantasy of television's "golden age." For a brief period, a number of talented people were involved in creating the weekly original drama, bearing their sponsors' names – *Kraft Television Theater; Philco Television Playhouse; Lux Video Theater*; and the only one still with its original name, *Hallmark Hall of Fame*

Figure 5.5 One of Ernie Kovac's funniest gags. By tilting the set, and situating the camera so that the tilt didn't show, he could pour milk sideways. Ernie Kovacs © Ediad Productions, 1997.

– that were performed live. The plays were written by the likes of Rod Serling and Paddy Chayefsky, distinguished figures in early television. Many directors of these shows went on to influential careers in film – Arthur Penn, who directed *Bonnie and Clyde* (1967), and John Frankenheimer, who directed *The Manchurian Candidate* (1962). A number of actors, like Paul Newman and James Dean, began their careers on live TV.

The dramas – *Marty*, written by Paddy Chayefsky, directed by Delbert Man in 1953, is perhaps the best remembered (and the most readily available on video) – were structured within the very constraints of their live-ness. They were set indoors, in a few, contained spaces, focused on dialogue and close-ups of the actors speaking, and intensively, almost obsessively, examined the small lives of small

Figure 5.6 Television did not allow for blackface, and African-American actors (Spencer Williams, Jr., Tim Moore, Alvin Childress) played Amos 'n' Andy, and Kingfish, on television. Getty Images.

people – anxiety-ridden, lonely, and contained. Containment is an appropriate metaphor for these dramas as it was for the decade of the 1950s in which they appeared. The sense of constraint was not only apparent in the sets that the actors and camera had to move about in quickly, or in the smallness of the characters' lives. The golden age dramas were also contained by the larger anxieties of their sponsors and networks, themselves afraid of addressing larger social issues at a time when intellectual inquiry could bring about the charge of Communist subversion. Dramatizing the emotional lives of little people in small spaces – such as Marty, the local butcher, who thinks himself too ugly and boring to get a date – did not create controversy, suited the limitations of the television studio, and managed to create accurate, if claustrophobic, images of a difficult period in recent American history (figure 5.7).

Technologies of live broadcasting   Live television was a unique event, literally. Each program was one of its kind, gone the instant it was broadcast, because, unlike film – and there was much filmed programming on early television, as there is now – television had no satisfactory recording medium available. Videotape did not become an option until later in the decade after CBS, in 1956, used tape to deliver its evening news broadcast to the West Coast. The only records we have before videotape are kinescopes: 16 mm films that were recorded by putting a camera in front of a TV monitor. They look terrible and were not very useful during their time (hence the poor quality of some of the stills reproduced here).

The experience of live television was therefore limited – mostly to New York City, where the shows originated (when rebroadcast around the country the dramas were, of course, no longer "live"), and subject to all the constraints presented by the inability to edit an ongoing stream of images. There was, in short, little control available to the makers of the show and to their sponsors. The latter, especially, wished for greater control. The networks themselves, and especially after coaxial cable made it possible to simulcast "live from coast to coast," wanted more control over their programming. Since live broadcast was partly about a minimum of control and a maximum of contained spontaneity, its days were numbered. The history of early television is very much about the tussle for control of programming, a struggle that the networks won, though the victory certainly did not bring about novel programming.

Figure 5.7 The constrained world of live TV. Joe Mantell as Angie and Rod Steiger as Marty in *Marty*, broadcast live on May 24, 1953, written by Paddy Chayefsky, directed by Delbert Mann. In this scene, the dialogue, "Well, what d'ya feel like doin' tonight?" . . . "I dunno, whad'you feel like doin'?" passed into the culture at large. *Marty* © Rhino Home Entertainment, 1995.

Commercial Television and the Continuity of Fragmentation

With the exception of PBS (as we will see, PBS is sponsored, though the system is somewhat different from the other networks) and premium cable channels, television is a commercial medium. Sponsorship is its driving force. Viewership – how many of us watch a particular show – is used to set rates for advertisers, thereby determining the commercial viability of a show. There is another determination as well, one that goes beyond profit and loss to the very structures of television and the process of watching it.

Sponsorship

Live television drama, comedy, and music in the early 1950s usually had a single sponsor, which meant that program content was largely in the sponsor's and not the network's hands. The name was in the title: *The Voice of Firestone, The Texaco Star Theater, Kraft Television Theater*. By the mid-1950s, this began to change. Networks moved to assert control over program content. When simultaneous coast-to-coast transmission became the norm in the second half of the decade, creating a wider audience that needed to be served by a variety of programming, the relative sophistication of live drama and comics like Sid Caesar and Ernie Kovacs became problematic. A New York and Los Angeles audience might appreciate Caesar's parody of an Italian movie, or a Paddy Chayefsky play about diminished, working-class life, but networks and the sponsors who purchased time on network programs became very concerned about how a Midwestern audience might respond. *Marty*, written in the rhythms of New York working-class dialect, might play well in that city, but what would a viewer in Kansas make of it? This may *not* have been a problem that concerned actual viewers. After all, the theatrical film version of *Marty* did well enough. But it was part of the concern that always goes with commercial sponsorship. Television programming – and motion pictures as well – are often based on what the networks, the studios, and the advertisers *think* audiences will or will not accept.

These concerns are deeply woven into the media design. They reflect the fact that sponsors pay networks to air television programs, and both network and sponsor demand a return on their investment. This always breeds fear of the audience or on behalf of it. Let me be clear: not fear *on the part of the* audience, but fear on the part of sponsor and network as to what the audience may or may not like or even understand. In reality, an audience is a collection of individuals, each with his or her own particular response. But to the media producer, the audience is a faceless mass, only understood by means of sampling – for example, from information gathered from the viewing diaries kept by a handful of viewers that constitute the Nielsen ratings (the Nielsen company acts on behalf of advertisers and the networks, surveying audiences to determine – through viewer diaries – who is watching what) or by means of focus groups. It might well be that audiences across the country would have responded positively to serious television drama of the kind produced during the "golden age." But it certainly would not be the *size* of audience that the sponsor and network would like. Size matters in an expensive and fiscally productive medium like television. The size of viewership is used not only as a measure, but also as a stick by means of which network and sponsor prod what goes on their air.

Production

Television's moment of high-mindedness – which included live drama, classical music concerts, and serious interviews with cultural figures – lasted little more than half a decade. Such programming was always only a small part of the schedule, which, from the beginning, was dominated by crime series, courtroom dramas, westerns, situation comedies, quiz shows – the variety of genres that wax and wane in popularity, but provide the bedrock of television programming. Production of these shows, supervised by the networks that programmed them and the advertisers who paid for them, became increasingly dispersed. Hollywood always had a hand in this, despite its constant anxiety that television would siphon off the already declining audience for motion pictures. Still, it understood the economic necessity of taking part in the new medium. Early on, many film studios established television production units.

In short, from the late 1950s on, television was produced by many different companies and the programming contracted into the kind of fare we still see today – news, quiz shows, police procedurals, talk shows, reality, amateur talent, situation comedies. The comfort zones for producers and viewers alike.

Origination   The early history of television is full of the fascination of change on the part of producers and viewers. But I would like to move from the early days of television to the present in order to investigate how the structure of production and reception work – how shows are made and how we understand them. Here I will pursue a slightly different approach and address the *form* of television and the way that form influences and affects the way we see it.

The news (and this includes news "magazines" like *60 Minutes, 20/20, Dateline NBC,* as well as morning news programs) is produced by the networks themselves. Other programming originates from a variety of sources, either developed by the networks or pitched to them or to various movie studios by independent producers. "Independent" should not be taken as meaning "small." Programs are created by movie studios, some of which, like 20th Century Fox, Universal, and Disney, are connected through ownership to a network. Major producers, like Dick Wolf (the *Law and Order* shows) and Jerry Bruckheimer (*CSI,* and a number of other shows) have ongoing relations with the networks.

A new show comes into being as follows. When the network is convinced by a writer and producer that a program idea has merit – meaning they believe they can get sponsorship and viewers – they will order a pilot, which the network will show to test audiences. If it tests well, they may order some further episodes and put it on the schedule. Once aired, if the show looks like it may be popular – that is, garner sufficient ratings – the network will order enough episodes for either part of a season or complete run, up to about 20, enough for "all new" episodes during the beginning of the season in middle to late September, during "sweeps" months (November, February, and May, when the Nielsen rating service does a concentrated poll of viewers), and sprinkled throughout the rest of the season.

The hoped-for result of this work is the addition of a new stream into the programming schedule that will catch the dedicated gaze of the viewer and a dedicated revenue stream from advertisers. This only rarely works as planned. Individual viewers are not the same as the ideal viewer posited by networks and advertisers, and new shows often do not catch our gaze. When shows don't work, they will either be shifted around the schedule to try and catch the eyes of viewers – who themselves are always shifting, these days to alternate programming on cable and online. Increasingly, a network will give a new show two or three airings and then kill it if the ratings are unpromising.

When programming does work, the networks have a predictable schedule, a predictable audience, and a predictable income from advertisers. The producers of the programs see a future in reruns, in syndication, and in future DVD sales. The viewer, if caught up in the flow, has a steady and dependable source of entertainment.

The process of creating a new show is interdependent and not contained within the expected boundaries. For example, 20th Century Fox, the studio owned by Rupert Murdoch, whose company also runs Fox television, makes the sitcom *My Name is Earl,* which is broadcast on NBC. The medical show *House* is made by NBC, which is part of a company that includes Universal film studios, but it is broadcast on Fox. Sometimes the process can be initiated by an individual. Perhaps the most interesting recent development of a hit TV series occurred when Shonda Rhimes, an African-American woman, worked with movie producer Mark Gordon and others to create *Grey's Anatomy* for ABC. Rhimes started as writer and went on to become executive producer and "show runner" (the person who writes and produces the show) – the only African-American woman to achieve that position.

These intricate processes of origination and production of programs lead to complications when the shows are sent into syndication – that is, sold to other networks or to companies that distribute them to local stations – or when they are put on DVD. Negotiations over who holds distribution rights to shows can be fierce, particularly because a great deal of money is at stake when a show goes into syndication after, and sometimes *during*, its initial run.

Scheduling   Ordering up a show is only part of the process. The real art of getting our eyes on the screen has been that of determining the time slot when a show will appear. The process is complicated – increasingly so as viewers record shows to watch them at a later time. There is the self-imposed "family viewing hour" from 8:00–9:00, during which the networks offer only family-friendly shows, thereby forestalling censorship that might come down if "adult" material were shown at an early hour. This hour is increasingly being filled by inexpensive programming: quiz and reality shows; occasionally a sitcom. Dramas appear at 9:00 and 10:00.

Otherwise, scheduling is based on how shows test on various audiences, undertaken in an attempt to understand not only what kinds of shows an audience might like, but when particular age groups might want to watch a particular show. Ratings will be analyzed to see how similar programs have done on various days and in different time periods. The competition will be studied in an attempt either to avoid putting a show up against a popular program on another network or to try to beat another network by putting a strong program against one of theirs. A new show may be placed after a popular program already on the schedule in order to provide it with a "lead in," the programmer hoping that the audience will stay tuned for the new show. Genres will often be grouped together: comedies on certain nights; dramas on others.

As soon as the schedule is set, sales people will be out drumming up advertisers, charging them a sliding scale throughout the season, the cost of a commercial depending on the popularity of a show. (The cost for a 30-second spot on the finale of *American Idol* was recently quoted at around $1.3 million.) Trailers advertising upcoming programming will be made, with loud music, fast editing, and portentous voice-over, and shown throughout the summer months, as well as in the middle of current shows – these days often superimposed as a graphic over a show in progress.

Episode and series

In an attempt to account for and categorize the great variety of TV programming, television producers, and some theorists, make a distinction in dramas and comedies between episodic television, in which each week's installment is a complete narrative, and a serial form, in which storylines are continued from one week to the next. The serial form was most evident in soap operas, those afternoon melodramas, whose form was an invention of radio, and in which characters and situations flow in open-ended stream, one love affair or another betrayal spinning off the next for as many years as the show could last. *Desperate Housewives*, a modern version of the soap opera, borrows and at the same time parodies the form. But its intention is the same: to capture our attention and build interest in characters and events that are ongoing and to create desire to come back and see more. This is how the series are encoded. The decoding process occurs every week when we tune back in and become part of the flow. The effect is a kind of personalization, a stake we have in the programming and, by extension, the programmers. We promise them our dedicated gaze week after week until we tire of the series and stop looking.

Episodic television is much more the rule. Although the characters are the same in show after show, and the general narrative remains the same, each week there is a different twist: a different situation with girl- or boyfriend; a different murder to solve. Recent shows like *Lost, 24*, and their various imitators, are hybrids. They are series, in that the characters and their situation remains the same, but they are also episodic in that, each week, another puzzling event or another threat emerges, requiring more effort, more danger, and, for the viewer, more puzzles to figure out.

The Televisual Gaze and the Concept of Flow

"Series" and "episodes" are large generic blocks under which the more familiar genres of comedy, melodrama, thriller, police procedural, and the rest are nested. The ways in which they are created and produced aim to attract our attention and win our trust and loyalty. But the very phenomenon of "attention" is extremely complex, because, no matter how well produced, how much careful choice we make in what to watch (and, increasingly – through the use of time-shifting technologies – when to watch), our gaze is controlled. What we see in a show has been predetermined, though we are free to interpret it as we will. Even more important, *how* we see is also predetermined. Unless we watch a non-commercial cable channel, or record our shows to skip past commercials, our viewing is determined by programming that is continually interrupted by advertising. Network and local television programming is based on a principle of discontinuity, on interruption and, at the same time, on a kind of enforced continuity, so that interruption becomes as seamless as possible.

Flow

Visual narratives, stories told through images and dialogue, are driven by continuity. As viewers, we want to move from moment to moment, event to event, place to place, by an invisible set of linkages that should create a sense of process, of a story moving effortlessly from its beginning to end. Every shot of someone looking at something, followed by a shot of what that someone is looking at; every movement in one shot that is followed by a shot that appears to continue that movement; and every link from point to point in a narrative strives to enforce this sense of continuity. Even a shift in place but not in time, an illusion of simultaneity – someone held captive by a bad guy while the FBI searches for him – is accepted as part of the narrative movement by carefully coded information in the dialogue and the visuals. A shift in time but not in place can be accomplished by visual information – a dissolve or a fade out and fade in – that we understand because we have seen the conventions many times and know their meaning.

The conventions of visual narration were established in film early in the twentieth century (we will examine them again and in more detail in chapter 5) and imported into television. But commercial television added a problematic element, something that disturbs narrative continuity: the commercial itself. Visual narratives, which are immediately present, absorbing, and demanding of attention, make integration of the commercial into the main program more difficult than it was in radio. Television had to create an alternative, or supplement, to the conventions of continuity and did so simply by presenting *as a given* interruption as part of continuity; interruption *as* continuity. Making the commercial break *obvious* and *inevitable* made it part of the programming flow. We are asked, even against our will, to accept commercials not as the interruption they are, but as part of our viewing experience, as part of the "flow" of program form and content.

Raymond Williams   Raymond Williams was a British critic and theorist who was an important founder of cultural studies. On a trip to the United States in the 1970s, suffering jet lag, he turned on the television set in his hotel room. Accustomed to British television, which at that time was dominated by the commercial-free BBC and one commercial channel that only ran ads at the beginning and end of each program, he was surprised by what American viewers take completely for granted: continuous interruption of a program by commercials. Thinking through this phenomenon, Williams reached some conclusions. Of course the very concept of "continuous interruption" was a contradiction that could only be accounted for by a learned response. We look at television, and television looks back at us, as a flow of discontinuities, discordant bits of information: fictional narratives interrupted by commercials, news interrupted by commercials, talk interrupted by commercials. Yet American viewers tend to accept this state of continual interruption as a given, as making up the stream of programming. From this, Williams formulated his concept of "flow":

> What is being offered is not, in older terms, a programme of discrete units with particular insertions, but a planned flow, in which the true series is not the published sequence of programme items but this sequence transformed by the inclusion of another kind of sequence, so that these sequences together compose the real flow, the real "broadcasting." Increasingly, in both commercial and public-service television, a further sequence was added: trailers of programmes to be shown. ... And with the eventual unification of these ... sequences, a new kind of communication phenomenon has to be recognized. (1974: 84–5)

"A new kind of communication phenomenon that called for a new kind of response." Just as early film-makers worked to create narrative flow, using cutting to maintain continuity from sequence to sequence, so television producers tried to incorporate interruption into the programming by combining program and commercials that flowed into and out of one another. Narrative programming for television is created with "natural" pauses in the action: a surprise discovery that will be revealed following the commercial; a significant look that indicates a character has recognized someone or something that will be revealed after the commercial break; an unexpected statement by a character made before the cut to commercial. These pauses don't prevent interruption, they prepare us for it, acting as a kind of pulling in of the breath that allows us to exhale slowly over the course of the commercial break. If producers really want to get our attention, they will announce the commercial break with a loud noise on the sound track. It is a sort of knock on the head to make us pay attention.

The flow of commercials that follow any given break create their own continuity, not through content – an ad for a prescription drug will be followed by an ad for a room freshener, itself followed by an ad for a Ford SUV, and then a promo for an upcoming show – but each commercial will be spliced to the next without a breath: no pause, no fade, no dissolve. The result is a series of linked discontinuities, *coded* as flow because they move together with a kind of inevitability and a growing tendency to intrude into the main programming. Increasingly, when the program resumes, a large banner promoting another show will appear at the bottom of the screen. (Of course, there is that other kind of intrusion through product placements, where "commercials" appear as a part of the set or the dialogue.)

Fragments and wholes: continuous interruption   Television wants us to read these fragments as ongoing and interconnected, the commercials as important as program content, all linked together and inevitable. In the most passive state of our viewing, this is exactly how we decode all of this, and the rhythms of our watching are controlled by the rhythms of show and commercial, alternating without pause. Of course, our viewing is not always passive. At least since the advent of the infrared remote control in the 1970s, viewers have been able to mute commercials or avoid watching them entirely by quickly switching to another channel. With or without a remote, one can always leave the room. Since the turn of the twenty-first century, time-shifting technologies such as DVRs (Digital Video Recorders) have allowed viewers to record and watch a program at a later time, zipping past commercial breaks. This is causing networks and advertisers much anxiety, which will eventually lead to newer technologies that will compel us to watch the commercials or embed them within the programming itself.

But if we forget intervening technologies for the moment and consider television in its intended form, we realize that it has set up an unusual, demanding, and constraining interaction between itself and its viewers. Radio – because sight is not involved – is a more *usable* medium than television, relatively undemanding, permitting listeners to move in and out of direct contact with its programming. While listening to the radio one can take a walk, drive a car, or accomplish other tasks. Television, in contrast, takes up a large amount of audio and visual space, demanding concentration in spite of the fact that it keeps shifting our concentration from moment to moment. In a sense, television uses us – or wants to – in its attempt to seal our attention within its flow of program and commercials. Our attention becomes part of the flow, our gaze enveloped, our response woven between narrative and advertisement. Radio, in its prime, acted as a kind of cultural assimilation machine, drawing a diversity of cultures into its mix. Television attempts an assimilation of the individual. Its form is constructed by the way it embraces our gaze, inviting us to overcome discontinuity and move with its flow, expecting equal attention to everything on its screen, privileging us as uniquely attentive to its messages.

Fragmentation and condensation

Television wants to lock in our gaze, demanding perceptual continuity within the fragmented flow of program and commercials. But the gaze of television out at us is variable. It can be constant or sporadic. Different programming looks at us, and asks us to look at it in slightly different ways. Fictional narratives – drama and comedy – create closed worlds in which characters interact and a plot unfolds in a narrative process that invites our attention as onlookers who respond emotionally to the events. We laugh at the jokes, snicker at sexual innuendos, recoil at the violence, anticipate the solving of a crime, and gag at the sight of a wound; we are engaged both within the narrative and as privileged viewers of it. This narrative strategy comes to television from the movies, where the narrative envelopes the viewer in the illusion of an ongoing story, directing us to look at characters, at what the characters are looking at, communicating emotion, promising resolution. In adapting this narrative strategy, television retains the sense of an ongoing process, whether it be the comedic world of *I Love Lucy* or *Two and a Half Men*, or the dramatic worlds of *Gunsmoke* or *Grey's Anatomy*. It limits them, contracting locations to a house, a workplace, or the city streets, and fragments them. Television drama and comedy programming are continuously incomplete. Each episode presents a small situation or a large problem to be solved, but is set up to make us prepared for the next episode. Even if a crime of the week is solved, the team – the police or crime-scene investigators – are always ready for more, as "scenes from next week's episode" assure us.

Eye contact

Television comedy and drama asks for a continuously anticipatory as well as participatory gaze. They ask us to look and to look forward to, enjoy the current episode and be prepared for next week's, all the while sitting through commercial interruption. They are complete and incomplete, engaging us in the present tense of the narrative and engaging our expectations for the future. A show like *24* plays on this expectation, pretending that each hour's segment actually takes place in the hour in which it is viewed (though actually the dramatic part of each hour's flow is only a bit over 40 minutes long, allowing for a full 20 minutes of commercials), promising the next hour of adventure in next week's episode.

It is an unstated rule of cinematic and televisual narrative fiction that, while we look at the characters, the characters never look at us. Ours is a privileged gaze into, even within, a fictional world whose characters must not acknowledge our presence. Our gaze is woven into theirs, and, if we are properly engaged, even the disruptions caused by commercials won't disturb our involvement. News, information, variety, and some game shows request a different gaze. The participants in non-dramatic genres pretend to look right at us and address us directly. "Welcome to *American Idol*. I'm Ryan Seacrest and we are live tonight …" A newscaster will gaze at us and say, as if she were just invited into the room, "Good evening." The desire is to breach the "fourth wall" of the television screen, to make eye contact with viewers, inviting them into the world of entertainment – where, in the case of *American Idol* or any other variety show, the performers themselves sing to the camera, our surrogate eye, consciously making contact with us – to create a bond of immediacy and sincerity.

This eye contact is unique to television. The knowing eye of a television anchor serves to focus and anchor our own gaze, to gain our trust so that he or she can relay information to us without our questioning it. On most newscasts, the reporters in the field address the anchor, who, in a sense, collects their information while remaining our mediator to the news. Imparting information requires the creation of confidence on the part of the receiver, and so the newscaster looks us in the eye. Similarly, a variety show performer makes eye contact to create a sense of intimacy. A quiz or reality show host wants us to join in the fun and addresses us as participants.

Questions of the gaze

The question is how we read or decode the gaze. Does a television viewer return the intimacy? Is this intimacy greater than the purely aural connection we make with the sounds coming from the radio? Does the happy gaze of the local news team or the serious gaze of a *60 Minutes* investigative reporter change our response to what we are seeing? How do we reconfigure our own response when the direct gaze ends, as it always does; as programming shifts from, for example, drama to news or comedy to reality? The answers are embedded in the overriding issue of codes and conventions, of the ways television has asked us to respond and our response to its invitation. The best means of understanding this is to examine how the televisual gaze is constructed by the way various genres request our attention, our look and assent. To start, we need to re-enter the flow and examine the mechanics of the way television is programmed, which in turn programs our response.

Thursday Evening

We can gather the various eddies of the television flow together, and examine larger issues of genres, by spending a few hours watching television. The evening I've chosen is Thursday, traditionally a night when many people are watching, and the shows are CBS's *Survivor* and *CSI*, and NBC's *My Name is Earl* and *The Office*. *Survivor* has continued for many seasons, while the NBC shows are relative newcomers and have become hits for their network, even as the viewership for *Survivor* falls. In their prime, these shows garnered a large audience, and they offer excellent examples of generic variety. (Even if they are no longer on the schedule, they will be available to watch in syndication or on DVD.) They will also give us an opportunity to look at the larger genres the shows belong to, so that, even though we are focusing on one night, we will be able to follow the flow and its contributors as we look at other examples.

Reality television

Survivor is a member of what appears to be a new genre, the "reality" show. But genres are never quite "new" in the sense of appearing suddenly with no perceivable antecedents. Reality shows are no exception, and they have an interesting pedigree.

One of their ancestors comes from cinema and is a specific subgenre of documentary film-making. It is called, after the French who named it, *cinéma vérité*. Developed in the late 1950s and early 1960s, *cinéma vérité* created the illusion that the camera was documenting an ongoing series of events without the intrusion of the film-maker. There is no voice-over narration in *cinéma vérité*, and a narrative seems to develop out of the spontaneous actions of the characters under observation. Reality shows attempt to create that illusion of unmediated observation. Although most of them have a host, who introduces events and talks to the participants, the producers hope to give viewers a sense of participation and surprise, of ongoing events observed.

A more immediate television ancestor of reality programming is a 1950s television show called *Candid Camera*, in which the host, Allen Funt, would put unsuspecting people through embarrassing situations, finally revealing that they were on television. MTV's *Punk'd* is a recent variant of the format. The attraction of the *Candid Camera* genre was the delight viewers took in looking at other people squirm, a form of voyeurism that current reality shows depend on. But *Candid Camera* did not have a narrative. It was similar to sketch comedy in its presentation of one-off observations of perplexed participants.

The storytelling part of reality shows came from the 1973 PBS series, *American Family*, which documented an "actual" family, the Louds, as they went through increasingly wrenching life processes, including divorce and the coming out of the family's gay son. MTV picked up the thread in 1992, but refined the genre by introducing an element of control and artifice. *The Real World* put "real" people into an artificial environment, forcing them to confront each other in ways that would not occur in reality. The results are edited (as was the case with *American Family*) in order to create and focus the drama. The drama acted as a kind of mirror for the audience, especially of young people, seeing and hearing people like them responding to familiar situations.

The oldest stream feeding "reality" TV is the quiz show, which goes all the way back to radio. This is a more complex genre than would first appear. On the surface, quiz shows simply involve contestants – "real" people – who are asked questions posed by a host. If the contestant answers correctly, he or she will win money or other prizes. Contestants who answer incorrectly will lose and disappear from the program. The concept of testing knowledge or skill in order to win is shared with card and board games – even computer games. In all cases, competition is rendered complex by adding various methods and obstacles to winning.

A number of elements enter the mix of television quiz shows that render them and their offshoots more than simple and sometimes less than harmless. A TV quiz show can be one long commercial, with rampant product placement and mini-commercials when the prizes are commodities rather than money. Any quiz program involves humiliation, the act of losing in which the loser is subjected to the invisible gaze of millions of viewers. Another problem is corruption.

Figure 5.8 Charles van Doren and Herb Stempel "competing" on the fixed quiz show, *Twenty-One* (1957). Everett Collection/Rex Features.

A defining moment in the history of television occurred in 1957, on an NBC quiz show named *Twenty-One*. The contestant was Charles Van Doren, a handsome college professor, the son of a respected poet and critic. His apparent intellectual acumen, his humility and good looks turned him into a celebrity, a cultural icon, the model of a public intellectual. He was perhaps the only intellectual, after Albert Einstein, to become so admired, so embraced by media and its audiences. He was on the cover of news magazines; he signed contracts to appear on other television shows. In a period of rampant anti-intellectualism, his was indeed a phenomenon, a thinking man who was also attractive and non-threatening. (See figure 5.8.)

Unfortunately, Van Doren's talent at knowing the answers to obscure questions was a fraud. Like all contestants on this and other shows, he was coached by the show's producers, and he was also fed the correct answers. Even after the scandal broke, he lied about his complicity. Two years passed before he admitted his part, resulting in humiliation beyond anything experienced by a losing contestant: he lost not only his celebrity but his position at Columbia University. Senate hearings upended his career and rumbled through the early foundations of television and the trusting gaze of its viewers.

Of course, it didn't put an end to quiz shows. After hiding in embarrassment for some years, they returned, and the long, long run of shows like *Jeopardy*, or even the flash-in-the-pans like *Who Wants To Be a Millionaire?* (popular enough to enter the phrase, "Is that your final answer?" into the cultural vocabulary) and its spin-off *Deal or No Deal*, with its complicated tricks and flashy sets, attest to the genre's popularity. The expectant gaze of participant and viewer, the desire for the contestant to win (or lose), as well as simple participation – can we guess more right answers than the contestant? – conspire to make the genre perpetually popular.

Reality programs are heirs to quiz shows and their game-show variants. Contestants are given problems to solve – most of them involving feats of physical endurance instead of knowledge – and there are losers. But people on most reality shows don't lose because they get something wrong; rather they lose because, for some reason, they displease the other contestants or the moderator. In the case of *American Idol*, a combination of talent and reality show, a democratic principle is at work, allowing the viewing audience – "America" – to vote for the winners by making multiple phone calls. This substitution of behavior for knowledge is part of a larger reconfiguring of the quiz show format. Rather than standing on a stage and answering questions, reality show contestants are placed in environments – various exotic locales, in the case of *Survivor* – and asked to perform stunts while playing roles in a larger story, forming self-sufficient communities, or "tribes" in *Survivor*'s jargon, going on treasure hunts for an "immunity idol," and plotting to get the better of the other tribes. At the beginning of one season, the series offered the promise of dividing "tribes" by race. This created exactly what it was intended to: a big buzz for the show. The racial gimmick lasted for one episode.

Like other programs in the reality show genre, *Survivor* is set up and edited as if it were a narrative, and a sequential one at that. Events occur one after the other as in an unfolding story. Gaps are filled in by the narrator/host, who summarizes things for the viewer, appears from time to time to present a "challenge" (usually involving physical endurance, like hanging off some structure until fatigue makes the contestant drop), and oversees the finale of each week's program, in which someone is "voted off the island." All the while, the contestants talk incessantly: they talk to each other, and they talk individually, addressing someone, though it's not clear who – the host, us? They don't quite make eye contact with the camera, but there is no indication of another person to whom they are directing their monologue. There is every indication that their incessant talking is not a linear process. In other words, the inserts of talk are taken at various times, or set up at specific times, to be edited into the final show that is put on the air.

Meanwhile, as they talk, there are cutaways to the other "tribe" members as they walk around, cook, and take part in other business; and to the wildlife of the particular location. Sometimes the videotape will be speeded up, so the characters look like they are zipping around. All of which adds up to the fact that someone is in control of this "reality," making the narrative, choosing the shots, determining how they will be ordered. The contestants *may* be speaking their minds, *may* be undergoing endurance tests, and *may* be voting each other off the island, but their reality is closely manipulated. Too much reality might be boring; carefully crafted expectation is the stuff of viewer interest. Expectation cannot be determined by spontaneous events, it has to be constructed; we viewers want a seamless narrative. We want reality manufactured to appear as an ongoing process with no boring quiet bits or periods of inaction.

This is clear in one episode of *Survivor Panama*, which has its own narrative occurring within the usual challenges and non-stop talking of the contestants. Here, Bruce, the oldest contestant, is sick (figure 5.9). His complaint is woven throughout the program; at one point another contestant says in voice-over that Bruce has been sick for ten or twelve days. Towards the end of the episode, poor Bruce is immobilized with stomach cramps, and the "medics" are finally called in to evacuate him. How much reality are we being exposed to here? Have the show's producers "really" allowed a man to get dangerously ill in order to create a drama and boost ratings?

If so, they ought to be guilty of reckless endangerment. Assuming that this is not the case, a larger question emerges. *Survivor* has an omniscient narrator – someone unseen, unheard, who is clearly ordering events and controlling what we see, if not what is actually happening. We are seeing Bruce suffer, which means that a camera is present: other people, beside the contestants, are taping the proceedings. And, of course, we can assume that the contestants are contracted to the production in ways that thoroughly cover the producers' liability.

The result of all this is an interesting kind of disconnectedness. The omniscient narration of a conventional dramatic program or movie asks us to forget the presence of the observing eye and allow our gaze to penetrate into the fictional world. But *Survivor* is meant to be nonfiction. On one level we are requested to observe the ongoing tale of Bruce's failing health, as if it were occurring in real time. At the same time, we can't help but ask why he is being allowed to suffer, even while we know that everything we see has already taken place and that were there any criminal negligence involved, we might have heard about it on that other form of "reality" programming, the news. (In fact, CBS does turn *Survivor* into "news" by following up Thursday's episode on its Friday morning *Early Show*, which is produced by CBS's news division.)

What is attractive about reality programming is that it allows us to have everything at once: the illusion of spontaneity, scantily clad people who talk more or less the way we do, conflict, mean-spiritedness, endurance, romance, someone winning and someone else losing, all in a controlled narrative environment. What's extremely attractive about reality programming for its producers and for the networks that carry it is that it is relatively cheap to make because there are no stars to pay, no high-priced writers, and a minimum of sets.

Survivor *and* American Idol   Before returning to our Thursday night line-up, and in order to further understand the phenomenon of "reality" programming, I want to digress a moment to investigate what happens when the reality format is combined with another genre, the amateur hour, which traces its lineage back to radio and earlier, to "live" community entertainment. *American Idol* is more than cheap to make: it was, during its heyday, a goldmine, attracting the highest number of viewers of any show running in its season, and garnering some of the highest prices for advertising. The talent showcased may not be so great, but that may be part of the attraction. The young people who perform are not (yet) overbearing celebrities, but are full of energy and delight in their work. With the help of the judges and guest stars from various kinds of popular music, their enthusiasm creates a genuinely genial atmosphere. The judges themselves combine kindness with pointed criticism as Simon Cowell doles out not only stinging (and accurate) remarks, but also the promise of a recording contract. He is the perfect judgmental father.

The narrative of *Idol* is as unsubtle as the singing. Typical of the amateur talent format, it mixes variety entertainment with judgment of the singers, both on the part of the judges and of viewers, who can vote many times for their favorite. During the main competition, one show is made up of performances, followed by another in which, with great suspense, some contestants are sent home. Continuity is maintained as the performers talk of their past and their drive to success, while each episode pushes their talents with a variety of popular musical formats. A story of developing stardom is told as each show develops both the contestants' poise – along with their wardrobe and hairstyle – in an ongoing act of grooming them into celebrity. Despite the fact that contestants are voted out each week, the larger narrative successfully sidesteps the humiliations that are embedded in many other reality shows – however stinging Simon's criticism may be. Taped interviews with the contestants and brief, behind-the-scenes sequences with the pop stars, who help them with their songs, offer a mix of humility and glitz, with a maximum of singing and minimum of humiliation. Unlike other reality shows, the environment of *American Idol* is show business itself and, rather than silly stunts, the test is talent and graciousness; the pressures are real and the judgments based – for the most part – on performance.

Thursday night comedy

We return to our Thursday evening and move on to the two NBC situation comedies that were programmed against *Survivor*: *My Name is Earl* and *The Office*. NBC, once the strongest of television networks, has been struggling of late to find its audience. A sign of a television network in trouble is the instability of its schedule, with shows being shifted around in search of an audience, rather than creating a stable schedule that viewers can depend on. (This means that, by the time you read this, these shows may be on at different times, different days, or not at all.) During the 1990s, NBC thrived with its Thursday line-up of comedies – an 11-year run of *Cheers* from 1982–93, followed by its spin-off, *Frasier*, which ran for another 11 years, followed by the 1989–98 run of *Seinfeld*. These three programs defined Thursday evening television and marked the maturation of the situation comedy genre, as old as television and radio, and whose roots can be traced back to the time of Shakespeare.

Comedy of humors   Sixteenth-century comedies of humors were based on an ancient belief that moods were controlled by elemental forces in the body, any one of which could become dominant and drive a personality. So, for example, a choleric humor would predispose a person to anger and ill temper, while a melancholic humor would create sadness, and phlegmatic humor, laziness. Modern situation comedy is similarly based on sets of characteristics, developed into characters who are defined by a narrow personality type that never changes and always responds to situations in the same way. A dumb character will always be dumb; a lecherous one will always make crude sexual remarks; a female character who cannot get a date will continue never to succeed in getting a date; a smart-aleck will always make wisecracks. The "situation" of situation comedy puts these narrow character types into an equally narrow set of circumstances, varied only within the spectrum of its characters' responses and set within an unchanging environment: an office, a bar, an apartment, the environs of a small town or a big city.

Situation comedy is made up of an unyielding set of conventions, an unchanging set of characters, and an unchanging physical environment. Situation comedy clearly raises the question of how we, as audience, remain interested in and respond to such a rigid set of conventions. Given such apparent lack of variety, what allows a sitcom to go on as long as some have? Familiarity with characters and the inevitability of their schemes, their fortunes and misfortunes, certainly. The sheer energy in keeping small but vital changes within the unchanging universe of the show. When that energy fails, so does viewer attention. Failure of a genre can be caused by a number of things. Sometimes the culture at large no longer responds to particular generic conventions; sometimes the lack of variation and the lack of invention within the generic conventions causes it to go stale. Regardless of the specifics that contribute to a show's failure, when the situation can longer yield laughs, the comedy fails.

Post-Seinfeld   Most of NBC's post-*Seinfeld*, post-*Frasier*, post-*Friends* sitcoms did not find an audience, and in an attempt to recapture its Thursday night pre-eminence the network tried moving two of its more popular comedies to the Thursday evening spot. *The Office* is based on a series that originated on the British Broadcasting Corporation (BBC). Ricky Gervais, a lead actor in the British series, is executive producer of the American version. British imports are not unusual in American television. Venerable old sitcoms like *All in the Family*, at least two recent quiz shows, *Who Wants To Be a Millionaire?* and *Deal or No Deal*, and *American Idol* all originated in England. For the translation to work, the show must shed all of its "foreign" elements and appear to be a native product. *The Office* does this by moving its location to Scranton, Pennsylvania, although the exteriors hardly matter, since most of the action takes place on a set made to look like a generic American office. The American version of the show retains the mock-documentary style of the original, allowing the characters to address the camera and providing for a shooting technique that departs from older sitcom conventions by appearing to be loose and spontaneous.

Three cameras and a laugh track   Conventionally, sitcoms were taped in front of live audiences, on a single set, using three cameras. This allowed for great speed because the show could literally be edited as it was performed – in a manner similar to the live TV dramas we discussed earlier – and the presence of an audience provided an excuse for adding a laugh track, which is still used to provide a measure of security for the producers of the program. If the audience sounds as if it were laughing hysterically, then viewers would hopefully join in. The laugh track is analogous to the musical score of a melodrama that will swell to propel emotions from screen to viewer during a climactic moment. The problem with a laugh track, however, is that it can be alienating. If the canned laughter is not met with an equivalent response from the viewer, the flow can be interrupted with an unwanted question – "why are things not as amusing as the synthetic laughter seems to say it is?" A show is headed for failure when the laugh track becomes a distraction, pointing only how unfunny a show is.

The alternative to the three-camera, live-audience convention is program production closer to film-making than television. Movies are made with one camera (the exception is that of complex actions sequences that can only be done once and therefore need to be covered from many angles). The one-camera format consumes more time and money, but permits greater flexibility. Rather than lighting an entire set for three cameras, any number of camera angles can be used, and each shot can be lit individually for greatest effect. With a single camera, a number of takes can be made and, during the editing process, the best takes can be used in assembling the show. More and more single camera sitcoms are taking advantage of their movie-like quality and doing away with the laugh track.

Cringe   *The Office* pushes the single-camera format by pretending that the camera is observing the characters as they go about their business, standing in for an unseen narrator, or perhaps for the viewer. This allows for an interesting substitution for the laugh track. Instead of telling us when to laugh – the idea being that if the audience laughs, even if the audience only exists as a sound effect, we should be laughing as well – the speeches made by the characters directly to the camera and the reactions of the characters to each other will clue us as to how we should respond. But this is situation comedy, and the response of the characters, and the audience, is always the same. *The Office* requires a response of cringing embarrassment, and uses that as its point of identification.

The situation is simple: a medium-sized office, whose business is selling paper products, is headed by Michael, a boss simultaneously clueless and narcissistic. He is played by Steve Carell, an actor who first came to prominence as a fake news reporter on Jon Stewart's *The Daily Show*, and who made his mark in the 2005 movie, *The 40-Year-Old Virgin*. Michael's "humor," his unchanging characteristic, is that he is unaware of his own stupidity and boorishness. He says what is on his mind, which is always banal and insulting. The embarrassed looks of his colleagues serve to pass comment on him. His assistant, Dwight, is even more dimwittedly self-important, alternately bullying and self-pitying. The rest of the staff are long-suffering, smarter than their boss and his flunky, and appearing diligent in contrast to their bosses' constant shirking, foolish plans, and bumbling lack of sensitivity. They all know better than Michael, and can only react with contempt and embarrassment, or, when it comes to the crunch, being sentimental and supportive.

Part of the subgenre of the workplace sitcom, which goes far back into television history and includes such shows as *MASH*, *The Andy Griffith Show*, *The Mary Tyler Moore Show*, and, arguably, *Cheers*, *The Office* substitutes workmates for dysfunctional family members. It pretends to indicate that we are all in the same boat, living lives of humorous desperation in circumstances that can be funny when they are not painful.

The Office *in the flow*   We are examining these programs in an artificial way, isolating them from the flow of program, commercial, promotions. Let's pay attention, for a moment, to the movement from program to commercials in our episode of *The Office*. We will find that the flow of material – in this case the juxtaposition of commercial and program – can create comic effects of its own. The pre-credit sequence of this episode involves a practical joke: the officious Dwight's office has been moved into the men's room. Dwight sits there like a fool while Kevin, one of his co-workers, comes out of the stall with a lit candle (a reference to how smelly the place is). Dwight reminds him to wash his hands. The opening credit sequence follows, ending with a brief fade out. The fade in reveals another office. A man walks into the cubicle area carrying a cupcake with a candle in it, which he places on another, younger man's desk. He says "Ta da … thanks for one solid year of great work, Jennings." The man answers, "It's '*Jenkins*,' sir." "You bet," says the older man, as he returns to his office. A voice-over butts in: "Hungry for a real celebration?" It turns out we are watching a commercial for Chili's restaurants; though, when it begins, we might have thought that we had returned to *The Office* itself.

Of course, any television viewer would know that a commercial will appear following the post-credit fade out, and, without knowing what kind of thinking went into preparing the network logs (the detailed schedules of programs and commercials that will appear on air during the broadcast day), it is impossible to know if the Chili's ad was purposely scheduled to appear exactly where it did, or if a programmer even knew the content of the ad when scheduling it. The point is that, if we ignore the flow, we miss the complete, sometimes ironic, occasionally confusing interplay of programmatic and commercial material. At the same time we need to ask, what is programmatic and what is commercial? The networks want to create shows that will attract viewers, who will in turn attract advertising. Advertisers want shows that will, in effect, be commercials for their commercials. They look at the flow from a different direction than viewers do. Because there is always the chance that we will swim against the flow, finding ways to get around or ignore commercials, the advertisers insist we stay with them. If programming can be so seamless that program and commercial can't be told apart, so much the better.

As I noted, *The Office* fits into the workplace variant of the situation comedy and serves to soothe an audience into believing that the office can serve as a surrogate for family. But the inhabitants of this sitcom are not a happy family, playing off each other's follies and enjoying each other's company. The best the characters can do is try to get the better of Michael and Dwight by playing tricks on them, or retreating into their own efficiencies, or getting done the work Michael won't do, while he is busy accomplishing such things as promoting Dwight from "Assistant to the Regional Manager" to "Assistant Regional Manager." If things get really bad and the office is under attack from the corporation that owns it, the group will band together.

This is a rare occurrence, however, and by substituting embarrassment for sentimentality, *The Office* winds up emphasizing the isolation and downright loneliness of the work experience. Even romance is painful as Jim and Pam endlessly exchange pained looks of unrequited love. The viewer's response to Michael's idiocy is likely to be a groan rather than a laugh – and a desire to run to your cubicle and hide, like many of the characters do. (See figure 5.10.)

Redneck humor   *The Office* is about middle-class job holders and is representative of that target audience of 18–49-year-old males that advertisers covet. *My Name is Earl,*

Figure 5.10 Michael gets a lesson in diversity on *The Office* (2005). *The Office* © Deedle-Dee Productions and Reveille LLC in association with Universal Media Studios, 2005.

which accompanies *The Office* on the Thursday schedule, creates an imaginary world of redneck wastrels and layabouts, who serve as objects not of cringing recognition, but of derision and hope. Its characters are the kind of stereotypes that television producers like to call "quirky," a term meant to convey the ordinary made to appear somewhat unusual. In *Earl*'s case, the quirkiness extends to a kind of crazy diversity. Earl's ex-wife, who is white, is married to an African-American and has a mixed-race child. His brother is a dimwit, but lives with a smart and sexy Hispanic maid. Earl himself is on a quest to right all the wrongs he has committed in his life, a narrative that drives all the episodes.

Also driving each show is Earl's voice-over, which guides us through the events, provides background, and facilitates the narrative. The voice-over has become popular across television genres, and can be heard in such shows as *Desperate Housewives* and *Grey's Anatomy,* where it provides wry commentary on events, somehow above the petty problems of the characters, inviting us to look on with concerned amusement. Earl's narrational voice is more knowing than his actual character and provides comic perspective for the episode and the entire series. Each episode is an attempt by Earl to make up for past misdeeds, to redeem himself. Male redemption is a narrative ploy used more often in film than television, perhaps because it is an easy way to close off a story rather than continue it from week to week. A character, who suddenly understands his sins and makes a move to correct or at least to understand them, packages a narrative tightly and guarantees a positive up tick in audience response. The world of *My Name is Earl* makes redemption an antic enterprise, allowing contact with comical characters – Earl's dumb brother, his scheming wife, his long-suffering father – and outrageous incidents, while at the same time offering a sentimental closure to each episode in which the shiftless character makes amends for his mistakes.

Both *The Office* and *My Name is Earl* are somewhat unusual among television sitcoms. *Earl* in particular moves the action outside the house or office, which are the centers of so much of the sitcom world. Even the characters of *The Office* occasionally bring their clueless behavior to the outside world. The characters of both are rarely treated sentimentally, and they all allow viewers a sense of superiority. Michael of *The Office* is insufferable and Earl and his comrades are too silly to provoke more than amused observation. Even more important, unlike most other contemporary sitcoms, they don't continually use sex as the springboard for plot and laugh lines. There are episodes of *My Name is Earl* in which he tries to make up for past sexual misdeeds, and the attraction of his brother, Randy, to Catalina is played up for how impossibly ridiculous it is. But the two shows do try to avoid the sexual innuendo and downright vulgarity (or at least play them up for laughs) that are commonplace in so many recent sitcoms, which are only occasionally very funny and sometimes a bit nasty.

How did NBC do with its attempt to revive comedy Thursday night? Not so well. It moved the popular *Will and Grace* – a long-running sitcom that went a small way to foreground gay characters – into the lead-in 8:00 slot, but that show ended with its

2006 season. NBC began the fall, 2006, season with *Earl* and *The Office* at the 8:00 PM slot, against *Survivor*. It hasn't been able to find a stable show for the 9:00–10:00 hour, which is held fast by CBS's very popular, though not always number one show, *CSI*. The result has been trying out other comedies – *Scrubs* and *30 Rock* (a genuinely funny show created by former *Saturday Night Live* personnel) – in an ongoing shift of timeslots that all but guarantees that viewers will be unable to settle into a comfortable viewing routine.

All in all, comedy is not faring well on television. Networks and producers are unsure of their audience; the clever writing that is essential to defining comic characters, and maintaining the rhythm of interchange between them, seems largely unavailable; the generic sitcom settings of home or workplace seem to be exhausted. *My Name is Earl* tries for a novel situation with suitably goofy characters, but can't get beyond repetition of the goofy. *The Office* seems bound mostly to make the viewer squirm. Only *30 Rock* seems able to capture the pleasurable silliness of the best of NBC's classic sitcoms.

Thursday night's dramatic genres

It is time to look at Thursday night's popular dramatic offering, *CSI*. As we have been doing with other genres, I want to enter the discussion by looking more broadly at dramatic television and their generic variables. This will enable us not only to understand *CSI* in more depth, but also to understand the range of dramatic programming available.

Like comedy, the generic array of television drama is limited, and imitation is rampant. When a particular genre becomes popular then more of the same will also be popular. This is the television version of Hollywood's "same only different" attempt to copy successful films into a series of imitations and sequels. In television, the tendency to build on success by imitation is intensive as well as extensive, with one show spawning versions of itself as well as imitations on other channels. There are, for example, three varieties of *Law and Order* and three of *CSI*. Because *CSI* is popular, there have been, at one time or another, three other crime-scene dramas: *NCIS* on CBS, *Crossing Jordan* on NBC, and *Bones* on Fox. (These shows have been so popular that they are influencing the culture at large: there has been a surge in college students wanting to major in forensics.) Series featuring the FBI are rampant: *Numbers, Without a Trace, Criminal Minds*. The hospital show, long a staple television genre, is having a revival. For a time, *ER* held pride of place of medical programs. Currently, *House* and *Grey's Anatomy* have revived it.

Desperate Housewives and the leavening of melodrama

It is important to stress that none of these genres are new. They are all traceable back to the earliest days of television and beyond. The forensic investigation is only the latest twist on the crime/detective genre; this and narratives about heroic doctors could be found in radio and movies in earlier days. The differences lie in the details – of crimes, of mutilated bodies, of production values themselves, the visual details of wide-screen, high-definition images; the desire to *see* more of bloody deaths and disease.

There is also a good deal of mixing of the genres. ABC's *Desperate Housewives* is a serious-comic parody of soap operas – anchoring itself in melodrama, leavening it with a dose of self-consciousness, taking itself seriously but not so seriously at the same time. I have noted earlier that soap opera was once one of radio's and, later, television's most popular forms. Soaps are a subgenre of melodrama, the genre that encompasses almost all other dramatic forms. Melodrama is about emotional excess, about the desire to feel and experience more. A soap opera (the term derives from the fact that the early radio version of soaps were sponsored by soap companies) is the perfect melodrama, filled with tears, threats, marriages gone bad, discovery of birth parents, evil people doing terrible things, sickness, and death. The difference between a soap opera and a self-contained melodrama, or even a melodramatic series, is that soaps never end. They can be stopped, but their narratives, instead of generating closure, keep generating new narrative threads.

Soap opera and the feminine　It has been theorized that soap opera is an intensively feminine form, its open-endedness and slow progression of events perfectly suited to the rhythms of a woman working at home. The *flow* of soap opera moves with the temperament and pace of a housewife's life. That life is no longer dominant. More and more women work outside of the home. The radio soap opera is all but gone and forgotten, and its television forms are diminishing. No wonder that when the soap reappears in the evening schedule, it does so in the guise of parody.

Desperate Housewives plays upon the conventions of soap opera, parodies them (by definition, parody exaggerates its target's characteristics and conventions), and plays a kind of counterpoint between its own seriousness and lack of seriousness. Danny Elfman's pizzicato score (Elfman is a prolific composer of film and TV scores, including *Spider Man* and *The Simpsons*), the voice-over narrator, whose slightly ironic tone distances us from the narrative she presumably oversees. A cynic might say that the show's success is actually due to the fact that it contains enough sexuality to keep the viewer properly, or improperly, engaged. Cynicism may be the last bulwark of a network programmer and television producer, but ultimately the viewer will see through it – we can only hope – and a program will survive on some other merits, or not survive at all. Audiences for *Desperate Housewives* fell off greatly after its first few seasons.

Lost　Another example of mixed genres is ABC's popular series, *Lost*. With its narrative built on the premise of plane crash survivors on a tropical island, it combines elements of *Survivor*, though without the pretense of observing "real" people; the old story of Robinson Crusoe stranded in the middle of the ocean; and, perhaps most interesting, some aspects of the computer game, *Myst*, which places the player on a strange island full of even stranger buildings, chambers, instruments, and characters. Out of these elements, *Lost* builds a web of mutual suspicion, profound paranoia, endless clues, and few answers. It parcels out bits of information and more and more questions from episode to episode, providing backstory (the characters' past that partially explains their activities on the island), and new discoveries. It mixes up chronology and fools our perceptions of things.

Lost makes the most of its constrained narrative space and its characters, alternatively frightened or ominous (figure 5.11). It responds to our daily feelings of insecurity by providing an ongoing story about paranoia writ large where enemies seen and unseen, past, present, and future, lurk and threaten. It provides as well a larger narrative of participation, where fans blog, create websites, and participate in trying to figure out the islands' mysteries.

Figure 5.11 *Lost*: John Locke faces the "Others" after they tied his father to some island ruins. The "Others" demand a sacrifice (2007). *Lost* © ABC Studios, 2007.

CSI, televisuality, and politics

CSI is less about paranoia than it is about fascination, attraction, and repulsion, about investigating and *seeing* all the possible woundings and mutilations of the human body. There are three varieties in the *CSI* group, and here I want to focus on the original, the Las Vegas *CSI*, the show that broke new ground not only in content, but in its style as well. In order to understand what *CSI* has done we need to digress once again and look at a bit of television history and, in particular, the history of visual style.

CSI: *style*   There has been a steady evolution of the way television programs – especially filmed programs – look. We discussed the single-camera style of some situation comedy, which allows for exterior shooting and more subtle lighting. This subtlety of visual style is noticeable across the board: current dramatic series are now composed with lighting like the most carefully made motion pictures.

The visual style of *CSI* can be traced back as far as the 1980s, to shows like *Beauty and the Beast*. But its main television precursor is *The X-Files*, the series that ran from 1993–2002. *The X-Files* was a nine-year celebration of paranoia, drawing on elements of science fiction, horror, the occult, and conspiracy theory. It drew on history as far back as the assassination of President John F. Kennedy (an event that still remains a subject of speculation and unease in American culture), tapped into the bizarre mass hallucination of alien abduction, and played on the fear of secret government operations replete with black helicopters and men in black (we have learned once again that the paranoia of fiction has a basis in fact: the government has kidnapped people and taken them to foreign countries to be tortured in the name of fighting terrorism). FBI agents Mulder and Scully searched for the truth of these fears, truths that were "out there" in a world of smoke and shadows.

The *mise en scène* of *The X-Files* was as dark as its narrative – though perhaps this should be stated the other way around: the dark, claustrophobic spaces of the show communicated the atmosphere of the murky stories being told. *The X-Files* made great use of very little, achieving its style and therefore its narrative strengths by showing just as much as necessary and hiding as much as possible. This was an economy of production that allowed for an excess of imagination.

The televisual style　　Like *The X-Files*, *CSI* is a visually intricate production. Like many current television shows that are made on film, the locations and sets are carefully lit and full of small details. Composition – the way a shot is put together within the frame – is artfully arranged, with people and objects positioned for best visual effect. This is a far cry from the low-contrast, low-resolution black and white of early television, and approaches in its artfulness the visual richness of motion pictures. (Figures 5.3 and 5.7 offer examples of what early television looked like.)

Television theorist John Caldwell coined the term "televisuality" to describe the complexity of style that, beginning in the 1980s, began to inscribe television images with a richness of detail and flourish of color and special effects – "to flaunt and display style." He points to a number of factors that made this "flaunting" possible, including advances in video technologies, a growing visual sophistication on the part of television producers and the technicians who made the images, and the increasing need to individuate programs out of the unending flow of programming that makes up the broadcast day. The *look* of a show, as well as the stories the show tells and the genre containing those stories, can be one of its special attributes, something that allows it to come to the surface of the flow and attract attention. Earlier I suggested that "flow" itself was the form of the television, or, more specifically, of the shared perceptual space of the television viewer and the programming that moves inexorably before her. But inevitably, as our discussion continued, we examined the programs themselves and the genres they belonged to, as if they could be pulled away from the flow. With the introduction of the concept of televisuality, I am suggesting that we can remove the program from the flow entirely and look at it as a stylistic, formal entity – as we did when examining the single-camera style of situation comedy, and as we also do when we watch a show online or on DVD.

Cool resolution　　Televisuality is created both *because of* and *in spite of* the technical limitations of the medium. In the famous words of Marshall McLuhan, the early media studies theorist, television is a "cool" medium. He was not referring to contemporary, quirky programming, but rather to the look of TV, its (at the time) low resolution, and the resulting low contrast, grayish hue of the screen. His point was that, lacking visual energy and definition – as opposed to the "hot" medium of film – television makes a strong demand on our gaze. We need to look closely and will ourselves into the flow of low-definition images.

McLuhan was right about early television's lack of definition and resolution. The standard black-and-white, 525 lines of resolutions (meaning that the electron beam that lights the phosphors on the back of a cathode ray tube scans at 525 times a second) yields an image without much definition. Combined with the small size of early television sets, and the uncertain quality of over-the-air transmission, early television was, in fact, hard to look at. That very difficulty was, as McLuhan points out, something viewers had to overcome through visual concentration. And they did: engagement, even communal engagement, with television began very soon after its introduction. Precisely because the image was poor, it forced both the producer of programs and the viewer to focus his gaze.

MTV   The visual style of early television depended on enclosed spaces and close-ups that could be easily contained within the small screen and low resolution. By the late 1950s, screen size increased to about 21 inches, and, by the late 1960s, screens became even larger and the move to all color transmission, which added more detail to the image, was complete. By the 1980s, new technologies, a tendency to look toward cinema for formal inspiration as well as content, and the ongoing need to attract the viewer's gaze, led to the development of stylistic subtleties: refinements in lighting; more complex compositions; and rapid editing. MTV, which began in 1981, played no small part in this transition. Unashamedly cinematic in the visual flourish of its music videos, and innovative in its editing, MTV didn't simply bring cinematic technique to television, but created a third form that combined the two and then influenced both in turn. That "third form" is the televisual style that opens the space of the television screen, explores the color palette, and rivets the viewer's gaze with rapid cutting.

To be sure, MTV music videos are commercials. Their purpose is to sell recorded music. But their form, sometimes surreal, always rhythmic, experimenting with color and black and white, often directed by established or new movie directors (Martin Scorsese filmed Michael Jackson's video, "Bad," in 1987; David Fincher, director of *Seven* and *Fight Club*, made Madonna videos), exemplified stylized excess. They refused the traditional constraints on composing and lighting scenes for television and instead exploited these constraints in order to break out of them. The editing of music videos became notorious, accused as the cause of, or response to, the short attention span of their viewers. Neither of these was true, and the fact of rapid editing, combined with an increasing density of the visuals, was responsible for heightened attention and a dedicated gaze.

The style of music videos spread across television and movies, part of that flow of cross-fertilization that marks all media as they respond to, imitate, improve upon, and compete against one another for our attention. The creators of network television shows began to create complex imaginative worlds with textured, dense visual spaces. With devices as simple as blowing dry ice onto the set to create a sense of depth, or as complex as digital imagery to create fantastic effects – like the journey through the wounds of a *CSI* victim – televisual space now equals film in its ability to communicate emotion and mood with as much eloquence as the dialogue.

High definition   The most important technological change to occur in recent years is that of moving television from a "cool" to a "hot" medium. "High definition," Marshall McLuhan wrote, as if prophesying the change, "is the state of being well filled with data." At almost twice the resolution of the current television image, high definition television approaches the movie image in clarity and color range. It is full of visual information and further supports the televisual style, enabling acute detail, subtle lighting, and careful composition and editing. Combined with a new generation of LCD and liquid plasma television receivers, the very experience of watching TV is converging toward the way we watch movies. And, while commercial television still requires our attention to the continual interruptions of the flow, its images – even the images of commercials, which themselves are increasingly being produced in high definition – are giving us more visual data than ever. The increase in visual data requires even more attention in order to be aware of all the details.

Seven, Law and Order, *and* CSI   This allows us to return to *CSI* and more fully appreciate that fact that it is one of the most stylized of current television shows, one of the most *televisual*. Its style is strongly influenced not only by *The X-Files*, its television ancestor, but by David Fincher's film *Seven* (1995), a serial killer movie with an intensely dark, claustrophobic visual style, a film fully as paranoid as *The X-Files* and which provides the cinematic element so important to the *CSI* "look." That *CSI* is so cinematic, that it uses the most technologically advanced digital effects to achieve that look, is no surprise. Its executive producer is Jerry Bruckheimer, whose film credits include *Beverly Hills Cop* (1984), *Top Gun* (1986), *The Rock* (1986), *Con Air* (1987), *Armageddon* (1998), *Black Hawk Down* (2001), and *Pirates of the Caribbean* (2003, 2006, 2007). In addition to the *CSI* collection, his company also produces *Without a Trace*, *Cold Case*, and the "reality" show, *The Amazing Race*. He brought, through the creators, producers, and directors of his various shows, a film-maker's intelligence to the making of television that pushed the medium's visual boundaries.

Each episode of *CSI* is tightly drawn in short, compact sequences, dramatically contoured to play out into a commercial and then resume, feeding us more narrative information. The cinematic style of each episode makes use of an intense color scheme, beyond the limited spectrum of conventional television. As in film – good film, at least – color and lighting are modulated to create mood. The flagship *CSI* series plays off the dazzle of Las Vegas, bright lights of the strip alternating with dark rooms in which unspeakable crimes have occurred. Interleaved are the stainless steel, and lucite spaces of the crime lab, fluorescent lit and blue-tinged, where montages of evidence processing are cut to a rhythmical sound track that allows hard, scientific work to appear less tedious, and much more speedy than it actually is. These spaces are filled with detail, an elaborate production design that requires an attentive gaze, on the part of the production, the characters, and the viewer of the program.

Generically, the *CSI* series are variations on the police procedural, itself a subgenre of detective and gangster narratives. The contemporary model of the genre is Dick Wolf's *Law and Order* and its variants. In all instances, the genre moves, within each episode, from crime to detection, examining the various steps along the way. *Law and Order* extends the procedure by including a trial in each episode, creating an extremely compact narrative structure in which events happen rapidly, each scene heavy with information that depends upon viewer attention and recognition of various codes of behavior and event. Heavy with information, but also empty of information. Such compact televisual narratives require that the viewer take much for granted and supply, quickly, the information that must be left out. This is an example of what McLuhan meant by "cool," and what we have been discussing under the rubric of coding and decoding. These programs depend on us to supply the narrative information offered in a look, a nod, a gesture of the hand, or a tone of voice.

CSI elevates the crime lab and its employees to the status of detectives and foregrounds not only their procedures, but also its subject: dead bodies and wounds. Much of the color and detail of the show is devoted to looking at disgusting things. The broken interiors of dead bodies become the object of the fascinated gaze of both the investigators in the narrative and the viewers of it. And they are as detailed and colorful as the crime lab in which they lie. (See figure 5.12.)

Figure 5.12 Body parts figure largely on *CSI*, as this popped eyeball demonstrates. *CSI* © Jerry Bruckheimer Television, CBS Paramount Network Television, 2006.

CSI is not merely an extension of the police procedural, but a strange variation on that other perennial popular television genre, the doctor show. All these genres and their variants create a paranoia of the body and pretend to offer a mastery of that paranoia. They speak of sudden, violent crime occurring next door, on the street, to us; of the body breaking, hurting, dying. They are the fictional parallel to the local news and its tales of homicide, fires, traffic accidents, devastating storms: a world of catastrophe. *CSI* merely ups the ante, reveling in blood splatter, splitting cartilage, and journeying through open wounds into the body's bloody, liquid interiors. But there is something more. *CSI* began in 2000, but in the wake of 9/11/2001 and the war in Iraq, when the unthinkable became visible, and grotesquely damaged and tortured bodies were no longer imagined but real, what we are shown on *CSI* becomes a representation of larger reality. Its stylized fiction brushes uncomfortably against reality. The producers of the show are aware of that.

Allegories of history In one of its most fascinating and curious episodes, aired February, 2006, the *CSI* team finds a tortured body in the desert, complete with a number branded into its skin. The narrative is filled with excruciating detail and odd characters, including popped eyeballs, bodily fluids, self-mutilation, an ancient manuscript, a dominatrix, and – typical of Bruckheimer's series – little hints about the private lives of its main characters. At its base, though, the episode concerns pharmaceuticals and a Nazi torturer named Sneller, who assumes his adopted family name of his Americanized brother, Wolfowitz, and works as a clinician performing drug trials while torturing people horribly. (See figure 5.13.)

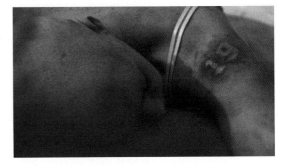

Figure 5.13 A victim of Nazi-like torture on *CSI* (2006). *CSI* © Jerry Bruckheimer Television, CBS Paramount Network Television, 2006.

When we peel away all the intricacies of plot, and move through the fascinating, revolting images of popped eyeballs, we are left with a question. Is the character's name, Wolfowitz, a random choice? Did Jerry Stahl, who wrote the episode (he is also a novelist of some note), or the *fourteen* co-, executive, supervising, and just plain producers of the show, plus Jerry Bruckheimer, not make the connection of their torturer character with a real-life Wolfowitz, Paul Wolfowitz, who happened to be former deputy Secretary of Defense and subsequently head of the World Bank? Paul Wolfowitz was one of the premier architects of the Iraqi War and is intimately tied to the government-approved torture of detainees at the Guantánamo military prison.

Many police procedurals base their episodes on stories "ripped from the headlines." But it is very rare for political allegory to be laid down as a matrix supporting the narrative of a popular television show, especially when, at this point in media history, the major desire of TV networks is not to offend anyone. The fact is that *CSI is* offensive, certainly if we compare its graphic images and narratives of sexual violence with the kind of content permissible just a few years ago. Perhaps, given its popularity, all the supervisors and producers of the show felt secure in permitting a comment on current history to poke out from the detached eyeballs, seminal fluids, frozen bodies, and a woman with a whip and create a political allegory in this, episode 615 of *CSI*, "Pirates of the Third Reich."

This episode of *CSI*, more than anything else on a Thursday night, spoke to the world – to war and torture, pain, and the seeming inability to learn from history. It is unusual even for *CSI*, not to mention all of our Thursday evening shows, indeed all of television, which tries to be as bland and simply entertaining as possible. If TV drama makes us worry at all, it also makes sure that a paternal figure – usually an FBI man with his young assistants – makes it as right as possible. It is the function of comedy, on the other hand, to indicate that, crazy as things are, somehow they will always come out right. But for one evening, at least, serious television brushed against an even more serious world.

Evolution of the Television Landscape

Bland, comedic, banal, melodramatic, violent, or political, television always manages to narrate our fears and pleasures as much as it narrates, or, perhaps more accurately, steers us in and out of the commercial messages that are the stream on which its programming floats and our attention flows. That a program occasionally bumps into the "real" world – as opposed, say, to the really fake worlds of "reality" shows – may be a coincidence, a statistical accident, or even a calculated response to a political climate of fear and repression.

TV makers are generally not a brave bunch, and there exist many pressure groups, who have the ear of the FCC, which is now fining the networks for what it perceives – or is told – are infractions against morality, or simply infractions that someone finds offensive. At the same time, the traditional networks are in competition with an enormous number of cable channels, a very few of which indulge in a freedom of expression that commercially sponsored television cannot hope to match, and over which the FCC has no control. The major networks' occasional forays into boldness – exemplified in the *CSI* Wolfowitz episode – may be part of "old" television's attempts to compete.

Cable

The fact is that the television landscape has changed greatly from the traditional model we have been investigating so far. The four networks – CBS, NBC, ABC, and Fox – now must survive in the sea of cable channels. Like so much of media, cable began as a technology, specifically a technological fix for the problem of getting a broadcast signal over mountains to communities that could not otherwise receive it. In media, necessity is always the mother of profit, and cable networks emerged that provided not only a signal, but specialized programming – recent movies, sports events, music, comedy – on a pay-per-view or subscription basis.

The physical construction of cable infrastructure – pulling cable over telephone poles or under the street – was an expensive proposition that economically and logistically seemed best undertaken by one company. This resulted in a lack of competition as companies whose main job was to build and operate cable negotiated with various counties or communities, usually paying them a percentage of their profits and offering local access channels. Cable subscribers received "basic" channels – usually including the networks and sponsored channels like CNN – for a set fee, paying extra for commercial-free channels like HBO.

All of this created many legal battles, much lobbying of the Federal Communications Commission, and a continuous changing of the rules until, today, not unexpectedly, a few telecommunications companies operate a number of cable franchises, some of them, like Time Warner and Comcast, owning the infrastructure *and* the distribution of content. In terms of viewership, cable or satellite – another distribution form mainly for communities not served by cable – serves almost everyone, not only in the United States, but internationally as well. Two of the most powerful media moguls, Rupert Murdoch, who owns Fox, and Silvio Berlusconi, Prime Minister of Italy, got their start developing European cable and satellite television services.

Diversity

Within the US, the popularity of cable is due to its promise of more and better programming. But the promise has turned into the obstacle of confusion. There are literally hundreds of cable and satellite channels, many of them clones of one another, cycling the same movies or old television series across the schedule and around the clock. Some – shopping channels, for example – broadcast 24-hour commercials. Some offer unique programming, like CSPAN's coverage of the House and Senate and talks by authors. TVLand offers the nostalgic solace of old television series. There are also very small outlets, available on a few satellite and cable line-ups – university channels presenting serious research, or Free Speech TV (FSTV) that provide news and documentaries to the left of the mainstream. Logo, a still small cable network that is part of the Viacom/MTV group, programs for the gay community.

Many cable channels, large and small, including BET (Black Entertainment Television) and the giant Univision (delivering Hispanic programming), serve racial and ethnic groups that are otherwise unrepresented or simply not catered to by network television. These cable networks originate programming or, in the case of Spanish-language networks, pick up the enormously popular soap operas, called *telenovelas*, from Latin American television, like Brazil's Globo. *Ugly Betty*, a sweet-tempered comedy-drama that was, for a while, a hit on ABC, was based on a Colombian soap opera.

We have seen how MTV, one of the oldest cable networks, generated a new televisual style. Among the other large cable networks, perhaps only HBO has created anything that could be considered new ideas in programming. Working within the greatly expanded freedom of a "private," subscriber-driven network (such networks are funded by the extra money we pay cable and satellite providers to receive them), thriving on a tradition of allowing the seven (at least) dirty words to be spoken, and reasonably explicit sexuality to be shown, HBO has developed series and original films in a variety of genres that go beyond the limited and repetitive programming of the old networks.

With few exceptions, HBO's series are in actuality elaborations of established television and movie genres. Its extremely popular series, *The Sopranos*, was a long extension of Martin Scorsese's 1990 film about lower-middle-class Mafiosi, *Goodfellas* (even using some of the same cast of that film). *Sex and the City* was a more explicit riff on some general sitcom postulates – in this instance, the tightly knit group of friends narrating their sexual adventures. Others, like *Six Feet Under* and *Big Love*, mixed situation comedy and melodrama in odd environments: a funeral home in the former; a Mormon polygamous household in the latter. But some of its shows push out in interesting directions. *The Wire* was an urban drama of some power and depth, treating the police and racial minorities with an insight rare on commercial television. Larry David, co-creator of *Seinfeld*, condensed most of the characters of that series into one persona, a smart, put-upon, bumbling, self-centered, self-righteous individual whose narcissism is a constant generator of anger in others and surprise in himself in the series *Curb Your Enthusiasm*.

Curb Your Enthusiasm pours the format of situation comedy through a funnel, into a character who reacts the same way to any situation: a funeral, a basketball game, a movie set, to become the catalyst for coincidences that may be as diverse as Larry tripping Shaquille O'Neal during a basketball game and then plying him with *Seinfeld* tapes in the hospital, or inadvertently hiring a chef with Tourette's Syndrome for his new restaurant, causing all the guests to join in a chorus of loud and joyous cursing in solidarity with their beleaguered cook. It is parody, self-satire, and cringe comedy; it is capable of creating self-recognition by creating a character who cannot recognize what a fool he is.

HBO's western, *Deadwood*, which was a kind of sequel to Robert Altman's 1971 film, *McCabe and Mrs Miller*, pushes against established generic boundaries by imagining a western settlement filled with connivers and cheats, dirty of body and mouth, speaking a fascinating artificial dialogue that occasionally borders on the Shakespearean.

None of this should either over- or undervalue what HBO is doing. It has freedom – too much in the eyes of current watchdog groups who complain to FCC about shows deemed immoral – and an audience that is as carefully, more narrowly, targeted as that of any other network. Its producers have the freedom and the money to do pretty much what they want, even to the extent of creating their own full-length feature films. That they too often fall into tricking out conventional material with more overt sexuality and certainly more four-letter words than the old networks may be the fate of any media outlet wanting to engage the largest audience possible.

The rise and fall of PBS

Lost between the commercial, over-the-air networks and the wide world of cable is the network that had promised the most, and arguably is now offering the least in alternative television. The ancestry of PBS lies in that part of the spectrum that the FCC cordoned off for educational broadcasting during "the freeze" in the late 1940s. It lies also in the early and brief attempts at cultural programming on network television in the 1950s, most especially a program called *Omnibus*, which knocked around CBS and ABC on Sunday afternoons, sponsored not by a commercial product, but by the Ford Foundation. *Omnibus* lived up to its title by presenting a wide variety of cultural events from poetry to drama to jazz, and Orson Welles playing King Lear, or composer-conductor Leonard Bernstein analyzing classical music.

The Ford Foundation also funded the early efforts of public television, which emerged under the guidance of the National Association of Educational Broadcasters, a group that formed the nucleus of public radio (discussed in chapter 4), along with other private foundations. Beginning in the mid-1950s, a number of universities and municipalities constituted what would become a strong, but loosely confederated, network of educational television stations. Some of these stations, like KCET in Los Angeles, WQED in Pittsburgh, WGBH in Boston, and WNET in New York still remain as important producers of PBS programming. The Public Broadcasting Act of 1967 created the government-funded Corporation for Public Broadcasting, which oversees PBS, its television network, and National Public Radio.

From the start, PBS stations faced challenges. Most of the frequencies originally allotted by the FCC for educational programming were on the high, UHF portion of the dial, so it took an additional FCC ruling to have television manufacturers build sets that could receive them. Funding was a problem from the beginning, as was political interference, the latter problem remaining to this day. In spite of these challenges, Public Television was a major cultural force in the second half of the twentieth century.

Community was a key idea for Public Television. Its audience has always been small, intelligent, and diverse. Rather than attempt to target most of it at one time, as the networks do, its programming clustered them by interest. Hence the now legendary "do it yourself" genres developed mostly by Boston's WGBH – Julia Child's cooking shows, home repair on *This Old House*, gardening on *Victory Garden* – shared expertise and engaged their viewers in process.

PBS children's programming　PBS soon built a solid reputation for well-researched, entertaining children's programming, notably with *Sesame Street* and *Mr Rogers' Neighborhood*. These shows provided gentle introductions to the basics of numbers and the alphabet as well as more complex notions of how a community functions and thrives. They were based on sound educational principles and were neither exploitative nor dumbed down. They spoke to children with a delighted and knowing voice. While the networks and local television provided visual babysitting, locking children's gaze into cheaply made animations, the Children's Television Workshop and other producers of PBS children's programs were using animation and puppetry, intelligently arranged sound and music, and educational theory. The programming attempted to address what most commercial television – in any genre, whether for children or for adults – largely evaded: a sense of community, a notion of sharing, and responsibility.

PBS documentaries   PBS and its contributing producers and film-makers also perfected the genre of the nature documentary. Drawing on diverse traditions – among them Walt Disney's 1953 film, *The Living Desert,* and early commercial television programs like *Zoo Train,* as well as the documentary traditions of the British Broadcasting Corporation – PBS, its affiliate stations, and the overseas programming it purchased created a visual and narrative catalogue of the natural world.

But the truly groundbreaking PBS achievement in documentary programming comes largely from the work of one film-maker, Ken Burns. His 1990 series, *The Civil War,* while coming late in the history of PBS, became its most popular series and quickly established a style of visual history as quasi-personal narrative. The Burns documentary style is simple: collect a large variety of archival photographs and personal letters and diaries; create visuals by panning and zooming around and into the photographs, dissolving from one to another, and create the aural experience with evocative background music while a number of voices read from the letters and diaries, ending with the narrator saying the name of the writer. The result is a narrative that seems to emerge effortlessly from personal recollection and carefully observed images.

The Civil War series is a curious mixture of political neutrality and Civil War sentimentality, ultimately too close to the general cultural nostalgia about a war and era that was, in fact, brutal and racist, but which lives on in re-enactments of battles and sometimes desperate attempts to hang on to what is euphemistically called "Southern culture" and "the war of Northern aggression." By being inoffensively sentimental and barely political, Burns was able to attract a large audience. Without doubt, information was imparted to viewers who rarely read history; by necessity much detail was left out; by choice, the politics of the Civil War were made subservient to the sentimentality of the personal.

Burns has gone on to make many documentaries for PBS, including one on the early pioneers of radio and on World War II. His visual style has become a cliché and even the basis for software that amateur photographers use to give their pictures the "Ken Burns Effect." This interesting infiltration of a televisual style into the general culture is tribute, perhaps, to the power of Burns's visuals, although it might also be a tribute to the ordinariness of the style itself. Ordinary or extraordinary, there is no question that Burns and PBS are now inextricably linked to the benefit of both. There is in Burns's work the stamp of authority that flows over the network itself.

PBS and the BBC   Many of PBS's nature and science shows, and almost all of its dramatic programming – including the WGBH flagship series, *Masterpiece Theater* – came from Britain, particularly the BBC. This, happily, exposed American viewers to British television, providing, in comedy shows like *Monty Python's Flying Circus,* a kind of television it would never otherwise see. It also allowed PBS to avoid the more expensive process of originating and producing its own dramatic fare. At the same time, the preponderance of BBC drama on PBS allowed it to trade on the idea of the cultural superiority of British television – an idea that rapidly collapses once a viewer sees the ordinary programming of British drama sitcoms (available on the cable network, BBC America), which are every bit as awful as the worst American ones. We can, in hindsight, foresee the dangers to PBS's standing in its dependence on British material. It built a reputation, in part, on material that was not its own, and has had continually to define its diversity to avoid the reputation of being only a high-culture network.

PBS in decline   Writing about PBS, I find myself unable to get out of the past tense. The evidence of its programming since the beginning of the twenty-first century seems to indicate that the network and its affiliates are imaginatively spent. So much of that programming, shows that distinguished it from commercial television, are now a staple on cable channels. Those wonderful, personal, informational do-it-yourself series have morphed into a variety of do-it-yourself fashion and celebrity cooking programs on cable channels like TLC and Bravo. Mixing information with "reality" techniques, these shows are made up of an excess of banal talk and speeded-up activity, with a minimum of detail on how to actually do it yourself.

Original drama, on such series as *American Playhouse*, and serious musical programs on *Great Performances*, has either disappeared or has been greatly compromised. History and politics have taken a beating. During the administration of George W. Bush, there were direct attempts to censor programs perceived as having a "liberal bias" – roughly translated as investigative reporting critical of the government. Kenneth Tomlinson, the political appointee who chaired the Corporation for Public Broadcasting – the unit that provides the budget to PBS – from 2002 to 2005 went after individuals and programs that he deemed "too liberal." Bill Moyers, a "liberal" commentator and producer of PBS documentaries was particularly singled out and monitored for content. Tomlinson was eventually relieved of his post because of inappropriate practices, and Bill Moyers has returned to the air.

But threats by the FCC to fine any broadcast that uses four-letter words has further cramped freedom of programming (many PBS affiliates were nervous over broadcasting Ken Burns's documentary on World War II because its participants used ordinary language with ordinary swearing). Under the constant threat that political displeasure will result in reduced funding, PBS and its contributing affiliates have largely ignored politics. Only the *Frontline* series or the occasional Bill Moyers documentary present investigative reporting that has something of a political bite.

PBS's non-commercial status has been largely abandoned. Despite the incessant fundraising marathons, during which many local stations show the most curiously banal self-help and sixties music programming, including shows on what to do with your money and old footage of Motown singers, almost every PBS program has backing from national and local businesses, corporations, and foundations. Shows are not interrupted with commercials, which are instead tastefully presented at the beginning and end of the program.

Thanks to a large private donation, NPR, the radio arm of the Corporation for Public Broadcasting, moves from strength to strength. But PBS has devolved from an alternative to commercial television to an increasingly irrelevant eddy in the television flow. The science and nature shows remain; the antiques programs are popular; nature documentaries continue. But PBS has fallen victim to timidity and an attempt to assuage its political obligations by trying to be many things to fewer and fewer people.

Globalization

The search for audience certainly exists beyond the boundaries of the United States. Media has joined most other corporate entities in a global expansion, which moves in many directions. We mentioned Rupert Murdoch, an Australian whose reach is world-wide and across media: satellite television, a US network and film studio, newspapers, and, most recently, the social networking site, MySpace. The Italian TV executive and Prime Minister Silvio Berlusconi has run a country and a media empire.

Media globalization and its effects are a source of contention and disagreement not only among media scholars, but also among the politicians and policy-makers who attempt to control it. There is no question that globalization concentrates media control into a very few hands, and that it offers access to many people. But access to what? TV Globo, the giant Brazilian satellite company, the fourth largest network in the world, supplies telenovelas (elaborately produced, enormously popular melodramas) around the world. MTV operates channels internationally. Are rock videos or melo-dramas the same in any language? The answer to the latter may be yes, indeed; though the power and the flexibility of the genre allow every culture to interpret the large passions, the sexual betrayals, and emotional tortures of melodrama in its own lights. MTV International not only exposes the world to American rock, but also exposes America to popular music from around the world. The result is a remarkable fusion of styles – for example, "world music," which has evolved into a genre of its own with some unusual influences from the Middle East, whose emigrants suffuse and enrich French and German cultures. These innovative blends, which might produce some-thing as strange and fascinating as Romanian country music, can be seen and heard on Link TV, a small American cable and satellite channel devoted to presenting global programming.

Globalization works in many directions. We've seen how British comedy has been translated into American television. *The Office* is the most current example of the phenomenon that goes all the way back to the popular 1970s series *All in the Family*, which was based on the British show *Till Death Do Us Part*. We've seen the importa-tion of a Latin American telenovela, *Ugly Betty*. NBC airs a quiz show, *Deal or No Deal*, franchised by a Dutch media company, Endemol, that licenses the show to about 20 different countries (it also franchises such reality programming as *Big Brother* and *Fear Factor*). This phenomenon may represent the worst side of media globaliza-tion, an instance where, for once, the United States can't be blamed for lowering the standards of culture worldwide. Instead, we can see a worldwide media developing as a set of programmatic guidelines – in this case the format for a quiz show – that is so culture-neutral it can be translated globally. As Endemol's website stated: "*Deal or No Deal* is the most flexible game show ever invented. It can play as huge primetime 90- or 60-minute weekly specials, or as a slot-winning 30, 40, or 50-minute daily stripped runs." The concept of flow, in such an instance, loses its linearity and can be imagined, spatially, as a vertical as opposed to horizontal event. *Deal or No Deal* is a formula held by a global media company that can be poured into any time slot on any over-air, cable, or satellite network, and into which can be poured a host and audience specific to the particular country that licenses the franchise. The elements of the formula need only be slightly altered to suit the language of the franchisee and the amount of production design it can afford.

Globalization can create resistance. In the Middle East, oil-rich countries have been able to create their own satellite networks. Al Jazeera, the news network that is produced in Qatar, is a particular irritant to US interests in the Middle East. It is an independent voice that contextualizes news and information within a more closely defined cultural and political perspective than the Western media. It is indicative of the possibilities that alternative voices can be heard, even if what is heard may not be to the liking of the dominant cultures. Al-jazeera now has an English language outlet.

Digital convergence

Abroad and at home, now, as in the beginning, it is technology and the search for profit that is determining rapid change in the ways in which the world watches television. It is curiosity that is making us, as viewers, look for and at different screens.

The FCC has mandated that, by 2009, analog broadcasting will end in order to be replaced by digital transmission. Why? Communications companies want the real estate of the electromagnetic spectrum that is currently used by analog broadcasting for cell phones and broadband Internet transmission. The FCC has auctioned off these frequencies to telecommunications companies with an estimated windfall of $10 billion dollars for a government sorely in need of cash.

Broadcasters want digital transmission because it will allow them either to broadcast a high-definition signal or to multicast a number of signals with different programming on each in order to create multiple income streams in addition to what television programs generate. The downside of this transition is that analog-only television receivers will no longer work without a converter box. Congress has allocated about $1 billion to help consumers – those who don't already have a cable or satellite box, which already receive digital signals – make the change.

Wandering eyes, multiple screens   Technology, policy, and the corporate search for profit are only as successful as the appetite of the audience for new sources for entertainment and information. There is no question that our eyes are wandering around, from the television to the computer screen, to the screens of our mobile phones, with increasing ease and frequency. Television is pursuing that wandering gaze by using the Internet as an extension of their on-air program and, increasingly, as an alternative way to deliver that programming. MTV has experimented with simultaneous transmission of programs on air along with alternative views – simultaneous backstage activity, for example – online. Some of the networks are self-syndicating, putting complete programs online, with limited advertising, the day after they air. All shows have a web presence, some more active than others. *Lost* has an "alternate reality" game site, as well as a mysterious, fake corporation online. Many networks are offering clips of their shows for downloading to cell phones. While it is hard to imagine how many people will be interested in watching television on a one-inch screen, it may account for why *24*, for example, is a show made up almost exclusively of close-ups.

When high-definition DVDs are more universally available, the cultural and economic structure of the audience will change even further. As the home theater "experience" (as marketers like to call it) becomes more satisfying, movie attendance will fall off even further than it has in past years. What this will mean to the public sphere, as more and more people stay at home and the experience of watching movies and watching television converges, will be interesting to see. As television providers continue to increase the amount of high-definition programming, and a greater number of consumers buy HD receivers, the televisual aesthetic will continue to develop, becoming more like film with all its subtleties of lighting and framing. Perhaps there will even be television with more of the subtlety and complexity of the best movies.

The End of Television?

In summary, we can say that there is today simply too much television and, with the Internet and cell phones, too many screens for visually based news and entertainment. The flow is self-interrupting. On the producer's side, viewership is becoming harder to track and, especially, to manage. On the audience side, there is too much choice, on the air, over cable and satellite, on the Internet. In place of a flow, we are faced with dozens of streams from which to choose. The smooth integration of program and commercial that represented television when there were only a few over-the-air channels exists still, but is much less dependable on all fronts than it once was, both on the side of programming and on the side of viewing. Cable, satellite, and Internet are offering distractions and an illusion of variety that seems to be rendering network television obsolete. DVR – digital video recording – is growing in popularity. Since it allows viewers the advantage of watching shows when they want, and skipping past commercials, it turns viewers into programmers and leaves programmers and advertisers without the ability to discover who is watching what and when. Of course, the very fact that commercials can be skipped negates – in the eyes of advertisers if not of viewers – the original purpose of television, to use various genres of entertainment to sell things.

Conventional television is becoming ephemeral and unpredictable. New shows receive massive pre-publicity and then disappear after a very few disappointing episodes, only to be replaced by another internationally syndicated game show. But at the same time, with DVRs, Internet downloads, and the increasing popularity and production of DVD collections of old and new television programs, TV has created its own archival memory. The popularity of these collections, along with the supplementary material – the interviews, commentaries, back-scene views, deleted scenes that are now an expected part of a DVD collection – further indicates that the flow can be interrupted, that viewers welcome not only old programming, but also programming uninterrupted by commercials. By creating an archive of television's past, television is given a value it has never had, a permanence that the daily flow of programming disallows. The business side of television worries that all of this is moving out of their control. The consumer and scholar are discovering that, when controlled, the mass media can be tamed to meet individual desire.

At the moment, despite all the choices available to viewers, and all the anxieties these choices are causing to producers, we are still watching television in real time – that is, the time in which shows are actually broadcast. The popularity of *American Idol* was proof. What we are watching, and how we are watching it, is changing, but, despite the varieties of screens at our disposal, the actual time we spend watching has been continually increasing over the years. The offer television made to us when it started, that it would be a window onto the world from the comfort of our homes, has been accepted as a way of life. More than a window, it is an extension of our public and private space – we embrace it; it embraces us in its flow. We like to watch television.

References

Television viewership is up, as cited by the Nielsen report, *Television Audience, 2006*: <http://www.nielsenmedia.com>).

A Brief History of Television

Nineteenth-century technologies
On early television, see William Uricchio, "Old Media as New Media: Television," *The New Media Book*, ed. Dan Harries (London: BFI Publishing, 2002), pp. 208–18.

Television on radio's heels
The website <http://www.tvhistory.tv/> provides many images of television sets from its invention to the present.

The woman's window on the world
Lynn Spiegel, in *Make Room for TV: Television and the Family Ideal in Postwar America* (Chicago, IL: University of Chicago Press, 1992), provides the best analysis of television and its role in the private sphere.

Early television programming
The comment on Ernie Kovacs comes from Lindsay Pack's article at: <http://www.museum.tv/>, a good source for much of television history.

Live television and the "golden age"

For a history of early television, its audience, and its economics, see William Boddy, *Fifties Television: the Industry and Its Critics* (Urbana: University of Illinois Press, 1990).

Commercial Television and the Continuity of Fragmentation

Production

A collection of essays detailing the history of Hollywood's relationship to television is found in Tino Balio (ed.), *Hollywood in the Age of Television* (Boston: Unwin Hyman, 1990). The complications of contemporary television production and distribution is outlined by Jacques Steinberg, "Digital Media Brings Profits (and Tensions) to TV Studios," *The New York Times* (May 14, 2006); <http://www.nytimes.com/2006/05/14/business/yourmoney/14studio.html>.

Origination

On Shonda Rhimes, see Lola Ogunnaike, " 'Grey's Anatomy' Creator Finds Success in Surgery," *The New York Times* (September 28, 2006); Pamela K. Johnson, "The Cutting Edge: Shonda Rhimes Dissects *Grey's Anatomy*" (September, 2005); <http://www.wga.org/writtenby/writtenbysub.aspx?id=883>.

For a discussion of television genres, see Jason Mittell, *Genre and Television* (New York and London: Routledge, 2004).

John Caldwell discusses the complexities and subtleties of programming in "Screen Practice and Conglomeration: How Reflexivity and Conglomeration Fuel Each Other," *The Oxford Handbook of Film and Media Studies*, ed. Robert Kolker (New York: Oxford University Press, 2007), pp. 327–64.

Episode and series

For a discussion of series, serial, and episode, see Jack Ellis, *Visible Fictions: Cinema, Television, Video* (London: Routlege and Kegan Paul, 1982). For soap opera, see the essays in Lynn Spiegel and Denis Mann, eds, *Private Screenings: Television and the Female Consumer* (Minneapolis: University of Minnesota Press: 1992).

The Televisual Gaze and the Concept of Flow

Raymond Williams

His essay on flow and the quotation is in *Television: Technology and Cultural Form* (Hanover and London: University Press of New England, 1974), pp. 72–112.

Thursday Evening

Reality television

On *Candid Camera*, see Charles B. Slocum, "The Real History of Reality TV Or, How Alan Funt Won the Cold War": <http://www.wga.org/>.

Mary Beth Haralovich and Michael W. Trosset, " 'Expect the Unexpected' ': Narrative Pleasure & Uncertainty Due to Chance in *Survivor*," *Reality TV: Remaking Television Culture*, ed. Susan Murray and Laurie Ouellette (New York and London: New York University Press, 2004), pp. 75–96.

A good summary of the 1950s quiz show scandal is at: <http://www.pbs.org/wgbh/amex/quizshow/peopleevents/pande02.html>. Robert Redford's 1994 film, *Quiz Show* is an excellent fictional accounting of this fiasco.

Desperate Housewives and the leavening of melodrama

A classic essay on soap operas and the feminine is by Tania Modleski, *Loving With a Vengeance: Mass-Produced Fantasies for Women* (Hamden, CT: Archon Books, 1994).

Lost

See J. Wood, *Living Lost* (New Orleans: Garrett County Press, 2007).

The televisual style

The quotation is from Caldwell, *Televisuality: Style, Crisis, and Authority in American Television* (New Brunswick, NJ: Rutgers University Press, 1995), p. 5. The discussion of television style and the image here depends upon Caldwell's work.

Cool resolution

Marshall McLuhan discusses cool media in *Understanding Media: The Extensions of Man* (Cambridge, MA, and London: MIT Press, 1994), pp. 22–32. His comment on high definition is on p. 22.

Allegories of history

A detailed plot summary of the *CSI* episode under discussion can be found at: <http://www.cbs.com/primetime/csi/episodes/615/>. Discussion of the make-up of police procedural is in Lorne Manly, "TVs Silver Age," *The New York Times* (May 6, 2007); <http://www.nytimes.com/2007/05/06/magazine/06tvland-t.html>.

Evolution of the Television Landscape

The rise and fall of PBS

A good, capsule history is on the PBS website: <http://www.cpb.org/>; and in James Day, *The Vanishing Vision: The Inside Story of Public Television* (Berkeley and Los Angeles: University of California Press, 1995).

Globalization

There is a wealth of material on the phenomenon. Two sources are Herbert Schiller, "Not Yet the Post-Imperialist Era," and Jack Banks, "MTV and the Globalization of Popular Culture," in Toby Miller (ed.), *Television: Critical Concepts in Media and Cultural Studies*, vol. IV (London and New York: Routledge, 2003), pp. 83–100; 100–20.

The Endemol website is: <http://www.endemol.com>.

Wandering eyes, multiple screens

John Borland, "*Lost* Finds Deeper Reality Online," CNet News (Oct., 28, 2005): <http://news.com.com>.

For various takes on television's future, see the essays in Lynn Spiegel and Jan Olsson (eds), *Television After TV: Essays on a Medium in Transition* (Durham, NC, and London: Duke University Press, 2004).

The End of Television?

Digital convergence

Stephen Labaton, "Transition to Digital Gets Closer," *The New York Times* (Dec. 20, 2005); <http://www.nytimes.com/2005/12/20/technology/20digital.html>.

CHAPTER SIX
Movies and Film

The cinema is an invention without a future.

Louis Lumière, pioneer of early film

What follows is a process of many parts: we will address the history of the movies, the ways in which they are made and seen, the differences between movies as "mass" art and unique artistic expression, and try to understand what happens when "movies" become "film" and enter the universe of "cinema." We will examine film genres and analyze some films in order to see how they work.

Film as Art

Of all the media we are discussing, film has, almost since its beginning, been seen, felt, and talked about as something special, something different, in a another category than radio and, later, television. Serious books about film were written beginning in the early twentieth century, when it was often described as the art form of the future. By the late 1960s, college courses in Film Studies appeared, and film schools, teaching the art and practice of making films, started up. With the exception of journalism, no other single medium has received such academic attention.

No other medium – with the possible exception of certain popular musical forms – has had the word "art" attached to it. And this leads us to reconsider a problem that was brought up in the first chapter of the book: how do we regard and evaluate the productions of media? "Art" is a term usually reserved for a unique work that is the product of an individual who has mastered a particular medium and can use it to express large ideas and complex emotions. Traditional forms of art are music, in the form of a symphony, a concerto, a string quartet; paint, marble or clay sculpture, oils or watercolors; words, in the form of literature: poetry, short story, novels, or a play; there is even a category called installation art, consisting of video or computer displays, configured by an artist in a gallery setting. Does film belong to these revered forms?

Film and the media design

Film is perfectly woven into the media design: it is made to be seen by large audiences; it depends upon genres and codes – in fact, film uses visual coding to provide a wealth of information from the smallest of gestures. It is a business, a big business with millions of dollars riding on any given production. Film is born of technology and, even though it is conservative in adopting new technologies, all aspects of its creation depend upon technological processes. Like other media, it is subject to evaluation in the form of film reviews. But here is where an important difference occurs between film and other media: it is evaluated closely, more closely than recorded music, certainly more than television, as something special. It is seen and addressed as a unique form of expression. If art lies in the eye of the beholder, then film is held as something worthy of analysis, description, criticism, condemnation, and praise – as art.

Movie vs. film

The very words we use to describe film demonstrate its dual nature as both art and popular entertainment. Like "watching TV," it is possible for us to simply "go to the movies," no matter what is playing – a generic act, watching a generic product, a way of passing an evening or just an excuse for getting out of the house. But we may also use the word "film" to refer to something more serious than the latest Steve Carell offering. The very word indicates seriousness. "I saw an interesting film last night." Some may use the word "cinema" when referring to the entire universe of film – the collaborative process of writing, producing, distributing, exhibiting, watching, and reviewing a film: "I'm a great fan of cinema." But, then again, Hollywood movie-makers, who are sometimes less serious than some of its viewers, refer to their product as "pictures" or "shows." There are no other media that have so many names to express the value we put on them, so many terms coded for seriousness or the lack thereof.

Moving pictures

Like television, which was dreamed of before technology made it possible, the mechanical reproduction of moving images was an age-old dream that preceded the invention of movies as we know them.

Photographic origins It should be no surprise by now that film, like so many of the media we have been discussing, is a product of nineteenth-century technologies. However, its origin is not in the electronics of telegraphy and telephony, like radio and television, but in photography, in the capacity of a piece of paper or strip of celluloid to carry a chemical coating that would react to light in a way that reproduced an image.

The desire to capture and preserve an image has a history that goes much farther back than the nineteenth century. Long before it was possible to make a chemical imprint of light and shadow, prehistoric artists were painting representations of the outside world on the walls of caves. Artists were always aware that the painted image was an interpretation of the world, and were perpetually curious about how an image of the world could be captured without any intervention, thereby making images as close to "reality" as possible.

In the seventeenth century, experimenters discovered that a pinhole in the side of an opaque, black box would cause an inverted image to be projected on the opposite side. Painters would actually get into the box, which was called a camera obscura (literally, "dark chamber") and trace the image. This satisfied part of the desire to capture the real world, but of course the camera obscura could only allow the image to be painted over, it could not make a permanent record of the thing itself. That was done when, in the early part of the nineteenth century, two Frenchmen, Joseph Niépce and Louis Daguerre, developed stable chemical processes to preserve an image. Once the chemistry was established, cameras and photography blossomed. Although some early photographers attempted to create the effects of painting in their photographs (a skill that survives to this day in the ability of image software to add brush strokes and other painterly effects to photographs), the desire to capture "reality" on film was too seductive to escape. (See figure 6.1.)

By the late nineteenth and early twentieth centuries, photographers such as Eugène Atget, Edward Steichen, and Alfred Stieglitz were discovering in photography a means of expression that explored the formal properties of their own medium: ways of composing, lighting, and developing an image that did not need to borrow from painting. Photography quickly branched into separate areas. We've discussed photojournalism and advertising photography in chapters 2 and 3. Photography as a form of aesthetic expression went in its own directions. It has its own body of criticism, and there are any number of sources where its development can be traced.

Here we are concerned with the particular branch of photography that led to the illusion of movement itself. There were pre-photographic attempts to create the illusion of movement, rotating drums with figures painted on them that, when viewed through slits, gave the illusion that the figures were moving. They bore fanciful names like kinetoscope, zoetrope, phenakistoscope, thaumatrope. By the second half of the nineteenth century, scientists like Eadweard Muybridge and Etienne-Jules Marey (who used a gun-like camera to take his pictures, resulting in the term "shooting" a photograph) experimented with sequential photographs of people and animals in motion. These were gradually combined with

Figure 6.1 One of the earliest photographs, made by the Frenchman, Joseph Niépce: dim, barely visible, ghostly. Science and Society Picture Library.

Figure 6.2 This famous series of sequential images, made in 1877, by Eadweard Muybridge proved that all four hooves of a horse left the ground during a gallop. Such images were a precursor of motion pictures. Science and Society Picture Library.

the older toys that created illusions of motion, leading eventually to a projected image that appeared to move. (See figure 6.2.)

Early film production William K. L. Dickson, an employee of Thomas Edison, pushed these experiments further. Edison originally wanted moving images to accompany his phonograph. In one sense, movies, for him, were an afterthought that happened to catch on and outstrip all the expectations Edison and Dickson had for them. Interestingly enough, similar work in developing the moving image was being carried out around the world. A kind of harmonious convergence of invention began a process that moved from the photograph to a filmstrip that was viewed in a machine, and then to projected images, resulting finally in the narrative, the storytelling film we are all familiar with.

I am not suggesting a "natural" or even inevitable progression. Most of the history of early film is the result of accident, intuition, and experimentation, all of which pleased both inventors and audiences, who asked for more of the same and responded well to attempts to complicate what they were seeing. Storytelling in film grew, in a relatively short time, rich and complex. But we must be careful. Most of early film is lost. It is estimated that up to 75 percent of the film made in cinema's early period is gone; the historical record is therefore spotty and we need to extrapolate from what we have and take an educated guess as to what most early filmgoers actually saw.

Figure 6.3 What an early viewer might have seen in the Kinetoscope was "The Kiss" (dir. William Heise, 1896).

Figure 6.4 The Kinetoscope: in the late nineteenth century this was the way to view a film. Science and Society Picture Library.

Early films by Edison and others were relatively simple, self-contained "attractions": two people kissing; a dancer; or, foreshadowing the exploitative image-making that would become so much a part of film-making, the electrocution of an elephant at Coney Island in 1903. These early strips were viewed in machines, placed in storefronts where passers-by would gather to watch them. Soon the machines were replaced by projection on a sheet – again in storefronts – and, as the images became more and more popular to ever-widening audiences, theaters devoted to the projection of films were built. (See figures 6.3 and 6.4.)

Unlike radio and television, the technologies of film were never very complex. The main obstacles involved developing standards of motion photography and projection, so that film could be manufactured and exhibited anywhere; and, most important, developing methods of story telling – narrative conventions – that would be instantly understood by a growing number of viewers. Audiences swelled during the first part of the twentieth century, and the venues where audiences would go to watch movies changed accordingly, leading to the elaborate "movie palaces" that were built in urban neighborhoods by the early 1920s. Each step in the process, on the side of production and of reception, was the result of curiosity, of technologies developed to enable the imaginative construction, of experiments in building visual narratives, and the eager and always positive response of a public, whose desire to see more spurred the production on: more films; more complex films. Before radio entered the home, the reconfigurations of space and time offered by the increasingly complex narratives of film, with its compelling illusions of larger-than-life characters who experienced larger-than-life emotions, propelled film rapidly into becoming the first non-print mass medium.

Economics and Art

The storytelling possibilities of film and the production processes that made the telling possible grew together, fueled by film's increasing popularity. The result was an increasing sophistication of film form, of the audience's comprehension of cinematic stories, and the economies of production that led, by the end of the first decade of the twentieth century, to something remarkable: imagination factories, the film studios, whose products were as controlled commodities as automobiles. One of the obstacles to thinking about film as art is the nature of its production. The studios, as we will see, considered their product as a manufactured object. They cared little about the "art" and a lot about the profit. The ability to "manufacture" film en masse has its own history that we need to follow. In so doing, we will discover that the *form* of film and its manufacture and economics go hand in hand.

From shot to story

We need to consider the work of some early film-makers, in the United States and abroad. As noted, the development of motion pictures occurred almost simultaneously around the world at the end of the nineteenth century. That development involved not only the means of putting an image on film, but also moving from that image – the smallest unit of a film, the shot – to the assemblage of the shots into a story by means of editing.

The Lumière Brothers, Georges Méliès, Edwin S. Porter   The earliest film-makers were curious about the ways in which films could show and tell. I pointed out that Edison's early films were the length of a shot – a few minutes – and showed a single idea, one attraction. In France, where advances in film were taking place at the same time, Auguste and Louis Lumière began making small documentaries of a train pulling into a station, of workers leaving their factory, of a gardener getting squirted with a hose. These may have been among the first films to have a public showing. As simple as they were, these early cinematic "attractions," also one shot in length, constituted little stories: they spoke of movement from one event to another, they invited the imagination and emotions to elaborate on a small event. There is a legend that, at the first screening of the Lumières' film of a train arriving at a station, the audience pulled back in fear (figure 6.5). True or not, it indicates the desire, indeed the necessity, to *believe* that an audience can be moved by what is seen on the screen.

These short, presentational films created pleasure and therefore an appetite for more: more films, more stories, more complexity. Film-makers began to create little fictions and imaginative worlds. In France, at the turn of the century, the French stage magician Georges Méliès was making fantasy films in his studio, using painted sets and elaborate costumes. In 1902. Méliès made what may have been the first science fiction film: *A Trip to the Moon*. In America, Edwin S. Porter, among others, was experimenting with editing – arranging shots so that a number of events related to one story, or a number of related stories, could be interconnected. Space and time were discovered to be storytelling – that is, narrative – elements that could be handled with as much flexibility as they were in literary fiction. In two surviving films, *The Life of an American Fireman* and *The Great Train Robbery* – both made for Edison's film-making company – Porter created scenes that took place at one time, but in different places, allowing one action such as the robbing of a train to be suspended, while another one, a square dance in town, was substituted, thereby creating expectation and suspense in the viewer. Editing allowed for the complicating of a story as well as involving the viewer; it concentrated the viewer's gaze and moved it across time and space. (See figures 6.6 and 6.7.)

Figure 6.5 In France, Auguste and Louis Lumière made films of actual events. One of the earliest of these was of a train arriving at the station (*L'Arrivée d'un train en gare à La Ciotat*, 1896).

D. W. Griffith   One of the most prominent figures in the early history of film was a Southern-born failed playwright, D. W. Griffith. Between 1908 and 1913, Griffith worked for a small New York company called Biograph, where he made some 500 short narrative films, and in the course of doing so experimented with various methods of cinematic storytelling. Looking through this enormous output of films, we can find the development of many visual narrative techniques that are still in use today.

For example, Griffith experimented with composition – how objects are arranged within the screen frame in ways that both please and direct the eye. Composition has the ability to include and exclude, to invite us to look closely at an important object, or a face expressing emotion, a gesture indicating happiness or despair. As a painter or a still photographer composes the picture with attention to the details he or she wants us to see, so Griffith played with the way the world could be framed and composed.

He also experimented with the ways in which movement within the screen frame could be carried over by means of editing from one shot to another. The process might involve nothing more complicated – at least not complicated to our eyes today – than getting a character out of one room and into another. The trick was to match movement, to cut from one gesture to the completion of that gesture in the next shot, to trick the viewer's eyes so that the cut itself would recede behind an illusion of a complete action. What Griffith and others were creating was continuity-cutting, the ability to manipulate scenes by cutting from shot to shot without the cut itself being visible. In the Hollywood style that was developed from Griffith's experiments, the edit would become invisible and the story being told became foregrounded. The development of continuity-cutting went hand in hand with the *kinds* of stories Griffith and his contemporaries were telling – melodramas, comedies, gangster films, Westerns – stories that would form the basis of the feature-length films that we refer to as the classical style of Hollywood cinema. (See figures 6.8 and 6.9.)

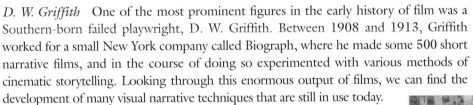

Figure 6.6

Figure 6.7

Figures 6.6–7 In *The Great Train Robbery* (1903), Edwin S. Porter alternated scenes of different actions occurring at the same time, providing a flexibility in storytelling.

Figure 6.8

Figure 6.9

Figures 6.8–9 These two images from D. W. Griffith's *The Lonedale Operator* (1911) look simple enough. But getting a character out the door and maintaining continuity across the cut was an important part of the early development of film.

Griffith went on to form his own film production company, where he made two of the earliest long-form films that remain touchstones of the silent film era. The first was *Birth of a Nation* (1915), a racist Civil War melodrama that glorified, and was responsible for the resurgence of, the Ku Klux Klan. Stung by the criticism the film received, Griffith tried to make good with *Intolerance* (1916), a huge, multi-part film on the theme of social injustice that attempted to cover enormous periods of history, editing back and forth among four separate story-lines involving ancient Babylon, the life of Jesus Christ, the Protestant Reformation, and modern capitalism. In both of these films Griffith developed the complex editing structures he had pioneered during the Biograph period. While Griffith was developing the long-form narra-tive film, others were experimenting too, not only with the form of film, but with its production methods, as increasing numbers of film-making studios started up in the early twentieth century.

The studio system

Film created a desire for more film. The attraction of the image and its stories, the empathies created by characters, the ability of film to enrapture the gaze, assured demand. As film-makers were busy discovering and trying out various ways to tell stories, businessmen were busy discovering ways to manufacture and sell them to a ready audience. As we discussed earlier, the Edison Company began exploiting film by the late nineteenth century, making films and dis-tributing them in a variety of venues. Edison also claimed to have proprietary rights on film-making equipment and formed the Motion Picture Patents Company, which was known to send in thugs to beat up people who tried to make movies without their equipment or permission.

Meanwhile, a number of East European immigrants, many of them salesmen, bookkeepers, or businessmen of various kinds, gravitated toward film distribution. They understood the demand and thought seriously about how to meet supply. They formed film-making companies and fled from the East to the West coast. In Los Angeles, real estate was cheap, the sun was out, and Edison's goons were absent. In the course of a relatively few years, through the process of forming and merging small companies, the studios, most of which still operate under their original names, were created. The names of Paramount, Warner Bros., 20th Century Fox, and Universal are still prominent. Others, like MGM and RKO (originally the high and low end of production in the prime of the studio period) and United Artists (formed by D. W. Griffith, the actor Douglas Fairbanks, and the comedian Charlie Chaplin as a distributor of important films), have dwindled to little more than a name. Columbia Pictures is owned by the Japanese electronics company, Sony, and has changed names to reflect this. None of them exists as an independent operation, but as a unit of a larger media company. Nonetheless, most of them still occupy the same real estate they created in the 1920s, and, however much changed in details, the production process is similar to what it was in the beginning.

Universal, MGM, and Erich von Stroheim The story of two of these studios, and one important film-making pioneer, is illustrative of how Hollywood and its style of film-making was born and flourished. Carl Laemmle (Uncle Carl, as he was known) began by operating a nickelodeon theater in Chicago. He expanded his operations by forming a studio in New York and buying out a small company in Hollywood, all of which would, by 1912, become Universal Pictures, an important early producer of a variety of small-budget films. Universal reached its high point in the early 1930s, when the studio produced *Frankenstein*, *Dracula*, and their many sequels, setting the generic standard for horror films. Today, Universal is part of the conglomerate made up of General Electric and NBC.

Early in the century, Marcus Loew went into business with Adolph Zukor (who would go on to head Paramount Pictures), operating a chain of theaters in New York. Like many early theater operators, he discovered that he needed to produce product in order to meet demand. He purchased a number of small studios in Hollywood, including Metro and another run by Samuel Goldwyn. Loew merged the two units and put Louis B. Mayer, a co-founder of Metro Pictures, in charge of production. Goldwyn left to start his own production company, but part of the buyout allowed his name to remain in MGM-Metro-Goldwyn-Mayer.

Erich von Stroheim was an important director in early American cinema. An immigrant from Austria, he began his career working for D. W. Griffith, and when he came to direct his own films, he was an obsessive perfectionist, deeply controlling and, within a cinematic universe that was already producing works of high sentimentality, cold-blooded in his outlook on the world. His concern for detail far outstripped his concern for budget. He went to work for Universal. His films, set in a mythical European city, narrated tales of lust, seduction, betrayal, and murder, infused with a kind of gleeful, sordid, irony – quite contrary to the sentimentality of Griffith. He took delight in the lurid, replacing the smarmy sexuality of more popular films with as direct a depiction of perversity as he could get away with. For Stroheim, decadence was a target, and a means. In *Foolish Wives* (1922), his second film, following *Blind Husbands* (1919), there is a character, a Count, who has seduced a mentally disabled woman. He is murdered in turn, and his body is stuffed down a sewer.

This kind of content did not go down well with the studio. But, more than content, Stroheim's methods – his concern for creating and dwelling on detail, his disdain for budget, for the economics of production – riled the studio. The production head at Universal was a young man named Irving Thalberg, who was charged with keeping the film-making process orderly and economical – two essential aims of the studio system in general, and the main tasks of a producer. Thalberg cut *Foolish Wives* down to a running length he thought was manageable. He then fired Stroheim from his next film, *Merry-Go-Round* (1922), and brought in another director to finish it.

Stroheim, undeterred, was in pre-production planning for an enormous project that he would make for Samuel Goldwyn's studio, an adaptation of Frank Norris's grim 1899 novel, *McTeague*. The novel was part of what has been called the "naturalist" school of American fiction, addressing the almost psychotically deprived and depraved lives of a lower-middle-class dentist and his pathologically stingy wife. Obsessive as always, Stroheim planned an almost page-by-page translation of Norris's novel to film, filmed partly on location, including a brutal final sequence in the desert of Death Valley. He assembled a cut that ran ten hours. Goldwyn would have none of it, and worked with Stroheim to whittle the film down to four hours, presumably to be shown in two parts. While this was going on, the merger occurred that created MGM, resulting in the departure of Goldwyn and the arrival of Louis B. Mayer. Mayer hired Irving Thalberg from Universal and gave him all but total control over production. Thalberg was no more sympathetic to Stroheim's artistry than he had been at Universal; he cut the film to two hours, gave a simpler title, *Greed*, fired the director (again!), and destroyed the remaining footage.

Rumors and legends persist that the lost reels exist in someone or another's basement. Partial reconstructions have been made in print and on film by using the stills of the lost footage. But *Greed* still exists only in this two-hour version and, mutilated or not, it is among the most powerful films of the silent era and among the most visually and narratively provocative films of any era. The experience pretty much ruined Stroheim's career as a director. He survived as an actor into the 1950s (he essentially plays himself in Billy Wilder's 1950 film, *Sunset Boulevard*). MGM, under Mayer and Thalberg, went on to be the prestige studio of the 1920s and 1930s, turning out melodramas and bright, often cloyingly sentimental films that were in every way anti-Stroheim in form and content.

The power of the studios   The point of this story is not to romanticize the misunderstood artist destroyed by crass, commercially minded bosses, but to emphasize that, in ways different from other media, film began and continued as a struggle between individuals with imaginative insight and those with business insight. The outcome of the struggle between Stroheim and MGM not only put an end to the director's career, but established a pattern that subordinated the director – and everyone else involved in the making of a film – to the producer, who controls the budget and oversees the making and distributing of a film, and studio boss, forcing the director to become just one staff member among many. (Throughout, I use the pronoun "him" for director advisedly: film directors were overwhelmingly male, with only three – Alice Guy-Blaché in the early silent period; Dorothy Arzner in the 1930s; and Ida Lupino in the 1950s – making Hollywood films before the 1970s, when a very few more women began joining the ranks.)

This imbalance of power is not unusual in any business model, media included. Newspaper reporters, for example, are subordinate to their editors, who are, in turn, subordinate to the publishers. Indeed, men like William Randolph Hearst were models for the new studio bosses. In 1941, when Orson Welles made *Citizen Kane* (which was in part a fictionalized biography of Hearst), Louis B. Mayer, whose studio employed Hearst's mistress, Marion Davies, offered to buy the negative from RKO, the studio where Welles made the film, and burn it! Welles went on to suffer a fate similar to Stroheim's – his film, *The Magnificent Ambersons* (1942), was cut and partly reshot by the studio – although, unlike Stroheim, he managed to continue making important films throughout his career into the 1970s, most of them outside of the studio system.

The production process   Once established, and lasting until the late 1950s, the studio system was a structure of power, control, and production. Everyone working for the studio, from the stars, the directors, and the writers, to the electricians and set decorators, were under contract and worked at the direction of the studio head, who in turn was subordinate to the studio's financial officer, who usually resided in New York and communicated long distance. The studio head and his producers chose the stories, chose who would star, who would direct, and, perhaps most important, set the film's budget. Anyone who disagreed with the choices would be suspended or fired. If a film fell behind schedule, or went over budget, much unpleasantness would ensue.

A film would be (and still is) made in parts. The script might be the product of any number of writers, some of whose names would appear in the credits, others not. As the script neared completion, the art director (also called the production designer) would plan the sets that would be built by studio carpenters and painters. Once in production, the director of photography, working with the film's director, would light and compose the various shots. When filming began, scenes would be – and still are – shot out of sequence, a technique carried over to television. Because a film narrative is built during the editing process, it isn't necessary to film the story in the order in which it will be told. If, for example, a number of scenes take place in a single location at different times in the narrative, all of them will be filmed together. If a star is only available for a given amount of time, all of her scenes will be shot. The process is further fragmented by breaking down any given scene into its component parts, filming various angles multiple times in order to supply the editor with as many choices as possible.

Once filming was over, the director, cast, and crew would move on to another film, while the editor and producer would set to work putting the film together, and the composer would write the music. The latter was and still is a fragmented process too. Film music is written as a set of "cues." There may be a full-length piece composed for the title sequence of the film, but the rest of the music is written to specific amounts of time to accompany specific scenes in the film.

The edited film would be taken out for previews. The director and producer might be looking on. The audience would fill out cards, and, depending on their responses, scenes might be recut or even reshot. At the same time, the studio's massive publicity machinery would be set into motion and the film would be distributed for viewings in theaters owned by the studios. If all the parts worked perfectly, if the film came in on time and within its budget, if the film's stars were in favor with the public and the studio publicity machine worked its magic, the film would turn a profit for the studio – though not for the film's participants, who were on salary.

Production today

Movie production today has not changed very much from the days of the studios. Though most retain their original names, the studios themselves, as I noted earlier, are no longer self-contained entities, but rather holdings of larger communications companies. A studio may still originate a project but, just as likely, a film idea may come from a star, an agent, or an independent producer or director. Financing may come from the studio for a large project; but smaller films have to be largely self-financed, sometimes with European capital. Stars and crewmembers are no longer under contract – though some may have contractual arrangements with particular studios – and have to be put together for each production, rather than coming "off the shelf" as was the case during the studio period. A film must still be made on schedule and within its budget, though the profits are now more widely shared than they were during the days of the studios.

Many of the basics of production and film-making methods have not changed that much since the studio days. Scriptwriting is still the product of many hands; filming is still done out of sequence; music is written after filming; the editor – who today works more closely with the director than she would have during the studio period – still shapes the final product. Instead of preview audiences writing note cards, the film will more likely be shown to carefully chosen focus groups. The producer may still require re-editing or even reshooting. A great deal of the film-making process is now left to computer-generated imagery, which we will examine later. And, certainly, independent film-making is allowing more individual voices to be heard.

The economies of visual narratives

The studio system produced profits for its owners. But it also produced narratives of good and evil, desire and sacrifice, of comic relief and moral uplift, emotional satisfaction that we can consider the profits paid to the audience. These narratives and their reception, collaborative by force of the production methods being practiced, and by the expectations of viewers, were the result of an intertwining of style and economics. The Hollywood style, that we began to outline earlier, and the studio production system were part and parcel of each other. The movies that emerged from the process created pleasure for the viewer, who paid for admission and completed the economy of production.

D. W. Griffith and his contemporaries worked to discover the best ways to create continuity from shot to shot, to tell stories economically, providing the details, the compositions, the facial expressions, and physical gestures that would work most effectively – and efficiently – to provide viewers with the visual information they needed to respond emotionally to the events on the screen. Once these efficiencies were established, they were repeated. The form and function of a film, the story it told and the ways it told it, and the ways it asked the audience to respond, were as refined as the production methods themselves. To understand this more fully, we need to depart from production and concentrate on reception, on how we see and understand a film. To accomplish this, we return to a concept we touched upon in the previous chapter: the gaze.

The eye drives the construction of film narrative

As visual media, film and television work by directing our gaze, guiding, sometimes forcing our eyes to see what needs to be seen, and providing enough visual information so that we understand what is seen. A central theory of Film Studies is based on the work of Laura Mulvey, who spoke of the gaze – of the characters in the film and the viewer looking at those characters – as the formal structuring principle of film. Mulvey thought of the gaze as highly gendered: men look at women, who become the object of the gaze; men the owner of it. In fact, ownership of the gaze shifts from character to character, and drives how we, the viewers, understand what we see.

The economies of the gaze involve the manipulation of two fundamental elements. The basic unit of any film – any visual narrative – is the shot, composed so that the arrangement of characters within the space of the frame orients us, providing details of time, place, and movement. Shots are controlled in turn by editing. As we have seen, narrative structure is created by cutting from shot to shot. Cutting allows movement from one space to another; it can accelerate time forward or move backward in time. Editing allows the representation of a number of narrative spaces occurring simultaneously so that subplots or "back stories" can be developed. Editing also moves the narrative forward by means of the play of the gaze across the edit from shot to shot.

Shot length and shot/reverse shot   Watch almost any American film, or any network drama or sitcom – watch them for form, not story. Count the length of the shots, from the moment a shot begins until it is replaced by another shot. You will find that the average length of a shot is about four to nine seconds. You will also discover that the majority of shots are cut on a particular kind of composition: one shot shows a character looking at someone or some object, and the following shot shows the person or object the character is looking at. Film is built on this counterpoint of gazes, with our own gaze locked in the exchange.

The narrative economy of this shot and cut, shot/reverse shot process allows a great deal of information to be communicated quickly. The "look" of a character is coded to be easily understood: surprise, sadness, fright, anger – any simple emotion is communicated by the furrow of a brow or movement of the mouth. Once we know the object of the "look" – a person holding a gun; a mysterious shadow; the movement of a door – we have already taken part in the process of narration. Something is happening, a chain of events, with characters responding. The chain of looks will be opened out in the course of a film by shots that establish place, and shots of objects the camera sees before the characters do, allowing us more knowledge than the characters have and thereby creating suspense as we wait until the characters catch up to what we already know. If the character does not respond with a look in a corresponding reverse shot, suspense is created until she does respond.

The dialogue sequence   Even though there are many variations that can be played upon it, the basic formal code of looking at a character/looking at what the character is seeing makes the process of filming and viewing all but automatic – or, more appropriately, economical. It is a relatively straightforward task for film-makers to set up the shots required, shoot them, and edit them into the appropriate pattern. Everyone involved in the process knows exactly what to do. This is nowhere more in evidence than in the way in which a simple dialogue – a conversation between two people – is shot and edited. It is almost *always* done in the same way. When it's not, you can be assured that someone, usually the director, is thinking about ways to make even this simple narrative event more interesting.

Figure 6.10

Figure 6.11

Figure 6.12

Figure 6.13

Figures 6.10–13 Continuity cutting: These frames are taken from a simple dialogue sequence in the film *Music and Lyrics* (dir. Mark Lawrence, 2007). The over-the-shoulder style is one of the basic conventions of film. *Music and Lyrics* © Warner Bros., 2007.

Here is how it works: a dialogue sequence will begin with a two shot: both characters in the frame talking to each other. Then the cutting will begin, over the shoulder of one character talking or listening to the other, followed by a reverse shot over the shoulder of the other character, talking to or listening to his or her partner in the dialogue. These over-the-shoulder shots will be punctuated by occasional close-ups or long shots of either of the characters listening or talking. At the end, there will be a return to the shot of both.

All of this is done with one camera, which means that each component shot is done separately, many times. This allows for many takes from which the complete dialogue will be built. It creates an economy during and after shooting. Look very carefully at the over-the-shoulder shots in the sequence, especially when the character over whose shoulder we are looking is talking. More often than not, if you can see lips moving, they won't be synchronized to the words, meaning this particular over-the-shoulder shot was not in sequence or that it had new dialogue dubbed in after editing. In fact, since a composition over the shoulder doesn't reveal facial characteristics, a stand-in can be used for the actor.

The economy *after* the shooting is even greater. With all the takes available, the director, producer, and editor can choose the best performances and cut them together. When a character is shot over the shoulder, the best reading of the dialogue can be lifted from one take and put into another. Likewise, a particularly bad reading can be done away with by choosing another take, or cutting away to a reverse shot. While the result of the cutting pattern is almost always the same, the flexibility it offers the film-makers to create the best possible example of the pattern is great. (See figures 6.10–6.13.)

The result is seamless by convention. There is nothing realistic about filmed dialogue sequences; we don't jump from one character to stand behind the shoulder of another when we look at two people talking. However, we see this pattern so often in film and television that we take for granted what we see and decode it as an ongoing conversation while being largely unconscious of the ways in which it was created. We discover again that other economy, of reception, of reading what we see on the screen quickly, interpreting it easily, responding as directed by the cutting, by the expression on characters' faces, by the movement of an eyebrow, by their gaze.

The same but different

An appropriate question at this point would be, "If the cutting patterns are the same across the field of visual narratives, why don't all films look alike?" The question becomes even more insistent when we understand that it is not only cutting patterns that are repeated. Like television (like all media), only with many more years of experience behind it, film depends on both repetitions of storytelling and the stories told. The shooting and cutting styles that make up the classical Hollywood cinema lay as a foundational structure beneath a limited and, at the same time, changing set of genres. The two dominant ones are comedy and melodrama, which are broken down into a number of subgenres, such as romantic comedy, domestic melodrama, action adventure, thriller, romance, science fiction, detective, gangster, and western. Within those genres, storylines follow fairly standard, even similar, patterns. Within the variation of their codes and conventions is where the cinematic imagination flourishes.

The old Hollywood joke is that, when a story is pitched – that is, proposed to someone with the money to make it – the first words are always, "It's the same as [name a popular and profitable film], only different." Creativity lives in the tension between "the same," familiar stories told in familiar ways that make producers happy because they like to build on past successes, and "different," varied with enough imagination to freshen the old story, enough style to engage the eye, enough passion to engage the emotions and, on the rarest of occasions, the mind. The creative tension is too often pulled in the direction of "the same." But when the balance tips, movies threaten to become film, and film moves into the realm of art.

Genres

Like all media, film works by means of genre. The classical Hollywood style of composing and cutting a film is itself a kind of genre, the genre of storytelling shared, to one degree or another, by all American film and narrative television. That style drives, in turn, the story genres that wax and wane, that have been varied in all but infinite ways, since the birth of cinema. Actually, cinematic (and television) genres existed in literature before they entered the media, or, more accurately, were consciously taken from literature in order to create recognizable forms of storytelling in a new medium.

Melodrama and comedy

There are, effectively, two overriding cinematic genres: melodrama and comedy. Melodrama deals in large emotional dynamics of love and hate, of loss and redemption; it is driven by internal reactions to external stimuli, but is largely the expression of emotions repressed, liberated, and then brought back into line. Even though it seemed to break new ground by focusing on gay characters, *Brokeback Mountain* (Ang Lee, 2005) was very much in the mold of conventional melodrama, with despairing lovers expressing desires outside the bounds of conventional behavior and paying for their transgressions with death and solitude. In melodrama, someone always pays for feeling too much.

Comedy is melodrama turned inside out. Emotions are too high; they outrun the plausible. Actions are exaggerated. A lover tries too hard, or tries the wrong ways to get the girl. But, unlike melodrama, no one loses in a comedy. The right guy gets the right girl. The bully, the stuffed shirt, loses in hilarious ways. Close same-sex friendships, which often appear unbreakable – recall *Wedding Crashers* (David Dobkin, 2005) or *The Forty-Year-Old Virgin* (Judd Apatow, 2005) – are always broken when the right girl is not only found, but convinced that the comic hero is the man for her.

Within comedy and melodrama live the many subgenres: domestic comedy or domestic melodrama; romantic comedy; the thriller or action-adventure film; the gangster film; the detective film; film noir; horror; science fiction. Any of these genres can also be parodied, their conventions taken to such an extreme that they suddenly become ridiculous. The recent spate of horror film parodies such as *I Know What You Did Last Summer* (Jim Gillespie, 1997) and *Scary Movie* (Keenan Ivory Wayans, 2000) indicates we are so familiar with genres that we can comfortably laugh at their excess.

Life span of genres

Any genre is a collaborative work, even a work of negotiation. Film-makers are always aware of the need to move around and press on generic boundaries, and every move, every variation, is very much laying a proposition before the audience: will you accept these variations? Are the basic generic boundaries still valid? Are they flexible enough to hold variations? Are *you*, the viewer, flexible enough to respond to variations in the only way I, as film-maker, understand – buying tickets or renting DVDs?

On a larger scale, genres, indeed every aspect of film- and television-making, also respond to history. The horror film started as early as silent film; its generic conventions were laid out by German film-makers such as Robert Wiene, Fritz Lang, and F. W. Murnau, working in the expressionist style. Expressionism, a form that spanned all art forms, attempted to re-create the mood of its characters – their intensity and often psychologically tortured states – in the environment the characters inhabited. The result, in film, was a kind of dream state of terrifying, dark worlds filled with frightening creatures. The very first Dracula movie, Murnau's *Nosferatu* (1922), was born of this movement, which was itself influenced by the horrors of World War I. (See figure 6.14.)

The horror film blossomed in America during the Depression, when the real monsters were economic catastrophe, but audiences were pleased to see their fears sublimated on the screen. Universal Studios released *Frankenstein* (James Whale) and *Dracula* (Tod Browning) in 1931, laying the basis of old dark houses, mad scientists, frightening but somehow attractive freaks of nature, scaring women and driving the townspeople mad, that lasts to this day through innumerable remakes and spin-offs. We are so deeply responsive to things going bump in the night – scared and thrilled to be scared (as long as we know we are actually safe) – that the horror genre keeps regenerating itself over and over.

Some genres rise and fall, even fall without rising again. Science fiction film is acutely sensitive to what goes on in the world. In the 1950s, when the United

States was frightened by atomic energy and encouraged to fear "alien" Communist ideologies, an easy transfer was made to movies about spaceships bringing soul-destroying aliens to earth. The science fiction film came to its grand summation in Stanley Kubrick's *2001: A Space Odyssey* (1968), where it was turned into a complex meditation on history and the evolution of consciousness (figure 6.15). The genre was revived in George Lucas's *Star Wars* in 1977, by fueling tales of outer space with generic elements of the war film, the western, even the Japanese Samurai movie. The genre has since waxed and waned according to how much it can reflect current cultural concerns and project them into the future.

Figure 6.14 *Nosferatu* (dir. F. W. Murnau, 1922). The first Dracula movie is also an example of the German expressionist style.

The western

I would like, for the moment, to concentrate on the western, a genre now in almost total eclipse. Once a mainstay of film (and, later, television) production, westerns are rarely made any more. The reasons for this are enlightening about genres in general, the Hollywood style in particular, and audience response.

But before examining its demise, I want to look closely at a western film that was popular in its time and one of the most influential films ever made: *The Searchers*. *Star Wars* is based on it in part (George Lucas even imitates a sequence from the film); so is Martin Scorsese's *Taxi Driver* (1976). Almost every film made by Steven Spielberg alludes to it in some way. The film itself demonstrates how an individual film artist can turn an established genre into an original, imaginative work, and it also helps us understand another aspect of the culture of film: the celebrity.

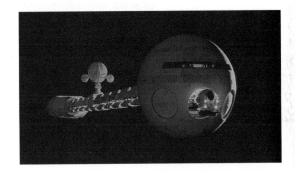

Figure 6.15 Visions of space travel that changed the look of science fiction film (*2001: A Space Odyssey*, dir. Stanley Kubrick, 1968). *2001: A Space Odyssey* © MGM/Turner Entertainment, 1968.

The Searchers   *The Searchers* was made by director John Ford and released in 1956. Ford, who made films within the studio system from 1917 through the late 1960s, specialized in the western and was responsible for setting many of its parameters. *The Searchers* stars John Wayne, who was, and remains long after his death, an icon of rugged heroism. John Wayne, the person, was not at all like the heroes he portrayed, but he represented in the minds of many film-goers what an American hero should be. *The Searchers* itself calls this heroism into question, in fact questions many things about the myths upon which the western is built. It does so by creating a rich narrative structure and a complex character, all of which confront a basic binary of the genre: white settlers who wish to settle the West, and the savage Indians who don't want them there.

Manifest destiny   By the mid-1950s, the western, which had established itself during the silent period, was among the most popular movie genres. Its conventions were simple, attractive, and intrinsically visual. In fact, it takes no more than a pair of images to codify the genre: the desert, indicating the wide-open frontier of the American West, and the lone image of the cowboy riding across it. Within that landscape, and embodied in that figure, were large cultural historical fantasies about the establishing of a middle-class domestic community in the wilderness through heroic struggle against the elements, outlaws, and Indians. All of this was part of the historical imperative of "manifest destiny," an almost mystical notion held during the nineteenth century that the United States had a right to claim the continent, and perhaps the world, as its own. The western presented a visual confirmation of this basic American cultural myth of endless opportunity and mobility, the justness of an individualist way of life pushing across the country, and the fantasy of the lone hero working in the cause of his country's expansion.

The western offered a container for cultural fears of the "other," embodied in the Indian – or, more accurately, the myth of the Indian – as a savage of the land who had to be rooted out to make room for civilization. During the 1950s, the western served as a reassuring antidote to the paranoid narratives of the science fiction film. There, the vast frontier of space delivered fearsome creatures who threatened to take over our minds and bodies. In the western, a more manageable frontier assured us that, even after the hardships of World War II, we were still a country on the make, that we could retain and even increase our supremacy in the world – and, perhaps most important, that there were still heroes to act on our behalf.

The western in the 1950s   At the same time, the place of America in the world, the traumas the country suffered in the wake of a world war, and the new demands being made on the culture itself began to gnaw away at the simplicity of the western genre. The cowboy, that unquestioned figure of individuality and trust, riding across the landscape and protecting the innocent townspeople from outlaws and Indians, began to grow more complex, even to have doubts about his place and his role as hero.

In light of the civil rights movement in the decades after the war, attitudes toward Indians began to change. Rather than portraying them as some elemental force of violence, something standing in the way of the westward movement of "civilization," Indians began to be understood both in and outside of film as individuals with complex, functioning cultures of their own. It took at least another decade for this understanding to take complete hold on the cultural imagination. When it finally did, by the late 1960s, the western was finished.

John Ford, the director of *The Searchers*, had been making westerns for some time, and immediately after World War II, in films like *Fort Apache* (1948), he began probing some of the givens of the genre. *The Searchers* brings these questions to the fore, while at the same time allowing all the right generic elements to thrive. The film's success is the tension it builds between what is expected of the western genre and the questions Ford poses within it.

The prisoner of the desert   A lone rider, Ethan Edwards, comes in from the desert and greets his family, who live in a small, exposed community. The rider may be an outlaw; he was a confederate soldier; while his family is adoring, the viewer is somewhat suspicious. Soon, the family and their home are destroyed by Indians, who carry away the hero's niece. The older niece is found dead; the hero and his nephew, who is part Indian, go on a long, obsessive quest to find the niece, Debbie. When they find her five years later, she has grown up and become a wife of the Indian tribe's leader, Scar. Ethan, suffering a pathological hatred of Indians, wants to destroy her because, he believes, she is no longer white. With the help of the Cavalry, Ethan and his part-Indian nephew, Martin, track down the marauding tribe; Ethan confronts Scar and, after the nephew kills him, scalps him. In a moment of redemption, Ethan, instead of killing Debbie, raises her up and carries her back to her family before riding off back into the desert. The "hero," helping to establish the family on the frontier, protecting it against primal forces that would destroy it, has, finally, no place in domestic space. He is a prisoner of his own heroism and, as the title song of *The Searchers* insists, must continue to wander.

A plot summary gives little information, especially about such a visually articulate film as this. Nor does it adequately explain the complexity of its main character, one of the most conflicted in film history. We will examine its formal properties, but first we need to pay attention to its hero, the actor who plays him, and, with that, attempt to understand the phenomenon of celebrity that is so much a part of media culture.

John Wayne, who plays Ethan Edwards, is, as we noted, still among the most well-known and admired of screen actors some 30 years after his death. He is still imagined by some as the embodiment of strong, masculine heroism. In "real life," Wayne was a fairly ordinary person with right-wing views. He was so non-heroic that, although his reputation rests on the western heroes he played and on the war films in which he led American troops to victory, he managed to avoid military service throughout his life. But celebrity has nothing to do with reality, and only a little to do with the roles that celebrities play as actors or singers. This calls for a digression.

Celebrity

We have spoken a lot about the concept of the gaze. Actors and actresses look at each other, we at them. The more we look, the more we seem to want to look some more. This has been true since film's beginning. Early film-makers kept their players anonymous, until audiences demanded to know not only who they were, but also what they were "as people." Television has never attracted quite as much celebrity interest as film. Think, for example, of how many actors and actresses you can name from television versus those you can think of in film. We tend to remember TV hosts or quizmasters or judges more than actors and actresses. Almost everyone has heard of Simon Cowell of *American Idol*. But Sandra Oh of *Grey's Anatomy*, or Sam Waterston of *Law and Order*? Perhaps not so many. Jennifer Aniston, who played a character millions of young women could identify with in *Friends*, seems to be a current exception to the rule. The reason, I think, is that most television players are young and, before their appearance in a series, not well known. As a series progresses, the actor stands well behind his or her character, and the character itself may be somewhat anonymous. We may remember Horatio from *CSI: Miami*, but what's the actor's name? How many contemporary viewers remember him from *N.Y.P.D. Blue*? How many even remember *N.Y.P.D. Blue*?

The demanding gaze

There was an old answer to this question of recognition, which was that movie stars appeared larger than life on the big screen. Their image, and their gaze, engulfed and engaged the viewer, as did the emotional dynamics of the stories they starred in. This is less true now. Even if we still go out to the movies (which we are doing less and less), the mall theater screens we see them on are not so large; and, more frequently, we are seeing movies on DVD at home, or even on our computers. But I think that, short of a big scandal, the celebrity machinery is still geared more toward movie stars than to the smaller figures on television.

This only partly answers the question of why, for example, we seem so interested in Brad Pitt and Angelina Jolie – despite the fact that neither have made very interesting movies of late. What, then, is so interesting about their reproductive capabilities, their on-again, off-again relationship, and the fact that they adopt children from poor countries? The fact is that actors can become celebrities quite separately from their roles as actors. With the help of celebrity magazines, which are as old as movies themselves, television shows, and gossip tabloids, actors turned celebrities may have many different narratives, various stories about their "lives."

Celebrity narratives

The primary celebrity narrative should be the films and shows that the star plays in. More accurately, that narrative is a *result* of the roles they play. Actors become identified with their roles, whether or not they are in any way like the characters they play. After all, the job of an actor is to act, to take on characteristics of a character, who may or may not have anything to do with who the actor is. But we tend to see the character in the actor, especially if the actor specializes in certain roles: Julia Roberts in romantic comedies; Jennifer Aniston as a somewhat bungling comic character; Samuel A. Jackson as a big, blustery, high-cursing action figure; Morgan Freeman as a sober, thoughtful character, the fantasy of an ideal African-American president. Earlier on, Humphrey Bogart was the icon of the movie tough guy; and, of course, John Wayne was the selfless, hard hero, the protector of those who needed to be saved by his tough skills.

The second narrative is the celebrity itself, created by publicity agents, and the array of magazines, tabloids, blogs, and television shows that traffic in star stories. The celebrity narrative may have little to do with acting talent or identification with a kind of role – as in the case of Brad and Angelina. A celebrity doesn't actually have to do anything but be a celebrity, created as such by all the available celebrity media. Think of Paris Hilton. Celebrity may grow out of the actor's extracurricular activities, excessive partying, too many divorces, or, increasingly, political involvement. Brad and Angelina, like the rock singer Bono, work on behalf of African poverty, for example. Some may have been performers at some time, but eventually begin to exist as the product of scandal, like Michael Jackson, or of unusual behavior, like Tom Cruise.

The least-known celebrity narrative is the actor's "actual" life – even though it is the one the tabloids seem most interested in. How she actually lives, her daily routine, what is actually going on in her head from moment to moment. There is a private life and then there is the celebrity narrative of the private, the story about marriage and divorce, children, drugs, parties. These may actually be part of a celebrity's daily exist- ence; but all we know is the story told. We are never privy to what anyone is thinking when, for instance, the alarm rings and they get out of bed.

The fascination with people with extraordinary public lives is irresistible, no more so than when they fall. The melodrama that is the genre in which their screen persona so often act becomes the melodrama of "real life" – or, at least, life that tabloid news- papers and television shows like *Entertainment Tonight* can convince us is real. Celebrity might therefore be constituted into a fourth narrative, the one shared between audience and the dramatic rise and fall of the celebrated person, tying the viewer's imagination to the emotional graph almost as much as would any genuinely fictional narrative. That we take a perverse pleasure in the fall of a celebrity is a fact of celebrity life in the stories we are told about it.

John Wayne and the undoing of the hero   John Wayne succeeded in extrapolating the narrative of his film roles into his public life. During the Vietnam War, when the American public violently split over support for an unwinnable and very deadly con- flict, Wayne came out loudly on the side of those in support of the war. He even directed and starred in a film, *The Green Berets* (1968), celebrating its soldiers and condemning those who opposed the war. The film was bad, but Wayne's political position tied in so neatly with his on-camera persona that he continued until and past his death as a heroic icon of the American right.

When we examine Wayne's character in *The Searchers*, we note that the power of celebrity can, in fact, outlive a role that attempts to attack its foundation. The point is that the film questions the western hero – and heroism in general – using Wayne's celebrity, and his past roles (he began acting in Ford westerns starting with *Stagecoach* in 1939), against the character he plays. Ethan Edwards is an obsessive racist. His quest after the Indians who killed his family is, at heart, the result of his horror that his niece has become a "squaw" (the word itself combines a misogynist and racist stereotype), has been violated and is therefore no longer white. In a core sequence of the film, Ethan views a group of white women the cavalry has set free from Indian captivity. The women act as if they are crazy, wide-eyed and hysterical, clutching rag dolls. "They ain't white!" Ethan yells, almost as hysterical as the women. The camera

Figure 6.16 In John Ford's *The Searchers* (1956), Ethan Edwards (John Wayne) looks at a group of white woman rescued from the Indians. His "look" combines hatred, fear, and confusion. *The Searchers* © Warner Bros., 1956, 1984.

tracks into his face, revealing a gaze that is at once full of hate, anger, and fear, and an agonized pity toward these women. The sequence is ambiguous. Are these women crazed, or have they become acclimatized to Indian culture and therefore disoriented when captured by the cavalry? Ethan's look reflects the uncertainty of the film's own position about Indians, an uncertainty that is emphasized when he meets his Indian antagonist, Scar. They act as mirror images, each one damaged by the violence committed on them and their people; each bent on revenge. (See figure 6.16.)

The Searchers uses the western genre and the landscapes of Monument Valley – which in all of John Ford's films becomes the mythic space of the American frontier – as a kind of closed universe in which questions of heroism, community building, racism, fears of the other, and of captivity, can be examined. The film was made at a time of racial change in the United States, which places this western movie in the midst of the contemporary struggle over civil rights. The film can no more solve racial tensions than could the culture that produced it. Neither can it solve its own internal questions about heroism nor justify the historical movement westward that required wiping out a race of people. What it manages to do is to make its genre responsible to the present moment, reflecting tensions occurring in the culture during the mid-1950s. The only thing it can do with certainty is indicate that obsession is the reverse side of heroism, and when coupled with racism is corrosive and ultimately destructive.

Ethan's change of heart, his saving of his niece rather than killing her as he intended to do, was as much a necessity of film-making at the time as it was a redemptive act on Ethan's part. His rage and hatred has no place in the new domestic order that he makes possible. *The Searchers* begins and ends in a perfect symmetry of inclusion and exclusion: Ethan rides in from the desert, viewed from the dark interior of a lone house in the wilderness; at the end, he rides back into the desert, viewed again from the dark and now protected interior of the house. The family he has reunited is secure. He is not. Neither is the heroism he represents. The door is closed on him. (See figure 6.17.)

Figure 6.17 The door opens in John Ford's *The Searchers* (1956). *The Searchers* © Warner Bros., 1956, 1984.

The end of the western

The Searchers was not the only 1950s western to question the givens of the genre, nor was the western the only genre to address the cultural anxieties of the decade. We noted that science fiction films abounded, and, with their relentless themes of alien invasion, they mirrored the society's hysteria about Communism taking over people's minds, first, and country, second. Because it is set in the future, but reflects our concerns in the present, science fiction can always be molded to fit the moment. But the western, which depends on the culture's mythologies of history, cannot keep changing as our ideas of the past change.

The western died. The slow, painful change in racial attitudes made it impossible to depict Indians as an undifferentiated, murderous, "other." In 1970, the director Arthur Penn made a western called *Little Big Man* in which the Indians refer to themselves as "human beings" and the white man is seen as the enemy. The film defined the end of Indian as savage primitive. Meanwhile, the Vietnam War, which the great western hero John Wayne so strongly embraced, was clarifying the fact that the United States could no longer wage war on a nation and try to destroy it, the way it did the Indian nations in the nineteenth century. By the late 1960s and early 1970s, *anti-westerns* were laying the ground for the genre's decline. Sam Peckinpah's *The Wild Bunch* (1969) and Robert Altman's *McCabe and Mrs. Miller* (1971) helped expose the contradictions and lies embedded in the genre's codes. *The Wild Bunch*, set in 1913, depicts the gang of outlaws as aging, unable to outlive their time, uncertain as to what side they should fight. They choose the wrong side – the Mexican government fighting a revolution of its people – and are destroyed. Peckinpah's film also clarifies the violence of the genre. Here, gunshots result in painful fountains of blood, and death comes in agonizing slow motion.

Altman's *McCabe and Mrs. Miller* abandons the desert for a cold, rainy Northwestern mining town, more interested in gambling and whoring than establishing a settlement with upstanding American values. Its "hero" is decidedly unheroic, and the bad guys are neither outlaws nor Indians (one of them happens to be an Indian, though it is not the point), but rather thugs sent in by mining interests who want to buy up the town. Even more, the visual spaces of this film are not the wide-open vistas of Monument Valley, but instead the closed inhospitable spaces of a town in a mudhole. The community in this film doesn't cohere; its hero, who eschews heroism and wants to save no one, dies alone in the snow.

An Italian director, Sergio Leone, made films like *The Good, The Bad, and The Ugly* (1966) that turned the generic gestures of the western into the equivalent of a western grand opera. Part parody, part homage, Leone's "spaghetti westerns" magnified the genre's conventions in ways that could only happen when viewers were becoming fully conscious, even self-conscious of them. Self-consciousness on the part of both the film-maker and the viewer is usually more than a genre can manage, and, predictably, the western is now all but gone, undone by changes in the historical imagination that used to feed it.

The end of the studio system

Gone too is the studio apparatus that supported the western. I pointed out earlier that, until the 1950s, the studio system provided talent, both on screen and off, all under contract. Everything was done in-house, almost literally "ordered up" and off the shelf. By the 1950s, contracts began running out, the old studio bosses were aging, and the blacklist – a result of the anti-Communist hysteria that permitted the government to accuse, and the studios to fire, anyone, including screenwriters, directors, and stars suspected of being "Communists" – was taking its toll. The studios blacklisted much of their best talent. Until the late 1940s, most of the studios also owned the movie houses that showed their pictures. The Supreme Court divested them of that monopoly and therefore of a guaranteed income. Income from audiences was falling as well, almost steadily since the late forties, as people moved to the suburbs and television took over as the preferred medium for visual narratives.

One result we have seen: while the names of the studios remain the same as when they were invented, they are now part of large media empires, and their product is one among many. During their heyday, the studios made movies. The studios today also make movies, but because of their placement within the larger media design, movies are not only a means of making money, but also a means of making more money by providing links to other profit centers. A movie itself is mediated by a number of forms and means of distribution. There is the traditional celluloid-based film, projected in a mall theater, though this is a fast-disappearing format soon to be replaced by digital projection. After a theatrical run, a movie will appear on DVD, often with "deleted scenes" and other supplements to give it renewed life. DVD sales often account for as much as half the profit for a film. The final outlets for a film are cable and then network television. A video game may be another outlet, particularly for an action film.

Film, Domestic and Foreign

We have been concentrating on the history and form of American film. The fact is that all countries, large and small, rich and poor, have film-makers, often using the medium for intense, creative, personal and political expression. Some have film-making industries. India produces more films than the United States, mostly in the form of elaborate, romantic, musical fantasies, and most for domestic consumption with DVD sales to Indian nationals living abroad. Other countries have much smaller output, sometimes the work of only a few film-makers, whose films travel the festival circuit (various film festivals – Cannes, Berlin, Toronto, Sundance, among the largest – feature big-budget films and smaller, independent, productions) and may be released on DVD.

The fact is that all of this production, big and small, domestic and foreign, conventional or wildly imaginative, is interrelated, and has been from the time film was invented. This relationship has always been filled with tension. Once Hollywood film-making was established and the studios began their stream of diverse, genre-based production of romance and adventure, comedy and melodrama, other countries didn't stand a chance. People the world over prefer American films. Many countries turned to state funding of film-makers and had to apply quotas: a certain percentage of the much-preferred American films could be shown in that country's theaters only when a percentage of home-made product was also shown.

But, despite the tension – perhaps because of it – there has also been a profound and energetic cross-fertilization of film-making styles. Foreign film-makers have absorbed, or imaginatively contended with, the Hollywood style; American film-makers have watched the work of foreign film-makers with interest, taking from them what they could, often working side by side when those film-makers came to the US.

From abroad

At the beginning of this chapter we spoke about the historical acceptance of film as an art form, a discourse that separates it from the mass media where it sometimes might more comfortably belong. We noted as well that, within the Hollywood system, individual directors were able to imprint a style, even a personality, on their films, imparting a visual and thematic coherence to all their works. We discussed John Ford, and need also to mention directors like Alfred Hitchcock, Frank Capra, and Howard Hawks, among others, who survived in Hollywood by making commercially successful films that also bore both coherence and complexity, that addressed moral, even political, issues, and that explored them by exploring cinema and its expressive powers, often playing with the forms of classical Hollywood cinema by turning them to their own imaginative ends.

From the beginning of film history, there have been directors outside the Hollywood mainstream – outside Hollywood itself – who have consciously set out to make films that would not be completely outside of the Hollywood system and its stylistic economics. They used cinematic language to construct narratives as demanding and complex as anything in the other visual arts or even written literature. Their work was influenced by the other arts and in turn influenced film-makers in an international exchange of cinematic innovation. We will look at some of their work.

Surrealism and fairy tale   Early in film history, artists who were experimenting in traditionally recognized media, such as painting and photography, turned to film as part of their expressive palette. In the 1920s, avant-garde visual artists created often abstract, sometimes surreal, films. The famous (or infamous) Spanish surrealist painter, Salvador Dali, collaborated with a young Spanish film-maker, Luis Buñuel, to create outrageous and sacrilegious films, like *Un chien Andalou* (1929) and *L'age d'or* (1930). Buñuel later worked on his own, perpetuating the surrealist urge in films like *Viridiana* (1961), with results sometimes bordering on blasphemy. The French poet and painter Jean Cocteau made a number of films, including a magical retelling of the "Beauty and the Beast" fairy tale (*La Belle et la Bête*, 1946). Films like these were crossovers, works by artists in other media turning to

Figure 6.18
Surrealism and the fairy tale, Jean Cocteau's *Beauty and the Beast* (1946). *Beauty and the Beast* © Comité Cocteau, 2000.

film as an alternative form of expression. More inherently cinematic forms were further developed by German film-makers, who came out of the artistic movement called expressionism; we mentioned this earlier when we explored the origins of the horror film genre. Among the most influential forms of film-making, expressionism was born out of the trauma that Europe suffered as a result of World War I. (See figure 6.18.)

Figure 6.19 In film noir, darkness swallows the light, and frightened faces peer out (*T-Men*, dir. Anthony Mann, 1947). *T-Men* © Eagle-Lion, 1947.

Expressionism and film noir   Not only born of trauma, but conveying it as well, expressionism attempts to externalize internal states of emotional turmoil. The spaces surrounding the characters reflect their torment: deep shadows, distorted shapes, characters groping their way through dreamlike landscapes. *Traum*, the root of "trauma," translates literally as "dream." German expressionist films, like *The Cabinet of Dr Caligari* (1919), were highly artificial, using painted sets and stylized acting. When the style emigrated to Hollywood – along with many of its practitioners – it influenced, as we've seen, the popular horror films made by Universal pictures in the early 1930s: *Frankenstein*, *Dracula*, and their many sequels and spin-offs, as well as films by Joseph von Sternberg. Expressionism was an influence on Orson Welles's *Citizen Kane*, which itself became an enormous influence on film-makers and helped create a style and genre of film called film noir. With its dark cityscapes and frightened characters scurrying in the shadows, film noir, particularly as it saturated gangster and private-eye films, became a major form in American film during the 1940s; it was revived by film-makers in the 1970s and continues as an influence to this day. (See figure 6.19.)

"Film noir" is a French term. American film-makers were not conscious of creating a new style when they began making these dark films in the 1940s. This should not be surprising. Historically, American film-making was largely an intuitive process. Producers, writers, directors, and stars may have had an idea of the broad generic bases of their work. If a Western or a gangster film was being made, everyone involved knew what they were doing and, more importantly, how to do it. In the early 1940s, some directors and directors of photography – the individual responsible for lighting the film, choosing the right lenses for the camera, and setting up a shot based in consultation with the director – may consciously have borrowed the dark, shadowy style of *Citizen Kane*. Writers would have been aware of the influence of detective fiction. But none of them – not even film reviewers – would have been conscious of starting an entirely new *kind* of film: tough, often brutal, films like *Murder My Sweet* (Edward Dmytryk, 1944), *Double Indemnity* (Billy Wilder, 1944), and *Raw Deal* (Anthony Mann, 1948).

Things were different in Europe, where film was taken more seriously as part of the general cultural scene. During World War II, when the Nazis controlled much of Europe, the showing of American films was not allowed. After the war, many years' worth of films from the US flooded in, and French film-goers noted the darkening tone, both visually and thematically, in the American films they were now able to see (*Citizen Kane*, made in 1941, premiered in France in 1946, and was reviewed by the famous French philosopher, Jean-Paul Sartre). They named the trend "film noir." It took almost 30 years for the label to become familiar to American film scholars and audiences, when it became one of the few terms from film criticism to enter the popular vocabulary.

Neo-realism   As Europe began to recover from the ravages of the war, a new kind of film began emerging there as well. Italian film-makers built a cinematic style out of the rubble that was left of their cities. With little money, borrowing film stock from the US Army Signal Corps, using non-professional actors, and filming on the streets, they created a form that they themselves called neo-realism. Films like Roberto Rossellini's *Open City* (1945) and Vittorio De Sica's *Bicycle Thief* (1948) were raw melodramas of poor people in the ruined cities of post-war Europe. Neo-realism became an influence on American film-makers, some of whom began moving out of the studio and onto the streets in order to capture the visual textures of a lived-in world. (See figure 6.20.)

Figure 6.20   A dramatic moment from Roberto Rossellini's *Open City* (1945). Neorealism told its stories on the street. *Open City* © Film Preservation Association, 1997.

The new wave   Neo-realism, noir, and the American gangster film together formed an influence on what became the most important movement in post-World War II film, the French new wave. Of the many film-makers who made up the movement, Jean-Luc Godard and François Truffaut are among the best known. Their films of the late 1950s and early 1960s – *Breathless, The 400 Blows, Jules and Jim* – seemed to be spontaneous eruptions of film-making energy with characters who were simultaneously tormented and freewheeling. Long, unedited shots taken with a hand-held camera, with editing that did not follow the conventions of the Hollywood style, created films that turned the cinema world upside down, spawning new cinematic movements across Europe and Latin America. For a few decades, it seemed as if a world cinema might emerge that would challenge in its complexity not only Hollywood, but also other forms of artistic expression.

American film felt the influence of the new wave as young directors – some of whom had received formal training in film school, all of whom had a sense of film history – came on the scene with European ideas of a counter-cinema. Arthur Penn's *Bonnie and Clyde* (1967), Francis Ford Coppola's *Godfather* films (1972, 1974) and *The Conversation* (1974), Martin Scorsese's *Mean Streets* (1973) and *Taxi Driver* (1976), among others, showed the influence of European "art cinema" and, however briefly, allowed some directors to ascend back to power in Hollywood.

A new American cinema

The ascension – or perhaps more accurately the resurrection – of the director meant that some chances were taken with the ways movie stories were told. The way Martin Scorsese's nervous camera style in *Mean Streets* and *GoodFellas* (1990) captured the point of view of small-time hoods in the streets of New York; or, in *Taxi Driver* (1976), the perspective of a man going slowly and thoroughly crazy, reflected much of the visual ingenuity of his European influences (and American as well – *The Searchers* and Alfred Hitchcock's *Psycho* [1960] are influences on *Taxi Driver*). Robert Altman came to Hollywood from the Midwest and, with *MASH* (the movie that spawned the television series), originated a style that probed space with a restlessly zooming camera, creating a sprawling cinematic canvas filled with characters whose lives keep criss-crossing each other in films that rethought conventional genres. One of them was *McCabe and Mrs. Miller,* which, as we saw earlier, was among the films that pushed the western genre so hard that it could not return to its original form. Many of the films by these new directors – like Steven Spielberg's *Jaws* (1975) and the *Godfather* – were extremely popular. They gave the Hollywood director newfound powers to create and control film-making – at least for a while.

Martin Scorsese reinvented the gangster genre as an extension of neo-realism, making the streets of New York the environment for men whose destructive behavior is at once funny and horrifying. Francis Ford Coppola engineered the genre into an embracing family melodrama, almost a gangster opera, in which the figures are larger than life, emotional about their lives and the murders they commit, self-protective, but in the end – like all gangsters in the movies – self-destructive. The two *Godfather* films were blockbusters, enormously popular and returning huge profits. So, too, was Steven Spielberg's *Jaws* (1975), a horror film with a strong sense of viewer engagement that the director learned from Alfred Hitchcock. Spielberg continued with a remarkable career that has mixed big special-effects movies like *Close Encounters of the Third Kind* (1977), *ET* (1982), and *War of the Worlds* (2005) with serious films that embrace painful memories of the Nazi destruction of the Jews in *Schindler's List* (1993), and ambiguous moral and political issues in *Munich* (2005).

Coppola did not survive the *Godfather* films. Although *Apocalypse Now* (1979), his surreal vision of war's nightmare, was a successful film, he slowly withdrew from the Hollywood scene, turning his attention to wine rather than film-making. Scorsese has survived with a career of well-made films, none of them blockbusters, almost all of them carrying on an urgent sense of exploration of cinematic possibilities. Spielberg understands that to make "personal" films, he also has to make popular ones, and he has alternated the two with amazing success.

But, with the exception of Spielberg, Scorsese, and a very few others, the director has not fared well. Keep in mind that, since the early days of the studio, the director was subordinate to the producer of a film, who wielded the power of the budget. When, in the 1970s, films that were identified with their director made money, the studios were happy to recognize it. Then it came to an end. A director named Michael Cimeno made *The Deer Hunter* (1978), a very popular film about the Vietnam War. His studio, the venerable United Artists – the company originally formed by D. W. Griffith, Charlie Chaplin, and Douglas Fairbanks in 1919, and at this point owned by a large insurance company – poured a lot of money into his next project, an epic-sized, slightly left-wing western, *Heaven's Gate* (1980). Perhaps the studio didn't know that the western was dead. Perhaps they could not predict that a very long, very slow, left-of-center western that cost millions might not go over well. Media companies are clever, but not infallible. The film failed catastrophically. It was drastically cut (shades of Stroheim's *Greed*). But nothing helped. United Artists was ruined, and Hollywood's affair with directors came, again, to an end.

Hollywood today

Today we are back in a period somewhat akin to the studio period, if only in the sense that most American film-making is largely anonymous, and the producer is back in full charge. A few American directors manage to retain some control over their work, and occasionally Hollywood will even attempt to create the reputation of a director based on the popularity of a film. M. Night Shyamalan is an example. His film, *Sixth Sense* (1999), was successful, his name exotic, his cinematic style not very interesting. There was an attempt to create a cult of personality, though this could not outlive the commercial failure of his subsequent films. Judd Apatow has been more successful. As director, producer, and writer, he has been the driving force behind a number of engaging (if occasionally vulgar) comedies like *The Forty Year Old Virgin* (2005), *Talladega Nights* (2006), *Superbad* (2007) and *Walk Hard: The Dewey Cox Story* (2007).

Personality is a quality that seems to be missing from much contemporary Hollywood production. The profits of the first weekend, not the reputation of a director or the attractions of an interesting cinematic style, are what drive Hollywood these days. Stars remain powerful draws, though in the process of containing costs, even they, with their enormous salary demands, are becoming victims of bottom-line mentalities. The fact is that first-run, theatrical releases do not always make the kinds of profits studios would like to see. What this means is that, like so many of the products offered by media companies, films are commodities in the circuit of exchange, and, in that circulation, your "eyeballs" – in the parlance of the business; your gaze, in the critical discourse we have been using – must be continually prompted and pleased in order to supply the money needed to keep the circulation moving.

Transnational cinema

A large part of this circulation has to do with the global reach of American media. We have discussed how American and European film-making were in a fairly constant state of mutual influence. This has turned into something of a one-way street, where talent from overseas is drawn to Hollywood and personality is transformed into a kind of universal style. Peter Jackson is a case in point. A New Zealander, he made his reputation with "slice and dice" exploitation films bearing titles like *Bad Taste* (1988), *Dead Alive* (1992), and *The Frighteners* (1996). A less bloody film, *Heavenly Creatures*, set in the remote New Zealand city of Christchurch in 1954, tells the story of two teenage girls who commit a murder. This film brought Jackson international attention and the directorship of the *Lord of the Rings* trilogy (2001–3), followed by the most recent remake of *King Kong* (2005).

Asia has been a particularly fertile ground for American film, as a market and as a source. The popularity of the martial arts genre, and the Hong Kong variants of the gangster film, have provided templates for American films, like Quentin Tarantino's *Kill Bill* (2003) and Martin Scorsese's *The Departed* (2006). The Hong Kong director John Woo started by making kung fu action movies in Hong Kong and then came to the United States, where he brought his arrhythmic, violent style to films like

Face/Off (1997) and *Mission: Impossible 2* (2000). Ang Lee, Taiwanese by birth, began his American career with an adaptation of a nineteenth-century novel, Jane Austen's *Sense and Sensibility* (1995), a costume drama in the manner of the PBS-BBC *Masterpiece Theatre* genre. But he quickly moved on to a variety of other genres, including a civil war film, *Ride With the Devil* (1999); a Chinese kung fu, romantic-operatic mix, *Crouching Tiger, Hidden Dragon* (2000); and a super-hero action film, *The Hulk* (2003). Lee's *Brokeback Mountain* (2005) is another kind of mix: a romantic melodrama, in a contemporary western setting, focusing on the emotional travails of a pair of male lovers. In the studio period, were the characters conventional, hetero-sexual, lovers, this emotionally fraught film would have been called a "weepie."

Some Asian directors have remained in their native countries, developed unusual cinematic styles, and achieved some international success. Wong Kar-wai has contin-ued working in his native Hong Kong, making films that are far from popular enter-tainments, but rather intense, complex ruminations on history and emotional engagement. His films – especially *In the Mood for Love* (2000) and *2046* (2004) – are wide-screen poems of people in small rooms, mixing memory and desire in richly colored, multifaceted images overlaid with a subtle and eclectic music track. Recently, he too has succumbed, coming to America to make an extraordinarily lyrical road movie, *My Blueberry Nights* (2007). Such films depend upon their visual and aural textures as much as – perhaps more than – the stories they are telling, which are oblique, moving in many directions, and ending without conclusion. They are about time, space, color, gesture, and sound as well as the people who are part of the visual and oral patterns. Wong Kar-wai maintains another tradition in contemporary cinema, often called the "art film." At the same time, he has reached into the global exchange of media culture, making music videos, notably DJ Shadow's rap, "6 Day War."

Global commerce

The commerce of film itself is becoming complicated by its global nature. The stu-dios, as we've seen, are parts of international media conglomerates. The larger the conglomeration, the tighter funding becomes for anything but a film that seems guaranteed to reap large returns. A look at the credits for almost any film that has not been solely financed by a studio, will reveal an amazing array of funders. *Crash*, a 2005 Academy Award winner, written and directed by Paul Haggis, is a well-made, highly melodramatic film that attempts to address the complexities of race relations through the chance encounter of a number of characters in Los Angeles. Its ancestry is a much more difficult, non-melodramatic film by Robert Altman, *Short Cuts* (1993), which was imitated by a 1999 film, *Magnolia*, directed by Paul Thomas Anderson. *Crash* lists 14 producers, including one of its stars, Don Cheadle. Its financial backers include two German production companies. The complexity of financing and production was such that, at Academy Award time, some of the pro-ducers got into a fight: lawsuits were filed and industry trade paper advertisements were taken out over who deserved production credits and who should receive what share of profits from the film.

The melodramatic improbabilities of *Crash* may dilute its seriousness, but even its rather uncontroversial treatment of racial conflict is a matter too close to the real world for Hollywood to handle. While the melodrama may have spilled over into fights for profits, the struggle for backing to *make* the film, and the need to find foreign backing for a small, even slightly controversial film is hardly unusual. Even a much admired and commercially viable director like Woody Allen found backing from the British Broadcasting Corporation, two other British backers, and a Luxemburg production company for his London-based film, *Match Point* (2005).

The concern about globalization is homogenization. If film – and any other media production, for that matter – is internationalized, will all film then look alike? Will we lose the individual, imaginative interventions that are necessary to keep cinema vital? Such questions bring us back to where we began – how does film, which is so often considered an "art form," survive? The answer, I think, lies in the vitality of this particular medium, in the ongoing desire for film-makers to keep reinventing cinema, probing it as a language that is complex, challenging, and evocative.

There will always be a huge, international audience for Hollywood and Hollywood-like film-making. At the same time, there will be a smaller audience for smaller, more inquisitive and thought-provoking films like those of Wong Kar-wai, or of the Austrian film-maker Michael Haneke, whose intense, demanding films – like *Code Unknown* (2000) and *Caché* (2005) – investigate the issues of racial diversity and of how we look at the world and how media looks at us. But even this very serious film-maker, who has worked in his native country and in France, has gone international with an English version of his gruesome "home invasion" film, *Funny Games* (2008).

Convergence

Technologies and illusions of vision

I have mentioned that the technologies of film were never very complex. They have developed from the optical and chemical bases of photography. The optical principle involves the ability to capture and manipulate a two-dimensional image that, because there is no actual depth, allows for the creation of illusions of depth. The way images are composed, the angle at which the camera is aimed at its subject, whether the foreground and background of the image are held in equal focus; and the way the lighting sculpts the image can all create a sense of space and depth that is highly manipulable. The lack of an actual third dimension permits film-makers to force a sense of depth by creating backgrounds with a false perspective.

From the earliest days of film, backgrounds have been faked – painted or projected behind the characters (most obviously in "rear-screen projection" sequences where the characters sit in a car while the moving background is projected on a screen behind them) – or where the background is actually placed in the foreground, photographed in a way that tricks the eye into reversing the spatial relationship. Rear-screen projection and matte painting are only the most simple effects film-makers use. The fact is that any given shot is likely to be a composite of different elements, taken or created at different times.

Given that an undeveloped piece of film can be exposed any number of times before it is developed, it is relatively easy to create a variety of effects by means of projecting different images that, when developed, will give the illusion of a complete space. The combinations of optical effects gave film-makers an enormous flexibility in creating representations of the real world, as well as imagining fantasy worlds, all of them articulated in great and convincing detail without the expense of location shooting or taking the actors out of the studio. It is part of the economy of film-making we discussed earlier.

CGI

CGI, or computer-generated imagery, has replaced all of these optical techniques in today's film-making. Its history can be traced back to an artist, John Whitney, who began experimenting with computer-generated art in the 1950s, and whose work was an influence on Stanley Kubrick's 1968 film, *2001: A Space Odyssey*. *2001* is a film that is, in part, about a computer that is not only intelligent, but sentient as well: it has consciousness. The film is a meditation about a future world dominated by computer design, filled with screens flashing data, and humans who act as the passive recipients of computer-generated information. *2001* also visualizes its worlds through the creation of special effects: spaceships waltzing across the universe; space stations; the surface of the moon; a voyage through infinity into an imaginative realm that could well exist within consciousness rather than outside it (see figure 6.15). Hardly the first science fiction film to use special effects – we can trace the genre and its imaginative spaces to a late German expressionist film, Fritz Lang's 1927 *Metropolis*, which was one of the first to create such imaginative detail by use of miniatures, matte shots, and rear- and front-screen projection.

2001 served as a catalyst for the advancement of special effects and the use of computers to create them. Initially, in the first *Star Wars* and Disney's *The Black Hole* (1979), for example, computers were used to control the careful synchronization of miniature and minute camera motions necessary to create convincing optical effects. George Lucas established Industrial Light and Magic, the special-effects unit of Lucasfilm that became a pioneer in CGI. By the 1980s, computers were beginning to be used to *generate* images as well as control them – *Star Trek II: The Wrath of Kahn* (1982) used a computer-generated sequence, and in *Young Sherlock Holmes* (1985) an animated figure, a knight in a stained-glass window that comes alive, was generated by computer.

The adaptation of CGI was rapid and became universal. From the metallic robot in *Terminator 2: Judgment Day* (James Cameron, 1991) to simple backgrounds, matte shots, and color effects, CGI processes are now used in all aspects of film-making, completely replacing older optical printing techniques. Look at the credits of any film, even one that appears to have been shot completely on location, and you will see a long list of CGI collaborators. The effects of this technical revolution are interesting.

The creation of fantastic worlds and the exercise of visual imagination have even fewer limitations than optical printing. Whatever can be designed on a computer, from fantastically detailed surroundings to human figures, can be transferred to the movie screen. In some instances, no sets need be built. Actors can perform in front of a blue or green screen that will be replaced with computer-generated actions and backgrounds at a later time. Actors themselves can be modeled, even replaced, by computer-generated figures, a common practice in action films.

Film has always played with our desire to see represented, even temporarily replaced, everyday reality with images and narratives that are more intense, more present than anything we might see out in the world. Machine-made images both expand the ability of film to generate these fictional realities and, at the same time, take some pressure off the imagination. Deliberation is replaced by expedience; creativity by graphical facility. When a creative process like CGI becomes ubiquitous and routine, it runs the risk of becoming too easy a fall back, a replacement for creativity.

George Lucas boasted that 95 percent of *The Revenge of the Sith* (2005), was computer-designed and animated. He also began trials in digital projection, showing the "film" not on celluloid, but from digital media in movie theaters. The fact is that chemically based, analogue recording of image and sound on strips of celluloid is all but obsolete. Not only are effects and background done digitally, so that it can be safely said that all films have a digital as opposed to a photographic *mise en scène*, but almost every film made is now converted to digital files for editing and image-processing. In fact, directors of cinematographers are often asked not to indulge in particular lighting techniques, but to leave those to digital compositing. The digital intermediary, as the digital files of a film ready for editing is called, is transferred back to celluloid for distribution to theaters. At the same time, a growing number of films are being shot in high-definition video. Digital editing has replaced the traditional process of working with strips of film, and has made editing relatively easy (as anyone who has worked with Final Cut Pro on their Mac knows). It offers even more flexibility in constructing a film's narrative. More and more theaters are converting to digital projection, carrying though Lucas's desire to put an end to celluloid and the enormous costs of striking prints and carting them around the country.

Like the changeover to sound that occurred in the late 1920s, all of this will call upon considerable resources, but with a difference: the change to sound remade cinema by calling on resources that were creative as much as they were financial and technical. Will digital cinematography develop into as subtle an expressive form as film, or will the demands for a flat, unnuanced image to be turned over to the digital compositors result in a different way, a different aesthetic for modeling cinematic space? We have seen that filmed television shows have gained the visual sophistication of film. Will film in turn be transformed into a visual sophistication of the digital?

Film-making for everyone

Another result of digitization is democratization. The ability to create and edit moving images has become inexpensive and readily accessible. Serious young film-makers are able to achieve professional results with relative ease and maximum imagination. Amateur movie-makers can receive instant gratification by putting their images online. The amazing growth of YouTube.com – and its billion-dollar purchase by Google – is a testament to the desire for people to show off their talent or their silliness in the quickest way possible. Interestingly enough, Hollywood producers scout YouTube for nascent talent. Judging by the majority of videos uploaded to the site, this might not seem to bode well for cinema's future and may seriously compromise any further hopes for film to reach the status of "art."

On the other hand, the future of cinema has always been in doubt, as noted in the epigraph of this chapter, voiced by one of the early pioneers of film. The "invention without a future" keeps reinventing itself. The desire and ability to imagine worlds cinematically satisfies a deep desire to see ourselves in alternative worlds. A critic has referred to ours as "the late age of film." More accurately, we are in another transitional age of film. New visions await.

References

Film as Art

Photographic origins
The classic discussion of the photographic origins of film is by the French critic, André Bazin, *What is Cinema?*, 2 vols, trans. Hugh Grey (Berkeley and Los Angeles: University of California Press, 1967, 1971). A good site for the history of photography is: <http://www.photographymuseum.com/>. There are many others, including sites for major museums.

Early film production
Tom Gunning's essay, "The Cinema of Attractions: Early Film, Its Spectator and the Avant-Garde," in *Early Film*, ed. Thomas Elsaesser and Adam Barker (London: British Film Institute, 1989), pp. 56–62, is the standard reference.

Economics and Art

The studio system
The classic study is the one by David Bordwell, Janet Staiger, and Kristin Thompson, *The Classical Hollywood Cinema* (New York: Columbia University Press, 1985). An excellent book on the founders of the studios is Neal Gabler's *An Empire of Their Own* (New York: Crown Publishers, 1988).

Universal, MGM, and Eric von Stroheim
For Erich von Stroheim and MGM, see David Cook, *A History of Narrative Film*, 4th edn (New York and London: W.W. Norton, 2004), pp. 193–203. See also Bud Schulberg, "Louis B. Mayer": <www.time.com>. A reconstruction of *Greed* using existing stills can be found in Herman Weinberg's *The Complete Greed of Erich von Stroheim* (New York: Arno Press, 1972).

The eye drives the construction of film narrative

The classic study of the "gaze" is Laura Mulvey's "Visual Pleasure and the Narrative Cinema," widely reproduced. It can be found in Leo Braudy and Marshall Cohen (eds), *Film Theory and Criticism*, 6th edn (New York: Oxford University Press, 2004), pp. 837–48.

The Searchers

Gary Wills's study, *John Wayne's America: The Politics of Celebrity* (New York: Simon and Schuster, 1997), is a good place to look for an analysis of Wayne, John Ford, and the fame of both. The connection of the film to the contemporary civil rights movement is made by Brian Henderson, in "The Searchers: An American Dilemma," *Film Quarterly* 34/2 (winter, 1980–81): 9–23.

Celebrity

All celebrity names are current as of this book's going to press. It is the nature of celebrity that its life is short. You may need to substitute current names.

For a study of Hollywood celebrity, see Marsha Orgeron, *Hollywood Ambitions: Celebrity in the Movie Age* (Middleton, CT: Wesleyan University Press, 2008).

From abroad

A study of post-World War II European cinema is Robert Kolker, *The Altering Eye*, online: <http://otal.umd.edu/~rkolker/AlteringEye>.

End of the studio system

There are many books about the Hollywood blacklist. Jon Lewis's essay, " 'We Do Not Ask You to Condone This': How the Blacklist Saved Hollywood," *Cinema Journal* 39 (2000): 3–30, is the best recent piece.

Global commerce

Discussion of the battle over the film *Crash* is reported by Sharon Waxman, " 'Crash' Producers Clash Loudly Over Credit and Payment," *New York Times*, (March 2, 2006); <http://www.nytimes.com/2006/03/02/movies/redcarpet/02cras.html>.

Convergence

CGI

A history of computer-generated imagery can be found at the website of Industrial Film and Magic: <http://www.ilm.com/inside_timeline.html> and at: <http://accad.osu.edu/~waynec/history/timeline.html>.

Film-making for everyone

The quotation "the late age of film" is by Paul Young, "The Negative Reinvention of Cinema: Late Hollywood in the Early Digital Age," *Convergence* 5 (1999): 24–50.

CHAPTER SEVEN
Digital Spaces

Today ... we have extended our central nervous system itself in a global embrace, abolishing both space and time as far as our planet is concerned.
Marshall McLuhan, *Understanding Media* (1994: 3)

*The book is an outmoded means of communicating information. And efforts to update it are hampered because, culturally, we give undue reverence to the form for the form's sake. Publish or perish, that's the highest call of our intellectual elite. But any medium that defines itself as a medium is in trouble: new*spapers, broadcast *TV*, broadcast *radio, and books. They are all faced with new and better means of doing what they do without regard to the limitations of any one medium.*
Jeff Jarvis, "The book is Dead. Long Live the Book,"
BuzzMachine (blog), May 19, 2006

All media have converged into the digital. Here we tell the history of computation and analyze the various interactions between individuals and the machine.

The Illusions of Digital Space

"We live in the late age of film." I quoted Paul Young's prophetic statement at the end of our discussion of film. We must add that we are living in the late age of all traditional media. Every media enterprise that we have discussed so far is contending with, moving to, replacing, and, in some rare instances, making peace with the digital realm.

The nineteenth-century analog technologies that drove "old media," as well as the twentieth-century media business models – the ways media products were produced, distributed, their audiences measured, and profits made – the very genres and narratives that inform media, as well as the basic relationships between the producers of media and its audience, are changing. If we are to believe the media producers, the digital world is challenging the way they make money, forcing them to think of new ways to create and make a profit from content. If we correctly understand our own activity as actors in the digital realm, we have become more immediately, more intimately, engaged in media, and are increasingly creating it ourselves.

Computers have succeeded in attaining the goal of all those nineteenth-century technological inventions that gave rise to modern media: they have made time and space completely malleable, flexible, and put them into our hands. Even more, computers, and networked computing especially, have created one of the great media illusions, an *alternate* space where information of all kinds, as well as a free exchange of words, images, and sounds – even personality, identity, and perhaps consciousness itself – are available within a kind of absence, a nowhere that is everywhere. There is a feeling that the Internet belongs to everyone, that everyone has access, and everyone has a place. Life online, it sometimes appears, is a comfortable substitute for life in the public sphere where people can roam, meet, exchange ideas, express themselves, and where self-expression can be shared and distributed, can charm other people, and can be used to make friends. There is a feeling that all the information one ever needs is available through Google, that all the community one needs might be found on a social networking site, and that all the imagination one needs is within the virtual world of *Second Life* or *World of Warcraft*. The World Wide Web *is* the new public sphere.

Computing presents itself as a present absence, a seemingly secure anonymity, or a glorious advertisement for oneself where one both is and isn't at the same time; it is a space that offers a notion of ownership, even omnipotence, and certainly control. This is completely at odds with the traditional media design, which, as we've seen again and again, places the audience in a receptive role, able to respond negatively by *not* viewing, listening, or reading, or by decoding media messages in ways that suit particular needs. In our relationship with traditional media, we are always aware that what we read, hear, and see has some kind of authorship behind it: someone writing and editing the newspaper column; producing, directing, and distributing a recording, a radio or TV show, or a movie. Advertising reminds us continuously that someone wants something from us, first our attention, then our fear or our desire, and then payment for the product. But at the keyboard and online, we seem to be in control and in intimate connection with something or someone, in a world both internal and external simultaneously.

"New media" is the general term used to describe these complex structures, artifacts, and the relationships and interactions we discover through the spaces represented on the computer. We need to explore the nature of the "new" and how the experience of user ownership, new to the media design and initially threatening to commercial media producers, has come about and exists in a process of seemingly constant change.

Enigma Machines

Analog vs. digital

In chapter 1, we examined the nineteenth-century origins of computation in the unusual relationship between Ada Lovelace – the daughter of the poet Lord Byron – and the mathematician Charles Babbage, who called her "the enchantress of numbers." Beyond the history of computation, we need to speculate about the basic concept of the "digital." On the level of technology, "analog" means "like," "continuous," or "corresponding to," and it refers to the physical medium, the electromagnetic spectrum, by means of which much media – radio, recorded sound, television, and film – are made and distributed. For example, in film-making, when a camera is running, light waves reflected from a subject enter the lens and hit a strip of film, causing a chemical change that, when developed, creates areas of light and shadow that correspond to those of the original subject. When a series of these images is projected, an illusion of movement is created, analogous to the movement recorded when the film was exposed. A voice in front of a microphone sets up vibrations that are translated into corresponding electronic waves that are amplified and set down on tape. Sounds and images can be carried in corresponding waves of the electromagnetic spectrum, transmitted, received, and reproduced on the radio or television. Reels of film with thousands of images are projected in a movie theater, creating the illusion of an ongoing world.

Digital is "not like." It is "discontinuous," a state of non-correspondence. A sound or light wave, rather than passing in a corresponding waveform state from source to recording medium, to listener or viewer, is instead translated into binary code, the zeros and ones that in multiple combinations represent the original source. The mediation effect is important here, because in digital reproduction the original and its representation pass through an intermediary form that preserves it, compresses it, and stabilizes it. Unlike an analog recording, the binary file is the result of digitizing text or image, and will not degrade. The file will yield the same information no matter how many times it is copied and reproduced. Recall our discussion of the traditional method of layering images to create the visual spaces of a film. The problem with that older method is that, each time an image is reprinted, its quality gets a little worse. The image on celluloid, even if left alone in a climate-controlled vault, degrades. A conventional magnetic recording of music or a movie will degrade by itself and lose quality each time it's copied. In contrast, a digital file, unless it becomes corrupted, will not change.

At the same time, a digital file can be manipulated much more easily than an analog image or sound. Computer code can be altered; the way information is stored, sampled, and compressed can be changed, sometimes for the worse (which is what is done by people intent on corrupting other people's machines), often for the better. The sampling and compression routines that capture the sound of an orchestra can be altered to accentuate certain frequencies, or bring out particular instruments.

The dialogue of a film has always been recorded, or "looped," after the film is edited so that the best reading of lines is created without any problem of synchronizing lip movement and sound. Now, using a digital process called Automated Dialogue Replacement, or ADR, this process creates perfect readings of lines that sound like they were recorded on the spot. The color of a film can be altered, added, or removed through manipulation of the digital files that all film becomes on the way to being edited.

Editing a film on celluloid is a cumbersome process because many physical strips of film need to be run through an editing machine, with the best ones chosen and physically spliced together. The digital files that make up a video recording are relatively simple to manipulate. They are easily stored and called up, editing patterns can be tried, discarded, and new ones created. The finished film can be digitally altered to look like traditional celluloid. With digital files, the entire industrial process of film-making can be homemade, manipulated on the desktop. Only creativity and imagination need be added.

A short digression on language and print

I want to digress for a moment to consider print, an analog process that is in some ways a forerunner of the digital. Letters are arbitrary, like the ones and zeros that are used to create a digital file. Letters, like numbers, don't stand for anything in the world. They and the words made from them are culturally determined forms. Four cows in a field can be photographed and recorded, and the resulting image will bear a resemblance to the thing itself. But "four" or "4," or the word "cow" or "field," not to mention the grammatical structure of a descriptive sentence, are the result of what was, once, an arbitrary creation of words and numbers and their meaningful arrangement (the notion that words are sometimes analogous to sounds does not hold up: French for the cow is *vache*, field is *champ*). The difference, of course, lies in the term "culturally determined." Binary "language" and computer code are the result of many determinations in the world of mathematics, developed to represent the world. But mathematics does not carry the larger, historical, weight of cultural determination and association that words and numbers do. Written and spoken language bears the weight of ages, coded with a great deal more than the binary numbers of a digital file.

The digital file now plays an important role in the preservation of language. The desire to save written language and images precedes one of the most important of digital endeavors, the collection and archiving of vast amounts of knowledge. Books, newspapers, catalogues, museums, and libraries were the original storage devices. They represent an undying desire to preserve what we know; they counter, to a large degree, the imperative of popular media to move on, to replace the old with the new and toss out the old (unless, of course, the old can be resuscitated for profit). Like any analog event, archives take up a great deal of space and will inevitably degrade over time. What's more, searching through them can be a difficult, though often rewarding, task. Working one's way through physical, analog, material creates a sense of connection, of one piece joining or leading to the discovery of another, and this is another way of thinking about analog versus digital: contiguous versus discrete.

A digital file contains discrete information, in the sense that the numerical code is made up of elements that are different from the source. Making the discrete contiguous, discovering ways to connect files and the information within them, *de*coding in ways that allow us to see the connections between things, has become perhaps the most important process computation has allowed. It is through the example of a searchable archive – a library – that the database emerges, becoming the basic structure of the digital world, where everything, text and images, social security and credit card numbers, MP3 and video files, email and Internet addresses, are stored, cross-referenced, made searchable, and ready for retrieval. Language, written and spoken, has now merged with the language of the machine.

Consciousness and the New Machine

Accessing and archiving information of all kinds, from any source, is one of the great accomplishments of modern computing. But we ask even more of these machines. Rather, we fantasize more. We dream of a machine with intelligence – more still, with consciousness. Indeed, modern computing began with this idea. The computer, a machine that manipulates numbers to create and search digital files, was fantasized in the imagination of a nineteenth-century poet's daughter and a mathematician-inventor, and was developed in the mid-twentieth century by the military. In World War II it was used to calculate the trajectory of armaments and to decode messages the German military was using to communicate. A British mathematician, Alan Turing, helped to create code-breaking computing, that was capable of deciphering German messages generated by the aptly named Enigma Machine. Turing also developed mathematical models for computing machines and code that made binary machine-thinking possible. Along the way he also laid the groundwork for an important school of computing science, Artificial Intelligence. "I propose to consider the question," Turing wrote in 1950, " 'Can machines think?' " To answer the question, he proposed an "imitation game" which, interestingly enough, was based on gender.

The Turing test An interrogator is placed in a room set apart from another space where there is a man (A) and a woman (B). Through a series of questions, the interrogator is asked to guess who is the man, and who the woman. "We now ask the question, 'What will happen when a machine takes the part of A in this game?' Will the interrogator decide wrongly as often when the game is played like this as he does when the game is played between a man and a woman?" If the answer is that the interrogator will have as much success with the machine as with the human being – that is, if the interrogator cannot ultimately tell if the response is coming from human or machine – intelligence may be ascribed to the machine.

The Turing test, as it has come to be called, not only sets the parameters for the study of Artificial Intelligence, but also, through its gendered participants, addresses something deeply embedded within our relationship with these machines: the intimacy experienced between a user and his or her computer. Following Turing, I would propose not a game, but a question. What is the nature of the intimacy so many people feel in regard to the computer? We think of it not as a tool, but as an extension of our selves. The computer seems not only to do tasks, but also to create a kind of undemanding environment for us in which the screen, unlike that of a television or a movie, becomes a personal space in which we can call forth almost anything. The intimacy is, at the same time, impersonal. The computer asks little of us, while at the same time, through the choices we make, the appearance of the screen we set up, the programs we choose, the websites we bookmark, the home pages we set up, it reflects us back to our selves and to others. If not a personality in itself, it becomes a kind of alternate, reflective, personality in the way no other media "appliance" can.

Frankenstein   This intimacy, the fantasy of the machine as conscious, intelligent entity, is not new. In fact, the only thing new about it is that it seems more possible, even probable, than it ever was. The dream of a mechanical or organic entity with intelligence and consciousness is as old as the Garden of Eden, where God created humans. In Greek mythology, Prometheus made men out of clay and gave them fire; Pygmalion created a woman out of ivory. In Jewish mythology of the Middle Ages, members of the shtetl created the Golem, a man of stone, to protect them. But the most enduring myth of man-made consciousness came from an early nineteenth-century contemporary of Ada Lovelace, Mary Shelley, who invented the scientist Frankenstein and his handmade monster. In Shelley's novel, the monster and his creator pursue each other into oblivion, the monster plagued with the inevitable questions of consciousness: "who am I" and "why?"

Frankenstein entered film and science fiction, morphing into various forms, but always maintaining the constant of the questions of consciousness. His mechanical versions were called "robot" or "android." We see them in Ridley Scott's film, *Blade Runner* (1982), where androids are given memories and are aware of their imminent deaths. Frankenstein's monster's computer version is reborn in HAL, the conscious, murderous computer of Stanley Kubrick's *2001: A Space Odyssey* (1968).

None of this is to suggest that we think of our computers as conscious entities. However, the myth of the conscious, non-human entity does seep into the sense of intimacy that we experience when working with them – a sense of ease and familiarity, of contact and response unavailable with any other electronic medium. We might call it the "computational embrace."

The personal machine

The machinery of intimacy developed steadily following World War II, though without apparent purpose. What I mean is that the "personal" computer was not in people's minds early on, when the machines were huge, hot, and cumbersome, run with vacuum tubes and using punch cards and linear recording tape for input and output. The US government put computing to civilian use, purchasing a UNIVAC from the Remington Rand Corporation to crunch numbers for the national census in 1951. The business machine company, IBM, developed mainframe computers to serve the workplace. The introduction of the transistor in late 1947 reduced the size and the heat of computing machines and began the process of shrinkage from room size to laptop. Developments followed in rapid order: the floppy disk was introduced in the 1960s, and magnetic core memory in 1953. Integrated circuits, developed in 1958, enabled increasing processing power in smaller sizes. As the machinery shrank, relatively simple operating systems capable of running them were developed. Bill Gates worked up a system called MS-DOS, which became the standard for small computers and the foundation for a computer software empire. Douglas C. Engelbart and others invented the mouse and developed graphical user interfaces in the 1960s. Commercialized by Apple computers in 1976 and then by Microsoft in its Windows operating systems, these became the extensions of the brain and body – the cybernetic connections of human and machine.

As with any technology, this development was not innocent or removed from cultural, political, and economic forces surrounding it. Nineteenth-century technologies had everything to do with expanding empires and the need to control communications throughout them. In the 1950s, with the post-World War II economy booming and corporations consolidating power, business developed a clear understanding of how computation would facilitate workloads and, more important for the corporate structure, reduce the number of people on payrolls.

The acceptance of computation in the home is more difficult to define. Somewhat akin to the ham operators, who helped pioneer radio transmission in the early 1920s, home-computing pioneers embraced the big, slow desktops that were becoming available in the mid- and late 1970s. In addition to the excitement of being on the leading edge of the science of tomorrow, a large part of the early attraction had to do with convenience (especially as word-processing programs improved) and entertainment. Computer games, begun in the early 1960s in MIT's laboratories, and reaching home with Atari's *Pong* in 1972, promoted acceptance. We will talk about computer gaming in detail later on.

One of the earliest uses of home computing was word processing. The transition from typewriter to a paperless system that allowed instant, clean revisions and quick searching capabilities was irresistible. Word processing is perhaps the one computer application that moved most quickly from curiosity to necessity, and it is interesting – in light of what we were discussing earlier about language and computing – that it is the written text that eased the transition. Words were the beginning of mediated communication between people. The written word was, and remains, the archive of our knowledge. The written word is the basis of computer programming, and programs to facilitate writing mediated the movement of the computer into the home. The language we use to describe electronic communication still depends on the old written word. We have been using the word "text" to describe a complete printed object as well as a coherent interplay of media object, audience, and cultural surround. Nowadays, "text" has been turned into a verb to describe the process of communicating in writing that occurs between individuals on their cell phones, which are miniature computers.

Online

On May 24, 1844, Samuel Morse telegraphed, in code, from Washington, DC, to Baltimore, Maryland: "What hath God wrought?" Perhaps a bit melodramatic, but the words did usher in telephony and a radical change in the way people communicated with each other. Emotion as well as information could be transmitted instantaneously. On October 29, 1969, Professor Leonard Kleinrock sent a packet of digitized text from one computer to another at UCLA. The text was meant to say "Login." The system crashed midway through transmission, and so the first word sent from one computer to another was "LO"! Once again, the way people communicated with each other began to change.

The Cold War and the highway

The way to the Internet starts with Morse's words; it received its technological push from Kleinrock. But, once again, it was the military that provided the initial path. In the late 1960s, the United States was fighting a "Cold War" with the then Soviet Union. This was a war of words and ideologies, of blacklists and atomic bomb scares, of stockpiling weapons, and real wars, like the Vietnamese conflict. The Cold War raged from the late 1940s until the early 1990s, when the Soviet Union fell apart. Almost every scientific discovery during that period was either made for, or put to use in, this struggle, "in the name of national security." Physical communication networks were built: the interstate highway system was created not primarily to move private automobiles and freight, but to facilitate evacuations and troop movements in the case of nuclear war. Virtual communication – another kind of highway – was being developed as well.

In October, 1957, the Russians beat the US into space by launching an earth-orbiting satellite called "Sputknik." The US responded with a major push into scientific and military development. One military research operation that emerged from this push was the Advanced Research Projects Agency, or ARPA, and one of their missions was to create a secure and attack-proof communications network. The result of their research, drawing on the work of Kleinrock and others, was ARPANet, a computer-based transmission system for bomb-proof military communications. ARPANet, opening into broader networks, was available for public use by the mid-1970s and quickly became known as a network for sharing academic research.

The progress from ARPANet to Internet happened quickly, as soon as protocols – technologies and programs – were created for transmitting and addressing digital packets of information. These protocols, called TCP/IP, were in place by the late 1970s and early 1980s, and remain the basis for Internet communications to this day. Primarily text-based, TCP/IP allowed for written communication and provided methods for addressing and moving these communications among multiple computers.

In the late 1980s, Tim Berners-Lee, an Englishman working at the Swiss physics laboratory, CERN, developed HTTP, Hypertext Transfer Protocol, which allowed for links to be embedded within text. In addition to communicating straightforward text messages, HTTP allowed linking, branching and redirecting text *and images*, so that users reading one thing could, with a click, go to another, thereby creating a web of interconnected sites. They could put up and link visuals to elaborate the text or be integrated with it. With a browser, a piece of software that interpreted and visualized HTTP (Berners-Lee called the browser that he developed "WorldWideWeb"), a new communications, storage, and information system was put into place.

Cultures of information

"The information superhighway" was the cliché that attempted to define the Internet. Clearly, "highway" was a useful if unconscious metaphor, linking the two Cold War projects of real and virtual roads of travel. The interstate highway system facilitated moving bodies. The Internet facilitated moving information and personalities. Like the telephone a century before, it was a kind of ventriloquist of consciousness. It threw our voices; it helped create a personality.

In our discussion of journalism in chapter 2, I attempted to pull some meaning out of the large, too-inclusive word, "information." An important thing to understand is that, whatever meaning we accept, or give, or allow to be given to that word at various times and from various sources, it is never neutral. We see from both the pre- and current history of the Internet that the information it transmits and holds is there for many purposes: from military to corporate; from academic to intensely personal. We know from all the horror stories about identity theft and sexual predation that some "information," useful when held by one person, is destructive when another person gets it. At the same time, it is necessary to acknowledge a basic curiosity that – to use the word in another context – informs all cultures. Consciousness is, in part, constructed by curiosity and its hunger to know more. That curiosity takes many forms and has different objects, and is mediated in different ways; it is hungry for information of all varieties.

"As We May Think"

As we've seen, long before the Internet there were libraries and archives of various kinds – physical storehouses of information. From the Renaissance on, thinkers attempted to conceptualize how knowledge could be collected and cross-referenced. But it was right after World War II that an idea appeared, born out of the need to organize wartime information. Vannevar Bush was an electrical engineer who worked on analog computation at MIT. He was interested in methods of collecting and retrieving information, using microfilm, an analog technology of the day. During the war, he headed the Office of Scientific Research and Development (that, among other things, oversaw the Manhattan Project, which was busy developing the atomic bomb). In 1945, he wrote an article, "As We May Think," in which he fantasized a machine he called the "memex …, a device in which an individual stores all his books, records, and communications, and which is mechanized so that it may be consulted with exceeding speed and flexibility. It is an enlarged intimate supplement to his memory." His device is an analog machine, using microfilm, but this idea of storage, retrieval, and cross-referencing would become the basis of the World Wide Web.

Fantasies of connection

Vannevar Bush's vision is the scientist's fantasy of harnessing and accessing knowledge, a means of enlarging intellectual scope, even the human spirit itself. He provided a goal and a model for an interconnected, always accessible, living database. The developers and theorists of the Internet and the World Wide Web realized the fantasy through the linking system of computers and files that could be created and accessed by anyone with a machine and a connection. As machines became smaller and more powerful, as interfaces became more intuitive, as the intimacy between person and machine grew through the increasing personalization of that machine, the computer became a kind of imaginative and often-creative extension of its user and the spaces into which the imagination could extend grew wider.

This sense of extension is a mark of difference from the media we have been discussing so far. We have examined the ways in which we interact with media, often decoding its messages based on our own individual and collective needs. Many media – radio, recorded music, film, even some television – can engage us on a deep personal level. But, as we have been saying, the unavoidable fact remains that all traditional media are one-way communications, produced for commercial gain, distributed through various networks that allow us only to choose, but not to contribute or alter in any major way. Because of the intimate connection, because of the varieties of *input* allowed by the computer, even without networked communication and the Internet, the creative relationship it affords is different from that established by traditional media.

Making Media

New creativity

One of the most enduring narratives both in and about literature, film, and television, indeed across all media, is the story of breaking *into* the media and "making it big." *American Idol* is only the most recent incarnation of this story, which inevitably involves hidden talent suddenly discovered, after much sacrifice and, in many versions of the narrative, resulting in momentary fame and ultimate unhappiness. The "making it" narrative is coded with a basic message about a desire for fame resulting in a lesson about knowing one's place and the dangers of trying to move out of it. It is safety coded on both ends, expressing a desire to make it big, and a caution about the unhappy outcomes of success. This forms the basis of almost all celebrity narratives.

Working one's way into media is itself a mediated process, an integration of talent and business – imagination and the means to get the productions of imaginations seen and heard by someone willing to pay for them. But the new medium of the computer has altered the narrative in some fundamental ways. Software makes music recording, mixing, and distributing a fairly simple process. Digital cameras and DVD recorders are inexpensive; digital editing systems allow a film to be constructed on any computer; self-distribution on the Web is as easy as having an URL. A web page can be designed by anyone (even someone without a knowledge of basic design principles), while music and videos can be uploaded and made available to anyone who knows the site's address. Production that still takes a long time, many resources, and great expense to accomplish in the world of professional media is now a relatively straightforward matter on the desktop. Garage bands no longer need all the expensive apparatus of recording and cutting disks and then getting them distributed. Young film-makers can bypass the complex process of funding, producing, making, and distributing their work.

New mediation

Can we bypass the big question? Does ease of production and distribution guarantee quality? Is everything created on the desktop worth being seen and heard by many people? These are the same questions we can ask about any media, large or personal, and the one response we have offered throughout our study is that audiences are good at judging for themselves, choosing, accepting, or rejecting. This holds true for the personal, immediate, works of computer-based music and video. The new processes of creativity and distribution that bypass "old" media still depend upon audience acceptance. The difference is that, just as in the process of creation and distribution, the process of recognition and judgment is exceptionally fast. When an amateur's video goes viral, worming its way to thousands, hundreds of thousands, of viewers by getting emailed and linked across the globe, the basic idea of distribution – controlled for maximum profit-making exposure – is turned upside down. Failure is measured not by a rapid decline in fame, but in less than expected hits on the website.

An example of the rapid fame and distribution of online content occurred in late 2005 when an editor of commercials, Robert Ryang, made a mock trailer for Stanley Kubrick's 1980 film, *The Shining*. Created with existing footage from the film, a new voice-over and some redubbed dialogue, the trailer made the film – which is both a parody of horror films and a serious exploration of decaying family relationships – appear to be a movie about a loving father and son, not a father who tries to kill his son. The result was an intervention into a well-known film, a parody of film trailers, which are a genre unto themselves, and a small act of amusing creativity that got distributed to and seen by an amazing number of people. Ryang commented, "I really didn't realize how fast the world moves." Movie producers expressed interest.

"I really didn't realize how fast the world moves." The statement can stand for everyone's reaction to the rapid development of online computation. Immediacy and change, two of the major elements of the media design, are the controlling elements of the online universe. No other media allows for such instantaneous communication coupled with such profound immersion and interactivity. It is speed taking place within a virtual space that the nineteenth-century inventors of telephony and telegraphy could only fantasize about; an immediacy that old media are still attempting to understand.

Social networking and the cultures of community

During the writing of this book, "MySpace.com" became one of the most talked-about and most popular sites on the Internet. In terms of design, it is a throwback to the early days of Internet visual ugliness. Its home page was design-challenged and barely functional. The home pages of its millions of members break every design rule in the book: they use multiple fonts, clashing colors, and, whether you want it or not, a music file that may or may not be to a visitor's taste, and which takes some effort to turn off. Some pages privilege exhibitionism over a desire for community; sexuality over – or in place of – personal communication. Fake celebrity sites abound. Commercial sites are growing. MySpace is proof of the fact that identities online are very fluid, and that anyone may be anyone else. But it is also proof of a playfulness that often expresses some genuine goodwill and desire for outreach, or simply curiosity about what might happen in the open social spaces of the online world.

It is a democratically open space. Even though its appeal is largely aimed at those in their teens and twenties, anyone can join; anyone can post; anyone can see and be seen – at least the way one wants to be seen. A combination of blog, personal diary, instant messaging, and exhibition, MySpace and its kin such as Facebook and Friendster constitute maps of personality, an open landscape for feelings, real or fantasized.

Is there danger here? Only if someone too innocent or too daring might act on the impulse to turn the virtual into the physical. This may be the fodder of television tabloids, like the NBC series *Dateline*, which attempted to brand itself by luring "Internet predators" into entrapment, so they can be filmed and then arrested. Convergence of media is a major event, and we will address it later, but this is a particular case of reverse engineering, of an older media creating discourses of fear out of new media. They turn that discourse into "news" (the show presents itself as a news program), but in reality they are exploiting any parent's real fear that their children will be prey to really disgusting older people by turning it into an exploitative performance in order to gain viewers. Online predation is now becoming a new genre, aligning itself with that much older story about the media audience, that it is passive, manipulable, and stupid. Are there dangers when someone creates an identity for public consumption? Certainly. But stories of predators luring people from their online anonymity into threatening situations have quickly become a narrative that parallels what may or may not go on in the virtual world.

Privacy

Online predation is part of the much larger issue of online privacy. Users of MySpace and other social sites may well think they are spending time in a comfortable, secure place among friends, a mini-culture of like-minded people, looking for some talk, some companionship. Exaggeration of appearance and habits is part of the interchange, part of the social game of hanging out online. The problem, of course, is that the Web is not private. The openness of social community sites means that anyone can look in, and MySpace has become a prowling ground not for predators (or not only for predators), but for head-hunters – of the employer variety. Some prospective employers, it has been reported, are doing background checks by looking at applicants' home pages and, it seems, turning them down for a job if their site portrays them as less than serious and dependable.

Role-playing, whether in an online game or with an online community of friends, is an intriguingly attractive proposition, and a multifaceted illusion. If you know that your identity will never be discovered, role-playing can be an adventure, a way to mediate your own personality, to say and show things you might never do in direct communications. But the Internet and all its subsidiaries – web, email, instant messaging – is open to discovery by anyone who knows how to get access, which is precisely part of its attraction; it's what we want from it: the public exploration of the private or manufactured self. Therefore, we need to be able to work within the limits of this contradiction and discover ways that anonymity, role-playing, confession, intimacy, *and* open access can coexist. We have spoken often of how media move us in and out of the public and private spheres. Here we find a space where the spheres do not simply overlap; they invade each other.

Their space

Within the larger economics of the media design, MySpace is more than a place for friends to gather and show off; it is a commercial site, a genre that advertisers are analyzing and exploiting. MySpace is owned by Rupert Murdoch's News Corporation, the multinational conglomerate that runs newspapers, the Fox network, cable news outlets, and the film studio 20th Century Fox. By July, 2006, MySpace.com was the most visited domain on the Internet. Advertisers have put an ad value on its home page of $1 million and create their own pages within MySpace to advertise their products. Wendy's page is kept by a hamburger. Almost 90,000 people signed in as "friends" of the hamburger. So much for online identities!

The site's popularity has fallen since that 2006 high (Facebook has gained in popularity), and will fluctuate, which is inevitable for a media entity that becomes a subject of such enormous media attention. We know that an important aspect of the media design involves rapid change and a restless sense of irrepressible novelty. The pace of novelty, of technological change, of users, producers, and corporate owners racing after the latest online phenomenon seems to accede what has taken place in any other media. It seems that every time users carve out an online space for themselves, that space is bought out. In the fall of 2006, Google purchased the video site YouTube for $1.65 billion.

Games

I want to pick up another thread in the discussion of computation and virtual spaces, even though separating the strands of computer activity is artificial because they are so closely intertwined. Creativity, archiving and accessing information, distribution of imaginative works, and social networking are all part of processes and engagements that are not only interactive but also deeply connected. Knowledge spaces, creative spaces, community spaces, great varieties of media spaces intersect, often in playful ways and ways of playing.

The ability to create profound immersion within an imaginary space made possible by the intimacy of user–computer interaction leads to one of the most controversial computer applications, the video game. Perhaps the earliest computer game was invented in the early 1960s at MIT, in the quaintly titled "Model Railway Club." It was, like almost all games that followed, a war game, called (what else?) *Spacewar!*, and it offers a start to understanding a complex component of the new media world.

Two rocket ships are maneuvered by various keys on the computer keyboard. The object is to have one rocket blow the other up before they collide. The collision path is built in and predetermined. If the player does nothing, the rockets will collide. The player otherwise controls the simple scenario of destroy or be destroyed. "Control" is the operative word. Unlike their predecessors, the old-fashioned shooting gallery or arcade target game – where the player, in a public place, stands in front of a machine, manipulating the controls in an effort to hit a moving target – video/computer games turn over as much control to the player as is possible within a game's particular context and genre. There is – as in so much computing – a deeply personal, emotional, relationship between player and game and the rules and methods of engagement. The level of engagement depends on the way a particular game is written – and the evolution of computer games is one of growing complexity, providing detailed visual spaces and complex interactions – whether the game is played as a stand-alone, with one or more players, or online in a "massively multiplayer online role-playing game" (MMORPG). (See figure 7.1.)

Figure 7.1 *Spacewar!*, developed at MIT in the early 1960s, is one of the earliest computer games.

MOOs and MUDs

Gaming evolved in a number of directions and developed a number of genres, following the development of computer power, the capabilities of graphic display, and the imagination of programmers. Early stand-alone games were often built to be played with a joystick-style controller and viewed on a television screen. Their graphics were blocky, and their movements stilted. Some used abstractions, like Tetris, or Pac Man, simple figures moving in vertical and horizontal directions. More imaginative developments were occurring online. Before the World Wide Web offered sophisticated graphical capabilities, there were the text-based *Dungeons and Dragons* worlds of MOOs and MUDs (Multi-Object Oriented and Multi-User Domain worlds), where verbal descriptions created imaginary characters or avatars, and spaces, rooms of various kinds, filled with objects that your avatar could pick up, pass to someone else, or attack in an ongoing exchange of places and identities. (See figure 7.2.)

Although, like any computer program, MOOs and MUDs were contained within the parameters allowed by the programmer, they were still remarkable examples of

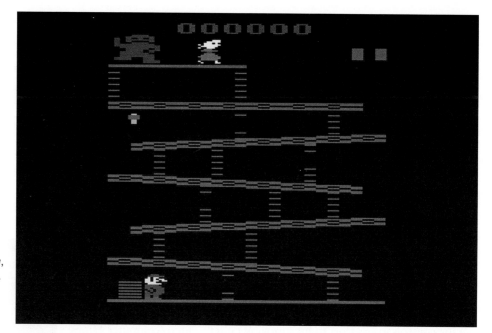

Figure 7.2 *Donky Kong*, an early computer game. Museum of Computing (www.museum-of-computing.org.uk).

creativity returned to the computer user. The capabilities of MOOs and MUDs lent themselves to expansion into educational use, allowing early versions of instant messaging between participants, often used by teachers to send communications between different classrooms, sometimes on different continents. They also helped introduce one of the ongoing, sometime troubling, always provocative phenomena of the online world, the false identity. An avatar can be anyone, of any gender, a representation of the player's fantasy. On the positive side, identity shifting is a useful strategy in gaming. Role-playing allows for strategizing and for changing tactics. Creating an avatar is also an act of liberation, a way of breaking free of confining identity, even of gender, and of imagining oneself into a gaming space. The negatives are similar to those that occur with social networking sites: manipulation and predation.

The player may still, physically, be rooted to one spot, seated in front of the computer. But the distinguishing mark of any computer game is the *un*rooting of the player, placing him in an imaginative realm over which he has some control. From one perspective, this should sound quite familiar. Overcoming temporal and spatial constraints has been the goal of media since their inception. But none of the other media allow direct manipulation of their imaginative, narrative spaces. We have already noted how computation takes the creation and distribution of imaginative works out of the hands of media producers; games add yet another element, of *creating* a narrative in a world that will change according to how the player interacts with it. The simple act of manipulating the representations of two space ships introduces an intervention that can stand as a metaphor for new digital media as a whole.

MMORPGs

MOOs and MUDs, those early versions of online, multiple player games, have evolved into the massively popular MMORPGs like *The World of Warcraft* (with an estimated 16 million users in 2008) and *Second Life*, which is less a game than a huge, virtual, social networking site. Although these games and sites still depend on text-based instructions, their worlds have been developed by sophisticated graphics through which avatars walk, ride, or fly. Characters are chosen, communities are formed, worlds are explored, and economies are set up. The player moves about the *mise en scène* of a complex virtual world, modifying her avatar, and even her surroundings, to suit her desires, role-playing within a community where every character is a creation of other users, accruing objects and wealth in an ongoing economy that is monetary, societal, and cultural. These online worlds have become so self-contained that players put up real money in order to play within the economic structures of imaginative worlds of the MMORPG. This has led some economists to study these online communities as a macrocosm of economic activity.

Like other social networking sites, *Second Life* is becoming rapidly commercialized. But it is also becoming a place for rehabilitation, where people with debilitating physical problems can create a space and avatars that allow mobility and healthy interchange. *Second Life* is so varied, so constantly changing and expanding, that it permits a great variety of activity and interaction (figure 7.3).

Figure 7.3 *Second Life*, a popular MMORPG in which real money is spent in a virtual world. *Second Life*. REUTERS/ Ho New.

First-person shooter

In a first-person shooter game, the player can be an active participant in a detailed landscape in which he or she joins with a character in a violent pursuit. These games, like Rockstar's *Grand Theft Auto* and its sequels, are often intimately tied to movies and offer interesting examples of the ways in which new and traditional media are interacting in a process of *remediation*, to use the term of Jay Bolter and David Grusin – by recreating old media inside of new. *GTA* began life as a 1977 movie, written and directed by Ron Howard. Its manifestation as a game involves a mutation from an external narrative *told* to the viewer and requesting emotional participation, to an interactive one, participated in directly, by assuming the point of view of a central character, who becomes an extension of the player, seeing him and seeing what he sees and manipulating his actions.

In a film, the narrative is built with a combination of point-of-view shots *of* and *from* a character, which are intercut with what is going on around the character and what she is supposed to be seeing. A film viewer cannot influence the events occurring within and around this interchange of glances. In a game version of a film, or a game using cinematic devices, these point-of-view techniques are part of a complex exchange of movements, tactics, actions, and reactions that change the character and his surroundings. Within the game space, a player can control point of view, looking at the character from various positions or directly through the character's eyes.

In *GTA San Andreas*, the game player can maneuver the main character, Carl, through a vast scenario and a varied landscape with a large cast of characters. *GTA* has a narrative as complex as any action movie, but the experience of playing the game is exponentially more complex than watching a movie, as the player makes one decision after another to manipulate the character, navigating him, bringing him into contact with other characters and events that change him and the course of the game. Events don't unfold, they are discovered; objects are found and made use of to further the character's progress. Things and events can't actually be created. Because a game is driven by a program, every possibility is always already built in; but so much is built in that the player experiences a sense of all but unlimited possibilities. (See figure 7.4.)

Popular stand-alone games like *Grand Theft Auto* create interactions not only between characters and player, but also between player and other gamers, since many of them can be joined online. Players organize conventions and communal contests. There is a cable channel devoted to gaming. Numerous websites have been created to guide newcomers through the game and to offer "cheats" or instructions on how to quickly discover the narrative avenues of the game. Most notorious of all is the violence inherent in first-person shooters, and, peculiar to *GTA*, the existence of a code on various websites that will unlock a pornographic scene, adding to its legendary status and its presumed danger.

Fears of the game

A consistent thread throughout our discussions of media has involved the discourse of concern about the moral dissolution threatened by almost every media form that

Figure 7.4 *Grand Theft Auto, San Andreas*, a first-person shooter with incredibly detailed graphics and interactions. *Grand Theft Auto, San Andreas*. REUTERS/ Ho New.

has appeared since the late nineteenth century. This discourse of fear is not unique to media alone. It is a general and dependable response to modernity as whole, a fear of the new and unknown, a certainty that exists within uncertainty: because something is new and popular – especially if it is popular among young people – it is threatening and, because threatening, dangerous. So, tabloid journalism was said to debase the seriousness of news reporting and our ability to understand the complexity of world events. Jazz, rock 'n' roll, hip-hop, or whatever might be the popular music of the moment, will loosen sexual constraints and incite violent behavior. Television will turn children into fat, passive dullards, and incite violent behavior. Computer games will cause young men – the majority of first-person gamers are young males – to be anti-social and will incite violent behavior.

The creators and the players of games like *Grand Theft Auto* seem to play consciously into this discourse of fear, as if it were another aspect of the game itself, part of its popularity and cultural context. *GTA* and its ilk are indisputably violent – or, more accurately, they *represent* violence in visual terms. Shootings and beatings are a major part of the action. The language the characters use is coarse, and sexuality – even without the hidden porn – is rampant. The basic premise of all such games is to seek, find, and kill the adversary. The skills required are so intense that the US military and – it is darkly rumored – al-Qaeda members adapt computer games for training purposes.

It would be amazing were there *no* comments made or alarms raised about how this skill for killing affected its players. Unfortunately, like all such alarms raised and studies made about media and violence, the results are inconclusive at best. What are the immediate real-world effects of computer games on behavior? Game theorist Henry Jenkins writes on his PBS website that the alarms themselves are problematic:

The moral panic over violent video games is doubly harmful. It has led adult authorities to be more suspicious and hostile to many kids who already feel cut off from the system. It also misdirects energy away from eliminating the actual causes of youth violence and allows problems to continue to fester.... If there is a consensus emerging around this research, it is that violent video games may be one risk factor – when coupled with other more immediate, real-world influences – which can contribute to anti-social behavior. But no research has found that video games are a primary factor or that violent video game play could turn an otherwise normal person into a killer.

That last phrase, "an otherwise normal person," stands, for now, as the best answer to the discourse of fear aimed at any media at any given time. We can use it to return to a more immediate issue that involves our notion of the computational embrace, the intimacy a computer user experiences within the virtual spaces of online worlds. The online communities of gamers, the various spaces for personal messaging, for aggregating friendships, are where "an otherwise normal person" can engage in what are rapidly become "normal" activities made available by new media technologies. When the once feared becomes the present norm, new media become part of the culture.

Convergence

Corporate designs

"Convergence" has been a topic running through our discussion of all media. We can now understand the complexity of the phenomenon. Traditional media – news, television, film, and the advertising that supports them – are all moving online and, in the process, reinventing themselves, often in interesting ways. But, in the digital realm, audiences have so far managed to outpace the producers. MySpace and YouTube were native to the Web, beginning as relatively small operations, growing in popularity *before* they were purchased by media giants – Murdoch's News Corporation in the case of MySpace, and Google in the case of YouTube. Google itself is an example of a media company that was invented, grew, and expanded within the space of the Internet, rather than coming in from outside. Television content, by contrast, had to be created by the networks and their corporate sponsors. Television's popularity was created from the outside in. Online, users are creating new genres and, in effect, selling them to corporate sponsors. Popularity in the digital world precedes corporate ownership.

Online commercialization and "ownership" bumps up against the unusual intimacy experienced by computer users that, online, expresses itself as a sense of entitlement and ownership. The development of the Internet roughly parallels radio's early history. The Internet was developed by engineers, computer scientists, and "hackers" – the computer equivalent of ham radio operators and a term that is used pejoratively today, but that originally referred to coders and people engaged in developing digital technologies. The Internet was peopled first by academics and then by enthusiasts who, starting with bulletin boards, moved the Web to a worldwide virtual community.

But it is already an act of nostalgia to look back at what seemed to be the people's medium. Cutting through the sentimental haze, we realize that what we are in fact seeing, for the first time in most people's lifetime, is the origin, growth, and corporate consolidation of a new mass media outlet. Again the parallel to radio is interesting. Radio, too, started full of high-minded hopes of being an educational medium. Advertisers, beginning with mostly local companies, slowly came to understand its potential for commercial exploitation. The potential realized, radio very quickly became a commercial medium. Commercialization of the Web is a study of a slightly slower embrace by advertisers and an example of the conservatism of older media.

Like radio, early online advertisers were small companies. Corporate sites came later, and were tentative, as big business waited to be sure that money could be made from the emerging medium. Computer companies and online services, providing technical information and software downloads, were present from the start, but even they were slow to comprehend the Web phenomenon. Microsoft is an interesting case study. Bill Gates created the company and made its fortune with desktop software. Microsoft waited a relatively long time to recognize the need to have a larger Web presence. When it did, it had to catch up with America Online and other service providers, and finally had to embed its browser (based on the original Mosaic browser developed at the University of Illinois's National Center of Supercomputing Applications in 1993) into its operating system, in order to regain its footing. The company also decided to branch out and become a media company. The history of Microsoft's attempts to move beyond its core products is a capsule of how media have adopted and adapted to the online environment. Like Google after it, Microsoft moved from computational applications to media ownership.

Microsoft's media adventures   Microsoft began Slate.com in 1996 as an experiment in an online subscription magazine. Bill Gates hired an experienced journalist, Michael Kinsley, to edit the magazine, and its content was rich, with fine opinion pieces and decent journalism. The very idea of charging for online content was not merely novel, it was adventurous, playing against an already well-developed culture of free access that was the founding spirit of the Internet. *Slate* abandoned the subscription model after a brief trial, and since then online magazines – and online versions of traditional magazines as well as newspapers – have had mixed success in any number of formats. Some magazines put some of their content online, while others insist on maintaining a subscription model. Almost all newspapers have free online access, with some charging for special features. *Slate* was eventually sold to the interactive unit of the company that publishes the *Washington Post* and *Newsweek*, relieving Microsoft of the unfamiliar job of running a magazine. Recently, *Slate* has joined with National Public Radio, co-producing their news magazine, *Day to Day*.

Microsoft's desire to merge its software market with other media continued with a joint venture with NBC – itself owned by General Electric, which also owns the movie studio Universal – a move that created both a cable news network and a website, both called MSNBC. The cable company has suffered the ups and downs that most other all-news channels have – though it is currently making its mark as the liberal alternative to Fox News – and its companion sites are well below Yahoo! in popularity. This fact has driven Microsoft to purchase the online site. Among its websites, MSN.com remains closely held and run by Microsoft.

The old Warner Bros. on the new frontier

In the early days of the Internet, corporations were timid and uncertain about their online presence. But by the late 1990s it seemed the Web had become a new frontier, on the other side of which lay untold fortune, and media companies in particular began to understand that their products – movies, music, news, even radio and television – needed to be aimed at the Internet, even if they weren't sure exactly what the target was, or even how they should aim at it. Caution and uncertainty were trampled by greed and necessity, nowhere more apparent than in the merger of Time Warner and America Online.

This was an important event because it envelops the history of media both old and new. Warner Bros., a studio that was itself the product of mergers early in the twentieth century, was founded by four brothers, children of immigrants: Harold, Albert, Sam, and Jack. They fled from the East Coast to Los Angeles to escape Edison's patents (see chapter 6) and proceeded to buy up two other film companies, Vitagraph and First National. They were pioneers, producing the first full-length film with synchronized sound sequences (*The Jazz Singer*, 1927), working with technology developed by AT&T, a company that also developed telephone and radio networking technology, including ownership of the first commercial radio station. Warner Bros. was largely responsible for creating the gangster film genre in the early 1930s with the films *Little Caesar* and *Public Enemy*, as well as bringing a touch of parody and inventiveness to animation with the *Looney Tunes* cartoon series.

The studio thrived with various ups and downs until, late in his life, Jack Warner sold the company to Seven Arts Ltd and, while it continued to make important films, continuing mergers forced Warner Bros. into a corporate unit rather than a stand-alone film studio. Briefly, in 1970s, in its then-current incarnation as Warner Communications, it owned the Atari game company. In 1989, Warner Communications merged with Time Inc., the remnants of the once powerful journalistic empire owned by Henry Luce. After the merger, the company grew into a huge media conglomerate, with publishing units and cable television outlets, including HBO.

Two other media companies were developing independently of Time Inc. and Warner Communications. Ted Turner, an Atlanta businessman, helped establish and define cable broadcasting with a variety of networks, including CNN, the first 24/7 cable news company. He also purchased the MGM and Warner Bros. film libraries, in the process restoring many damaged and fading prints that might have otherwise disappeared. These films helped program Turner Classic Movies, which remains the best movie archive on cable television.

In 1991, Steve Case and others took an online bulletin-board service, named it America Online, and proceeded to build the first and, until recently, most popular Internet portal, a place where beginners could feel secure within the wide-open and unknown spaces of the online world. At this point, convergence became a cascade: Time Warner, the company that resulted from the merger of Time Inc. and Warner Communications, bought Turner Broadcasting in 1996. In 2000, AOL and Time Warner engaged in what was then the biggest corporate merger ever, costing $183 billion. An immediate result of this alliance was a clash in ideas of how to administer old film media, old news media, and new online media. AOL's founder, Steve Case, resigned from the AOL Time Warner board and wrote a column in the *Washington Post* in 2005, decrying the merger, taking responsibility for its failure, and urging for a separation of the units. His comments make an interesting case study of what happens when media worlds collide:

> Each of the four units would benefit from the separation. Time Warner Cable would be better positioned to compete effectively against aggressive communications companies like Verizon and the new AT&T – and it would lose little in being divorced from the Time Warner movie and television companies, as few benefits have ever materialized from having Time Warner Cable and Turner Broadcasting under the same roof. Time Warner Entertainment (Warner Bros., New Line, HBO and Turner Broadcasting) could build on its strength as one of the world's leading entertainment companies, and more vigorously embrace new technologies and new distribution channels. Time Inc. would be able to grow from being a traditional magazine company into a multifaceted media and information company, focused on expanding its brands well beyond magazines.
>
> AOL would be the fourth company, and perhaps the one with the greatest potential. At a time when some of the fastest-growing enterprises in our economy are Internet leaders – such as Google – shareholders would benefit from seeing AOL return to its roots in the Internet sector. A split into separate companies has one other advantage for shareholders: Investors who don't believe in the promise of one of these endeavors could sell their shares in that business and double up in their holdings in other parts of the former Time Warner empire.

In Case's arguments we can see how conflict over technologies, media mentalities, and the ever-present bottom line of corporate profits foreshadowed the ongoing problems of media convergence.

The conglomerate did not divide. The various parts just tried to ignore one another. Time Warner dropped AOL from its corporate title. Though still nominally part of the company, AOL is currently trying to rebrand itself as a broadband service provider and has fallen in popularity as more people find they need less handholding in the virtual world. The merger and its failure are significant in many ways. The clash of management is an important indicator of the difficulties faced by media old and new as they try to find a place in the online universe. The delivery systems are so different, the audiences so much more difficult to identify and segment, the sources of income so uncertain, the technology changes so rapid, that even with a responsive and collaborative management, making online enterprises work is complex and without guarantees of success.

Under production head Jack Warner, the original Warner Bros. had built a successful and extremely creative movie studio over the course of many decades. *Time* magazine, under its founder, Henry Luce, was an important journalistic force throughout the early and mid-twentieth century. Each knew their media and its audience – and its audience, in turn, knew what to expect from the films and the publications. As merged entities, without strong personalities at their head, both the studio and the magazine seemed to lose if not all creative steam, then at least the distinctive identity they had each forged with certain kinds of movie-making on one hand and a certain kind of journalism on the other. AOL never had a "creative" center as such. It was formed as an aggregator and entry point, a way to make the Internet, then as now a confusing place for beginners, accessible and easy. Steve Case was not Jack Warner or Henry Luce; he was a dot-com entrepreneur, someone who understood the potential of new media, worked up a business, and nursed it until it became attractive to an old media company looking for space in the new market. Ted Turner *did* have the kind of personal and creative flair of his older predecessors. He was perhaps the closest relative to the old media barons. He gave up control over his companies soon after the AOL Time Warner merger. I doubt anyone outside of the business community can name the individuals currently running Time Warner, or – perhaps with the exception of Rupert Murdoch – any big media company, or keep up with the ongoing change of executives as each in their turn tries to maneuver the new landscape. This is not only a sign of the anonymity of corporate ownership, but also of the fact that, in new media, it is individual users and their communities that are of the most active interest.

The work of art in the age of digital reproduction

At this point, we need to examine the discourse of the last few paragraphs and think back through some issues that have worked their way throughout our discussion of the media design. What is the purpose of lamenting the end of the "great man" history of the media, or even applying the notion of individual creativity to what we have already determined is a work of collaboration among many individuals on the side of both production and reception? We certainly can't romanticize the old movie studios. Jack Warner was a boss who subordinated talent to profit at every turn. It may be only coincidence that his studio turned out so many important films among its general output of generic works of banal predictability. Given all the producers involved in a television series, it may be only coincidence that original narratives emerge from *Law & Order* or *CSI*. Despite individual marks of creativity online, many videos on YouTube do not fall into the ranks of imaginative genius.

We can't, of course, dismiss individuality. There surely will be artists who continue to emerge across media, though the way we identify them will be different from the way we identify them in small-audience art. But, as always, we need to understand that the artists who create large-audience, mass media works will continue to actually be collaborative groups: 14 producers, one writer, one director for a television show; a songwriter, his group, and the A&R (artists and repertoire) person, the arranger, and the record producer, all of whom create the final CD. The corporate people will increasingly be scattered across the universe of media holdings, doing their work under the umbrella of one giant company like Time Warner, or General Electric-Universal,

Disney, The News Corporation, and on and on in an ever-thinning group of large companies whose chief goal is owning as much as possible.

Individual creativity and the Internet

The Internet is going through a kind of recapitulation of the history of old media forms. Like cinema, which was developed by individuals before it turned into a product for corporate image factories, the Internet was and remains a place where individual creators of all kinds thrive, alone or under an academic umbrella. There are digital artists who express themselves through existing software, such as Flash animations, Quicktime videos, and Java programming, taking full advantage of the interactive structures available to online programming. An example of such work can be found in the University of Southern California's Labyrinth Project. Scholars have long turned to digital imaging and database archiving to create imaginative ways of displaying and analyzing their investigation, as in the University of Virginia's pioneering Institute for Advanced Technology in the Humanities. Programmers are using open-source code to develop new online applications that will enable more flexible means toward imaginative expression. And, as we have seen, individuals, unconnected to any institution, happy amateurs enjoying various levels of creativity, are creating a variety of artifacts from music to goofy videos and often finding their work catapulted around the Web.

If we follow the analogy to film history, we might ask whether artists of stature will emerge from all of this activity. A more pertinent question would be how will we define art, artist, and stature in this new creative environment, and will they and their media survive increasing corporate control? Will university departments emerge as the new "studios," sheltering and nurturing digital artists? Will Internet content be defined by and segregated within its three major domains: educational (.edu), government (.gov), and corporate/business (.com, .net)? Perhaps the domains themselves will emerge as three overriding genres, providing unique accessibility, varying opportunities, and specific formats for creativity, information, and commercial development. (There is no denying that some corporate sites are using Flash- and Java-driven graphics to high creative advantage.) Overriding these domains, there may well be various tiers of service and accessibility. The telecommunications companies, like Comcast and Time Warner, that run the "pipes" that carry networked communications would like to charge large and small customers for various levels of service. The large media corporations, for example, would pay for high-speed broadband to carry film and television programs. Small users, people who put their videos online, would have to deal with slower connections.

Politics, policy, ownership

The future of online creativity, indeed the very nature of how creativity will manifest itself, is impossible to predict, even based on current examples. What is possible to predict is that the "old" media will continue to search for ways to make money from their products, even though, at this moment, it seems that most of that content will be recycled old media. Movie studios and television networks are providing some add-ons by means of interactive websites with fan news, games, and behind-the-scenes material, but mostly they are finding ways to charge for downloading films and programs. The networks, for example, are putting complete shows online with some commercials. But their major efforts are currently directed not so much toward creating content as toward protecting it. Copyright and intellectual property issues have quickly risen to the surface, often eclipsing creativity by challenging who owns it. Copyright concerns need to be understood within larger contexts of ownership and media power. We need to recover some ground.

Intellectual Property

Recorded music and the right to copy

By the early 1990s, the business of music was going through the same process as all other media: simultaneous contraction and expansion. Record labels were merging along with the corporations that owned them. Hip-hop and rap were defining new markets. CD sales were booming. Sampling then changed all the equations.

"Sampling" is a word with a number of meanings, all of them pertinent to media studies. For advertisers and producers, the statistical meaning of the word – taking a sample of audience response and extrapolating it to a larger group – is important, because their job is to gather or imagine a representative sample of their potential audience and attempt to create the programming that will draw this audience. For a rap artist, sampling pre-existing music means creating the strong counterpoint between the verbal rhythms of the lyric and a tonal background that promises a musical resolution, but always remains in tension to the rhythm of the rap. In the digital world, sampling refers to what happens when an analog signal is converted to a digital file. Digital compression is enabled by sampling parts of the analog stream that can then be recreated when the file is played back. This allows the MP3 compression standard, developed by the Moving Pictures Expert Group, to create small, but high-quality, files.

Because of sampling and the development of peer-to-peer (P2P) networks that enabled online users to download files, single tunes or entire albums suddenly became available to everyone free of charge. It should be pointed out that, even before MP3s, even before it became easy to burn CDs, people were making their own mixes of music by recording various tracks onto cassette tapes. But, still, a vinyl record or a CD had to be purchased, or at least some effort needed to be spent recording tunes off the radio. MP3s, however, changed, for a while at least, the producer-CD-radio play-listener design of recorded music. Songs were free for the taking. A personal mix of favorites was as easy as downloading files and burning them to a CD. More and more software, much of it also free, made this extremely easy.

Needless to say, this upset the music business a great deal. It also interfered with the royalty system, the means by which artists get paid every time their work is performed. (It is beyond the scope of our discussion here, but it should be noted in passing that recording artists, unless they are extremely popular, often do not get a fair distribution of royalties for their work.) Copyright law at its best offers protection to content owners. However, it can be argued that downloading a song for personal use is not very different from recording a song off the air (which has not brought legal sanctions) for personal use. But industry practices are rarely reasonable when an income stream is perceived to be under attack. Their response is often out of proportion to the threat, and it takes them a while to reach a compromise with a situation that is, ultimately, out of their control.

Sony in trouble   In 2003, the Recording Industry Association of America (RIAA) sued Internet service providers and individuals for illegally downloading music files. They sued the major downloading site, Napster, in particular. Four college students were found guilty and fined. A 12-year-old girl settled out of court by apologizing and paying a $2,000 fine for downloading some 200 songs. Napster shut itself down as a free music site. The lawsuit was a public relations disaster for the RIAA, and it got worse. In November, 2005, Sony released a CD, Van Zant's *Get Right with the Man*, one of whose songs is called "There Ain't Nobody Gonna Tell Me What To Do." Sony thought it knew what to do. In this instance, the company was concerned not so much with downloading music but with burning it onto home-made CDs. They programmed the Van Zant's CD to download a "rootkit" onto the user's machine to prevent copying. Unfortunately, the program created a vulnerability that allowed other malicious software to be deposited on the infected hard drive. The result was more disastrous still. Music lovers proclaimed a boycott against Sony, who recalled the CD and issued software designed to remove the offending code.

This episode was not without its historical ironies. In 1984, Universal Studios had sued the Sony Corporation over its newly introduced Betamax technology. Betamax was a home videotape format that eventually gave way to the VHS standard. Universal's complaint was that the technology would be used for copyright infringement, allowing individuals to copy their films for free. The case went to the Supreme Court, and it ruled in favor of Sony and their recording technology. The ruling was a win not only for Sony and for the public's right to record television and movies, but also for the various technologies, from videotape to DVD burners, that aimed to perfect an easy process of copying and storing recorded images and sounds.

What is copyright and IP?

Copyright is part of the larger issue of intellectual property, a complex set of legal rules and opinions that, essentially, attempts to address who owns the products of creativity. Copyrights in the United States are administered by the Copyright Office of the Library of Congress. Can an idea be copyrighted, that is, legally marked as owned by someone? Not until it is given physical manifestation: the written or published word, the screenplay or the film made from it, the recorded song or a guitar chord chart, a written piece of software, an electronic device. The creator owns the copyright as soon as the material is fixed in tangible form. Yet, as we've just discussed, there are many "creators" involved in the transformation of a cinematic idea into an actual movie, a musical idea into a saleable CD, and so on. If that's so, who owns the copyright (or patent, if we extend the problem to devices) on the finished work? Is it the creator who had the original idea, or the company that publishes the book, produces the film, or distributes the CD, or manufactures the device?

Go to the reverse side of the title page of this book. You will see the entry "© 2009 Robert Kolker." As author of the book, I hold its copyright, which means that, to a certain extent, I own it. It is my intellectual property. Actually, however, what I "own" are the intangible contents of the book. Wiley-Blackwell Publishing owns "the appearance of the work," and "all intellectual property rights, of whatever nature, in the Appearance of the Work and in the Title." This is, in fact, an excellent combination for protection. If someone attempts to copy anything in the book without permission, they have both the publisher and me to answer to. Of course it's not that simple. Another basic principle of US copyright law is that titles are not eligible for copyright protection, so if someone used the title, *Media Studies: An Introduction*, in a completely dissimilar format, there would most likely be no legal problem.

So many conditionals – "if," "might," "most likely...." Copyright law has been in effect, and periodically updated, since shortly after the US Constitution was ratified. It protects an author or other creator of a tangible object from having their work stolen. At the same time, in recognition that intellectual property needs circulation in the public sphere, the law also has a time limit. For example, any work published in the United States before 1923 is in the public domain. After that, there is a sliding scale, depending on when the work is published, with the general rule that copyright lasts the life of the author plus 70 – in some cases 95 – years before the work goes into the public domain. Once in the public domain, the work is available to be used (with appropriate citation) by anyone, anywhere. But a work of complex authorship, like a movie, may have "underlying rights" held by the author of the novel from which the film was made, or by the composer, or by the actors or their estate, who claim ownership of their image, even after they are dead. Even while a work is under copyright, there is a legal option to use a very small part of it without notifying or paying its owner called "fair use." You may quote a few sentences from *Media Studies: An Introduction* without contacting the publisher or me, as long as you cite your source. Like copyright itself, fair use has many, many restrictions as to how much use of a given work is "fair," in what context it is used – there is, for example, some greater leeway to fair use in an academic setting.

Before the Internet, copyright was rarely an issue for anyone but large corporations and famous authors. The Internet changed all that. As a free and open space, with a marked sense of communal intimacy, coupled with the ease of moving digital files around the world, the Internet makes it difficult to enforce the restrictions surrounding copyrighted material. Because copying and distributing files is so easy, it has come to be widely considered a right, even a communal obligation. After all, people had been adapting the creative ideas of others, or tape-recording songs from the radio, burning their own CDs, making a mix of favorites and passing it along to friends long before digital technologies came along. The Internet made the process easier and more global. But it also made it visible. The pushback, the lawsuits, the "cease and desist" orders generated by the content owners – the RIAA and the media companies – were less a matter of income than the reassertion of power in a new environment that appears to them uncontrollable.

Who is winning or losing in this battle over copyright? Not so much the artists, whose music is being shared online, who are often not paid fairly by their record labels. Besides, there are many bands that don't find file-sharing a threat. Book publishers, who put part or all of their books online, report that they do not, generally, find that sales are affected. CD sales continue to fall as new businesses have emerged from the downloading battles. Some of the old P2P networks like Napster now charge for downloading, with part of the revenue going to the record companies. The Apple Corporation, having always served a small audience with its computers, developed and marketed the iPod and the music downloading site, iTunes, and with them launched itself into a premier money-making position by legally selling music and videos, a portion of the income going to artists who created the tunes. Meanwhile, the Internet continues to be a place where new music and new video thrives, absent the control of large media companies – until, that is, they discover a potential money-making site and, like Google and YouTube, gobble it up.

From Modernity to Postmodernity

The computer screen is, of course, only one point of media convergence. The mobile phone has created a number of convergent streams and a variety of ways for users to further define interactions – some might say interferences – between public and private spheres. The private is brought out of doors, as people talk to friends in public spaces. Old media becomes portable, as tunes and video images reside on or are transmitted to mobile devices. New media is undocked, as Internet and Web communications are available on mobiles. Writing is becoming reinvented. The use of abbreviations for speedy communications goes as far back as the days of ham radio operators talking to each other in Morse code. "Texting" (itself a neologism barely a few years old) is busy converging language and grammar into the smallest possible, still understandable, fragments. Starting as shorthand, transforming itself into code, private and public simultaneously – txtN enables prv8 cmUnik8shnz n public – an accomplishment that is both playful, ever more necessary to thumb-based typing, and quite possibly detrimental to written language in general. The technologies of modernity that permitted a virtual uprooting of the self, carrying the voice, delivering images, creating and distributing alternative, fictional spaces, have turned public and private spheres inside out. The mobile phone has moved everything into the open. With older media, we could discriminate between the public space of movies and the private, domestic, space filled by radio and television. The landline telephone was part of the private sphere, allowing intimate voice communications. The mobile phone is anything but private or intimate, and its screens that allow photographic and video images to appear, to be taken, to be transmitted anywhere, move us from the modern to the *post*modern, a state in which there are no boundaries.

In the postmodern state, public and private are interchangeable. Everything is open and identity itself is fluid. This has its positive and negative sides. Postmodern communications allow us to be anywhere at any time; but this fluidity moves in many ways. Media companies create new ways to deliver media and then find new ways to keep track of how that media is used, where it is used, and how. Our clicks are tracked in order to find out what websites we have visited and how often. Our sites on social networks are scanned by both potential employers and sexual predators. Our cell-phone messages – all of them, voice and text – are recorded in databases for potential government surveillance. In short, the more control we believe we are exercising, the more control is passed on; the more communications devices we buy, the more personal information becomes readily for sale or for spying on; the more playfully we create identities for ourselves, the more our identities are available for others to do well or ill by.

Whose identity?

The state of fluid identity has risks. A world that is open to communications of all kinds and where capitalism, the "free" market, is the economy of choice, where digital spaces are open to shifting identities and assumed anonymity, there will be shifting dangers, great and small. The real problems lay not only within the narratives of predation, of identity theft, of unknown and unwanted surveillance, but also in the area of access. And when we speak of access we come back to the too real and always present story of race and class. Throughout our study, we have been considering the ways race has been a dominant force, in early radio and across the history of popular music, and as a rapidly growing presence in Hispanic media. But new media, indispensable in so many ways, is still not available to everyone, and the lines that are drawn are classic. The majority of Internet users remain educated white Americans. The one area in which the customary divides do not apply is gender. Among all users, women lag only somewhat behind men in Internet usage.

By the time you read this, the racial and class imbalance will certainly have improved, and, as always, statistics tell only a small part of the story. Public access increases throughout the US in schools and libraries, and Internet usage in general is growing rapidly across the board. But the digital divide remains, in the United States and even more in developing countries. And because of the convergence of all old media into the digital and the rapid emergence of new media as the dominant form of entertainment and communications, this divide simply keeps a large number of people on the margins. It might be argued that, given the potential of online anonymity and the Internet's global reach, race and class ultimately do not matter; everyone is equal online; everyone can be anyone online. But equality cannot be achieved without presence, and dreams of a virtual, global community are always challenged by economics, access, and politics.

Media and Politics

In our discussion of journalism in chapter 2, we examined some of the direct relationships of media and politics. Some newspapers and their owners have had enormous influence over the politics of their day. On a daily basis, journalism – in print, on the air, on the Internet – is involved in the reporting and discussion of politics. Elections, candidates, policies, and ideologies are discussed, sometimes heatedly, often informatively. In chapter 4, we discussed the Federal Communications Commission, established in the 1930s to oversee communications policy and control the electromagnetic spectrum. The FCC usually follows the changing ideologies of the parties in power, and more often than not has been handmaiden to media corporations, allowing the mergers that form giant companies, dividing the electromagnetic spectrum to benefit the highest bidders. Recently, the FCC has bowed to other pressures from special interest groups, with an attempt at government censorship by fining networks for broadcasting material deemed inappropriate by conservative groups.

Journalism reports on politics. The FCC exercises political power over parts of the media. The media create content and own it, have power over it. Many people, because of economics or geography, have no access to it. Understanding this, we need to think about politics in a larger sense, about politics as power, about the ways a culture creates limits and controls itself and attempts to impose dominant beliefs on the various subcultures that make it up, which includes the cultures and subcultures that cannot take part, and who have no power at all. In liberal democracies – democracies believing in open elections, free markets, and the basic ideology of equality for all its members – the culture, or subcultures, choose by election those who will wield power over the public sphere. Elections are therefore managed by politicians through the media to the greatest degree possible. Mediation is the tool of power.

That power extends into the private sphere as well, where policy affects the ways in which people live, effectively determined by constraints of income, by race and class, access to education, to medical care. Media politics – media power – operates at the intersections of public and private spheres. In the broadest sense, media is part of the dominant political culture. The media speaks the discourse of power. Newspapers may contain editorials against government policy and elected officials, but all mass-circulation papers pretend to objectivity, an ideological stance that is coded as support for the political status quo. No mainstream newspaper calls for radical change in the way we are governed. *CSI* may slip in an episode that covertly alludes to policies of torture, but by and large their focus on blood and body parts and detection is out to shock us and then reassure us – as do all police procedurals – that those in power will, through local police or the FBI, look out for our best interests. Comedies, on the big or smaller screens, assure us that despite differences (and against all evidence in the everyday world), the "family," in the workplace or at home, will pull together for the common good. Reality programming is coded with images that offer us the illusions of adventure and sport, safely contained in a narrative space that allows us to look in without any risk. Advertising is the lubricant of economic and political stability. As long as advertising works, and as long as we decode advertisements by purchasing what is being sold (which includes political candidates and policy), the society and its cultures remain in balance.

All along we have been arguing that the media is not a simple one-way street, that the old arguments about a passive audience held captive by media, who spoonfeed it less than mediocre material, do not account for the complex relationships that any one member of an audience, or an entire subculture, builds by responding in particular ways to particular media forms. The sense of active participation in media remains no less true, but is certainly compromised, when we understand that the power does remain one-sided. We choose and we are free to respond to what is offered us. These offerings may change as audience response and interest changes. But creation and delivery of content – even given the creativity allowed by the World Wide Web – remain lopsided, and may become more so.

This returns us to our arguments about online media and helps us understand why there is so much churn and so much power-grabbing going on in the face of a new media design where the power seems to have shifted more toward individuals and away from the corporations that are historically accustomed to supplying individuals with information and entertainment. If anyone with access is free to create content, or if any pre-existing content can be digitized, sampled, altered, and shared across a very large, very free network (the parody of *The Shining* mentioned earlier is an example), then the comfortable supply chain where the media distribute content to a large audience is disrupted. There is some threat to power, at least until power finds a way to exert control.

The dream of community

Instant communication throughout a global community is a fantasy that has bloomed with the advent of every new electronic media. The "global village" that Marshall McLuhan dreamed of, that Internet users believe in, is a technological possibility that faces insurmountable national and ideological obstacles. The marginalizing of economic and cultural minorities is only one such obstacle. The open forum for hateful individuals and groups that *call* for marginalization is another; state censorship of access, such as occurs in China, and the increasing incorporation of the Internet in capitalist countries are others still. But beyond such problems is the culture of modernity itself. Modernity is defined by fragmentation, by the loss of unifying myths, narratives, and beliefs that make for coherence and unity. That's why we, as modernity's children, as beginners in the postmodern world, are always searching for coherence, even if it is the fragile coherence of exaggerated identity on a social networking site.

The discourses of modernity

The media are the creations and the tools of modernity: they represent not only technology and the way technology is used, but also the ways we *think* about technologies. Modernity permits a boundless curiosity and thrives on a willingness to embrace complexity and change over and over again. The postmodern world allows us to expand our curiosity with a sense of free interchange across boundaries.

Look back to the epigraph that begins this chapter.

> The book is an outmoded means of communicating information. And efforts to update it are hampered because, culturally, we give undue reverence to the form for the form's sake. Publish or perish, that's the highest call of our intellectual elite. But any medium that defines itself as a medium is in trouble: news*papers*, *broadcast* TV, *broadcast* radio, and books. They are all faced with new and better means of doing what they do without regard to the limitations of any one medium.

This comes from a blog, one of the most recent and powerful media developed out of the Internet. Blogs are postmodernity in action, allowing for instant communication of fragmented ideas. Blogs are always new. More than journalism, they are old the instant they are posted. While a thread of discussion may keep an idea alive for a while, even allowing an argument to influence old media, or policy itself, it always gives way to the next posting, the next idea, the next rant.

The very title of Jeff Jarvis's blog, "BuzzMachine," indicates that it is about current ideas, in this instance springboarded into the blogosphere by a former newspaper man now so taken by instantaneous communication that blogging is his major occupation. Jarvis gives voice to an old idea that is restated every time a new form of technological mediation occurs, sometimes as a caution, here as something to embrace. The idea can be briefly stated as "out with the old and outmoded and in with the new and immediate." New media will render old media obsolete. We have seen the argument woven throughout discussion: printed newspapers are rendered obsolete by online editions; radio is rendered obsolete, first by television, then by the iPod or satellite; movies will be rendered obsolete (as Hollywood feared in the early 1950s) by television; movie-going is rendered obsolete by DVDs. Now we are told that books are obsolete because of the Internet.

Are old forms of media dead? Recall that one of the designs of media is the struggle between the new and the outmoded, the value given to novelty and the devaluation of the "old-fashioned." But we have seen that, converge as they might, the old media thrive within the new and apart from the new. Newspapers are turning small profits, even if they are not enough to satisfy stockholders. Radio in all its manifestations thrives. Television is constantly reinventing itself, even if the reinvention is too often a reconfiguration of the old. Film is always in a process of rediscovering its possibilities. Advertising, as media's medium, is becoming ever more ubiquitous. Book sales are declining but hardly dead. Look around your campus bookstore. Even as they converge toward the digital, media are still maintaining their identities and a respectable part of their audience.

There is an assumption in Jarvis's comment that is important to consider. He implies that the old media are limited, while the new, the digital, are not. This idea goes back at least as far as Vannevar Bush's "As We May Think." Modernity's dream is that its vast fragments can somehow all be linked: that knowledge, expression, institutions, all the products of modern culture, can be made to cohere, or at least be revealed and somehow connected. The digital state allows us to access everything ever expressed, interact with it, and connect its parts. The truth is more nuanced. Any medium of whatever kind is contained by its own limitations, which is why radio is not television or film journalism. The digital world and online communications have limits of their own – impermanence being a major one; a lack of easy discrimination between the important and the unimportant, the authentic and the fake another. (False identities on a social networking site or in a virtual-world game is one thing; bad information posing as good is another.) The lack of universal access is, perhaps, the most limiting of all.

The real question is not about the lifespan or usability of one medium or another, or even a qualitative judgment about whether one medium is better or more important than another. The real question is always about the ways a culture and its members configure the media and are configured by it in turn. We see and are seen through a wonderful variety of media. They are becoming more interrelated, one with the other, as are the individuals and the cultures that use them. The more media converge, the greater their diversity. But a perfect coherence and diversity is not possible and probably not desirable. Many people, even entire cultures, fear modernity and struggle against it. That struggle can sometimes be counterproductive, even hateful. Denying the new, violently or not, is always a diversion from important matters at hand. It is a deadly irony, when the expression of such resistance makes use of the tools of modernity to rail against it, as do various Internet hate groups and defenders of media morality, who use the Internet to spread their unpleasantness.

At the same time, embracing modernity brings as many responsibilities as it does possibilities. It takes alertness rather than passive acceptance; the ability to discriminate – in the positive sense of being able to separate the valuable from the nonsensical; the usable from junk; the entertaining from the debasing. In the end, defenders and antagonists of the new, those who take pleasure from the media and those who hate it, those who use media or use media to do harm to its users, make up the variety of cultures that *are* the media.

In the end, convergence occurs within our consciousness, and we need to understand that enormous complexity.

References

The quote is from Jeff Jarvis, "The book is Dead. Long Live the Book," Jeff Jarvis, BuzzMachine (blog), May 19, 2006: <http://www.buzzmachine.com/2006/05/19/the-book-is-dead-long-live-the-book/>.

The Illusions of Digital Space

A short digression on language and print
A fascinating collection of essays on pre-computer archiving is found in Neil Rhodes, (ed.), *The Renaissance Computer* (London and New York: Routledge, 2000).

For theories of the database, see Lev Manovich's *The Language of New Media* (Cambridge, MA, and London: MIT Press, 2001), which addresses the concept of the database as metaphor for all computing.

Consciousness and the New Machine

The Turing test
Turing's essay is "Computing Machinery and Intelligence," *Mind* (1950): 433–60; <http://loebner.net/Prizef/TuringArticle.html>.

The personal machine
A useful history of computing is at: <http://trillian.randomstuff.org.uk/~stephen/history/timelines.html>.

Online
For background, see Stephen White's "Brief History of Computing": <http://trillian.randomstuff.org.uk/~stephen//history/>.

Leonard Kleinrock's logs are at: <http://www.lk.cs.ucla.edu/first_words.html>.

The history of Arpanet is at: <http://www2.dei.isep.ipp.pt/docs/arpa.html>. >.

"As We May Think," Vannevar Bush's article, is available at: <http://www.theatlantic.com/doc/194507/bush>.

Making Media

The quote is from Marshall McLuhan, *Understanding Media: The Extensions of Man* (Cambridge, MA, and London: MIT Press, 1994), p. 3.

The story of *The Shining* trailer is in David M. Halbfinger, "His 'Secret' Movie Trailer is No Secret Anymore," *New York Times* (September 30, 2005); <http://www.nytimes.com/2005/09/30/movies/30shin.html>.

Sources dealing with MySpace privacy issues and corporate ownership are: Alan Finder, "For Some, Online Persona Undermines a Résumé," *New York Times* (June 11, 2006): <http://www.nytimes.com/2006/06/11/us/11recruit.html>; Gavin O'Malley, "Social Media Sites Start Snagging Big-Name Marketers," *Advertising Age* (June 6, 2006): <http://adage.com/digital/article?article_id=109706&search_phrase=Social+ Media+Sites+Start+Snagging+Big-Name+Marketers>.

Games

MOOs and MUDs
For a discussion of the genres of computer games and their relation to film, see Paul Young, "Film Genre Theory and Contemporary Media: Description, Interpretation, Intermediality," in *The Oxford Handbook of Film and Media Studies*, ed. Robert Kolker (New York: Oxford University Press, 2008), pp. 224–59.

MMPORGs

You can trace the number of online game-players at: <http://www.mmogchart.com>.

On the economics of virtual worlds, see Edward Castronova, *Synthetic Worlds: The Business and Culture of Online Games* (Chicago and London: University of Chicago Press, 2005).

On *Second Life* and disabled users, see Rob Stein, "Hope in a Virtual World: Online Identities Leave Limitations Behind" (*Washington Post*, October 6, 2007); <http://www.washingtonpost.com/wpdyn/content/article/2007/10/05/AR2007100502391.html>.

First-person shooter

On repurposing media, see Jay David Bolter and Richard Grusin, *Remediation: Understanding New Media* (Cambridge and London: MIT Press, 1999).

Fears of the game

Henry Jenkins, "Reality Bytes: Eight Myths about Video Games Debunked": <http://www.pbs.org/kcts/videogamerevolution/impact/myths.html>. See also Toby Miller, "Gaming for Beginners," *Games and Culture* 1 (January, 2006): 5–12.

A classic essay on the dangers of online predation is Julian Dibbell's "A Rape in Cyberspace, or How an Evil Clown, a Haitian Trickster Spirit, Two Wizards, and a Cast of Dozens Turned a Database into a Society," which can be found at: <http://www.juliandibbell.com/texts/bungle.html>.

The old Warner Bros. on the new frontier

The classic history of Warner Bros. is Nick Roddick, *A New Deal in Entertainment: Warner Brothers in the 1930s* (London: The British Film Institute, 1983). Timelines for the various mergers of Warner Bros. with other companies are at: <http://www.cjr.org> and <http://www.ketupa.net/time2.htm>. See also Patricia Aufderheide, "Competition and Commons: The Public Interest in and after the AOL-Time Warner Merger," *Journal of Broadcasting & Electronic Media* 46/4 (December 2002): 515(17).

The quotation from Steve Case comes from "It's Time to Take It Apart: My Case for Dividing the Media Giant," *Washington Post* (December 11, 2005); <http://www.washingtonpost.com/wpdyn/content/article/2005/12/10/AR2005121000099.html>.

Individual creativity and the Internet

The Institute for Advanced Technology in the Humanities is at: <http://www.iath.virginia.edu/>; the Labyrinth Project can be found at: <http://college.usc.edu/labyrinth/>.

Intellectual Property

Recorded music and the right to copy

A reasoned discussion about the legalities of file-sharing is David L. Lange's "Students, Music and the Net: A Comment on Peer-to-Peer File Sharing" (2003): <http://www.law.duke.edu/journals/dltr/articles/2003dltr0021.html>. Your university probably has its own guidelines and they should be consulted.

Details on RIAA lawsuits can be found on the website of the Electronic Frontier Association: <http://www.eff.org>.

For Sony and the rootkit, see Tom Zeller, Jr, "The Ghost in the CD," *The New York Times* (November 14, 2005); <http://www.nytimes.com/2005/11/14/business/14rights.html>; and Dan Mitchell, "Rootkit of All Evil," *The New York Times* (November 19, 2005); <http://www.nytimes.com/2005/11/19/business/media/19online.html>.

What is copyright and IP?

There are many authoritative sites explaining copyright. Start with the source, the US copyright office: < http://www.copyright.gov/ >.

A CNN report of the RIAA out-of-court settlement is found at: <http://www.cnn.com/2003/TECH/Internet/09/09/music.swap.settlement/>.

From Modernity to Postmodernity

Whose identity?

Up-to-date surveys of Internet usage can be found at: <http://www.pewinternet.org/>.

Media and Politics

Some studies on race and the online world are: Anna Everett, "Click This: From Analog Dreams to Digital Realities," *Cinema Journal* 43 (2004): 93–8; Mark B. N. Hanson, "Digitizing the Racialized Body or The Politics of Universal Address," *SubStance* 33/2 (2004): 107–33; Josh Adams and Vincent J. Roscigno, "White Supremacists, Oppositional Culture and the World Wide Web," *Social Forces* 84/2 (2005): 759–78.

Index

Note: Page numbers in *italics* refer to figures.